Study Guide

for use with

Statistical Techniques in Business and Economics

Tenth Edition

Robert D. Mason
Late of The University of Toledo

Douglas A. Lind
The University of Toledo

William G. Marchal
The University of Toledo

Prepared by
Walter H. Lange
The University of Toledo

 **Irwin
McGraw-Hill**

**Boston   Burr Ridge, IL   Dubuque, IA   Madison, WI   New York   San Francisco   St. Louis
Bangkok   Bogotá   Caracas   Lisbon   London   Madrid
Mexico City   Milan   New Delhi   Seoul   Singapore   Sydney   Taipei   Toronto**

Irwin/McGraw-Hill

A Division of The McGraw-Hill Companies

Study Guide for use with
STATISTICAL TECHNIQUES IN BUSINESS AND ECONOMICS

5 6 7 8 9 0 MAZ/MAZ 9 3 2 1

ISBN 0-07-303928-4

http://www.mhhe.com

PREFACE

This study guide is especially designed to accompany the Tenth Edition of Statistical Techniques in Business and Economics by Robert D. Mason, Douglas A. Lind and William G. Marchal. It can also be used alone, or as a companion to most other introductory statistics texts. It provides a valuable source of reinforcement for the material in the text. The chapters in the text and the study guide are parallel in topics, notation, and the numbering of formulas. Students will attain the most benefit if they study the textbook first, and then read the corresponding chapter in the study guide. The major features of the study guide include:

- **Chapter Goals**. They are listed first and stress the main concepts covered and the tasks students should be able to perform after having studied the chapter. It is recommended that students refer to the goals before reading the chapter to get an overview of the material to be studied and again after completing the chapter to confirm mastery of the material.

- **Brief Introduction.** A brief Introduction follows the goals. In capsule form the material covered in previous chapters is tied with that covered in the current chapter, thus maintaining continuity throughout the book.

- **Definitions**. Key words are defined and used in their correct statistical context.

> **Key Words** are in a text box for easy reference.

- **Formulas.** The formulas are placed in a formula box for easy reference.

> **Formula box** is used to emphasize formulas.

- A **glossary** follows the chapter discussion. The glossary provides definitions of the key words used in the chapter and is a handy reference.

- **Chapter Problems.** Chapter problems, including solutions, come next. In this section the step-by-step method of solution is presented along with an interpretation of the results. The values are kept small to emphasize the concept.

- **Exercises.** Following the chapter problems is an exercise. The student completes the exercise and checks the answer in the answer section at the end of the guide. Thus the student can check his/her comprehension of the material as they progress through the chapter.

- **Chapter Assignments.** Chapter assignments cover the entire chapter and are intended to be completed outside the classroom. Part I of the assignment consists of multiple-choice questions, Part II is problems, with space for students to show essential work and a box for the answers. The pages are perforated, so that assignments can be torn out and handed in to the instructor for grading.

For this revised edition we wish to thank Temelon G. Rousos for his invaluable assistance in reviewing the manuscript and checking the accuracy of the solutions to the problems, the exercises, and the assignments. A special thanks to Danuta T. Lange who prepared the camera-ready copy for this publication.

Walter H. Lange
Douglas A. Lind

TABLE OF CONTENTS

CHAPTER 1
WHAT IS STATISTICS?

Chapter Goals

After completing this chapter, you will be able to:

1. Define what is meant by statistics.

2. Explain what is meant by descriptive statistics and inferential statistics.

3. Distinguish between a qualitative variable and a quantitative variable.

4. Distinguish between a discrete variable and a continuous variable.

5. Distinguish between nominal, ordinal, interval, and ratio levels of measurement.

6. Define the terms mutually exclusive and exhaustive.

Introduction

No doubt you have noticed the large number of facts and figures, often referred to as *statistics*, that appear in the newspapers and magazines you read, the television you watch (especially sporting events) and in the grocery stores where you shop. A simple figure is called *statistic* (singular). A few examples:

- The best performing stock last year was Yahoo. It went up 301% in 1997. (*Smart Money*, February, 1998).

- The worst performing stock last year was Molten Metal Technology. It was down 98% in 1997. (*Smart Money*, February, 1998).

- During the summer as many as 6,000 cars a day go through the south entrance of Grand Canyon National Park. (*Highways*, February 1998).

- The International Federation of Organic Agricultural Movements is a 570-member organization in more than 100 countries. (*Organic Gardening*, March 1998).

- Stock prices recently jumped to record highs this week. The Dow Jones Industrial average closed at 8546. (*Wall Street Journal, March* 2, 1998)

The Yahoo stock price increase of 301 percent is a statistic (singular). The Dow Jones average of 8546 is a statistic. A collection of figures is called statistics (plural). An example from the March 2, 1998 *USA Today* daily feature on the "Markets" is shown:

Markets	
Dow Jones industrial average	8545.72
Nasdaq composite	1770.51
T-bond, 30 year yield	5.92%
Gold, oz. Comex	$299.10
U.S. dollar, yen per dollar	126.10

You may think of statistics simply as a collection of numerical information. However, *statistics* has a much broader meaning.

> **Statistics:** The science of collecting, organizing, presenting analyzing, and interpreting data to assist in making more effective decisions.

Note in this definition of statistics that the initial step is the collection of pertinent information. This information may come from newspapers or magazines, the company's human relations director, the local, state, or federal government, universities, nonprofit organizations, the United Nations, and so on. A few actual publications of the federal government and others are:

- *Statistical Abstract of the United States*, published annually by the U.S. Department of Commerce.
- *Monthly Labor Review*, published monthly by the U.S. Department of Labor.
- *Survey of Current Business*, published monthly by the U.S. Department of Commerce.
- *Social Security Bulletin*, published annually by the U.S. Social Security Administration.
- *Crime in the United States*, published annually by the U.S. Federal Bureau of Investigation.
- *Hospital Statistics*, published annually by the American Hospital Association.
- *Vital Statistics of the United States*, published annually by the National Center for Health Statistics.

If the information is not available from company records or public sources, it may be necessary to conduct a *survey*. For example, the A.C. Nielsen Company surveys about 1200 homes on an ongoing basis to determine which TV programs are being watched, and Gallup surveys registered voters before an election to estimate the percent that will vote for a certain candidate. These firms also sample the population regarding food preference, what features in automobiles are desirable, and what appliances consumers will most likely purchase next year.

Fortune annually surveys 12,600 senior executives, outside directors, and securities analysts to evaluate the companies in their industry to find the ten most admired firms, and the least admired firms. Each executive is asked to rate a list of firms on eight attributes, namely innovativeness, quality of management, quality of products and services, long-term investment value, financial soundness, employee talent, social responsibility to the community and the environment and wise use of corporate assets. Each attribute is rated on a scale of zero (poor) to ten (excellent). The ten most admired companies are listed in the table.

Rank	Company
1	General Electric
2	Microsoft
3	Coca Cola
4	Intel
5	Hewlett-Packard
6	Southwest Airlines
7	Berkshire Hathaway
8	Disney
9	Johnson & Johnson
10	Merck

Source: *Fortune*, March 2, 1998

Why Study Statistics?

Statistics is required for many college programs for three reasons.

1. Numerical information is everywhere. If you look in various newspapers (*USA Today, Wall Street Journal*), magazines (*Time, Business Week, Sports Illustrated, People*) you will be bombarded with numerical information. You need to be able to determine if the conclusions as reported are reasonable. Was the sample large enough? You must be able to read and interpret the charts or graphs.

2. Statistical techniques are used to make decisions that affect our lives. Insurance companies use statistics to determine the premiums you pay for automobile insurance, the Environmental Protection Agency uses various statistical tools to determine air quality in your area, and the Internal Revenue Service uses statistical surveys to determine if your tax return should be subject to an audit.

3. Knowledge of statistical methods will help you understand why decisions are made and give you a better understanding of how they affect you.

Descriptive and Inferential Statistics

The definition of statistics referred to collecting, organizing, and presenting numerical information. Data stored in a computer's memory or in a filing cabinet are of little value. Techniques are available that organize this information in a more meaningful form. Such aids are called *descriptive statistics*.

> *Descriptive statistics*: Methods of organizing, summarizing, and presenting data in an informative way.

A statistical tool designed to describe the movement of a series of numbers over a long period of time (such as production, imports, wages and stock market trends) is called a line chart. The line chart below, for example, depicts the upward movement of the Dow Jones average of 30 industrials year-end closing prices since 1985.

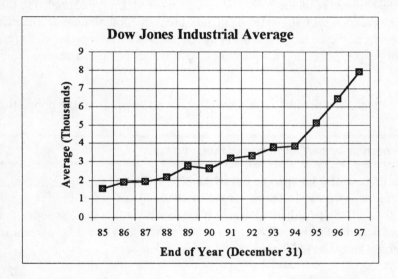

Notice how easy it is to describe the trend of stock prices: The price of the 30 industrials, as represented by the Dow, rose somewhat steadily from about 1800 in 1987 to over 8500 in early 1998.

Another descriptive measure is referred to as an average. Some examples are:

*   The 1998 Toyota Sienna minivan averages 12 miles per gallon in city driving, 30 miles per gallon highway driving and 19 miles per gallon overall. (*Consumers Reports*, March, 1998)

*   The average price of vehicles wholesaled at United States automobile auctions in 1997 was $9,992, down from an average price of $10,069 in 1996. (*NADA/NAAA Auction Net*, February, 1998)

*   Herman Warsaw set the world record in 1985 by averaging 70 bushels of corn per acre on a 100.4 acre field. (*Farm Journal*, January, 1996)

*   The median (an average) price of homes sold in 1997 in Lucas County was $64,500 (*The Blade*, January 18, 1998)

The Bureau of Labor Statistics describing the labor force in the United States reported that the average number of employed persons in 1997 was 133,900,000 and the average number of unemployed people was 5,400,000. Averages and other descriptive measures are presented in Chapter 3.

A second aspect of statistics is called *inferential statistics*.

Inferential statistics: The methods used to find out something about a population, based on a sample.

This branch of statistics deals with problems requiring the use of a sample to infer something about the *population*.

Population: A collection of all possible individuals, objects, or measurements of interest.

A population might consist of all the 7,425,000 people in North Carolina, or all 480,000 people in Wyoming. Or, the population might consist of all the teams in the Canadian Football League, the PE ratios for all chemical stocks, or the total assets of the 20 largest banks in the United States. A population, therefore, can be considered the total collection of people, prices, ages, square footage of homes being constructed in Flint, Michigan in 1998, and so on.

To infer something about a population, we usually take a *sample* from the population.

Sample: A portion, or part, of the population of interest.

A sample might consist of 2,000 people out of the 32,268,000 people in California, 12 headlights selected from a production run of 1000 for a life test, or the three scoops of grain selected at random to be tested for moisture content from a 15-ton truckload of grain. If we found that the three scoops of grain consisted of 9.50 percent moisture, we would infer that all the grain in the 15-ton load had 9.50 percent moisture. We start our discussion of inferential statistics in Chapter 5.

Types of Variables

There are two types of variables, *quantitative* and *qualitative*.

Qualitative variable: A variable that has the characteristic of being nonnumeric.

A classification of students at your university by the state of birth, gender, or college affiliation (Business, Education, Liberal Arts, etc.) is an example of a qualitative variable.

Quantitative variable: A variable being studied that can be reported numerically.

Examples of quantitative variables include: the balance in your checking account, the ages of the members of the United States Congress, the speeds of automobiles traveling along I-70 in Kansas, the number of customers served in the Commodore Barber Shop last week, or the number of new single family homes constructed by Reynolds Construction Company last year in Erie, Pennsylvania.

There are two types of quantitative variables, *discrete* and *continuous*.

> *Discrete variable*: A quantitative variable that can only assume certain values. There is usually a "gap" between the values.

Examples of discrete variables are: the number of children in a family, the number of customers in a carpet store in an hour, or the number of commercials aired last hour on radio station WEND. A family can have two or three children, but not 2.445, or WEND can air five or six commercials, but not 5.75. Usually discrete variables result from counting.

> *Continuous variable:* A quantitative variable that can assume any value within a range.

Examples of continuous variables are: the amount of snow for the winter of 1998-99 in Toronto, Ontario, the pressure in a tire, or a person's weight. Typically, continuous variables are the result of measuring something. We can measure the pressure in a tire, or the amount of snow in Toronto.

Levels of Measurement

Data may be classified into four categories or levels of measurement. These categories are nominal, ordinal, interval, and ratio.

Nominal Level Data

When data can only be classified into categories, we refer to it as being the *nominal* level of measurement.

> *Nominal level*: A level of measurement in which the data are sorted into categories with no particular order to the categories.

At this level the categories have no particular order or rank and are *mutually exclusive.*

> *Mutually exclusive*: An individual, object, or measurement is included in only one category.

For example, the Office of Special Education, U.S. Department of Education, gave these counts of the number of handicapped children 3 to 21 years old who were in special education programs.

Type of Handicap	Number Served
Visual impairments	23,000
Serious emotional impairment	401,000
Speech impairments	996,000
Deaf-blindness	2,000
Learning disabilities	2,354,000
Mental retardation	519,000
Hearing impairments	60,000
Orthopedic impairments	52,000
All others	718,000
Total	5,125,000

The data is nominal level of measurement because it can only be classified into categories and it is immaterial what order the type of handicap is listed. Mental retardation could be listed first, serious emotional impairment second, and so on. The categories are mutually exclusive meaning that the type of handicap a child has can be counted into only one category. And such categories are said to be *exhaustive*.

> *Exhaustive:* Each individual, object, or measurement must appear in a category.

This means that a handicapped child enrolled in the program must appear in one of the categories. Chapter 14 deals with data that is nominal level of measurement.

To summarize, nominal level data has these properties:

- Data categories are mutually exclusive, so an object belongs to only one category.
- Data categories have no logical order.

Ordinal Level Data

The *ordinal* level of measurement implies some sort of ranking.

> *Ordinal level*: A level of measurement that presumes that one category is ranked higher than another category.

An example of ordinal level of measurement follows: undergraduate students in a basic statistics class were classified according to class rank.

Class Rank	Number
Freshman	13
Sophomore	17
Junior	9
Senior	5

Note that the categories are mutually exclusive meaning that a student can only be counted in one category. A student cannot be a freshman and a sophomore at the same time. Also, the categories are exhaustive meaning that a student must appear in one of the categories.
In addition, a ranking of students is implied meaning that juniors are ranked "higher" than sophomores. Chapter 15 deals with tests involving ordinal level of measurement.

To summarize, ordinal level data has these properties:

- Data categories are mutually exclusive and exhaustive.
- Data categories have some logical order.
- Data categories are ranked or ordered according to the particular trait they possess.

Interval Level Data

The *interval level* of measurement is the next highest level.

> *Interval level:* Includes the ranking characteristics of the ordinal scale and, in addition, the distance between values is a constant size.

Temperature on the Fahrenheit scale is an example. Suppose the high temperature for the last three days was 85, 73, and 78 degrees Fahrenheit. We can easily put the readings in a rank order, but in addition we can study the difference between readings. Why is this so? One degree on the Fahrenheit temperature scale is a constant unit of measure for all three days. Note in this example that the zero point is just another point on the scale. It does not represent the absence of temperature, just that it is cold! Test scores are another example of the interval scale of measurement.

In addition to the constant difference characteristic, interval scaled data have all the features of nominal and ordinal measurements. Temperatures are mutually exclusive, that is, the high temperature yesterday cannot be both 88 and 85 degrees. The "greater than" feature of ordinal data permits the ranking of daily high temperatures.

The properties of the interval scale are:

- Data categories are mutually exclusive.
- Data categories are scaled according to the amount of the characteristic they possess.
- Equal differences in the characteristic are represented by equal differences in the numbers assigned to the categories.

Ratio Level Data

The *ratio level* of measurement is the highest level of measurement.

> *Ratio level*: Has all the characteristics of the interval scale, but additionally there is a meaningful zero point and the ratio of two values is meaningful.

Weight, height, and money are examples of the ratio scale of measurement. If you have $20 and your friend has $10, then you have twice as much money as your friend. The zero point represents the absence of money. That is, the zero point is fixed and represents the absence of the characteristic being measured. If you have zero dollars, you have none of the characteristic being measured.

The properties of the ratio level are:

- Data categories are mutually exclusive.
- Data categories are scaled according to the amount of the characteristic they posses.
- Equal differences in the characteristic are represented by equal differences in the numbers assigned to the categories.
- The point 0 reflects the absence of the characteristic.

Glossary

Statistics: The science of collecting, organizing, presenting, analyzing, and interpreting data to assist in making more effective decisions.

Descriptive statistics: Methods of organizing, summarizing, and presenting data in an informative way.

Inferential statistics: The methods used to find out something about a population, based on a sample.

Population: A collection of all possible individuals, objects, or measurements of interest.

Sample: A portion, or part, of the population of interest.

Qualitative variable: A variable that has the characteristic of being nonnumeric.

Quantitative variable: A variable being studied that can be reported numerically.

Discrete variable: A quantitative variable that can only assume certain values. There is usually a "gap" between the values.

Continuous variable: A quantitative variable that can assume any value within a range.

Nominal level: A level of measurement in which the data are sorted into categories with no particular order to the categories.

Mutually exclusive: An individual or object can be included in only one category.

Exhaustive: Each individual, object, or measurement must appear in a category.

Ordinal level: A level of measurement that presumes that one category is ranked higher than another category.

Interval level: Includes the ranking characteristics of the ordinal scale and, in addition, the distance between values is a constant size.

Ratio level: Has all the characteristics of the interval scale, but additionally there is a meaningful zero point and the ratio of two values is meaningful.

CHAPTER 1 ASSIGNMENT

WHAT IS STATISTICS?

Name _____   Section _____   Score _____

Part I   Classify the following sets of data as qualitative or quantitative.

_____ 1.   The height of each member of a basketball team

_____ 2.   The religious affiliations of school faculty members

_____ 3.   Scores of students on the first statistics exam

_____ 4.   The Olympic track and field world records

_____ 5.   The color of Labrador puppies in a litter

Part II   Classify the following sets of data as continuous or discrete.

_____ 6.   The number of sit-ups

_____ 7.   The acceleration of an automobile

_____ 8.   The number of pairs of shoes sold at a shoe store

_____ 9.   The temperature of an oven

_____ 10.   The diving depth of a submarine

Part III   Identify the measurement scale for each of the following.

_____ 11.   Classification of automobile make

_____ 12.   The temperature readings in Nome, Alaska

_____ 13.   College major

_____ 14.   Number of traffic fatalities

_____ 15.   Military rank

_____ 16.   Time required to complete a crossword puzzle

_____ 17. Order of finish in the 1996 Glass City Marathon

_____ 18. Number of people at a business meeting

_____ 19. Years in which Huntington Bank stock split

_____ 20. The hair color of employees at Jones City Hardware

Part IV   Select the correct answer and write the appropriate letter in the space provided.

_____ 21. The collection of all possible individuals, objects, or measurements is called

   a. a sample.
   b. a ratio measurement.
   c. a population.
   d. an inference.

_____ 22. Techniques used to organize, summarize, and present the data that have been collected are called

   a. populations.
   b. samples.
   c. inferential statistics.
   d. descriptive statistics.

_____ 23. An individual, measurement, or object that can appear in only one category is said to be

   a. mutually exclusive.
   b. exhaustive.
   c. inferential.
   d. descriptive.

_____ 24. Techniques used to determine something about a population, based on a sample, are called

   a. descriptive statistics.
   b. inferential statistics.
   c. populations.
   d. samples.

_____ 25. A difference between the interval scale and the ratio scale is

   a. the interval scale cannot be ranked.
   b. the zero point on the interval scale is arbitrary.
   c. the ratio scale does not meet the exhaustive criteria.
   d. the interval scale does not meet the mutually exclusive criteria.

CHAPTER 2
DESCRIBING DATA: FREQUENCY DISTRIBUTIONS AND GRAPHIC PRESENTATION

Chapter Goals

After completing this chapter, you will be able to:

1. Organize data into a frequency distribution.

2. Portray a frequency distribution in a histogram, a frequency polygon, and a cumulative frequency polygon.

3. Develop a stem-and-leaf display.

4. Present data using such graphic techniques as line charts, bar charts, and pie charts.

Introduction

This chapter begins our study of *descriptive statistics*. Recall from Chapter 1 that when using descriptive statistics we merely describe a set of data. For example, we want to describe the entry level salary for a select group of professions. We find that the entry level salary for accountants is $28,000, for systems analysts $30,000, for infectious disease specialists $70,000, and so on. This unorganized data provides little insight into the pattern of entry level salaries which makes conclusions difficult.

This chapter presents a technique that is used to organize raw data into some meaningful form. It is called a *frequency distribution*. Then, to better understand the main features of the data, we portray the frequency distribution will in the form of a frequency polygon, a histogram, or a cumulative frequency polygon.

Frequency Distributions

A *frequency distribution* is a useful statistical tool for organizing a mass of data into some meaningful form.

> *Frequency Distribution*: A grouping of data into categories showing the number of observations in each mutually exclusive category.

As noted, a frequency distribution is used to summarize and organize large amounts of data.

The steps to follow in developing a frequency distribution are:

1. Decide on the number of classes or the class interval.

2. Tally the observations into the appropriate classes.

3. Count the number of tallies in each class.

As an example, the lengths of service, in years, of a sample of eleven employees are given.

Length of Service (in years)					
4	3	2	10	6	6
5	8	4	8	4	

The eleven observations are referred to as **raw data** or ungrouped data. To organize the lengths of service into a frequency distribution we first set up groups called **classes.** We decided to use classes 1 up to 3, 3 up to 5, and so on. Then we **tally** the lengths of service into the appropriate classes. Finally, we count the number of tallies in each class as shown.

Lengths of service	Tallies	Number of employees
1 up to 3 years	/	1
3 up to 5 years	////	4
5 up to 7 years	///	3
7 up to 9 years	//	2
9 up to 11 yrs.	/	1
Total		11

How many classes should there be? A common guideline is from 5 to 15. Having too few or too many classes gives little insight into the data. The size of the class interval may be a value such as 3, 5, 10, 15, 20, 50, 100, 1,000, and so on.

Class Interval: The size or width of the class.

The class interval can be approximated by text formula [2-1]

$$\text{Class Interval}\,(i) = \frac{\text{highest value} - \text{lowest value}}{\text{number of classes}} \qquad [2-1]$$

Each class has a lower class limit and an upper class limit. The lower limit of the first class is usually slightly below the smallest value and is a multiple of the class interval.

In the previous example, the smallest number of years of service is 2. Therefore, we selected 1, which is slightly below 2, as the lower limit of the first class. The lower limit of the second class is 3 years, and so on.

The number of tallies that occurs in each class is called the *class frequency*.

Class frequency: The number of observations in each class.

In the example, the class frequency of the lowest class is 1. For the next higher class it is 4. The class midpoint divides a class into two equal parts.

Class midpoint: The point halfway between the upper and lower limit of a class.

Note that the class midpoint is also called the *class mark*.

In the example, the class midpoint of the 5 up to 7 class is 6 found by (5 + 7)/2. The class interval is the distance between the lower limit of two consecutive classes. It is 2 found by subtracting 1 (the lower limit of the first class) from 3 (the lower limit of the second class).

Suggestions on Constructing Frequency Distributions

When constructing frequency distributions, follow these guidelines:

1. *The class intervals used in the frequency distribution should be equal.* Unequal class intervals present problems in graphically portraying the distribution. However, in some situations unequal class intervals may be necessary in order to avoid a large number of empty classes.

2. *Text formula [2-1] above is based on the number of classes, and is useful for determining the class interval.*

3. *The class interval (i) can also be estimated based on the number of observations.* To estimate the class interval based on the number of observations, use text formula [2-2] which uses logs to the base ten. Note in the formula that you multiply 3.322 times the **log** of the number of frequencies. To find the log of 60 using a scientific calculator, enter 60 then depress the **log** key for base ten logarithms. The display will show: 1.77815125.

$$i = \frac{\text{Highest value} - \text{Lowest value}}{1 + 3.322 \ (\text{log of the total frequencies})} \qquad [2-2]$$

4. *Your professional judgement can determine the number of classes.* Too many classes or too few classes might not reveal the basic shape of the distribution. A general rule is that it is best to use at least 5 and not more than 15 classes when constructing a frequency distribution.

5. *The "2 to the k rule" is also used to determine the number of classes.* To estimate the number of classes we select the smallest integer (whole number) such that $2^k \geq n$ where n is the total number of observations. Suppose a set of data has 60 observations. If we try $k = 5$, *we get* $2^5 = 32$, which is less than 60, so we try $2^6 = 64$, which is greater than 60. Thus the recommended number of classes is 6. The table is based on the *"2 to the k rule."*

2 to the *k* Rule for Number of Classes	
Total Number of Observations	Recommended Number of Classes
9 – 16	4
17 – 32	5
33 – 64	6
65 – 128	7
129 – 256	8
257 – 512	9
513 – 1,024	10

6. *The lower limit of the first class should be an even multiple of the class interval.* Suppose a sample of weight losses ranged from 25 pounds to 64 pounds. We want to organize the weight losses into a frequency distribution with an interval of 6 pounds. The lower limit of the first class would be 24, found by multiplying 4, the even multiple, by 6, the class interval.

7. *Avoid overlapping stated class limits.* Class limits such as 4-6 and 6-8 should not be used. Use 4 up to 6, then 6 up to 8. This way you can determine in which class to tally 6.

8. *Try to avoid open-ended classes.* Open ended classes cause serious graphing problems and make it difficult to calculate various measures described in Chapters 3 and 4.

Relative Class Frequency

It is often helpful to know what percent the class frequencies are of the total number of observations.

> *Relative class frequency*: It shows what percent each class is of the total number of observations (frequencies).

The relative class frequency is found by dividing each of the class frequencies by the total number of frequencies.

Using the distribution of the lengths of service of the eleven employees, the relative frequency for the 1 up to 3 year class is 0.0909 found by 1/11 = 0.0909 = 9%. Thus 9% of the employees had 1 up to 3 years of service.

The relative frequencies for the remaining classes are shown.

Length of service (in years)	Number of employees	Relative Frequency	Found by
1 up to 3 years	1	0.0909	1/11
3 up to 5 years	4	0.3636	4/11
5 up to 7 years	3	0.2727	3/11
7 up to 9 years	2	0.1818	2/11
9 up to 11 years	1	0.0909	1/11
Total	11	1.0000	

Stem-and-Leaf Displays

A stem and leaf display is a combination of sorting and graphing.

> *Stem-and-Leaf Display*: A statistical technique for displaying a set of data. Each numerical value is divided into two parts: The leading digit(s) become the *stem*, and the trailing digits the *leaf*. The stems are located along the main vertical axis, and the leaf for each observation along the horizontal axis.

To develop a **stem-and-leaf chart** the first step is to locate the largest value and the smallest value. This will provide the range of the stem values. The **stem** is the leading digit or digits of the number, and the **leaf** is the trailing digit. For example, the number 15 has a stem value of 1 and a leaf value of 5. For another problem the number 231 has a stem value of 23 and a leaf value of 1.

The following are the amounts spent (in dollars) in the grocery store by a sample of 12 people.

$12	$28	$32	$24	$17	$6
$34	$18	$22	$42	$36	$26

The range of values is from $6 to $42. The first digit of each number is the stem and the second digit is the leaf. The first customer (upper left) spent $12. Hence, the stem value is 1 and the leaf value is 2. The completed display after each trailing digit is arranged from low to high is shown.

Leading Digit	Trailing Digit
0	6
1	278
2	2468
3	246
4	2

Graphic Presentation of a Frequency Distribution

To get reader attention a frequency distribution is often portrayed graphically in a histogram or some other type of chart.

Histogram

The simplest type of a statistical chart is called a *histogram*.

> *Histogram:* A graph in which the classes are marked on the horizontal axis and the class frequencies on the vertical axis. The class frequencies are represented by the heights of the bars and the bars are drawn adjacent to each other.

For the length of service for the sample of eleven employees a histogram would appear as shown:

Note that to plot the bar for the 5 up to 7 years (which has a midpoint of 6 years) we drew lines vertically from 5 and from 7 years to 3 employees on the *Y*-axis and then connected the end points by a straight line. The histogram provides an easily interpreted visual representation of a frequency distribution.

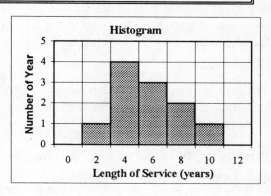

Frequency Polygon

A second type of chart used to portray a frequency distribution is the *frequency polygon*.

> *Frequency Polygon*: A graph that consists of line segments connecting the points formed by the intersection of the class midpoints and the class frequency.

For the frequency polygon, the assumption is that the observations in any class interval are represented by the class midpoint. A dot is placed at the class midpoint opposite the number of frequencies in that class. For the distribution of years of service, the first plot is made by going to 2 years on the *X*-axis (the midpoint) and then going vertically on the *Y*-axis to 1 and placing a dot.

This process is continued for all classes. Then the dots are connected in order.

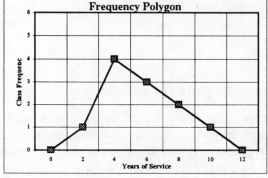

Normal practice is to anchor the frequency polygon to the *X*-axis. This is accomplished by extending the lines to the midpoint of the class below the lowest class (0) and to the midpoint of the class above the highest class (12).

Cumulative Frequency Polygon

A *less-than-cumulative frequency polygon* reports the number and percent of observations that occur less than a given value.

> ***Less-Than-Cumulative Frequency Polygon***: A graph that shows the number of observations below a certain value.

Before we can draw a cumulative frequency polygon we must convert the frequency distribution to a cumulative frequency distribution. To construct a less-than-cumulative frequency distribution we add the frequencies from the lowest class to the highest class.

Length of service (in years)	Class Frequency	Cumulative Frequency	Found by
1 up to 3 years	1	1	1
3 up to 5 years	4	5	4 + 1
5 up to 7 years	3	8	5 + 3
7 up to 9 years	2	10	8 + 2
9 up to 11 years	1	11	10 + 1

The cumulative frequencies are plotted on the vertical axis (Y-axis) and the lengths of service on the Y-axis.

It may be helpful to plot the cumulative frequencies on the left side of the vertical axis and the percent of the total on the right side as shown in the following polygon.

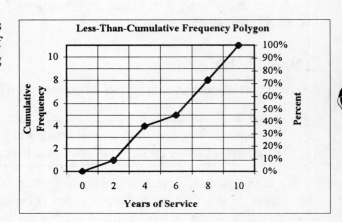

Other Graphical Techniques

Several other charts are discussed in this section. Each is designed to emphasize certain characteristics in the data. The simple **line chart** displays information over a period of time. Time is always scaled on the horizontal axis. In the line chart the values for various periods are connected by a line.

As an example, shown is a line chart illustrating the year-end closing stock price of the Microsoft Corporation from the years 1986 through 1997. The prices ranged from about $6.00 in 1996 to $130 in 1997.

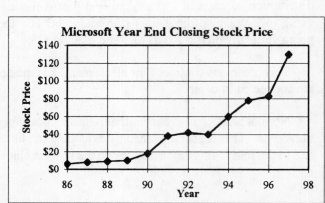

The **bar chart** is often used to display categories. For a bar chart, the data for each period are represented by bars. The bars can be shown as vertical or horizontal bars. As an example, shown below are the revenues, in billions of dollars, for the top four retailers for 1997.

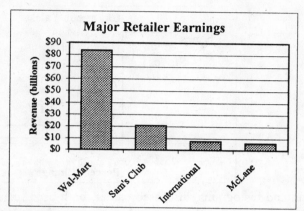

As the name implies, a **two-directional bar chart** presents such changes as profit or loss over a period of time. As an illustration, here are the percent increases and decreases in sales for selected electronic items from 1990 to 1998.

Item	Percent Change
TV sets	+40
Stoves	-12
Microwave ovens	+92
Telephones	-30
Refrigerators	+21

We organize the increases from high to low.

Item	% Increase
Microwave ovens	92
TV sets	40
Refrigerators	21

Then we rank the decreases from low to high.

Item	% Decrease
Stoves	-12
Telephones	-30

The increases are plotted in the form of bars to the right of the origin (0) and the decreases to the left of 0.

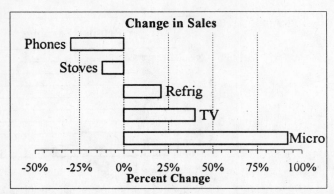

Note that bar charts and histograms, discussed earlier, both used rectangles to represent the data. The difference between the two graphs is that the bars in a histogram touch each other because the data is continuous.

Another popular chart is **a pie chart.** Its purpose is to show the relative comparison between parts of a total. Suppose we want to show where our tax dollar goes.

Tax Dollar Distribution	
Category	Percent
Roads	20
Education	40
Welfare	15
Salaries	18
Miscellaneous	7

After drawing a circle (pie) we put 0 on the top and go around the circle in increments of 5.

To plot the percent going for roads we draw a line from 0 to the center of the circle and another line from the center to 20. Then 20 + 40 = 60 and this area represents the amount going for education. This process is continued for the remaining items.

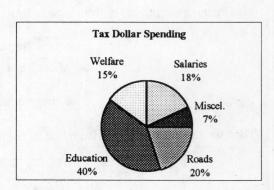

Misuses of Statistics

You must be careful that you do not mislead or misrepresent your data when you construct charts and graphs. In Problems 6 and 7 we present several examples of charts and graphs that could be misleading. Whenever you see a chart or graph, study it carefully. Ask yourself: What is the writer trying to show me? Could the writer have any bias?

Glossary

Frequency Distribution: A grouping of data into categories showing the number of observations in each mutually exclusive category.

Class Interval: The size or width of the class.

Class frequency: The number of observations in each class.

Class midpoint: The point halfway between the upper and lower limit of a class.

Relative class frequency: It shows what percent each class is of the total number of observations (frequencies).

Stem-and-leaf display: A statistical technique for displaying a set of data. Each numerical value is divided into two parts. The leading digit(s) become the stem, and the trailing digits the leaf. The stems are located along the main vertical axis, and the leaf for each observation along the horizontal axis.

Histogram: A graph in which the classes are marked on the horizontal axis and the class frequencies on the vertical axis. The class frequencies are represented by the heights of the bars and the bars are drawn adjacent to each other.

Frequency polygon: A graph that consists of line segments connecting the points formed by the intersection of the class midpoint and the class frequency.

Less-than-cumulative frequency polygon: A graph that shows the number of observations below a certain value.

Note to students:

Recall that on the first page of this chapter there was a listing of the chapter goals. A brief discussion of the chapter highlights and a glossary of terms followed these goals. Now come several problems and the solution to each of the problems. They are intended to give you a detailed solution to a real-world problem, corresponding to each of the problems discussed.

Chapter Problems

Problem 1

A sample of 30 homes sold during the past year by Gomminger Realty Company was selected for study. (Selling price is reported in thousands of dollars.)

$76	$94	$71	$78	$80	$67	←Low
80	82	67	88	72	78	
85	76	84	82	98	80	
72	82	90	95	94	99	←High
91	70	82	86	78	77	

Organize these data into a frequency distribution and interpret your results.

Chapter 2

Solution

First, observe that the home with the lowest selling price was $67 thousand and the highest was $99 thousand. We decided to let $65 be the lower limit of the first class and the class interval to be $5. Thus, the first class will be $65 up to $70 and the second class $70 up to $75, and so on.

Next, the selling prices are tallied into each of the classes. The first home sold for $76 thousand, therefore, the price is tallied into the $75 thousand up to $80 thousand class. The procedure is continued, resulting in the following frequency distribution.

Observe that the largest concentration of the data is in the $80 up to $85 thousand class. As noted before, the class frequencies are the number of observations in each class. For the $65 up to

Selling Price ($000)	Tallies	Number of Homes
$65 up to $70	//	2
$70 up to $75	////	4
$75 up to $80	///// /	6
$80 up to $85	///// ///	8
$85 up to $90	///	3
$90 up to $95	////	4
$95 up to $100	///	3

$70 class the class frequency is 2, and for the $70 up to $75 class the class frequency is 4. This indicates that two homes sold in the $65 up to $70 thousand price range and four in the $70 up to $75 thousand range.

It is also clear that the interval between the lowest and highest selling price in each category is $5 thousand. How would we classify a home selling for $70 thousand? It would fall in the second class. Homes selling for $65,000 up through $69,999.99 go in the first class, but a home selling for more than this amount goes in the next class. So the $70,000 selling price puts the home in the second class.

The class midpoint is determined by going halfway between the lower limit of consecutive of classes. Halfway between $65 and $70 is $67.5, the class midpoint.

Exercise 2.1

Check your answers against those in the ANSWER section.

This is the first in a series of exercises designed to check your comprehension of the material just presented. It is suggested that you work all parts of the exercise. Then check your answers against those given in the answer section of this study guide.

The Jansen Motor Company has developed a new engine to further reduce gasoline consumption. The new engine was put in 20 mid-sized cars and the number of miles per gallon recorded (to the nearest mile per gallon).

29	32	20	30	39
27	28	21	36	20
27	18	32	37	29
30	23	25	19	30

Develop a frequency distribution. Use a class interval of 5, with 15 as the lower limit of the first class.

Problem 2

Based on the information from Gomminger Realty in Problem 1, develop a histogram.

Solution

The class frequencies are scaled on the vertical axis (Y-axis) and the selling price on the horizontal (X-axis). A vertical line is drawn from the two class limits of a class to a height corresponding to the number of frequencies. The tops of the lines are then connected.

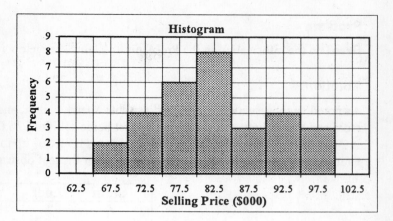

Exercise 2.2

Check your answers against those in the ANSWER section.

Use the Jansen Motor Company data in Exercise 2.1 to construct a histogram.

Problem 3

Based on the information from Problems 1 and 2, construct a frequency polygon.

Solution

The class frequencies are scaled on the vertical axis (Y-axis) and the class midpoints along the horizontal axis (X-axis). The first plot is at the point 67.5 on the X-axis and 2 on the Y-axis. To complete the frequency polygon, the midpoint of the class below the first class and above the last class are added. This allows the graph to be anchored to the X-axis at zero frequencies.

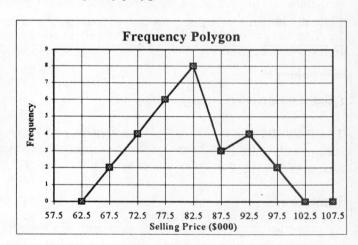

Exercise 2.3

Check your answers against those in the ANSWER section.

Use the Jansen Motor Company data in Exercise 2.1 to construct a frequency polygon..

Chapter 2

Problem 4

Based on the information in the Problems 1, 2, and 3, develop a stem-and-leaf chart.

Solution

As noted, an observation is broken down into a leading digit and a trailing digit. The leading digit is called the **stem** and the trailing digit the **leaf**. The first home sold for $76,000. The $000 were dropped, so the stem value is 7 and the leaf value is 6. The actual data ranges from $67 up to $99 so the stem values range from 6 to 9 using an increment of 10. The usual practice is to order the leaf observations from smallest to largest.

Stem	Leaf
6	77
7	0122667888
8	00022224568
9	0144589

The display shows that there is a concentration of data in the $70 up to $80 and the $80 up to $90 group. There were 10 homes that sold for more than $70 but less than $80. Specifically one sold for $70, one for $71, two for $72, two for $76, one for $77, and three sold for $78.

Exercise 2.4

Check your answers against those in the ANSWER section.

Use the Jansen Motor Company data in Exercise 2.1 to construct a stem-and-leaf chart.

Problem 5

Based on the information in Problem 1

a. Construct a less-than-cumulative frequency polygon.
b. Estimate the price below which 75 percent of the homes were sold.
c. Estimate the number of homes sold for less than $72,000.

Solution

A less-than-cumulative frequency distribution is constructed by using the class limits. The first step is to determine the number of observations "less than" the upper limit of each class. Two homes were sold for less than $70 and six were sold for between $65 and $75 thousand. The six is found by adding the two that sold for $65 to $70 thousand and the four that sold for between $70 and $75 thousand. The cumulative frequency for the fourth class is obtained by adding the frequencies of the first four classes. The total is 20, found by 2 + 4 + 6 + 8. The less-than-cumulative frequency distribution would appear as:

Class limits ($000)	Class frequency	Cumulative frequency
$65 up to $70	2	2
$70 up to $75	4	6
$75 up to $80	6	12
$80 up to $85	8	20
$85 up to $90	3	23
$90 up to $95	4	27
$95 up to $100	3	30

a. To construct a less-than-cumulative frequency polygon the upper limits are scaled on the X-axis and the cumulative frequencies on the Y-axis. The cumulative percents are placed along the right-hand scale (vertical). The first plot is $X = 70$ and $Y = 2$. The next plot is 75 and 6, As shown, the points are connected with straight lines (see the following chart).

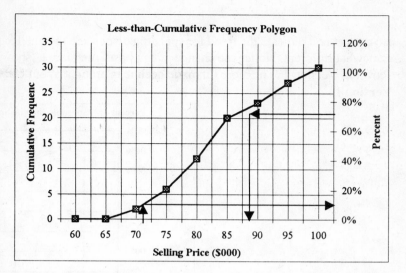

b. To estimate the amount for which less than 75 percent of the homes were sold, a horizontal line is drawn from the cumulative percent (75) over to the cumulative frequency polygon. At the intersection, a line is drawn down to the X-axis giving the approximate selling price. It is about $88 thousand. Thus, about 75 percent of the homes sold for $88,000 or less.

c. To estimate the percent of the homes that sold for more than $72,000 first locate the value of $72 on the X-axis. Next, draw a vertical line from the X-axis at 72 up to the graph. Draw a line horizontally to the cumulative percent axis and read the cumulative percent. It is about 12%. Hence, we conclude that about 12 percent of the homes were sold for less than $72,000.

Exercise 2.5

Check your answers against those in the ANSWER section.

Use the Jansen Motor Company data in Exercise 2.1.

a. Construct a less-than-cumulative frequency polygon..
b. Estimate the percent of the automobiles getting less than 30 miles per gallon.
c. Twenty percent of the automobiles obtain how many miles per gallon or less?

Problem 6

The percent of disposable income (disposable income is the amount of income left after taxes) spent for groceries for the period from 1975 to 2000 is shown below. Draw a line chart to depict the trend.

Year	Disposable Income spent on groceries
1975	13.0%
1980	12.3%
1985	11.2%
1990	10.1%
1995	9.5%
2000	9.3% (estimated

Solution

The time is scaled at five-year intervals on the horizontal or X-axis. The percent of disposable income spent for groceries is scaled on the vertical or Y-axis. Two different versions are shown. In each version the first point is plotted by going up from 1975 on the X-axis to 13%. The second point is plotted by going up from 1980 to 12.3. This process is continued for the remaining periods. The dots are connected with straight lines.

Note that in Version 2 the vertical axis did not start from zero. Technically this is called a scale break. That is, we started at 8 and ended at 14. In Version 1 we scaled the vertical axis from 0 to 14. Both versions are correct and indicate the trend for spending disposable income for groceries however, the visual impact is somewhat different. Notice the change in emphasis. Version 2 "shows" a more dramatic decline than is shown in Version 1. The more dramatic decline is brought about because of the use of the scale break.

Version 1

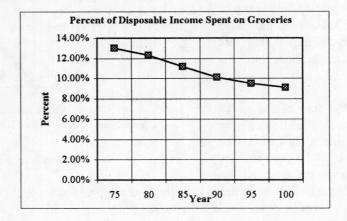

Version 2 - Misuse

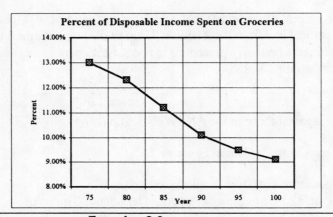

Exercise 2.6

Check your answers against those in the ANSWER section.

The expenditures on research and development for the Hennen Manufacturing Company are given below. Construct a simple line chart.

Year	Expenditure ($000)
1991	94
1992	103
1993	115
1994	145
1995	175
1996	203
1997	190

Problem 7

Refer to Problem 6. Develop a simple bar chart for the percent of disposable income spent for groceries.

Solution

The usual practice is to scale time along the horizontal axis. The height of the bars corresponds to percent of disposable income spent for groceries. Two different versions are shown. In each·version, to form the first bar, draw parallel vertical lines from 1975 up to 13.0%. Draw a line parallel to the X-axis at 13.0% to connect the lines. This process is continued for the other periods. Note that in Version 2 the vertical axis did not start from zero. Technically this is called a scale break. That is, we started at 8 and ended at 14. In Version 1 we scaled the vertical axis from 0 to 14. Both versions are correct and indicate the trend for spending disposable income for groceries. However, the visual impact is somewhat different. Notice the change in emphasis. Version 2 "shows" a more dramatic decline than is shown in Version 1. The more dramatic decline is brought about because of the use of the scale break.

Version 1

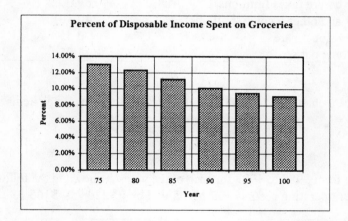

Version 2 – Misuse

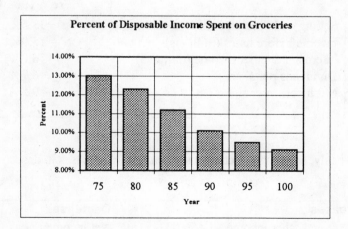

Problem 8

A comparison of selected earnings for the first quarters of 1988 and 1997 of the Moon Petroleum Corporation is to be made. The amounts are:

	First Quarter Earnings Ended March 31	
	1997	**1988**
Selling and other operating costs (millions)	$220.70	$165.300
Income before taxes (millions)	789.00	938.600
Interest and other income (millions)	40.70	15.900
Dividends per share	0.55	0.375
Net income per share	3.05	3.370

Depict the percent changes from 1988 to 1997 for each of the selected items in the form of a two-directional bar chart.

Solution

The percent change from 1988 to 1997 for each of the items is shown in the following table. The percent change for selling and other operating costs is +33.5%, found by [($220.7 − $165.3) / $165.3] 100.

	Percent Change From 1988 to 1997
Selling and other operating costs (millions)	+33.5%
Income before taxes (millions)	− 15.9%
Interest and other income (millions)	+156.0%
Dividends per share	+46.7%
Net income per share	− 9.5%

As noted previously, the usual practice is to arrange the increases in descending order and the decreases in ascending order.

Increases		Decreases	
Interest and other income	156.0%	Net income per share	− 9.5%
Dividends per share	46.7%	Income before taxes	− 15.9%
Selling costs	33.5%		

The percent increases from 1988 to 1997 are plotted to the right of the centerline of 0. The percent decreases are plotted to the left of the centerline.

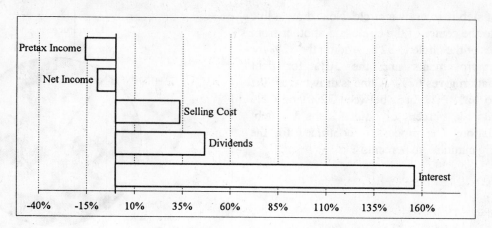

Exercise 2.8

Check your answers against those in the ANSWER section.

A real estate company is studying the changes in the type of living quarters in a large city. A sample of 800 family units in 1987 and 1997 yielded the following results:

	Frequency	
Type of Living Quarters	**1997**	**1987**
High rise apartments	210	200
Multiple family house	260	240
Single family house	270	320
Mobile home	60	40
Condominiums	75	60
Total	875	860

Depict the percent changes from 1987 to 1997 for the five types of living quarters in the form of a two-directional bar chart.

Problem 9

The purpose of home equity loans by the Home Bank and the percent of each type of loan relative to the total is shown. Portray the home equity loans information in the form of a pie chart.

Loan Purpose	Percent Of Total	Cumulative Percent
Home improvement	32	32
Debt consolidation	30	62
Car purchase	11	73
Education	10	83
Other	9	92
Investments	8	100

Chapter 2

Solution

The first step is to draw a circle. Next draw a line from 0 to the center of the circle and another from the center of the circle to 32%. Adding the 32% for home improvements and the 30% for debt consolidation gives 62%. A line is drawn from the center to 62%. The area between 32% and 62% represents the percent of equity loans for debt consolidation. The process is continued for the remaining cumulative percents.

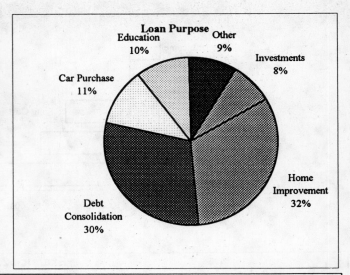

Exercise 2.9

Check your answers against those in the ANSWER section.

The data below depicts new cars sold in the United States during the year, classified by manufacturer.

Manufacturer	Cars Sold (Millions)
General Motors	3100
Ford	1900
Chrysler	800
Toyota	800
Honda	800
Nissan	500
Other	<u>1100</u>
Total	9000

Portray these data in the form of a pie chart.

CHAPTER 2 ASSIGNMENT

DESCRIBING DATA: FREQUENCY DISTRIBUTIONS AND GRAPHIC PRESENTATION

Name _____ Section _____ Score _____

Part I   Select the correct answer and write the appropriate letter in the space provided

_____ 1.   A grouping of data into categories giving the number of observations in each category is called a(an)
    a   bar chart.
    b. frequency distribution.
    c. pie chart.
    d. cumulative frequency distribution.

_____ 2.   The distance between consecutive lower class limits is called the
    a. class interval.
    b. frequency distribution.
    c. class midpoint.
    d. class frequency.

_____ 3.   The class midpoint is
    a. equal to the number of observations.
    b. found by adding the upper and lower class limit and dividing by 2.
    c. equal to the class interval.
    d. all of the above.

_____ 4.   The number of observations in a particular class is called the
    a. class interval.
    b. class frequency.
    c. frequency distribution.
    d. none of the above.

_____ 5.   A bar chart is used most often when
    a. you want to show frequencies as compared to total observations.
    b. you want to show frequencies by class intervals.
    c. you want to display frequencies by category.
    d. you want to organize data along certain time interval.

_____ 6.   In a *relative frequency* distribution
    a. the class frequencies are divided by 100.
    b. the data are related to each other rather than mutually exclusive.
    c. the class frequency is divided by the total number of observations.
    d. the frequencies are added together to give a relative set of numbers.

_____ 7. For a line chart involving time in years and dollar values, the horizontal or *X*-axis would be used to represent
   a. the dollar variable.
   b. the time variable.
   c. the class interval.
   d. the class frequency.

_____ 8. The size of the class intervals for a histogram can be found by:
   a. consecutive lower class limits divided by 2.
   b. consecutive lower class limits divided by the total number of observations.
   c. consecutive lower class limits divided by the number of desired classes.
   d. consecutive lower class limits divided by the number of frequencies in each class.

_____ 9. A pie chart requires at least what level of data?
   a. nominal
   b. ordinal
   c. interval
   d. ratio

_____ 10. A graphic representation of a frequency distribution constructed by connecting the class midpoints with lines is called a
   a. histogram.
   b. line chart.
   c. pie chart.
   d. frequency polygon.

Part II Show all of your work. Write the answer in the space provided.

11. Shown below are the net sales for the J. M. Smucker Company, a leading marketer of jams and jellies. Use the data to construct a line graph.

Smucker's Net Sales	
Year	Sales (millions
1986	249
1987	268
1988	292
1989	345
1990	399
1991	425
1992	454
1993	462
1994	478
1995	511
1996	529
1997	543

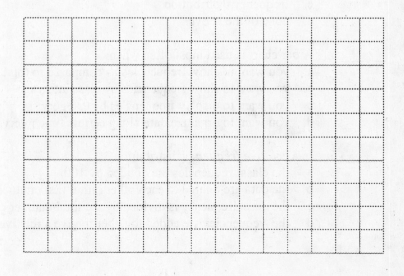

12. The following is a breakdown of the expenditures of the Ohio Division of Wildlife for 1997. Construct a pie chart.

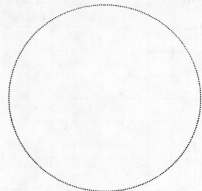

Category	Amount (millions)
Administration	1.9
Education	4.1
Law enforcement	2.8
Wildlife officers	5.5
Fish management	7.8
Wildlife management	7.8
Operations	7.6
Capital improvements	6.6

13. Listed are the weights of the 1998 Super Bowl Champion Denver Broncos starting lineup. Organize the data into the following:

228	209	195	305	324	215
241	291	181	242	234	320
190	210	230	263	194	205
326	333	186	225	279	255

a. Frequency distribution (use a class interval of 30, with 180 as the lower limit of the first class)

b. Cumulative frequency distribution

c. Draw a histogram for the data.

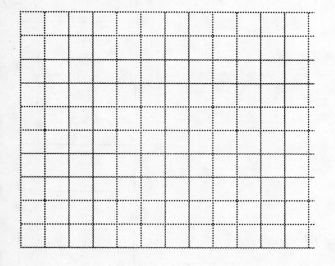

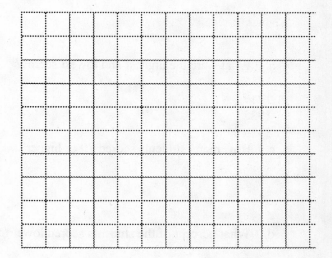

31

d. Develop a frequency polygon.   e.   Draw a less-than-cumulative frequency polygon

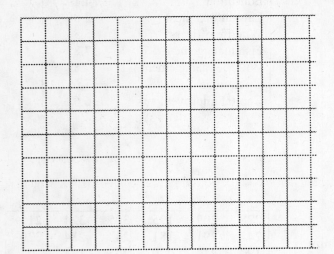   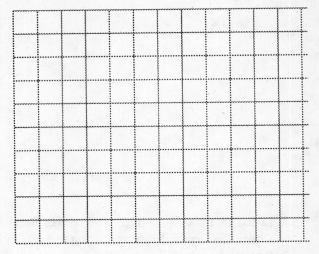

14. The following stem and leaf plot shows the scores on a recent test of Pre-Calculus students.

STEM	LEAF
5	6 8
6	1 2 2 4 8
7	0 4 6 6
8	0 4 4 6 6 6 6 6
9	0 2 6
10	0

a.   How many students took the test?

a.

b.   What were the highest and lowest scores?

b.

c.   How many students scored 70 or higher?

c.

d.   What percent of the students scored lower than 70?

d.

CHAPTER 3
DESCRIBING DATA: MEASURES OF LOCATION

Chapter Goals

After completing this chapter, you will be able to:

1. Calculate the arithmetic mean, median, mode, weighted mean, and geometric mean for a set of observations.

2. Explain the characteristics, use, advantages, and disadvantages of each measure of central tendency.

3. Identify the position of the arithmetic mean, median, and mode for both a symmetrical distribution and a skewed distribution.

Introduction

What is an average? It is a single number used to describe the central tendency of a set of data.

Examples of an average are:

- In 1998 the five year average return on a 12 stock portfolio assembled in 1995 was 17.8%. (*Better Investing*, March 1998)

- The average length of the school year for students in public schools in the United States is 180 days.

- Magazines ended 1997 on a high note with a record number of pages of advertisements. The top ten had an average of 31 ad pages per issue. (*Advertising Age*, January 26, 1998).

- The median asking price for a group of houses listed for sale by a Toledo realtor is $128,000.

- "The difference between America's average, or mean, income of $25,466 and its median income of $17,587 is at an all time high…"(*The Census Bureau's Income Statistics Branch*, April 1998)

There are several different types of averages. We will consider five: the arithmetic mean, the median, the mode, the weighted mean, and the geometric mean.

Measures of Central Tendency

The purpose of a measure of central tendency is to pinpoint the center of a set of observations.

> *Measure of central tendency*: A single value that summarizes a set of data. It locates the center of the values.

The arithmetic mean, or simply mean, is the most widely used measure of central tendency.

> *Arithmetic mean*: The sum of observations divided by the total number of observations.

The mean is calculated as follows:

$$\boxed{\text{Population mean } = \frac{\text{Sum of all values in the population}}{\text{Number of values in the population}}}$$

In terms of symbols, the formula for the arithmetic mean of a population is:

$$\boxed{\mu = \frac{\Sigma X}{N} \qquad [3-1]}$$

Where:

μ	stands for the population mean.
N	stands for the number of items in the population.
X	stands for a particular value.
Σ	indicates the operation of adding all the values. It is pronounced "sigma."
ΣX	is the sum of the X values. It is pronounced "sigma X."
[3-1]	indicates the formula number from the text.

Any measurable characteristic of a population is called a *parameter*.

$$\boxed{\textit{Parameter}: \text{A characteristic of a population.}}$$

In terms of symbols, the formula for the arithmetic mean of a sample is:

$$\boxed{\overline{X} = \frac{\Sigma X}{n} \qquad [3-2]}$$

Where:

$\overline{X}$	stands for the sample mean; it is read "X bar".
n	stands for the number of values in the sample.
X	stands for a particular value.
Σ	indicates the operation of adding all the values.
ΣX	is the sum of the X values.
[3-2]	is the formula number from the text.

The mean of a sample, or any other measure based on a sample data, is called a *statistic*.

$$\boxed{\textit{Statistic}: \text{A characteristic of a sample.}}$$

"The mean weight of a sample of laptop computers is 15 pounds," is an example of a statistic.

Note that in both of the above formulas the mean is calculated by summing the observations and dividing by the total number of observations.

As an example, the Kellogg Company had quarterly earnings per share of: $0.89, $0.77, $1.05, $0.79, and $0.95.

$$\mu = \frac{\Sigma X}{N} = \frac{(\$0.89 + \$0.77 + \$1.05 + \$0.79 + \$0.95)}{5}$$

$$= \frac{\$4.45}{5} = \$0.89$$

The mean quarterly earning per share is $0.89.

In some situations the mean may not be representative of the data.

As an example, the annual salaries of five executives are: $40,000, $42,000, $44,000, $48,000, and $300,000. The mean is:

$$\mu = \frac{\Sigma X}{N} = \frac{(\$40,000 + \$42,000 + \$44,000 + \$48,000 + \$300,000)}{5}$$

$$= \frac{\$474,000}{5} = \$94,800$$

Notice how the one extreme value ($300,000) pulled the mean upward. Four of the five executives earned less than the mean, raising the question whether the arithmetic mean value of $94,800 is typical of the salary of the five executives.

Properties of the Mean

As stated, the arithmetic mean is a widely used measure of central tendency. It has several important properties.

- Every set of interval level and ratio level data has a mean.
- All the data values are used in the calculation.
- A set of data has only one mean, that is, the mean is unique.
- The mean is a useful measure for comparing two or more populations.
- The sum of the deviations from the mean equal 0, that is:

$$\boxed{\Sigma(X - \overline{X}) = 0 \qquad [3-3]}$$

Weighted Mean

The *weighted mean* is a special case of the arithmetic mean. It occurs when there are several observations of the same value.

> *Weighted mean*: The value of each observation is multiplied by the number of times it occurs. The sum of these products is divided by the total number of observations to give the weighted mean.

In general, the weighted mean of a set of numbers, designated $X_1, X_2, X_3, \ldots X_n$, with the corresponding weights $w_1, w_2, w_3, \ldots, w_n$ is computed by:

$$\overline{X}_w = \frac{w_1 X_1 + w_2 X_2 + w_3 X_3 + \cdots + w_n X_n}{w_1 + w_2 + w_3 + \cdots + w_n} \qquad [3-4]$$

The weighted mean is particularly useful when various classes or groups contribute differently to the total. For example, the coronary care unit of a hospital consists of nurses' aides who are paid $8 per hour, nurses' assistants who earn $10 per hour, and registered nurses who earn $15 per hour.

It would not be accurate to say the average hourly wage for the coronary unit is $11 per hour ($8 + $10 + $15) / 3 unless there were the same number of people in each group.

Suppose the coronary care unit has ten employees: two aides who earn $8 per hour, 3 nurses' assistants who earn $10 per hour and five registered nurses who earn $15 per hour. The weighted mean is:

$$\overline{X}_w = \frac{w_1 X_1 + w_2 X_2 + w_3 X_3 + \cdots + w_n X_n}{w_1 + w_2 + w_3 + \cdots + w_n}$$

$$= \frac{(2 \times \$8) + (3 \times \$10) + (5 \times \$15)}{2+3+5} = \frac{\$16 + \$30 + \$75}{10} = \frac{\$121}{10} = \$12.10$$

Thus the weighted mean is $12.10.

The Median

It was pointed out that the arithmetic mean is often not representative of data with extreme values. The *median* is a useful measure when we encounter data with an extreme value.

> *Median*: The midpoint of the values after all observations have been ordered from the smallest to the largest, or from largest to smallest. Fifty percent of the observations are above the median and 50 percent are below the median.

To determine the median, the values are ordered from low to high, or high to low, and the middle value selected. Hence, half the observations are above the median and half are below it. For the executive incomes, the middle value is $44,000, the median.

$40,000 $42,000 $44,000 $48,000 $300,000

⇑

median

Obviously, it is a more representative value in this problem than the mean of $94,800.

Note that there were an odd number of executive incomes (5). For an odd number of ungrouped values we just order them and select the middle value. To determine the median of an even number of ungrouped values, the first step is to arrange them from low to high as usual, and then determine the value half way between the two middle values.

As an example, the final grades of the six students in Mathematics 126 were: 87, 62, 91, 58, 99, and 85. Ordering these from low to high:

$$58 \quad 62 \quad 85 \quad 87 \quad 91 \quad 99$$
$$\Uparrow \quad \Uparrow$$

The median grade is halfway between the two middle values of 85 and 87. The median grade is 86. Thus we note that the median (86) may not be one of the values in a set of data.

Properties of the Median

The major properties of the median are:

- It can be computed for ratio level, interval level, and ordinal-level data.
- It is not influenced by extreme values.
- Fifty percent of the observations are greater than the median.
- It is a unique value for a set of data.
- It can be computed for an open-ended frequency distribution if the median does not lie in the open-ended class.

The Mode

A third measure of central tendency is the *mode*.

> *Mode*: The value of the observation that appears most frequently.

The mode is the value that occurs most often in a set of raw data. The dividends per share declared on five stocks were: $3, $2, $4, $5, and $4. Since $4 occurred twice, which was the most frequent, the mode is $4.

Properties of the Mode

- The mode can be found for all levels of data (nominal, ordinal, interval, and ratio).
- The mode is not affected by extreme high or low values.
- A set of data can have more than one mode. If it has two modes it is bimodal.
- It can be used as a measure of central tendency for open-ended distributions.
- A disadvantage is that a set of data may not have a mode because no value appears more than once.

Geometric Mean

The geometric mean is used to determine the mean percent increase from one period to another. It is also used in finding the average of ratios, indexes, and growth rates.

> *Geometric mean*: The *n* th root of the product of *n* values.

The formula for finding the geometric mean is:

$$GM = \sqrt[n]{(X_1)(X_2)\cdots(X_n)} \qquad [3-5]$$

37   Chapter 3

Where:

X_1, X_2, etc. are data values.

n is the number of values.

$\sqrt[n]{\ }$ is the n th root

The geometric mean can be used for averaging percents. Suppose the income as percent of sales for McDermoll International for the past 4 years is: 0.4, 2.9, 2.1, and 2.2 percent. The GM is 1.5 percent, found by:

$$GM = \sqrt[n]{(X_1)(X_2)\cdots(X_n)}$$
$$= \sqrt[4]{0.4 \times 2.9 \times 2.1 \times 2.2}$$
$$= \sqrt[4]{5.3592} = 1.521 = 1.5$$

Another application of the geometric mean is to find average percent increase over a period of time. Text formula [3-6] is used:

$$\boxed{GM = \sqrt[n]{\dfrac{\text{Value at end of period}}{\text{Value at beginning of period}}} - 1 \qquad [3-6]}$$

Selecting an Average for Data in a Frequency Distribution

The mean, median, and mode of a set of data are usually not all equal. However, if they are identical the distribution is a *symmetrical distribution*.

> *Symmetrical distribution*: A distribution that has the same shape on either side of the median.

The following chart shows the useful life of a sample of 51 batteries. Note the symmetrical bell-shape of the distribution. In a symmetrical distribution the mean, median and mode are equal.

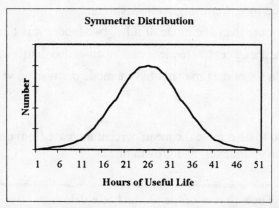

If the distribution is not symmetrical it is said to be skewed and the relationship between the mean, median, and mode changes. If the long tail is to the right, the distribution is said to be a *positively skewed distribution*.

> *Positively skewed distribution*: The long tail is to the right; that is, in the positive direction. The mean is larger than the median or the mode.

The following chart shows the years of service for a group of employees at an old manufacturing plant that **was** revitalized with a new product line and experienced a hiring surge about 13 years ago. It is a positively **skewed** distribution. The mean is larger than the median which is larger than the mode.

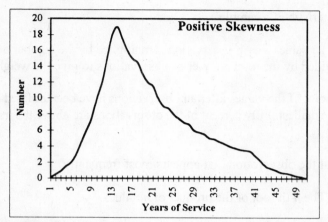

For a *negatively skewed distribution* the mean is the smallest of the three measures of central tendency (**because** it is being pulled down by the small observations). The mode is the highest of the three measures.

> *Negatively skewed distribution*: The long tail is to the left or in the negative direction. The mean is smaller than the median or mode.

The following chart shows the years of service for a group of teachers in a school system that has an **experienced** staff and has not hired many staff in recent years. The mean is smaller than the median which is **smaller** than the mode.

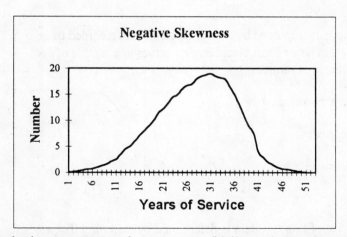

In skewed distributions the mode always appears at the apex or top (highest point) on the curve, and the mean **is pulled** in the direction of the tail. The median always appears between the mode and the mean, regardless of **the direction** of the tail.

Chapter 3

Glossary

Measure of central tendency: A single value that summarizes a set of data. It locates the center of the values.

Arithmetic mean: The sum of observations divided by the total number of observations.

Parameter: A characteristic of a population.

Statistic: A characteristic of a sample.

Weighted mean: The value of each observation is multiplied by the number of times it occurs. The sum of these products is divided by the total number of observations to give the weighted mean.

Median: The midpoint of the values after all observations have been ordered from the smallest to the largest, or from largest to smallest. Fifty percent of the observations are above the median and 50 percent are below the median.

Mode: The value of the observation that appears most frequently.

Geometric mean: The *n* th root of the product of *n* values.

Symmetrical distribution: A distribution that has the same shape on either side of the median.

Positively skewed distribution: The long tail is to the right; that is, in the positive direction. The mean is larger than the median or the mode.

Negatively skewed distribution: The long tail is to the left or in the negative direction. The mean is smaller than the median or mode.

Chapter Problems

Problem 1

A comparison shopper employed by a large grocery chain recorded these prices for a 340-gram jar of Kraft blackberry preserves at a sample of six supermarkets selected at random.

a. Compute the arithmetic mean.

b. Compute the median.

c. Compute the mode.

Supermarket	Price X
1	$1.31
2	1.35
3	1.26
4	1.42
5	1.31
6	1.33
Total	$7.98

Solution

a. The mean price of this raw data is determined by summing the prices for the six jars and dividing the total by six. Recall the formula for the mean of a sample was given previously. See Formula [3-2].

$$\overline{X} = \frac{\Sigma X}{n} = \frac{\$7.98}{6} = \$1.33$$

b. As noted above the *median* is defined as the middle value of a set of data, after the data is arranged from smallest to largest. The prices for the six jars of blackberry preserves have been ordered from a low of $1.26 up to $1.42. Because this is an even number of prices the median price is halfway between the third and the fourth price. The median is $1.32.

Prices Arranged from Low to High:

$1.26 $1.31 $1.31 $1.33 $1.35 $1.42
⇑   ⇑

$$Median = \frac{\$1.31 + \$1.33}{2} = \$1.32$$

Suppose there are an odd number of blackberry preserve prices, such as:

$1.31 $1.31 $1.33 $1.35 $1.42

The median is the middle value ($1.33). Of course, to find the median, the values must first be ordered from low to high.

c. The mode is the price that occurs most often. The price of $1.31 occurs twice in the original data and is the mode.

Exercise 3.1

Check your answers against those in the ANSWER section.

The number of semester credit hours for seven part-time college students is: 8, 5, 4, 10, 8, 3, and 4.

Compute the:
a. mean
b. median
c. mode

Problem 2

The hourly wages for a sample of plumbers were grouped into the following frequency distribution. Since the wages have been grouped into classes, we refer to the following distribution as being *grouped* data.

a. Compute the arithmetic mean.

b. Compute the median.

c. Compute the mode.

Hourly Wages		Number f
$8 up to	$10	3
$10 up to	$12	6
$12 up to	$14	12
$14 up to	$16	10
$16 up to	$18	7
$18 up to	$20	2
		40

Solution

a. The arithmetic mean of this sample data, grouped into a frequency distribution, is computed by formula [3-7].

$$\overline{X} = \frac{\Sigma fX}{n} \qquad [3-7]$$

Where:

$\overline{X}$ is the designation for the arithmetic mean.
X is the mid-value, or midpoint, of each class.
f is the frequency in each class.
fX is the frequency in each class times the midpoint of the class.
ΣfX is the sum of these products.
n is the total number of frequencies.

It is assumed that the observations in each class are represented by the midpoint of the class. The midpoint of the first class is $9.00, found by ($8.00 + $10.00)/2. For the next higher class, the midpoint is $11.00.

Wage Rate	Frequency f	Class Midpoint X	fX
$8 up to $10	3	$9.00	$27.00
$10 up to $12	6	11.00	66.00
$12 up to $14	12	13.00	156.00
$14 up to $16	10	15.00	150.00
$16 up to $18	7	17.00	119.00
$18 up to $20	2	19.00	38.00
Total	40		$556.00

Using formula [3-7] the arithmetic mean hourly wage is $13.90, found by

$$\overline{X} = \frac{\Sigma fX}{n} = \frac{\$556.00}{40} = \$13.90$$

The median of data grouped into a frequency distribution is found by applying formula [3-8] as follows:

$$Median = L + \frac{\frac{n}{2} - CF}{f}(i) \qquad [3-8]$$

Where:

L is the lower limit of the class containing the median.
n is the total number of frequencies.
f is the frequency in the median class.
CF is the cumulative number of frequencies in the class immediately preceding the class containing the median.
i is the width of the class containing the median.

The hourly wage distribution of a sample of plumbers is repeated and a column giving the cumulative frequencies added.

Wage Rate	Frequency f	Cumulative Frequency CF
$8 up to $10	3	3
$10 up to $12	6	9
$12 up to $14	12	21
$14 up to $16	10	31
$16 up to $18	7	38
$18 up to $20	2	40

Median Class ⇒ (points to the $12 up to $14 row)

The median class is located by dividing the total number of observations by 2. Thus, $40/2 = 20$. The class containing the 20th plumber can be located by referring to the cumulative frequency column in the above table. Notice that 9 plumbers earn less than $12. And, 21 plumbers earn less than $14. Thus, the 20th plumber earns some amount between $12 and $14, the lower limit ($L$) of that class is $12. This class in the middle of the distribution is designated as the *median class*.

The cumulative number of frequencies (CF) in the class preceding the median class is 9. The number of frequencies (f) in the median class is 12. The width of the median class (i) is $2.00. Solving for the median:

$$\text{Median} = L + \frac{\frac{n}{2} - CF}{f}(i) = \$12 + \frac{\frac{40}{2} - 9}{12}(\$2.00) = \$12 + \frac{11}{12}(\$2.00) = \$12 + \$1.83 = \$13.83$$

The *mode* is the value that occurs most often. For data grouped into a frequency distribution, the mode is the midpoint of the class containing the most observations. There are more observations (12) in the $12 up to $14 class than in any other class. The midpoint of the class is $13, which is the mode.

We computed three measures of central tendency for the hourly wage data. Observe that the mean ($13.90), the median ($13.80), and the mode ($13.00) are all different. Generally, this is the case. What measure of central tendency to select to represent the data will be discussed shortly.

Exercise 3.2

Check your answers against those in the ANSWER section.

The annual exports of 50 medium-sized manufacturers were organized into a frequency distribution. (Exports are in $ millions.)

Exports	Frequency
$6 up to $9	2
9 up to 12	8
12 up to 15	20
15 up to 18	14
18 up to 21	6

Compute the:
a. mean   b. median   c. mode

Problem 3

At Sarasota College there are 10 instructors, 12 assistant professors, 20 associate professors, and 5 professors. Their average annual salaries are $34,000, $45,000, $58,000, and $68,000, respectively. What is the weighted mean salary?

Solution

The number of faculty for each rank is not equal. Therefore, it is not appropriate simply to add the average salaries of the four ranks and divide by 4. We have a better method for weighting the averages. In this problem the salaries for each rank are multiplied by the number of faculty in that rank, the products totaled, then divided by the number of faculty. The result is the weighted mean.

$$\overline{X} = \frac{w_1 X_1 + w_2 X_2 + w_3 X_3 + w_4 X_4}{w_1 + w_2 + w_{31} + w_4}$$

$$= \frac{10(\$34,000) + 12(\$45,000) + 20(\$58,000) + 5(\$68,000)}{10 + 12 + 20 + 5}$$

$$= \frac{\$2,380,000}{47}$$

$$= \$50,638$$

Exercise 3.3

Check your answers against those in the ANSWER section.

During the past month an electronics store sold 31 model EL733 calculators for $30 each, 42 model EL480 calculators for $10 each, 47 model FX115 calculators for $20 each, and 63 model BA35 calculators for $24 each. What is the weighted mean price of the calculators?

Problem 4

From 1984 to 1998 the number of hospital net beds sold by Wagoner Enterprises increased from 5 to 300. Compute the mean annual percent increase in the number of hospital beds sold.

Solution

The geometric mean (GM) annual percent increase from one time period to another is determined using formula [3-6].

$$GM = \sqrt[n]{\frac{\text{Value at the end of the period}}{\text{Value at the start of the period}}} - 1 \qquad [3-6]$$

Note that there are 14 years between 1984 and 1998, so, $n = 14$.

$$GM = \sqrt[14]{\frac{300}{5}} - 1 = \sqrt[14]{60.0} - 1 = 1.33971 - 1 = 0.3379$$

For those with a $\sqrt[x]{y}$ key on their calculator, the geometric mean can be solved quickly by:

$$GM = \sqrt[n-1]{\frac{300}{5}} - 1 = \sqrt[14]{60.0} - 1$$

Using $\sqrt[x]{y}$	Display
$300 \div 5 =$	60
Depress $\sqrt[x]{y}$	
Depress 14	1.33971
Depress $-1 =$	0.33971, or about 34%

The value 1 is subtracted, according to formula [3-6], so the rate of increase is 0.33971, or 33.971% per year. The sale of hospital beds increased at a rate of almost 34% per year.

Exercise 3.4

Check your answers against those in the ANSWER section.

In 1983, thirty acres of woods was valued at $475 per acre. In 1998 the acreage was valued at $1850 per acre. What is the geometric mean annual percent increase in value?

CHAPTER 3 ASSIGNMENT

DESCRIBING DATA: MEASURES OF LOCATION

Name _____   Section _____   Score _____

Part I   Select the correct answer and write the appropriate letter in the space provided.

_____ 1.   The arithmetic mean is computed by
   a.   summing the values and dividing by the number of values.
   b.   finding the middle observation and dividing by 2.
   c.   finding the value that occurs most often.
   d.   electing the value in the middle of the data set.

_____ 2.   To compute the arithmetic mean at least the
   a.   nominal level of measurement is required.
   b.   ordinal level of measurement is required.
   c.   interval level of measurement is required.
   d.   ratio level of measurement is required.

_____ 3.   The value that occurs most often in a set of data is called the
   a.   mean.
   b.   median.
   c.   mode.
   d.   geometric mean.

_____ 4.   What level of measurement is required to determine the mode?
   a.   nominal
   b.   ordinal
   c.   interval
   d.   ratio

_____ 5.   For a symmetric distribution
   a.   the mean is larger than the median.
   b.   the mean, median and the mode are equal.
   c.   the mean is smaller than the median.
   d.   the mode is the largest value.

_____ 6.   Which of the following is *not* true about the arithmetic mean.
   a.   all the values are used in its calculation
   b.   half of the observations are always larger than the mean
   c.   it is influenced by a large value
   d.   it is found by summing all the values and dividing by the number of observations

_____ 7. In a *negatively* skewed distribution
     a.   the mean and median are equal.
     b.   the mean is larger than the median.
     c.   the mean is smaller than the median.
     d.   the median and the mode are equal.

_____ 8. What level of measurement is required for the median?
     a.   nominal
     b.   ordinal
     c.   interval
     d.   ratio

_____ 9. The Dow Jones Industrial Average increased from 961 in 1980 to 8900 in the first quarter of 1998. The annual rate of increase is best described by the
     a.   geometric mean.
     b.   weighted mean.
     c.   median.
     d.   mode.

_____ 10. What is the shape of a frequency distribution with an arithmetic mean of 12,000 pounds, a median of 12,000 pounds, and a mode of 12,000 pounds?
     a.   flat
     b.   symmetric
     c.   geometrically skewed
     d.   positively skewed

Part II   Find the answers to each of the following questions. Show essential calculations.

11. **A** study was conducted about the number of people running a red light at a particular intersection. The **number** of violators for a sample of seven days is:

         6   12   7   12   8   4   5

    a.   Compute the sample mean.

a.

    b.   What is the median?

b.

c.   What is the mode?

c.

d.   Describe the skewness.

d.

12. A shipment of packages to the Solomon Company included 10 packages weighing 7.4 pounds, 12 weighing 8.2 pounds and 6 weighing 8.7 pounds. What is the **average weight of a package?**

12.

13. The average daily attendance for eight large employers in Lucas County is as follows:

    95.7%,   95.3%,   95.5%,   95%,   94.7%,   93.7%,   93.8%   90.7%.

Find the average daily attendance for the county.

13.

14. From 1981 to 1997 the net sales for the J.M. Smucker Company increased from $157 million to $543 million. Compute the mean annual percent increase in net sales.

14.

15 . The Ohio Bureau of Employment gathered the following sample information on the number of hours unemployed workers spent looking for work last week.

Hours spent Searching	Number of Unemployed
0 up to 10	3
10 up to 20	7
20 up to 30	15
30 up to 40	10
40 up to 50	5
TOTAL	40

a. Determine the mean

a.

b. Determine the median

b.

c. Determine the mode

c.

CHAPTER 4
DESCRIBING DATA: MEASURES OF DISPERSION

Chapter Goals

After completing this chapter, you will be able to:

1. Compute and interpret the range, the mean deviation, the variance, and the standard deviation from raw data.

2. Compute and interpret the range, the variance, and the standard deviation from grouped data.

3. Explain the characteristics, uses, advantages, and disadvantages of each measure of dispersion..

4. Understand Chebyshev's Theorem and the Normal, or Empirical Rule, as they relate to a set of observations.

5. Compute and interpret quartiles and the interquartile range.

6. Construct and interpret box plots.

7. Compute and understand the coefficient of variation and the coefficient of skewness.

Introduction

In Chapter 2 we discussed methods of organizing data into a frequency distribution and presented various graphical techniques. In Chapter 3 measures of central tendency were examined. A direct comparison of two sets of data based only on two measures of central tendency can be misleading.

For example, suppose a statistics instructor had two classes, one in the morning and one in the evening; each with six students. In the morning class (AM) the students' ages are: 18, 20, 21, 21, 23, and 23 years. In the evening class (PM) the ages are 17, 17, 18, 20, 25, and 29 years. Note that for both classes the mean age is 21 years but there is more variation or dispersion in the ages of the evening students.

This chapter considers several measures of dispersion, namely, the *range*, the *mean deviation*, the *variance*, the *standard deviation*, the *interquartile range*, and *quartile deviation.*

Range

Perhaps the simplest measure of dispersion is the *range*.

> *Range*: The difference between the highest and lowest value in a set of data.

The formula for range is:

$$\text{Range} = \text{Highest value} - \text{Lowest value} \qquad [4\text{-}1]$$

In the introduction to this chapter an example was given where a statistic instructor had two classes with the ages indicated:

A.M. Class: 18, 20, 21, 21, 23, 23   **P.M. Class**: 17, 17, 18, 20, 25, 29

The range for the classes is:

A.M. Class: (23 – 18) = 5   **P.M. Class**: (29 – 17) = 12

Thus we can say that there is more spread in the ages of the students enrolled in the evening (P.M.) class compared with the morning (A.M.) class.

The characteristics of the range are:

- Only two values are used in the calculation.
- It is influenced by extreme values.
- It is easy to compute and understand.
- It can be distorted by an extreme value.

The range has two disadvantages. It can be distorted by a single extreme value. Suppose the same statistics instructor has a third class of five students. The ages of these students are given in the table.

| 20, 20, 21, 22, 60 |

The range of ages is 40 years, yet four of the five students' ages are within two years of each other. The 60-year old student has distorted the spread. Another disadvantage is that only two values, the largest and the smallest, are used in its calculation.

Mean Deviation

In contrast to the range, the *mean deviation* considers all the data.

Mean Deviation: The mean of the absolute values of the deviations from the arithmetic mean.

In terms of symbols, the formula for the mean deviation is:

$$MD = \frac{\Sigma \left| X - \overline{X} \right|}{n} \qquad [4-2]$$

Where:
X is the value of each observation
$\overline{X}$ is the arithmetic mean
n is the number of observations
| | indicates absolute value

The mean deviation is computed by first determining the difference between each observation and the mean. These differences are then averaged without regard to their signs. For the PM statistics class the mean deviation is 4.0 years, found by

$X - \overline{X}$				Absolute deviation
$\mid 17 - 21 \mid$	=	$\mid -4 \mid$	=	4
$\mid 17 - 21 \mid$	=	$\mid -4 \mid$	=	4
$\mid 18 - 21 \mid$	=	$\mid -3 \mid$	=	3
$\mid 20 - 21 \mid$	=	$\mid -1 \mid$	=	1
$\mid 25 - 21 \mid$	=	$\mid -4 \mid$	=	4
$\mid 29 - 21 \mid$	=	$\mid -8 \mid$	=	8
			Σ =	24

then

$$\overline{X} = \frac{\Sigma \mid X - \overline{X} \mid}{n} = \frac{24}{6} = 4$$

The parallel lines $\mid \mid$ indicate absolute value. To interpret, 4.0 years is the mean amount by which the ages differ from the arithmetic mean age of 21.0 years for the PM students.

Variance and Standard Deviation

The disadvantage of the mean deviation is that the absolute values are difficult to manipulate mathematically. The problem of absolute values is eliminated by squaring the differences from each value and the mean. These squared differences are used both in the computation of the *variance* and the *standard deviation*.

> *Variance:* The arithmetic mean of the squared deviations from the mean.

> *Standard Deviation:* The square root of the variance.

Squaring units of measurement, such as dollars or years, makes the variance cumbersome to use since it yields units like "dollars squared" or "years squared." However, by calculating the standard deviation, which is the positive square root of the variance, we can return to the original units, such as years or dollars. Because the standard deviation is easier to interpret, it is more widely used than the mean deviation or the variance.

Population Variance

The formula for the population variance for ungrouped data, that is, data not tabulated into a frequency distribution, is:

$$\sigma^2 = \frac{\Sigma (X - \mu)^2}{N} \qquad [4-3]$$

Where:

σ^2 is the symbol for the population variance.

X is a value of an observation in the population.

μ the arithmetic mean of the population.

N is the total number of observations in the population.

The major characteristics of the variance are:

1. All the observations are used in the calculations.

2. It is not influenced by extreme observations.

3. The units are somewhat difficult to work with. (They are the original units squared.)

    The standard deviation is the square root of the variance. The formula for the standard deviation of a population is:

$$\sigma = \sqrt{\frac{\Sigma(X-\mu)^2}{N}} \qquad [4-4]$$

Sample Variance – Conceptual Formula

The conversion of the population variance formula to the sample variance formula is not as direct as the change made when we went from the population mean formula to the sample mean formula. Recall that we replaced μ with $\overline{X}$ and N with n. The conversion from population variance to sample variance requires a change in the denominator. Instead of substituting n, the number in the sample, for N, the number in the population, we replace N with $(n-1)$. Thus the formula for the sample variance is:

$$s^2 = \frac{\Sigma(X-\overline{X})^2}{n-1} \qquad [4-5]$$

Where:

s^2 is the symbol for the sample variance. It is pronounced as "s squared."

X is the value of each observation in the sample.

$\overline{X}$ is the mean of the sample.

n is the total number of observations in the sample.

    Changing the denominator to $(n-1)$ seems insignificant, however the use of n tends to underestimate the population variance. The use of $(n-1)$ in the denominator provides an appropriate correction factor.

Sample Variance – Computational Formula

We can show that the term $\sum(X-\overline{X})^2$ is equal to $\sum X^2 - \frac{(\sum X)^2}{n}$.

Hence the computational formula for the sample variance is:

$$s^2 = \frac{\sum X^2 - \dfrac{(\sum X)^2}{n}}{n-1} \qquad [4-6]$$

This formula is somewhat easier to use because it avoids all but one subtraction.

Standard Deviation – Computational Formula

The sample standard deviation is used as an estimator of the population standard deviation. The sample standard deviation is the square root of the sample variance. The formula is:

$$s = \sqrt{\frac{\sum X^2 - \dfrac{(\sum X)^2}{n}}{n-1}} \qquad [4-7]$$

Interpretation and Uses of the Standard Deviation

Recall that the standard deviation is used to measure the spread of the data. A small standard deviation indicates that the data is clustered close to the mean, thus the mean is representative of the data. A large standard deviation indicates that the data are spread out from the mean and the mean is not representative of the data.

Chebyshev's Theorem

We can use Chebyshev's theorem to determine the percent of the values that lie within a specified number of standard deviations of the mean.

Chebyshev's theorem: For any set of observations (sample or population), the minimum proportion of the values that lie within k standard deviations of the mean is at least $1 - 1/k^2$, where k is any constant greater than 1.

The theorem holds for any set of observations regardless of the shape of the distribution.

The Empirical Rule

Chebyshev's theorem is concerned with any set of values: that is the distribution of values can have any shape. If the distribution is approximately symmetrical and bell shaped then the *Empirical Rule* or **Normal Rule** as it is often called is applied.

> **Empirical Rule**: For a symmetrical, bell-shaped frequency distribution, approximately 68 percent of the observations will lie within plus and minus one standard deviation of the mean; about 95 percent of the observations will lie within plus and minus two standard deviations of the mean; and practically all (99.7 percent) will lie within plus and minus three standard deviations of the mean.

The rule states that:

- The mean, plus and minus one standard deviation, will include about 68% of the observations.
- The mean, plus and minus two standard deviations, will include about 95% of the observations.
- The mean, plus and minus three standard deviations, will include about 99.7% of the observations.

Relative Dispersion

Suppose we want to compare the variability of two sets of data that are measured in different units—one in dollars and the other in years. How can this be done? The *coefficient of variation* is used.

> **Coefficient of variation**: The ratio of the standard deviation to the arithmetic mean, expressed as a percent.

The formula for coefficient of variation for a sample is:

$$CV = \frac{s}{X}(100) \qquad\qquad [4-9]$$

It is a measure of relative dispersion. To compute the coefficient of variation the standard deviation is divided by the mean and the result is multiplied by 100. This measure reports the standard deviation as a percent of the mean.

If, for example, in a study of executives the coefficient of variation for incomes is 29 percent and for their ages it is 12 percent, we would conclude that there is more relative dispersion in the incomes of the executives than in their ages.

Characteristics of the coefficient of variation are:

- It reports the variation relative to the mean.
- It is useful for comparing distributions with different units.

Skewness

The measures of central tendency and the measures of dispersion are both descriptive characteristics of a set of data. A third characteristic of a distribution is its *skewness*. As noted before, a **symmetric** distribution has the same shape on either side of the median and it has no skewness. For a **positively skewed** distribution the long tail is to the right, the mean is larger than the median or the mode, and the mode appears at the highest point on the curve. For a **negatively skewed** distribution the mode is the largest value and is at the highest point of the curve, while the mean is the smallest.

> *Coefficient of skewness:* A measure to describe the degree of skewness.

The formula for computing the coefficient of skewness is:

$$sk = \frac{3(\text{mean} - \text{median})}{\text{Standard deviation}} \qquad [4-10]$$

The coefficient of skewness, designated sk, measures the amount of skewness and may range from -3.0 to $+3.0$.

The major characteristics are:

- It may range from -3.00 up to $+3.00$.
- A value of 0 means the distribution is symmetric.

Other Measures of Dispersion

The variance and the standard deviation are the most widely used measures of dispersion. However there are several others which include *Quartiles*, *Deciles*, and *Percentiles*.

Quartiles

Recall that the median divides data that has been placed in an array, such that half the values are below the median and half are above the median. If we divide the lower and upper set of values into two equal parts we have quartiles. Quartiles divide a set of data into four equal parts.

> *First Quartile* The point below which one fourth or 25% of the ranked data values lie. (It is designated Q_1)

> *Third Quartile* The point below which three fourths or 75% of the ranked data values lie. (It is designated Q_3)

Logically the median is the Second Quartile (designated Q_2). The values corresponding to Q_1, Q_2 and Q_3 divide a set of data into four equal parts.

Two other measures of dispersion are *interquartile range* and *quartile deviation*.

> *Interquartile range*: The distance between the first and third quartile.

> *Quartile deviation*: Half the interquartile range.

Both of the measures are concerned with the middle 50 percent of the observations, or data. An advantage of these two measures is that they are easy to compute and they are not affected by extremely large or small values. A disadvantage is that not all observations are used in their calculation.

Deciles and Percentiles

Just as quartiles divide a distribution into 4 equal parts, deciles divide a distribution into ten equal parts, and percentiles divide a distribution into 100 equal parts

For example: If you were told that your Scholastic Aptitude Test score was in the 9th decile, you could assume that 90 percent of those taking the test had a lower score than yours and that 10 percent had a higher score. A Grade point Average in the 55th percentile means that 55 percent of students have a lower GPA than yours and that 45 percent have a higher GPA.

The procedure for finding the quartile, decile and a percentile for ungrouped data in an ordered array is generalized using text formula [4-10].

$$L_p = (n+1)\frac{P}{100} \qquad [4-10]$$

Where:
L_p refers to the location of the desired percentile.
n is the number of observations.
P is the desired percentile

Note that this is a generic formula for percentiles, deciles and quartiles.

For example, if you had a set of data with 49 observations in ordered array and wanted to locate the 78 percentile, then let $P = 78$ and $L_p = (n+1)\frac{P}{100} = (49+1)\frac{78}{100} = 39$. Thus you would locate the 39th observation .

If you wanted to locate the 6 decile, then let $P = 60$ and $L_p = (n+1)\frac{P}{100} = (49+1)\frac{60}{100} = 30$. Thus you would locate the 30th observation. Note that the 6 decile equals the 60 percentile

Box Plots

A *box plot* is a graphical display that helps us picture how a set of data is distributed relative to the quartiles.

> *Box plot*: A graphical display based on quartiles.

To construct a box plot we need five pieces of data: the minimum value, Q_1 ,(the first quartile), Q_2 the median, Q_3 (the third quartile) and the maximum value. The details for constructing and interpreting a box plot are found in Problem 10 of the Chapter Problems.

Glossary

Range: The difference between the highest and lowest value in a set of data.

Mean Deviation: The mean of the absolute values of the deviations from the arithmetic mean.

Variance: The arithmetic mean of the squared deviations from the mean.

Standard Deviation: The square root of the variance.

Chebyshev's theorem: For any set of observations (sample or population), the minimum proportion of the values that lie within k standard deviations of the mean is at least $1 - 1/k^2$, where k is any constant greater than 1.

Empirical Rule: For a symmetrical, bell-shaped frequency distribution, approximately 68 percent of the observations will lie within plus and minus one standard deviation of the mean; about 95 percent of the observations will lie within plus and minus two standard deviations of the mean; and practically all (99.7 percent) will lie within plus and minus three standard deviations of the mean.

Coefficient of variation: The ratio of the standard deviation to the arithmetic mean, expressed as a percent.

Coefficient of skewness: A measure to describe the degree of skewness.

First Quartile The point below which one fourth or 25% of the ranked data values lie. (It is designated Q_1)

Third Quartile The point below which three fourths or 75% of the ranked data values lie. (It is designated Q_3)

Interquartile range: The distance between the first and third quartile.

Quartile deviation: Half the interquartile range.

Box Plot: A graphical display based on quartiles.

Chapter Problems

Problem 1

A sample of the amounts spent in November for propane gas to heat homes of similar sizes in Duluth revealed these amounts (to the nearest dollar):

$191 $212 $176 $129 $106 $92 $108 $109 $103 $121 $175 $194

What is the range? Interpret your results.

Solution

Recall that the range is the difference between the largest value and the smallest value.

$$\text{Range} = \text{Highest Value} - \text{Lowest Value} = (\$212 - \$92) = \$120$$

This indicates that there is a difference of $120 between the largest and the smallest heating cost.

Problem 2

Using the heating cost data in Problem 1, compute the mean deviation.

Solution

The mean deviation is the mean of the absolute deviations from the arithmetic mean. For raw, or ungrouped data, it is computed by first determining the mean. Next, the difference between each value and the arithmetic mean is determined. Finally, these differences are totaled and the total divided by the number of observations. We ignore the sign of each difference. Formula [3-2] for the sample mean and formula [4-2] for the mean deviation are shown below.

Sample Mean

$$\overline{X} = \frac{\Sigma X}{n} \quad [3-2]$$

Mean Deviation

$$MD = \frac{\Sigma |X - \overline{X}|}{n} \quad [4-2]$$

The table below shows the data values, each data value minus the mean, and the absolute value of the deviations from the mean.

In other words, the signs of the deviations from the mean are disregarded.

Payment X	$|X - \overline{X}|$		Absolute Deviations
$191	|$+48 |	=	$48
212	| +69 |	=	69
176	| +33 |	=	33
129	| −14 |	=	14
106	| −37 |	=	37
92	| −51 |	=	51
108	| −35 |	=	35
109	| −34 |	=	34
103	| −40 |	=	40
121	| −22 |	=	22
175	| +32 |	=	32
194	| +51 |	=	51
$1,716			$466

$$\overline{X} = \frac{\Sigma X}{n} = \frac{\$1,716}{12} = \$143.00$$

$$MD = \frac{\Sigma |X - \overline{X}|}{n} = \frac{\$466}{12} = \$38.83$$

The mean deviation of $38.83 indicates that the typical electric bill deviates $38.83 from the mean of $143.00.

Problem 3

Using the same heating cost data in Problem 1, compute the variance and the standard deviation.

Solution

The sample variance, designated s^2, is based on squared deviations from the mean. For ungrouped raw data, it is computed using formula [4-5] or [4-6].

Formula [4-5]

$$s^2 = \frac{\Sigma(X - \overline{X})^2}{n-1}$$

Formula [4-6]

$$s^2 = \frac{\Sigma X^2 - \frac{(\Sigma X)^2}{n}}{n-1}$$

Computing the sample variance both ways:

X	$X - \overline{X}$	$(X - \overline{X})^2$	X^2
$191	$48	2,304	36,481
212	69	4,761	44,944
176	33	1,089	30,976
129	−14	196	16,641
106	−37	1,369	11,236
92	−51	2,601	8,464
108	−35	1,225	11,664
109	−34	1,156	11,881
103	−40	1,600	10,609
121	−22	484	14,641
175	32	1,024	30,625
194	51	2,601	37,636
$1,716	0	20,410	265,798

$$s^2 = \frac{\Sigma(X - \overline{X})^2}{n-1} = \frac{20,410}{12-1} = 1,855.45$$

or

$$s^2 = \frac{\Sigma X^2 - \frac{(\Sigma X)^2}{n-1}}{n-1}$$

$$= \frac{265,798 - \frac{(1,716)^2}{12}}{12-1} = 1,855.45$$

The standard deviation of the sample, designated by s, is the square root of the variance. The square root of 1,855.45 is $43.07. Note that the standard deviation is in the same terms as the original data, that is, dollars.

Exercise 4.1

Check your answers against those in the ANSWER section.

The manager of a fast-food restaurant selected several cash register receipts at random. The amounts spent by customers were $12, $15, $16, $10, and $27. Compute the:

a. range
b. the mean deviation
c. the sample variance
d. the sample standard deviation.

Problem 4

The office manager of the Mallard Glass Company is investigating the ages in months of the company's personal computers currently in use. The ages of 30 units selected at random were organized into a frequency distribution. Compute the range.

Age to the Nearest Month	Number of Personal Computers
20 up to 25	3
25 up to 30	5
30 up to 35	10
35 up to 40	7
40 up to 45	4
45 up to 50	1

Solution

The range is the difference between the lower class limit of the lowest class and the upper class limit of the highest class.

$$\text{Range} = \text{Upper Class Limit} - \text{Lower Class Limit}$$
$$\text{Range} = 50 - 20 = 30 \text{ months}$$

Problem 5

Using the ages of the personal computer equipment in Problem 4, compute the variance and the standard deviation.

Solution

Formula [4-8] is used to compute the standard deviation of grouped data.

$$s = \sqrt{\frac{\Sigma fX^2 - \frac{(\Sigma fX)^2}{n}}{n-1}} \qquad [4-8]$$

Where:
s is the symbol for the sample standard deviation.
X is the midpoint of a class.
f is the class frequency.
n is the total number of sample observations.

Applying this formula to the distribution of the ages of the personal computers in Problem 4, the standard deviation is 6.39 months.

Age to the Nearest Month	f	Class Midpoint X	fX	fX²
20 up to 25	3	22.5	67.5	1,518.75
25 up to 30	5	27.5	137.5	3,781.25
30 up to 35	10	32.5	325.0	10,562.05
35 up to 40	7	37.5	262.5	9,843.75
40 up to 45	4	42.5	170.0	7,225.00
45 up to 50	1	47.5	47.5	2,256.25
	30		1010.0	35,187.50

$$s = \sqrt{\frac{\Sigma fX^2 - \frac{(\Sigma fX)^2}{n}}{n-1}}$$

$$= \sqrt{\frac{35,187.50 - \frac{(1010)^2}{30}}{30-1}}$$

$$= 6.39 \text{ months}$$

The variance is the square of the standard deviation.

$$s^2 = (6.39)^2 = 40.83$$

Problem 6

Use the age of the Mallard Glass word processing equipment (Problem 5) to compute the interquartile range and the quartile deviation.

Solution

The interquartile range and the quartile deviation are computed by:

$$\boxed{\text{Interquartile range} = Q_3 - Q_1 \qquad [4-11]}$$ $$\boxed{\text{Quartile deviation}, Q.D. = \frac{Q_3 - Q_1}{2} \qquad [4-14]}$$

Where:
Q_3 is the third quartile.
Q_1 is the first quartile.

The formula for the first and third quartiles is:

$$\boxed{Q_1 = L + \frac{\frac{n}{4} - CF}{f}(i) \qquad [4-12]}$$ $$\boxed{Q_3 = L + \frac{\frac{3n}{4} - CF}{f}(i) \qquad [4-13]}$$

Where:
L is the lower limit of the class containing the first (or third) quartile.
n is the total number in the sample.
CF is the cumulative number of frequencies occurring before the class containing the first (or third) quartile.
f is the number of frequencies in the class containing the first (or third) quartile.
i is the width of the class interval containing the first (or third) quartile.

The calculations for Q_1 and Q_3 are similar to those for the median (Q_2) discussed in Chapter 3.

To find Q_1: The first step is to search for the class in which Q_1 is located. Note there are 30 word processors. One-fourth of 30 is 7.5. Refer to the following table. Count down in the class frequency column. The first cumulative frequency is 3, the next 8, found by 3 + 5, the next is 18, found by 3 + 5 + 10, and so on.

Age (Stated Limits)	Class Frequency		Cumulative Frequency
20 up to 25	3	COUNT	3
25 up to 30	5	DOWN	8
30 up to 35	10		18
35 up to 40	7		25
40 up to 45	4		29
45 up to 50	1		30
	30		

Note in the cumulative frequency column that 3 word processors have been in use less than 25 months. Eight processors have been in use less than 30 months. The 7.5 processors must be in the 25 up to 30 age class.

Using the formula [4-12], the values to find first quartile (Q_1) are:
$L = 25$, the lower limit of the class containing the first quartile.
$n = 30$, the total number of word processors in the sample.
$CF = 3$, the cumulative number of frequencies occurring prior to the class containing the first quartile.
$f = 5$, the number of frequencies in the class containing the first quartile.
$i = 5$, the width of the 25 up to 30 class.

Computing the first and third quartile.

$$Q_1 = L + \frac{\frac{n}{4} - CF}{f}(i) \qquad\qquad Q_3 = L + \frac{\frac{3n}{4} - CF}{f}(i)$$

$$= 25 + \frac{\frac{30}{4} - 3}{5}(5) \qquad\qquad = 35 + \frac{\frac{3(30)}{4} - 18}{7}(5)$$

$$= 29.5 \qquad\qquad\qquad\qquad = 38.21$$

Fifty percent of the word processors have been in use more than 29.5 months but less than 38.21 months. The interquartile range is 8.71, found by $Q_3 - Q_1 = 8.71$ months. The quartile deviation is:

$$Q.D. = \frac{Q_3 - Q_1}{2} = \frac{38.21 - 29.5}{2} = \frac{8.71}{2} = 4.355 \text{ months}$$

Exercise 4.2

Check your answers against those in the ANSWER section.

The weekly income of a sample of 60 part time employees of a fast-food restaurant chain was organized into the following frequency distribution.

Weekly Incomes	Number of Employees
$100 up to $150	5
150 up to 200	9
200 up to 250	20
250 up to 300	18
300 up to 350	5
350 up to 400	3

a. Compute the standard deviation

b. Compute the quartile deviation,

Problem 7

A sample of the business faculty at state supported institutions in Ohio revealed the mean income to be $52,000 for 9 months with a standard deviation of $3,000. Use Chebyshev's Theorem and the Empirical Rule to estimate the proportion of faculty who earn more than $46,000 but less than $58,000.

Solution

To find the proportion of faculty who earn between $46,000 and $58,000 we must first determine k; k is the number of standard deviations above or below the mean.

$$k = \frac{X - \overline{X}}{s} = \frac{\$46,000 - \$52,000}{\$3,000} = -2.00$$

$$k = \frac{X - \overline{X}}{s} = \frac{\$58,000 - \$52,000}{\$3,000} = 2.00$$

Applying Chebyshev's Theorem: $1 - \dfrac{1}{k^2} = 1 - \dfrac{1}{2^2} = 0.75$

This means that at least 75 percent of the faculty earn between $46,000 and $58,000.

The Empirical rule states that about 68 percent of the observations fall within one standard deviation of the mean, 95 percent are within plus and minus two standard deviations of the mean, and virtually all (99.7%) will lie within three standard deviations from the mean. Hence, about 95 percent of the observations fall between $46,000 and $58,000, found by $\overline{X} \pm 2s = \$52,000 \pm 2(\$3,000)$. So if we conclude that we have a bell shaped distribution, most of the observations fall within the interval.

Problem 8

Recall from Problem 7, a study of business faculty at state supported institutions in Ohio revealed that the arithmetic mean salary for nine months is $52,000 and the standard deviation of the sample is $3,000. The study also showed that the faculty had been employed a mean of 15 years with a standard deviation of 4 years. How does the relative dispersion in the distribution of salaries compare with that of the lengths of service?

Solution

The coefficient of variation measures the relative dispersion in a distribution. In this problem it allows for a comparison of two distributions expressed in different units (dollars and years). Formula [4-9] is used.

$$CV = \frac{s}{\overline{X}}(100) \qquad [4-9]$$

For the salaries:

$$CV = \frac{\$3,000}{\$52,000}(100)$$
$$= 5.8\%$$

For the length of service:

$$CV = \frac{4\,\text{years}}{15\,\text{years}}(100)$$
$$= 26.7\%$$

The coefficient of variation is larger for length of service than for salary. This indicates that there is more relative dispersion in the distribution of the lengths of service relative to the mean than for the distribution of salaries.

Problem 9

The research director of a large oil company conducted a study of the buying habits of consumers with respect to the amount of gasoline purchased at full-service pumps. The arithmetic mean amount is 11.50 gallons, and the median amount is 11.95 gallons. The standard deviation of the sample is 4.5 gallons. Determine the coefficient of skewness. Comment on the shape of the distribution.

Solution

The coefficient of skewness measures the general shape of the distribution. A distribution that is symmetrical has no skewness and the coefficient of skewness is 0. Skewness ranges from −3 to +3. The direction of the long tail of the distribution points in the direction of the skewness. If the mean is larger than the median, the skewness is positive. If the median is larger than the mean, the skewness is negative. The coefficient of skewness is found by formula [4-10]. For this problem:

$$sk = \frac{3(\overline{X} - \text{median})}{s}$$
$$= \frac{3(11.50 - 11.95)}{4.5}$$
$$= -0.30$$

This indicates that there is a slight negative skewness in the distribution of gasoline purchases from full-service pumps.

Exercise 4.3

Check your answers against those in the ANSWER section.

An automobile dealership pays its salespersons a salary plus a commission on sales. The mean biweekly commission is $990, the median $950, and the standard deviation $70.

a. Estimate the percent of salespersons that earn more than $885, but less than $1095.

b. Is the distribution of commissions positively skewed, negatively skewed, or symmetrical?

c. Compute the coefficient of skewness to verify your answer.

Problem 10

Listed below are the selling prices (in thousands of dollars) of a sample of 15 homes sold by agents working in Lucas County, Ohio.

$20	$56	$65	$17	$26	$90	$13	$27
$16	$68	$86	$80	$50	$25	$92	

Determine the first and third quartiles and the median for the data.

Solution

The first step is to organize the data into an ordered array from smallest to largest:

13   16   17   20   25   26   27   50   56   65   68   80   86   90   92

To locate the first quartile, let $P = 25$ and $L_p = (n+1)\dfrac{P}{100} = (15+1)\dfrac{25}{100} = 4$

Then locate the 4th observation in the array which is 20. Thus $Q_1 = 20$ or $20,000.

To locate the third quartile, let $P = 75$ and $L_p = (n+1)\dfrac{P}{100} = (15+1)\dfrac{75}{100} = 12$

Then locate the 12th observation in the array which is 80. Thus $Q_3 = 80$ or $80,000.

To locate the median, let $P = 50$ and $L_p = (n+1)\dfrac{P}{100} = (15+1)\dfrac{50}{100} = 8$

Then locate the 8th observation in the array which is 50. Thus $Q_2 =$ the median $= 50$ or $50,000.

In the above example with 15 observations the location formula yielded a whole number result. Suppose we were to add one more observation (95) to the data list.

13   16   17   20   25   26   27   50   56   65   68   80   86   90   92   95

What is the third quartile now?

To locate the third quartile, let $P = 75$ and $L_p = (n+1)\dfrac{P}{100} = (16+1)\dfrac{75}{100} = 12.75$

Then locate the 12th and 13th observation in the array which are 80 and 86. The value of the third quartile is 0.75 of the distance between the 12th and 13th value. We must calculate $0.75(86 - 80) = 4.5$ Thus $Q_3 = (80 + 4.5) = 84.5$ or $84,500.

Problem 11

Use the selling price of homes data from Problem 8 to develop a box plot.

Solution

The first step is to identify the five essential pieces of data:

67

Minimum value = 13, $Q_1 = 20$, $Q_2 = 50$ $Q_3 = 80$,   Maximum value = 92

The next step in drawing a box plot is to create an appropriate scale along the horizontal axis. Next, we draw a box that starts at $Q_1 = 20$, and ends at $Q_3 = 80$. Inside the box we place a vertical line to represent the median 50. We then extend horizontal lines from the box to the minimum (12) and the maximum (92).

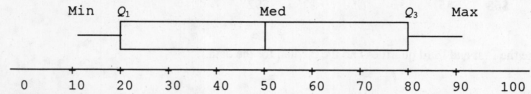

The box plot shows that the middle 50 percent of the homes sold for between $20,000 and $80,000. Also the distribution is somewhat positively skewed, since the line from Q_3 (80) to the Maximum (92) is longer than the line from Q_1 (20) to the minimum (13). In other words the 25% of the data to the larger than the third quartile is spread out more than the 25% of the data less than the first quartile.

Exercise 4.4

Check your answers against those in the ANSWER section.

Listed below are the selling prices (in thousands of dollars) of a sample of 20 homes sold by agents working in Franklin County, Ohio.

| $86 | $61 | $148 | $81 | $39 | $142 | $152 | $140 | $65 | $28 | $85 |
| $90 | $92 | $25 | $50 | $85 | $85 | $82 | $120 | $137 |

Determine the following:

a. the first quartile

b. the third quartile.

c. the median

d. Draw a box plot for the data.

CHAPTER ASSIGNMENT 4

DESCRIBING DATA: MEASURES OF DISPERSION

Name _____   Section _____   Score _____

Part I   Select the correct answer and write the appropriate letter in the space provided.

_____ 1. The mean deviation
   a.   is the average of all the numbers..
   b.   is the midpoint of the range.
   c.   is how far each value is from the median.
   d.   is the average of how far each value is from the mean.

_____ 2. The sum of the deviations from the mean is
   a.   equal to the mean.
   b.   equal to zero.
   c.   always positive.
   d.   equal to the median.

_____ 3. The square of the standard deviation is equal to
   a.   the mean.
   b.   the variance.
   c.   the median.
   d.   the mean deviation.

_____ 4. The coefficient of skewness
   a.   is always positive.
   b.   may range from –3.00 up to 3.00.
   c.   is a measure of relative dispersion
   d.   is equal to the range.

_____ 5. Suppose the coefficient of skewness was equal to –2.50.
   a.   A mistake was made because it cannot be negative.
   b.   The distribution is positively skewed.
   c.   Fifty percent of the observations are less than –2.50.
   d.   The mean is smaller than the median.

_____ 6. The coefficient of variation
   a.   is found by dividing the standard deviation by the mean and multiplying the result by 100.
   b.   is a measure of relative dispersion.
   c.   is reported in percent.
   d.   all of the above are correct.

_____ 7. The range of a sample of 10 values is 5 and the largest observation is 50. The lowest value is
   a.   40   c.   55
   b.   45   d.   cannot be computed from the data given

_____ 8. What is the shape of a frequency distribution with an arithmetic mean of 800 pounds, median of 758 pounds, and a mode of 750 pounds?
   a.   negatively skewed
   b.   symmetric
   c.   geometrically skewed
   d.   positively skewed

_____ 9. The quartile deviation and the interquartile range are:
   a.   both based on the median.
   b.   both based on the mean deviation.
   c.   related in that the square of the former is equal to the later.
   d.   based on the middle 50 percent of the observations.

_____ 10. According to the Empirical Rule, what percent of the observations are within 2 standard deviations of the mean?
   a.   50
   b.   68
   c.   99.7
   d.   95

Part II   Find the answers to each of the following questions. Show essential calculations.

11. The revenues of the top eleven personal computer manufacturers are given (in hundred millions).

| 15 | 17 | 23 | 26 | 27 | 35 | 72 | 88 | 91 | 98 | 102 |

   a.   Compute the range.

   a. [box]

   b.   Compute the mean deviation.

   b. [box]

   c.   Compute the standard deviation.

   c. [box]

d. Compute the quartiles and the median.

$$Q_1$$

$$Q_2$$

M

e. Draw a box plot for the data.

f. Describe the skewness.

f.

12. The CTC is studying the number of passengers riding the bus from Rocky River, Ohio to downtown Cleveland during the morning rush hour. A sample of 50 busses revealed the following number of passengers. Determine:

Number of Passengers	f
15 up to 20	3
20 up to 25	8
25 up to 30	12
30 up to 35	15
35 up to 40	7
40 up to 45	5

a. The range.

b. The standard deviation.

a.

b.

c. The first and third quartile.

$$Q_1$$

$$Q_2$$

d. The quartile deviation.

d.

71

13. The mean number of gallons of gasoline pumped per customer at Ray's Marathon Station is 9.5 gallons with a standard deviation of 0.75 gallons. The median number of gallons pumped is 10.0 gallons. The arithmetic mean amount of time spent by a customer in the station is 6.5 minutes with a standard deviation of 2 minutes.

a. According to Chebyshev's Theorem, what proportion (percent) of the customers spend between 3.30 minutes and 9.70 minutes at the station?

a.

b. According to the Empirical Rule, what proportion of the customers pump between 8.00 gallons and 11.00 gallons?

b.

c. Compute coefficient of variation for both the time spent at Ray's Marathon and the gasoline pumped. Comment on the relative dispersion of the two distributions.

c.

d. Compute the coefficient of skewness for the number of gallons pumped. Interpret it.

d.

CHAPTER 5
A SURVEY OF PROBABILITY CONCEPTS

Chapter Goals

When you have completed this chapter, you will be able to:

1. Define probability.

2. Describe the classical, the empirical, and the subjective approaches to probability.

3. Understand the words: experiment, event, and outcome.

4. Define the terms: conditional probability and joint probability.

5. Calculate probabilities, applying the rules of addition and the rules of multiplication.

6. Use a tree diagram to organize and compute probabilities.

7. Calculate a probability using Bayes' Theorem.

8. Determine the number of permutations and the number of combinations.

Introduction

Chapters 2, 3 and 4 emphasized *descriptive statistics*. In those chapters we described methods used to collect, organize, and present data, as well as measures of central tendency, dispersion, and skewness used to summarize data. A second facet of statistics deals with computing the chance that something will occur in the future. This facet of statistics is called *inferential statistics*.

An inference is a generalization about a population based on information obtained from a sample. Probability plays a key role in inferential statistics. It is used to measure the reasonableness that a particular sample could have come from a particular population.

Probability Defined

Probability allows us to measure effectively the risks in selecting one alternative over the others.

> *Probability*: A value between zero and one inclusive describing the relative possibility (chance or likelihood) an event will occur.

Probability is expressed either as a percent or as a decimal. The likelihood that any particular event will happen may assume values between 0 and 1.0. A value close to 0 indicates the event is unlikely to occur, whereas a value close to 1.0 indicates that the event is quite likely to occur.

To illustrate, a value of 0.60 might express your degree of belief that tuition will be increased at your college, and 0.50 the likelihood that your first marriage will end in divorce.

In our study of probability we will make extensive use of several key words. They are: *experiment, outcome*, and *event*.

> *Experiment*: A process which leads to the occurrence of one (and only one) of several possible observations.

For example, you roll a die and observe the number of spots that appear face up. The experiment is the act of rolling the die. Your survey company might be hired by Ford to find out how many consumers plan to buy a new American-made car this year. You contact 5,000 consumers. The act of counting the consumers who indicated they would purchase an American-made car is the experiment.

> *Outcome*: A particular result of an experiment.

One outcome of the die-rolling experiment is the appearance of a 6. In the experiment of counting the number of consumers who plan to buy a new American made car this year, one possibility is that 2,258 plan to buy one, another outcome is that 142 plan to buy one.

> *Event*: A collection of one or more outcomes of an experiment.

Thus, the *event* that the number appearing face up in the die-rolling experiment is an even number is the collection of the *outcomes* 2, 4, or 6. Similarly the event that more than half of those surveyed plan to buy a new American made car is the collection of the outcomes 2,501 , 2,502, 2,503, and so on all the way up to 5,000.

Approaches To Probability

Two types or classifications of probability are discussed: the objective and subjective viewpoints. Objective probability is subdivided into classical or a *priori* probability and the empirical or *posteriori* concept.

Classical Probability

Classical probability is based on the assumption the outcomes of an experiment are equally likely.

> *Classical Probability*: Based on the assumption that outcomes of an experiment are equally likely.

To find the probability of a particular outcome we divide the number of favorable outcomes by the total number of possible outcomes as shown in text formula [5-1].

$$\text{Probability of an event } = \frac{\text{Number of favorable outcomes}}{\text{Total number of possible outcomes}} \qquad [5-1]$$

For example, suppose you take a multiple-choice examination and have no idea which one of the choices is correct. In desperation you decide to guess the answer to each question. The four choices for each question are the outcomes. They are equally likely, but only one is correct. Thus the probability that you guess a particular answer correctly is 0.25 found by 1/4.

Empirical Probability

Another probability concept is based on relative frequencies.

> *Relative frequency*: Occurs when the number of times an event happens is divided by the total number of observations.

The probability of an event happening in the long run is found by observing what fraction of the time similar events happened in the past.

$$\text{Probability of event happening} = \frac{\text{Number of times event occurred in past}}{\text{Total number of observations}}$$

To find a probability using the relative frequency approach we divide the number of times the event has occurred in the past by the total number of observations. Suppose the Civil Aeronautics Board maintained records on the number of times flights arrived late at the Newark International Airport. If 54 flights in a sample of 500 were late, then, according to the relative frequency formula, the probability a particular flight will be late is 0.108, found by 54/500.

Subjective probability

If there is little or no past experience on which to base a probability, a probability may be determined subjectively. Thus you evaluate the available opinions and other subjective information and then make a decision and arrive at a probability.

> *Subjective probability*: The likelihood of an event happening is assigned by an individual based on whatever information is available.

Subjective probability is based on judgment, intuition, or "hunches." The likelihood that the horse, Sir Homer, will win the race at Ferry Downs today is based on the subjective view of the racetrack oddsmaker.

Some Rules of Probability

In the study of probability it is often necessary to combine the probabilities of events. This is accomplished through both rules of addition and rules of multiplication. There are two rules for addition, the special rule of addition and the general rule of addition.

Special Rule of Addition

The special rule of addition states that the probability of the event A or the event B occurring is equal to the probability of event A plus the probability of event B. The rule is expressed by using text formula [5-2]:

$$P(A \, or \, B) = P(A) + P(B) \qquad [5-2]$$

To apply the special rule of addition the events must be mutually exclusive.

> *Mutually exclusive:* The occurrence of any one event means that none of the others can occur at the same time.

When a single die is rolled once, for example, a 2 and a 6 cannot both appear at the same time. A computer chip cannot be defective and not defective at the same time.

If an experiment has a set of events that includes every possible outcome, then the set of events is called *collectively exhaustive.*

> *Collectively exhaustive:* At least one of the events must occur when an experiment is conducted.

For example: In a die-tossing experiment every outcome will be either an even number or an odd number. Thus the set is collectively exhaustive.

Venn Diagram

Venn diagrams, developed by English logician J. Venn, are useful for portraying events and their relationship to one another. They are constructed by enclosing a space, usually in a form of a rectangle, which represents the possible events. Two mutually exclusive events such as A and B can then be portrayed—as in the following diagram—by enclosing regions that do not overlap (that is, that have no common area).

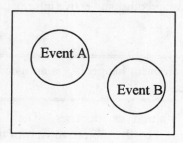

> *Complement rule:* A way to determine the probability of an event occurring by subtracting the probability of an event **not** occurring from 1.

This is expressed using text formula [5-3].

$$P(A) = 1 - P(\sim A) \qquad [5-3]$$

This formula could be written as:

$$P(A) + P(\sim A) = 1$$

In some situations it is more efficient to determine the probability of an event happening by determining the probability of it not happening and subtracting from 1.

General Rule of Addition

What if the events are not mutually exclusive? In that case the general rule of addition is used. The probability is computed using the text formula [5-4].

$$P(A \ or \ B) = P(A) + P(B) - P(A \ and \ B) \qquad [5-4]$$

Where:

P(A)   is the probability of the event A.
P(B)   is the probability of the event B.
P(A and B)   is the probability that both events A and B occur.

For example, a study showed 15 percent of the work force to be unemployed, 20 percent of the work force to be minorities, and 5 percent to be both unemployed and minorities. What percent of the work force are either minorities or unemployed? Note that if P (unemployed) and P (minority) are totaled, the 5 percent who are both minorities and unemployed are counted in both groups—that is, they are double-counted. They must be subtracted to avoid this double counting. Hence,

P (unemployed or minority) = P (unemployed) + P (minority) – P (unemployed and minority)
                              = 0.15 + 0.20 – 0.05
                              = 0.30

These two events are not mutually exclusive and would appear as follows in a Venn diagram:

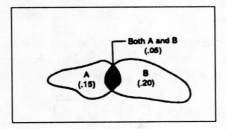

Rules of Multiplication

There were two rules of addition, the general rule and the special rule. We used the general rule when the events were not mutually exclusive and the special rule when the events were mutually exclusive. We have an analogous situation with the rules of multiplication. We use the general rule of multiplication when the two events are not independent and the special rule of multiplication when the events are independent.

> *Independent events*: The occurrence of one event has no affect on the probability of the occurrence of any other event.

When we want to find the probability that two events will both happen, we use the concept known as *joint probability*.

> *Joint probability*: A probability that measures the likelihood that two or more events will happen concurrently (at the same time).

Another probability concept is called *conditional probability*.

> **Conditional probability**: The probability of a particular event occurring, given that another event occurred.

Probability measures uncertainty, but the degree of uncertainty changes as new information becomes available. Symbolically, it is written $P(B|A)$. The vertical line (|) does not mean divide; it is read "given" as in the probability of B given that A happened.

General Rule of Multiplication

The general rule of multiplication is used to combine events that are not independent—that is, they are dependent on each other. For two events, the probability of the second event is affected by the outcome of the first event. Under these conditions, the probability of both A and B occurring is given in formula [5-6].

$$P(A \text{ and } B) = P(A) \times P(A|B) \qquad [5-6]$$

Where $P(B|A)$ is the probability of B occurring given that A has already occurred. Note that $P(B|A)$ is a conditional probability.

For example, among a group of twelve prisoners, four had been convicted of murder. If two of the twelve are selected for a special rehabilitation program, what is the probability that both of those selected are convicted murderers?

Let A_1 be the first selection (a convicted murderer) and A_2 the second selection (also a convicted murderer). Then $P(A_1) = 4/12$. After the first selection, there are 11 prisoners, 3 of whom are convicted of murder, hence $P(A_2|A_1) = 3/11$. The probability of both A_1 and A_2 happening is:

$$P(A_1 \text{ and } A_2) = P(A_1) \times P(A_2|A_1)$$
$$= \frac{4}{12} \times \frac{3}{11}$$
$$= 0.0909$$

Special Rule of Multiplication

The special rule of multiplication is used to combine events where the probability of the second event does not depend on the outcome of the first event.

The probability of two independent events, A and B, occurring is found by multiplying the two probabilities. It is written as shown in text formula [5-7].

$$P(A \text{ and } B) = P(A) \times P(B) \qquad [5-7]$$

As an example, a nuclear power plant has two independent safety systems. The probability the first will not operate properly in an emergency $P(A)$ is 0.01, and the probability the second will not operate $P(B)$ in an emergency is 0.02. What is the probability that in an emergency both of the safety systems will not operate? The probability both will not operate is:

$$P(A \text{ and } B) = P(A) \times P(B)$$
$$= 0.01 \times 0.02$$
$$= 0.0002$$

The probability 0.0002 is called a joint probability, which is the simultaneous occurrence of two events. It measures the likelihood that two (or more) events will happen together (jointly).

Bayes' Theorem

Bayes' Theorem is used to revise the probability of a particular event happening based on the fact that some other event had already happened.

For example, we have three machines each producing the same items. Machine A produces 10 percent defective and Machines B and C each 5 percent defective. Suppose each machine produces one-third of the total production. Since Machine A produces one-third of all the parts, we naturally expect that prior to any experiment the probability of a defective being produced by Machine A is 0.33. Logically, the 0.33 is called a *prior probability*.

Prior probability: The initial probability based on the present level of information.

A part is selected at random. It was found to be defective. The question is: what is the probability that it was produced by Machine A? As noted above, Machine A produces twice as many defective parts as Machines B and C. (A produces 10%, B and C 5% each). Since we discovered that the part selected was defective, the probability it was manufactured by Machine A is now greater than 0.33. Bayes' Theorem will give us this revised probability. The text formula is [5-8]

$$P(A_1|B) = \frac{P(A_1) \times P(B|A_1)}{P(A_1) \times P(B|A_1) + P(A_2) \times P(B|A_2) + P(A_3) \times P(B|A_3)} \quad [5-7]$$

The probabilities to be inserted in the formula are:

$P(A_1)$ = Probability the part was produced by Machine A = 0.33
$P(A_2)$ = Probability the part was produced by Machine B = 0.33
$P(A_3)$ = Probability the part was produced by Machine C = 0.33
$P(B|A_1)$ = Probability of a defect being produced by Machine A = 0.10
$P(B|A_2)$ = Probability of a defect being produced by Machine B = 0.05
$P(B|A_3)$ = Probability of a defect being produced by Machine C = 0.05

$$P(A_1|B) = \frac{0.33(0.10)}{0.33(0.10) + 0.33(0.05) + 0.33(0.05)} = \frac{0.033}{0.033 + 0.0165 + 0.0165} = \frac{0.033}{0.066} = 0.50$$

Chapter 5

Hence, the probability that the defective part was manufactured by Machine A is increased from 0.33 to 0.50. We revised upward the probability that the part was produced by Machine A, because we obtained the additional information that the part selected was defective. This revised probability is called a *posterior probability*.

> *Posterior probability:* A revised probability based on the benefit of additional information

Principles of Counting

In previous examples it was not difficult to count the possible outcomes. However, sometimes the number of possible outcomes is quite large, and listing all the possibilities would be time consuming, tedious, and error prone. Three formulas are very useful for determining the number of possible outcomes in an experiment. They are: the *multiplication formula*, the *permutation formula*, and the *combination formula*.

Multiplication Formula

The general rule of multiplication is used to combine events that are dependent on each other.

> *Multiplication formula:* If there are *m* ways of accomplishing one thing, and *n* ways of accomplishing another, there are *m* times *n* ways of doing both.

In terms of a formula:

$$\text{Total number of arrangements} = (m)(n) \qquad [5-8]$$

Permutation Formula

The permutation is an arrangement of objects or things wherein order is important. That is, each time the objects or things are placed in a different order, a new permutation results.

> *Permutation:* Any arrangements of *r* objects selected from a single group of *n* possible objects.

The formula for the number of permutations is:

$$_nP_r = \frac{n!}{(n-r)!} \qquad [5-9]$$

Where:
P   is the number of permutations, or ways the objects can be arranged.
n   is the total number of objects.
r   is the number of objects to be used at one time.

The Combination Formula

One particular arrangement of the objects without regard to order is called a *combination*.

> **Combination**: The number of ways to choose *r* objects from a group of *n* possible objects without regard to order.

The formula for the number of combinations is:

$$_nC_r = \frac{n!}{r!(n-r)!} \qquad [5-10]$$

Where:

C   is the number of different combinations.
n   is the total number of objects.
r   is the number of objects to be used at one time.

Glossary

Probability: A value between zero and one inclusive describing the relative possibility (chance or likelihood) an event will occur.

Experiment: A process which leads to the occurrence of one (and only one) of several possible observations.

Outcome: A particular result of an experiment.

Event: A collection of one or more outcomes of an experiment.

Classical Probability: Based on the assumption that the outcomes for an experiment are equally likely

Relative frequency: Occurs when the number of times an event happens is divided by the total number of observations.

Subjective probability: The likelihood of an event happening is assigned by an individual based on whatever information is available.

Mutually exclusive: The occurrence of any one event means that none of the others can occur at the same time.

Collectively exhaustive: At least one of the events must occur when an experiment is conducted.

Complement rule: A way to determine the probability of an event occurring by subtracting the probability of an event **not** occurring from 1.

Independent events: The occurrence of one event has no affect on the probability of the occurrence of any other event.

Joint probability: A probability that measures the likelihood that two or more events will happen concurrently (at the same time).

Conditional probability: The probability of a particular event occurring, given that another event occurred.

Prior Probability: The initial probability based on the present level of information.

Posterior probability: A revised probability based on the benefit of additional information.

Multiplication formula: If there are *m* ways of accomplishing one thing, and *n* ways of accomplishing another, there are *m* times *n* ways of doing both.

Permutation: Any arrangements of *r* objects selected from a single group of *n* possible objects.

Combination: The number of ways to choose *r* objects from a group of *n* possible objects without regard to order.

Chapter Problems

Problem 1

Dunn Pontiac has compiled the following sales data regarding the number of cars sold over the past 60 selling days. Answer the following questions for the sales data shown.

a. What is the probability that two cars are sold during a particular day?

b. What is the probability of selling 3 or more cars during a particular day?

Dunn Pontiac Sales Data	
Number of Cars Sold	Number of Days
0	5
1	5
2	10
3	20
4	15
5 or more	5
Total	60

c. What is the probability of selling at least one car during a particular day?

Solution

This problem is an example of the relative frequency type of probability, because the probability of an event happening is based on the number of times the particular event happened in the past relative to the total number of observations.

a. The events are mutually exclusive. That is, if a total of two cars are sold on a particular day, four cannot be sold. The probability that exactly two cars are sold is:

$$P(2 \text{ cars}) = \frac{\text{Number of days two cars were sold}}{\text{Total number of days}} = \frac{10}{60} = 0.1667$$

b. The probability of selling three or more cars is found by using a special rule of addition given in formula [5-2]. Let *X* represent the number of cars sold. ($\geq$ is read "greater than or equal to." The notation > would be just greater than.) Then:

$$P(X \geq 3) = P(3) + P(4) + P(5 \text{ or more}) = \frac{20}{60} + \frac{15}{60} + \frac{5}{60} = \frac{40}{60} = 0.67$$

Interpreting, three cars or more are sold 67 percent of the days.

c. The probability of selling at least one car is determined by adding the probabilities of selling one, two, three, four, and five or more cars. Again let X be the number of cars sold, then

$$P(X \geq 1) = P(1) + P(2) + P(3) + P(4) + P(5 \text{ or more})$$

$$= \frac{5}{60} + \frac{10}{60} + \frac{20}{60} + \frac{15}{60} + \frac{5}{60} = \frac{55}{60} = 0.9166 = 0.92$$

The same result can also be found by using the complement rule. The probability of the occurrence of a particular event is obtained by computing the probability it did not occur and then subtracting that value from 1.0. In this example, the probability of not selling any cars is 5/60 = 0.08, then (1 – 0.08)= 0.92.

$$P(X \geq 1) = 1.0 - P(0)$$

$$= 1.0 - \frac{5}{60} = (1 - 0.08) = 0.92$$

Exercise 5.1

Check your answers against those in the ANSWER section.

A study was made to investigate the number of times adult males over 30 visit a physician each year. The results for a sample of 300 were:

Number of Visits	Number of Adult Males
0	30
1	60
2	90
3 or more	120
Total	300

a. What is the probability of selecting someone who visits a physician twice a year?

b. What is the probability of selecting someone who visits a physician?

Problem 2

A local community has two newspapers. The *Morning Times* is read by 45 percent of the households. The *Evening Dispatch* is read by 60 percent of the households. Twenty percent of the households read both papers. What is the probability that a particular household in the city reads at least one paper?

Solution

If we combine the probabilities (0.45, 0.60, and 0.20), they exceed 1.00. The group that reads both papers, of course, is being counted twice and must be subtracted to arrive at the answer. Letting T represent the *Morning Times*, and D the *Evening Dispatch*, and using the general rule of addition, formula [5-4]:

$$P(T \text{ or } D) = P(T) + P(D) - P(T \text{ and } D)$$
$$= 0.45 + 0.60 - 0.20$$
$$= 0.85$$

Thus, 85 percent of the households in the community read at least one paper.

Exercise 5.2

Check your answers against those in the ANSWER section.

The proportion of students at Pemberville University who own an automobile is 0.60. The proportion who live in a dormitory is 0.20. The proportion who both own an automobile and live in a dormitory is 0.12. What proportion of the students either own an auto or live in a dorm?

Problem 3

The probability that a bomber hits a target on a bombing mission is 0.70. Three bombers are sent to bomb a particular target. What is the probability that they all hit the target? What is the probability that at least one hits the target?

Solution

These events are independent since the probability that one bomber hits the target does not depend on whether the other hits it. The special rule of multiplication, formula [5-7], is used to find the joint probability. B_1 represents the first bomber, B_2 the second bomber, and B_3 the third bomber.

$$P(\text{all } 3 \text{ hit target}) = P(B_1)P(B_2)P(B_3)$$
$$= (0.70)(0.70)(0.70)$$
$$= 0.343$$

Hence the probability that all three complete the mission is 0.343.

The probability that at least one bomber hits the target is found by combining the complement rule and the multiplication rule. To explain: The probability of a miss with the first bomber is 0.30, found by $P(M_1) = 1 - 0.70$. The probability for M_2 and M_3 is also 0.30. The multiplication rule is used to obtain the probability that all three miss. Let X be the number of hits.

$$P(X > 0) = 1 - P(0)$$
$$= 1 - [P(M_1)][P(M_2)][P(M_3)]$$
$$= 1 - [(0.30)(0.30)(0.30)]$$
$$= 1 - 0.027 = 0.973$$

Thus, the likelihood that at least one of the bombs hit the target is 0.973.

Exercise 5.3

Check your answers against those in the ANSWER section.

A side effect of a certain anesthetic used in surgery is the hiccups, which occurs in about 10 percent of the cases. If three patients are scheduled for surgery today and are to be administered this anesthetic, compute the probability that:

a. all three get hiccups

b. none get hiccups

c. at least one gets hiccups

Problem 4

Yesterday, the Bunte Auto Repair Shop received a shipment of four carburetors. One is known to be defective. If two are selected at random and tested:

a. What is the probability that neither one is defective?

b. What is the probability that the defective carburetor is located by testing two carburetors?

Solution

a. The selections of the two carburetors are not independent events because the selection of the first affects the second outcome. Let G_1 represent the first "good" carburetor and G_2 the second "good" one.

$$P(G_1 \text{ and } G_2) = P(G_1) \times P(G_2|G_1)$$

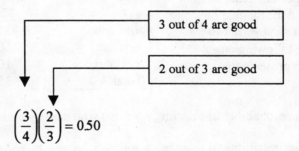

3 out of 4 are good

2 out of 3 are good

$$\left(\frac{3}{4}\right)\left(\frac{2}{3}\right) = 0.50$$

Hence, the probability that neither of the two selected carburetors is defective is 0.50.

b. The probability that the defective carburetor is found requires the general rule of multiplication and the general rule of addition.

In this case the defect may be detected either in the first test or in the second one. The general rule of multiplication is used. Let D_1 represent a defect on the first test and D_2 on the second test. The probability is:

$$P(\text{find the defect}) = P(G_1) \times P(D_2|G_1) + P(D_1) \times P(G_2|D_1)$$

$$= \left(\frac{3}{4}\right)\left(\frac{1}{3}\right) + \left(\frac{1}{4}\right)\left(\frac{3}{3}\right) = 0.50$$

To explain further, the probability that the first carburetor tested is good is $P(D_1) = \frac{3}{4}$. If the first one selected is good, then to meet the requirements of the problem the second one sampled must be defective. This conditional probability is $P(D_2|G_1) = 1/3$. The joint probability of these two events is 3/12 or $\frac{1}{4}$. The defective part could be found on the first test $P(D_1)$. Since there is one defect among the four carburetors the probability that it will be found on the first test is $\frac{1}{4}$. If the defect is found on the first test then the three remaining parts are good. Hence the conditional probability of selecting a good carburetor on the second trial is 1.0 $P(G_2|D_1)$. The joint probability of a defective part being followed by a good part is $\frac{1}{4}$, found by $P(D_1)$ x $P(G_2|D_1) = (1/4)(3/3) = \frac{1}{4}$. The sum of these two outcomes is 0.50.

Exercise 5.4

Check your answers against those in the ANSWER section.

Ten students are being interviewed for a class office. Six of them are female and four are male. Their names are all placed in a box and two students are selected to be interviewed.

a. What is the probability that both of those selected are female?

b. What is the probability that at least one is male?

Problem 5

A large department store is analyzing the per-customer amount of purchase and the method of payment. For a sample of 140 customers, the following cross-classified table presents the findings.

Payment Method	Amount of Purchase			
	B_1: Less than $20	B_2:$20 up to $50	B_3: $50 or more	Total
A_1: Cash	15	10	5	30
A_2: Check	10	30	20	60
A_3:Charge	10	20	20	50
Total	35	60	45	140

a. What is the probability of selecting someone who paid by cash or made a purchase of less than $20?

b. What is the probability of selecting someone who paid by check and made a purchase of more than $50?

Solution

a. If we combine the events "Less than $20" ($B_1$) and "Cash payment" ($A_1$), then those who paid cash for a purchase of less than $20 are counted twice. That is, these two events are not mutually exclusive. Therefore, the general rule of addition formula [5-4] is used.

$$P(A_1 \text{ or } B_1) = P(A_1) + P(B_1) - P(A_1 \text{ and } B_1)$$

$$= \frac{30}{140} + \frac{35}{140} - \frac{15}{140} = \frac{50}{140} = 0.36$$

The probability of selecting a customer who made a cash payment or purchased an item for less than $20 is 0.36.

b. Conditional probability is used to find the probability of selecting someone who paid by check (A_2) and who made a purchase of over $50 ($B_3$)

There are two qualifications: "paid by check" and "made a purchase of over $50." Referring to the table, 20 out of 140 customers meet both qualifications, therefore, $20/140 = 0.14$.

This probability could also be computed in a three-step process.

1. The probability of selecting those who paid by check (A_2) is $60/140 = 0.43$.

2. Of the 60 persons who paid by check, 20 made a purchase of over $50. Therefore $P(B_3|A_2) = 20/60 = 0.33$

3. These two events are then combined using the general rule of multiplication, formula [5-6].

$$P(A_2 \text{ and } B_3) = P(A_2)P(B_3|A_2)$$
$$= (0.43)(0.33) = 0.14$$

Exercise 5.5

Check your answers against those in the ANSWER section.

Five hundred adults over 50 years of age were classified according to whether they smoked or not, and if they smoked, were they a moderate or heavy smoker. Also, each one was asked whether he or she had ever had a heart attack. The results are given.

| | **Heart Attack** | | |
	Yes	No	Total
Do not smoke	30	220	250
Moderate smoker	60	65	125
Heavy smoker	90	35	125
Totals	180	320	500

a. What is the probability of selecting a person who either has had a heart attack, or who is a heavy smoker?

b. What is the probability of selecting a heavy smoker who did not have a heart attack?

Problem 6

The probability that a person has "BLEEBS," a rare disease that occurs in young baseball players is 0.02. If a person has BLEEBS, the probability that the individual is diagnosed as having it is 0.80. On the other hand, if an individual does not have BLEEBS, the probability of being diagnosed as having it is 0.05. Given that a person is diagnosed as having BLEEBS, what is the probability that the person really does not have it?

Solution

This problem is solved using Bayes' Theorem. The various parts of the problem are as follows:

$P(B)$ is the probability of having BLEEBS. It is 0.02.

$P(NB)$ is the probability of not having BLEEBS. It is 0.98.

$P(D|B)$ is the probability of being diagnosed as having BLEEBS, given that the person has the disease. It is 0.80.

$P(D|NB)$ is the probability of being diagnosed as having BLEEBS, given that the person does not have the disease. It is 0.05.

$P(NB|D)$ is the revised probability of not having BLEEBS, given that the diagnosis is that of having BLEEBS.

A useful device for displaying conditional and joint probabilities is called a tree diagram. The tree diagram will be used to solve the above problem. The initial relationships are as follows.

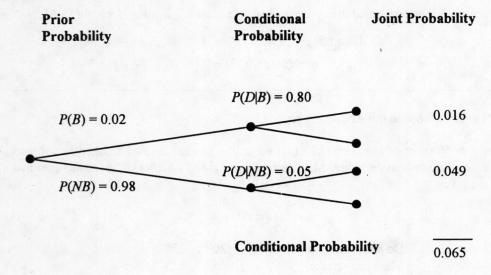

The computational form of Bayes' Theorem formula [5-8] is repeated.

$$P(NB|D) = \frac{P(NB)P(D|NB)}{P(B)P(D|B) + P(NB)P(D|NB)}$$

$$= \frac{(0.98)(0.05)}{(0.02)(0.80) + (0.98)(0.05)} = 0.754$$

Interpreting, this means that even though a person is diagnosed as having BLEEBS, the probability of not actually having it is 0.754.

To explain this problem further, everyone falls into one of the two categories, they have BLEEBS or they don't. Only two percent of the population actually have the condition [$P(B) = 0.02$] and 98 percent do not [$P(D|B) = 0.80$], but some people are diagnosed as having BLEEBS, when they actually do not [$P(D|NB) = 0.05$]. These are actually false positive readings.

The denominator of Bayes' Theorem computes the fraction of the population that are diagnosed as having BLEEBS. That fraction is obtained by combining the two joint probabilities as follows:

$$P(B) = P(B) \times P(D|B) + P(NB) \times P(D|NB) = (0.20)(0.08) + (0.98)(0.05)$$
$$= 0.065$$

The 0.065 is the fraction of the population that will be diagnosed as having BLEEBS. However, some of those diagnosed actually have the condition [$P(B) \times P(D|B) = 0.02)(0.80) = 0.016$] and some while diagnosed as having BLEEBS actually do not [$P(NB) \times P(D|NB) = (0.98)(0.05) = 0.049$]. We are interested in the fraction that are diagnosed as having the condition but really don't [$(0.049/0.065) = 0.754$]. This result may seem rather startling, because more than 75 percent of the time the test results are actually incorrect. This indicates that the test for BLEEBS is not very discriminating.

Exercise 5.6

Check your answers against those in the ANSWER section.

A test on probability is to be given next week. Suppose 75 percent of the students study for the test and 25 percent do not. If a student studies for the exam, the probability that he or she will pass is 0.90. If the student does not study, the probability that he or she will pass is 20 percent. Given that the student passed the test, what is the probability he or she studied?

Problem 7

A deli bar offers a special sandwich for which there is a choice of five different cheeses, four different meat selections, and three different rolls. How many different sandwich combinations are possible?

Solution

Using the multiplication formula, there are five cheeses (c), four meats (m), and three rolls (r). The total number of possible sandwiches is 60 found by:

$$cms = (5)(4)(3) = 60$$

Exercise 5.7

Check your answers against those in the ANSWER section.

The Swansons are planning to fly to Hawaii from Toronto with a stopover in Los Angeles. There are five flights they can take between Toronto and Los Angeles and ten flights between Los Angeles and Hawaii. How many different flights are possible between Toronto and Hawaii?

Problem 8

Three scholarships are available for needy students. Their values are: $1,000, $1,200, and $1,500. Twelve students have applied and no student may receive more than one scholarship. Assuming all twelve students are in need of funds, how many different ways could the scholarships be awarded?

Solution

This is an example of a permutation because a different assignment of the scholarships means another arrangement. Jones could be awarded the $1,000 scholarship, Sinski the $1,200 scholarship, and Peters the $1,500 scholarship. Or, Sinski could be awarded the $1,000, Seiple the $1,200 one, and Orts the $1,500 scholarship, and so on.

$$_nP_r = \frac{n!}{(n-r)!} = \frac{12!}{(12-3)!} = \frac{12 \times 11 \times 10 \times 9!}{9!} = 1,320$$

Where:

n is the total number of applicants

r is number of scholarships.

Exercise 5.8

Check your answers against those in the ANSWER section.

A company has four plumbers. If there are repairs to be done at eight households, in how many different ways can the households be assigned to the plumbers?

Problem 9

The basketball coach of Dalton University is quite concerned about their 40 straight losses. The frustrated coach decided to select the starting lineup for the DU-UCLA game by drawing five names from the 12 available players at random. (Assume that a player can play any position.) How many different starting lineups are possible?

Solution

This is an example of a combination because the order in which the players are selected is not important. Jocko, Camden, Urfer, Smith, and Marchal is the same starting lineup as Smith, Camden, Marchal, Jocko, and Urfer, and so on.

$$_nC_r = \frac{n!}{r!(n-r)!} = \frac{12!}{5!(12-5)!} = \frac{12 \times 11 \times 10 \times 9 \times 8 \times 7!}{5 \times 4 \times 3 \times 2 \times 1 \times 7!} = \frac{95,040}{120} = 792$$

Where:

n is the total number of available players.

r is the number in the starting lineup.

Exercise 5.9

Check your answers against those in the ANSWER section.

A major corporation has branch offices in eight major cities in the United States and Canada. The company president wants to visit five of these offices. How many different trip combinations are possible?

CHAPTER 5 ASSIGNMENT

A SURVEY OF PROBABILITY CONCEPTS

Name _____   Section _____   Score _____

Part I   Select the correct answer and write the appropriate letter in the space provided.

_____ 1.   Which of the following statements regarding probability is always correct?
   a.   A probability can range from 0 to 1.
   b.   A probability close to 0 means the event is not likely to happen.
   c.   A probability close to 1 means the event is likely to happen.
   d.   all of the above are correct.

_____ 2.   According to the classical definition of probability
   a.   all the events are equally likely.
   b.   the probability is based on hunches.
   c.   the number of successes is divided by the number of failures.
   d.   one outcome is exactly twice the other.

_____ 3.   The observation of some activity or the act of taking some measurement is called
   a.   an outcome.
   b.   an event.
   c.   a probability.
   d.   an experiment.

_____ 4.   The particular result of an experiment is called
   a.   an outcome.
   b.   an event.
   c.   a probability.
   d.   an experiment.

_____ 5.   An event is the collection of one or more
   a.   outcomes.
   b.   combinations.
   c.   probabilities.
   d.   experiments.

_____ 6.   If A and B are mutually exclusive events then $P(A$ or $B)$ equals
   a. $P(A) + P(B) - P(A$ and $B)$
   b. $P(A) \times P(B)$
   c. $P(A) + P(B)$
   d. $P(A|B) + P(B|A)$

_____ 7. If A and B are independent events, then $P(A$ and $B)$) equals
  a. $P(A) + P(B|A)$.
  b. $P(A) \times P(B)$.
  c. $P(A) + P(B)$.
  d. $P(A|B) + P(B|A)$.

_____ 8. Which formula represents the probability of the complement of event A?
  a. $1 + P(A)$
  b. $1 - P(A)$
  c. $P(A)$
  d. $P(A) - 1$

_____ 9. The simultaneous occurrence of two events is called
  a. prior probability
  b. subjective probability
  c. conditional probability
  d. joint probability

_____ 10. If the probability of an event is 0.3, that means
  a. the event has a 70% chance of not occurring.
  b. the complement of the event has a 30% chance of occurring.
  c. the event has a 30% chance of not occurring.
  d. the complement of the event has a 70% chance of not occurring.

Part II Answer each question below. Be sure to show all of your work.

11. A recent study of young executives showed that 30 percent run, 20 percent bike and 12 percent do both. What is the percent of young executives who run or bike?

11.

12. A survey of advertising jobs indicates that 92 percent are completed on time. Assume that three jobs are selected for study.
  a. What is the probability they are all completed on time?

a.

  b. What is the probability that at least one was not completed on time?

b.

13. Today's local newspaper lists 20 stocks "of local interest." Of these stocks, ten increased, five decreased and five remained unchanged yesterday. If we decide to buy two of the stocks, what is the likelihood that both increased yesterday?

13.

14. Six employees of a marketing firm had effectiveness ratings as follows: 0.72, 0.46, 0.59, 0.64, 0.81 and 0.76. Find the probability of selecting an employee with the indicated effectiveness rating.
    a. Greater than 0.75.   b. Less than 0.75 but greater than 0.5.

    c. Greater than the mean.   d. Not less than 0.9.

a.

b.

c.

d.

15. The manager of Solomon Enterprises, a stock brokerage firm, bought four suits, six shirts, and ten ties. If all the items coordinate with each other, how many outfits are possible?

15.
1140

16. The United Way Campaign of Greater Toledo had fifteen applications for funding this year. If eight of these applications can be funded, how many different lists of successful applications are there?

16.

17. Rob Yelton, a management trainee at Vater Trucking, Inc., drives to work 60 percent of the time and takes the bus the rest of the time. When he drives himself, he is late 5 percent of the time and when he takes the bus he is late 20 percent of the time. Rob was late to work this morning. What is the likelihood that he took the bus?

17.

18. A market analyst is hired to provide information on the type of customers who shop at a particular store. A random survey is taken of 100 shoppers at this store. Of these 100, 73 are women. The shoppers are grouped in three age categories, under 30, 30 up to 50 and 50 and over. The data is summarized below.

	Women	Men	Total
Under 30	30	8	38
30 to 50	25	14	39
50 & over	18	5	23
Totals	73	27	100

Let W be the event that a randomly selected shopper is a woman.
Let A be the event that a randomly selected shopper is under 30.

a. Find the probability of ~W.

a.

b. Find the probability of A.

b.

c. Find the probability of A and W.

c.

d. Find the probability of A or ~W.

d.

e. Find the probability of A given W.

e.

CHAPTER 6
DISCRETE PROBABILITY DISTRIBUTIONS

Chapter Goals

After completing this chapter, you will be able to:

1. Define the terms probability distribution and random variable.

2. Distinguish between discrete and continuous probability distributions.

3. Calculate the mean, variance, and standard deviation of a discrete probability distribution.

4. Describe the characteristics of the binomial probability distribution.

5. Compute probabilities using the binomial probability distribution.

6. Describe the characteristics of the hypergeometric distribution.

7. Compute probabilities using the hypergeometric distribution.

8. Describe the characteristics of the Poisson distribution.

9. Compute probabilities using the Poisson distribution.

Introduction

In the previous chapter we discussed the basic concepts of probability and described how the rules of addition and multiplication were used to compute probabilities. In this chapter we expand the study of probability to include the concept of a *probability distribution*.

Probability Distributions

A probability distribution shows the possible outcomes of an experiment and the probability of each of these outcomes.

> *Probability distribution*: A listing of all the outcomes of a random experiment and the probability associated with each outcome.

How can we generate a probability distribution?

As an example, the possible outcomes on the roll of a single die are:

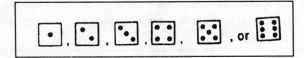

Each face should appear on about one-sixth of the rolls. The table shows the possible outcomes and corresponding probabilities for this experiment. It is a discrete distribution because only certain outcomes are possible and the distribution is a result of counting the various outcomes.

Number of Spots on Die	Probability		
	Fraction		Decimal
1	1/6	=	0.1667
2	1/6	=	0.1667
3	1/6	=	0.1667
4	1/6	=	0.1667
5	1/6	=	0.1667
6	1/6	=	0.1667
Total	6/6	=	1.0000

There are several important features of the discrete probability distribution:

1. The listing is exhaustive; that is, all the possible outcomes are included.

2. The total (sum) of all possible outcomes is 1.0.

3. The probability of any particular outcome is between 0 and 1 inclusive. (see the table above.)

4. The outcomes are mutually exclusive, meaning, for example, a 6 spot and a 2 spot cannot appear at the same time on the roll of one die.

This discrete probability distribution, presented above as a table, may also be portrayed in graphic form:

By convention the probability is shown on the Y-axis (the vertical axis) and the outcomes on the X-axis (the horizontal axis). This probability distribution is often referred to as a uniform distribution.

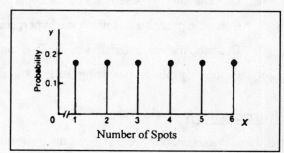

A probability distribution can also be expressed in equation form.

For example:

$$P(X) = 1/6, \text{ where } X \text{ can assume the values } 1, 2, 3, 4, 5, \text{ or } 6.$$

Random Variable

A *random variable* is a value determined by the outcome of an experiment.

> ***Random Variable:*** A quantity resulting from an experiment that, by chance, can assume different values.

A random variable may have two forms: discrete or continuous. A *discrete random variable* may assume only distinct values and is usually the result of counting.

> ***Discrete random variable***: A variable that can assume only certain clearly separated values resulting from a count of some item of interest.

For example, the number of highway deaths in Arkansas on Memorial Day weekend may be 1, 2, 3,... Another example is the number of students earning a grade of B in your statistics class. In both instances the number of occurrences result from counting. Note that there can be 12 deaths or 15 B's but there cannot be 12.63 deaths or 15.27 B grades.

Does this rule out the possibility that a discrete random variable may assume fractional values? No. A study of stock prices might reveal that 20 stocks increased by one-eighth of a point ($0.125) and that 12 increased by one-fourth of a point ($0.25). Note that the random variable itself may assume fractional values, but there is some distance between these values. In the stock example the result is still a count—that is, 12 stocks increased by $0.25.

The second type of distribution is a continuous random variable

> **Continuous random variable**: A variable that can assume one of an infinitely large number of values within certain limitations.

For example, in a high school track meet, the winning time for the mile run may be reported as 4 minutes 20 seconds, 4 minutes 20.2 seconds, or 4 minutes 20.2416 seconds, and so on, depending on the accuracy of the timing device.

In brief, if the problem involves counting something, the resulting distribution is usually a discrete probability distribution. If the distribution is the result of a measurement, then it is usually a continuous probability distribution.

What is the difference between a random variable and a probability distribution? A probability distribution lists all the possible outcomes as well as their corresponding probabilities. A random variable lists only the outcomes.

We will examine the continuous random variable and the continuous probability distribution in Chapter 7.

Mean, Variance, and Standard Deviation of a Probability Distribution

In Chapter 3 we computed the mean and variance of a frequency distribution. The mean is a measure of central tendency and the variance is a measure of the spread of the data. In a similar fashion the mean (μ) and the variance (σ^2) summarize a probability distribution.

The mean, or expected value, of a probability distribution is its long-run average. It is computed by the following formula:

$$\mu = E(X) = \Sigma\left[XP(X)\right] \qquad [6-1]$$

This formula directs you to multiply each outcome (X) by its probability $P(X)$; and then add the products.

While the mean describes the center of a probability distribution, it does not tell us anything about the spread in the distribution. The variance tells us about the spread or variation in the data. The variance is computed using the following formula:

$$\sigma^2 = \Sigma\left[(X-\mu)^2 P(X)\right] \qquad [6-2]$$

Chapter 6

The steps in computing the variance using formula [6-2] are:

1. Subtract the mean (μ) from each outcome (X) and square these differences.
2. Multiply each squared difference by its probability $P(X)$.
3. Sum these products to arrive at the variance.

The standard deviation (σ) of a discrete probability distribution is found by taking the square root of σ^2, thus $\sigma = \sqrt{\sigma^2}$.

Binomial Probability Distribution

One of the most widely used discrete probability distributions is the binomial probability distribution. It has the following characteristics:

1. An outcome of an experiment is classified into one of two mutually exclusive categories—namely, a success or a failure.
2. The data collected are the result of counts.
3. The probability of a success stays the same for each trial. So does the probability of a failure.
4. The trials are independent, meaning that the outcome of one trial does not affect the outcome of any other trial.

Illustrations of each characteristic are:

1. Each outcome is classified into one of two mutually exclusive categories. An outcome is classified as either a "success" or a "failure." For example, 40 percent of the students at a particular university are enrolled in the College of Business. For a selected student there are only two possible outcomes—the student is enrolled in the College of Business (designated a success) or he/she is not enrolled in the College of Business (designated a failure).
2. The binomial distribution is the result of counting the number of successes in a fixed sample size. If we select 5 students, 0, 1, 2, 3, 4, or 5 could be enrolled in the College of Business. This rules out the possibility of 3.45 of the students being enrolled in the College of Business. That is, there cannot be fractional counts.
3. The probability of a success remains the same from trial to trial. In the example regarding the College of Business, the probability of a success remains at 40 percent for all five students selected.
4. Each sampled item is independent. This means that if the first student selected is enrolled in the College of Business, it has no effect on whether the second or the fourth one selected will be in the College of Business.

Constructing a Probability Distribution

To construct a binomial probability distribution we need to know: (1) the number of trials, designated n, and (2) the probability of success (π) on each trial.

The binomial probability distribution is constructed using the formula [6-3]:

$$P(x) = \frac{n!}{x!(n-x)!}(\pi)^x(1-\pi)^{n-x} \qquad [6-3]$$

Where:

n is the number of trials

x is the number of observed successes

π is the probability of success on each trial

The mean (μ) and variance (σ^2) of a binomial distribution can be computed by these formulas.

$$\mu = n\pi \qquad [6-4]$$

$$\sigma^2 = n\pi(1-\pi) \qquad [6-5]$$

Hypergeometric Probability Distribution

To qualify as a binomial distribution, the probability of a success must remain constant. What if this requirement is not met? This usually happens when the size of the population is small and samples are drawn from the population and not replaced. This causes the probability of a success to change from one trial (or sample) to the next. This means the trails are not independent.

For example, if a class consisted of 20 students, 12 males and 8 females, what is the probability of selecting two people to serve on a committee who are both female? If Ms. Smith was selected on the first trial, she cannot be selected again because she is already on the committee. Thus the outcome of the second trial depends on the outcome of the first trial. The probability of a female on the first selection is 8/20, and if a female is selected first there are 7 females out of the 19 remaining students. Hence the probability of selecting two females for the committee is 0.147 found by (8/20)(7/19).

This assumes that the population is finite, that is, the number in the population is known.

> *Finite population*: A population consisting of a small number of individuals, objects, or measurements.

This probability may also be calculated using the hypergeometric distribution, which is described by the formula:

$$P(x) = \frac{(_sC_x)(_{N-s}C_{n-x})}{(_NC_n)} \qquad [6-6]$$

Where:

N is the size of the population.
S is the number of successes in the population.
n is the size of the sample or the number of trials.
x is the number of successes in the sample.
C is the symbol for a combination.

In the example $N = 20$, $S = 8$, $n = 2$, and $x = 2$. Therefore,

$$P(2) = \frac{(_8 C_2)(_{20-8} C_{2-2})}{(_{20} C_2)}$$

$$= \frac{\left(\dfrac{8!}{2!6!}\right)\left(\dfrac{12!}{0!12!}\right)}{\left(\dfrac{20!}{2!18!}\right)} = 0.147$$

Hence, the probability of selecting two students to serve on a committee and having that committee consist of two females is 0.147. This is the same probability we computed earlier.

Poisson Probability Distribution

Another discrete probability distribution is the *Poisson probability distribution*.

Poisson probability distribution: Has the same four characteristics as the binomial, but in addition the probability of success (π) is small, and n, the number of trials, is relatively large.

The formula for computing the probability of a success is:

$$P(x) = \frac{\mu^x e^{-\mu}}{x!} \qquad [6-7]$$

Where:

$P(x)$ is the probability to be computed for a specified value of x.
x is the number of occurrences (successes).
μ is the arithmetic mean number of occurrences (successes) in a particular interval of time.
e is the mathematical constant 2.71828.

Note that the mean number of successes, μ, can be determined in Poisson situations by $n\pi$, where n is the total number of trials and π is the probability of success.

$$\mu = n\pi \qquad [6-8]$$

As an example where the Poisson distribution is applicable, suppose electric utility bills are based on the actual reading of the electric meter. In 1 out of 100 cases the meter is incorrectly read ($\pi = 0.01$). Suppose the number of errors that appear in the processing of 500 customer bills approximates the Poisson distribution (n = 500). In this case the mean number of incorrect bills is 5, found by $\mu = n\pi = 500\ (0.01)$.

Using formula [6-7], finding the probability of exactly two errors appearing in 500 customer bills is rather tedious. Instead we merely refer to the Poisson distribution in Appendix C. Locate by $\mu = (5.0)$ at the top of a set of columns. Then find the x of 2 in the left column and read across to the column headed by 5.0. The probability of exactly 2 billing errors is 0.0842.

GLOSSARY

Random Variable: A quantity resulting from an experiment that, by chance, can assume different values.

Discrete random variable: A variable that can assume only certain clearly separated values resulting from a count of some item of interest.

Continuous random variable: A variable that can assume one of an infinitely large number of values within certain limitations.

Probability distribution: A listing of all the outcomes of a random experiment and the probability associated with each outcome.

Finite population: A population consisting of a small number of individuals, objects, or measurements.

Poisson probability distribution: Has the same four characteristics as the binomial, but in addition the probability of success (π) is small, and n, the number of trials, is relatively large.

CHAPTER PROBLEMS

Problem 1

Bill Russe, production manager at Ross Manufacturing, maintains detailed records on the number of times each machine breaks down and requires service during the week. Bill's records show that the Puret grinder has required repair service according to the following distribution. Compute the arithmetic mean and the variance of the number of breakdowns per week.

Number of Breakdowns Per Week	Weeks	Probability
0	20	0.333
1	20	0.333
2	10	0.167
3	10	0.167
Total	60	1.000

Solution

The arithmetic mean, or expected number of breakdowns per week for the probability distribution is computed using formula [6-1].

The arithmetic mean number of times the Puret machine breaks down per week is 1.168. The variance of the number of breakdowns is computed using formula [6-2].

Number of Breakdowns Per Week x	Probability $P(x)$	$xP(x)$
0	0.333	0.000
1	0.333	0.333
2	0.167	0.334
3	0.167	0.501
Total		1.168

Number of Breakdowns Per Week x	Probability $P(x)$	$(x - \mu)$	$(x - \mu)^2 P(x)$
0	0.333	0 – 1.168	(1.364)(0.333) = 0.454212
1	0.333	1 – 1.168	(0.028)(0.333) = 0.009324
2	0.167	2 – 1.168	(0.692)(0.167) = 0.115564
3	0.167	3 – 1.168	(3.356)(0.167) = 0.560452
			Total 1.139552

The variance of the number of breakdowns per week is about 1.140. The standard deviation of the number of breakdowns per week is 1.07, found by $\sqrt{1.139552} = 1.0674 = 1.07$.

Exercise 6.1

Check your answers against those in the ANSWER section.

The safety engineer at Manellis Electronics reported the following probability distribution for the number of on-the-job accidents during a one-month period.

Number of Accidents	Probability
0	0.60
1	0.30
2	0.10

a. Compute the mean

b. Compute the variance.

Problem 2

An insurance representative has appointments with four prospective clients tomorrow. From past experience she knows that the probability of making a sale on any appointment is 1 in 5 or 0.20. Use the rule of probability to determine the likelihood that she will sell a policy to 3 of the 4 prospective clients.

Solution

First note that the situation described meets the requirements of the binomial probability distribution. The conditions are:

1. There are a fixed number of trials—the representative visits four customers.

2. There are only two possible outcomes for each trial—she sells a policy or she does not sell a policy.

3. The probability of a success remains constant from trial to trial—for each appointment the probability of selling a policy (a success) is 0.20.

4. The trials are independent—if she sells a policy to the second appointment this does not alter the likelihood of selling to the third or the fourth appointment.

If S represents the outcome of a sale and NS the outcome of no sale, one possibility is that no sale is made on the first appointment but sales are made at the last 3.

$$(NS, S, S, S)$$

These events are independent, therefore the probability of their joint occurrence is the product of the individual probabilities. Therefore, the likelihood of no sale followed by three sales is $(0.8)(0.2)(0.2)(0.2) = 0.0064$. However, the requirements of the problem do not stipulate the location of NS. It could be the result of any one of the four appointments. The following summarizes the possible outcomes.

Location of NS	Order of Occurrence	Probability of Occurrence
1	NS, S, S, S	$(0.8)(0.2)(0.2)(0.2) = 0.0064$
2	S, NS, S, S	$(0.2)(0.8)(0.2)(0.2) = 0.0064$
3	S, S, NS, S	$(0.2)(0.2)(0.8)(0.2) = 0.0064$
4	S, S, S, NS	$(0.2)(0.2)(0.2)(0.8) = \underline{0.0064}$
		0.0256

The probability of exactly three sales in the four appointments is the sum of the 4 possibilities. Hence, the probability of selling insurance to 3 out of 4 appointments is 0.0256.

Problem 3

Now let's use formula [6-3] for the binomial distribution to compute the probability that the sales representative in Problem 2 will sell a policy to exactly 3 out of the 4 prospective clients.

Solution

To repeat, formula [6-3] for the binomial probability distribution is:

$$P(x) = \frac{n!}{x!(n-x)!}(\pi)^x(1-\pi)^{n-x} \qquad [6-3]$$

Where:

x is the number of successes, 3 in the example.

n is the number of trials, 4 in the example.

π is the probability of a success, 0.20.

$(1-\pi)$ is the probability of a failure, $= 0.80$ found by $(1 - 0.20)$.

The formula is applied to find the probability of selling an insurance policy to exactly 3 out of 4 potential customers.

$$P(x) = \frac{n!}{x!(n-x)!}(\pi)^x(1-\pi)^{n-x}$$

$$= \frac{4!}{3!(4-3)!}(0.20)^3(0.80)^{4-3} = 0.0256$$

Thus the probability is 0.0256 that the representative will be able to sell policies to exactly 3 out of the 4 clients visited. This is the same probability as computed earlier. Clearly, formula [6-3] leads more directly to a solution, and better accommodates the situation where the number of trials is large.

Exercise 6.2

Check your answers against those in the ANSWER section.

It is known that 60 percent of all registered voters in the 42nd Congressional District are Republicans. Three registered voters are selected at random from the district. Compute the probability that exactly 2 of the 3 selected are Republicans, using :

a. The rules of probability

b. The binomial formula.

Problem 4

In Problems 2 and 3 the probability of 3 sales resulting from 4 appointments was computed using both the rules of addition and multiplication and the binomial formula. A more convenient way of arriving at the probabilities for 0, 1, 2, 3, or 4 sales out of 4 appointments is to refer to a binomial table. We will now use the binomial table to determine the probabilities for all possible outcomes.

Solution

Refer to Appendix A, the binomial table. Find the table where n, the number of trials, is 4. Within that table find the row where $x = 0$, and move horizontally to the column headed $\pi = 0.20$. The probability of 0 sales is 0.410. The list for all possible outcome number of successes is:

Binomial Probability Distribution	
$n = 4$	$\pi = 0.20$
Number of Successes (x)	Probability
0	0.410
1	0.410
2	0.154
3	0.026
4	0.002
	*1.000

*'Slight discrepancy due to rounding.

Problem 5

Use the information regarding the insurance representative, where $n = 4$ and $\pi = 0.20$, to compute the probability that the representative sells more than two policies. Also determine the mean and variance of the number of policyholders.

Solution

The binomial table (Appendix A) can be used to determine the probability. First, note that the solution must include the probability that exactly 3 policies are sold and exactly 4 policies are sold, but not 2. From Appendix A, $P(3) = 0.026$ and $P(4) = 0.002$. The rule of addition is then used to combine these mutually exclusive events.

$$P(\text{more than } 2) = P(3) + P(4)$$
$$= 0.026 + 0.002$$
$$= 0.028$$

Thus the probability that a representative sells more than 2 policies is 0.028. Suppose the question asked is: "What is the probability of selling three or more policies in four trials?" Since there are no outcomes between "greater than 2" and "less than 3", the answer is exactly the same (0.028).

To determine the mean and the variance of a binomial we use formulas [6-4] and [6-5]. $\mu = n\pi = 4(0.20) = 0.80$. The variance is $\sigma^2 = n\pi(1-\pi) = 4(0.20)(0.80) = 0.64$. So the standard deviation is $\sqrt{0.64} = 0.80$. Thus if the sales representative has several days with 4 appointments, typically he/she will sell 0.80 policies.

Exercise 6.3

Check your answers against those in the ANSWER section.

Labor negotiators estimate that 30 percent of all major contract negotiations result in a strike. During the next year, 12 major contracts must be negotiated. Determine the following probabilities using Appendix A:

a.   no major strikes

b.   at least 5

c.   between 2 and 4 (that is 2, 3, or 4).

Problem 6

Alden and Associates write weekend trip insurance at a very nominal charge. Records show that the probability a motorist will have an accident during the weekend and file a claim is quite small (0.0005). Suppose Alden wrote 400 policies for the forthcoming weekend. Compute the probability that exactly two claims will be filed. Depict this distribution in the form of a chart.

Solution

The Poisson distribution is appropriate for this problem because the probability of filing a claim is small ($\pi = 0.0005$), and the number of trials n is large (400).

The Poisson distribution is described by formula [6-8]:

$$P(x) = \frac{\mu^x e^{-\mu}}{x!} \qquad [6-8]$$

Where:

x is the number of successes (claims filed). In this example $x = 2$

μ is the expected or mean number of claims to be filed $\mu = n\pi = (400)(0.0005) = 0.2$

e is a mathematical constant equal to 2.718.

The probability that exactly two claims are filed is 0.0164, found by

$$P(2) = \frac{\mu^x e^{-\mu}}{x!} = \frac{(0.2)^2 (2.718)^{-0.2}}{2!} = 0.0164$$

This indicates that the probability is somewhat small (about 0.0164) that exactly 2 claims will be filed.

The calculations to determine the probability 0.0164 were not shown above. As noted previously, a more convenient way to determine Poisson probabilities is to refer to Appendix C. To use this table, first find the column where $\mu = 0.20$, then go down that column to the row where $X = 2$ and read the value at the intersection. It is 0.0164.

The probabilities computed using formula [6-8] and those in Appendix C are the same. But those from the Appendix can be determined much more rapidly. The complete Poisson distribution is shown at the right and a graph for the case where $\mu = 0.20$ is shown below. Note the shape of the graph. It is positively skewed, and as the number of claims increases, the probability of a claim decreases.

Poisson Probability Distribution $\mu = 0.2$	
Number of Claims	Probability
0	0.8187
1	0.1637
2	0.0164
3	0.0011
4	0.0001
	1.0000

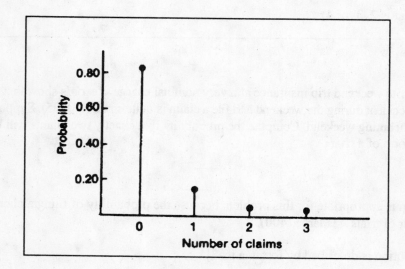

The probability of a typographical error on any page is 0.002. If a textbook contains 1,000 pages, compute the probability there are:

a.   No typos on a page

b.   At least 2 typos on a page.

Problem 7

The government of an underdeveloped country has 8 loans payable, 5 of which are overdue. If a representative of the International Monetary Fund randomly selects 3 loans, what is the probability that exactly 2 are overdue?

Solution

Note in this problem that successive observations are not independent. That is, the outcome of one sampled item influences the next sampled item. Because the observations are not independent, the binomial distribution is not appropriate and the hypergeometric distribution is used. To repeat formula [6-6] for the hypergeometric distribution:

$$P(x) = \frac{(_sC_x)(_{N-s}C_{n-x})}{(_NC_n)} \qquad [6-6]$$

Where:
N is the population size
S is the number of successes in the population
n is the number sampled
x is the number of successes in the sample.

The problem asks for the probability of exactly 2 loans overdue in a sample of 3, so $x = 2$ and $n = 3$. There are 8 loans in the population, 5 of which are overdue, so $N = 8$ and $S = 5$.

The probability is computed as follows:

$$P(x) = \frac{(_sC_x)(_{N-s}C_{n-x})}{(_NC_n)} = \frac{\left(\frac{5!}{2!3!}\right)\left(\frac{3!}{1!2!}\right)}{\left(\frac{8!}{3!5!}\right)} = \frac{30}{56} = 0.536$$

Interpreting the probability that exactly 2 of the 3 sampled loans are overdue is 0.536.

Exercise 6.5

Check your answers against those in the ANSWER section.

A retailer of personal computers just received a shipment of 30 units of a new model. The store has a quality agreement with the manufacturer which states that four of the machines are to be selected for a thorough performance check. If more than one fails a performance test the shipment is returned. Suppose the retailer did not know that 5 of the 30 incoming personal computers are defective. Compute the probability that exactly two computers selected at random are defective.

CHAPTER 6 ASSIGNMENT

DISCRETE PROBABILITY DISTRIBUTIONS

Name _____ Section _____ Score _____

Part I   Select the correct answer and write the appropriate letter in the space provided.

_____ 1. A listing of all possible outcomes of an experiment and the corresponding probability is called:
   a.   a random variable.
   b.   the complement rule.
   c.   the normal rule.
   d.   a probability distribution.

_____ 2. A probability distribution that can assume only certain values within a range is called
   a.   a discrete probability distribution.
   b.   a continuous probability distribution.
   c.   a random variable.
   d.   a Poisson probability distribution.

_____ 3. Which of the following is **not** a requirement of the binomial distribution?
   a.   the trials must be independent
   b.   the probability of a success changes from one trial to the next
   c.   the sample size must be fixed
   d.   only two outcomes are possible

_____ 4. The mean of a discrete probability distribution is also called the
   a.   variance.
   b.   standard deviation.
   c.   expected value.
   d.   median.

_____ 5. Which of the following statements is true about a Poisson probability distribution?
   a.   The probability of a success is small.
   b.   The sample size is small.
   c.   Probability changes after each trial.
   d.   The outcome of one trial affects the outcome of another trial.

_____ 6. Which distribution would be most appropriate if one wanted to find the probability of selecting three Republicans from a sample of 15 politicians?
   a.   binomial
   b.   discrete
   c.   hypergeometric
   d.   Poisson

_____ 7. A discrete distribution is usually the result of
   a.   a measurement.
   b.   a count.
   c.   a small sample.
   d.   a small probability.

8. Which of the following is **not** a requirement for a discrete probability distribution?
   a. The sum of the probabilities is equal to 1.00.
   b. The probability of each outcome is between 0 and 1.00.
   c. The outcomes are mutually exclusive.
   d. The trials are independent.

9. To construct a binomial probability distribution, we need to know
   a. the mean and standard deviation.
   b. only the mean.
   c. the size of the sample.
   d. the number of trials and probability of success.

10. The difference between the binomial distribution and the hypergeometric distribution is
   a. the binomial requires a large sample.
   b. the mean and the variance are equal for the binomial.
   c. the probability of a success is not the same for all trials in the hypergeometric.
   d. the trials are not independent for the binomial.

Part II   Using the appropriate distribution answer the following questions. Show all your work. Write your answer in the answer box provided.

11. The number of connections on the Internet during any two minute period is given by the following distribution:

Number of times	Proportion
0	0.1
1	0.2
2	0.1
3	0.4
4	0.2

a. Determine the mean number of times a connection is made during a two minute period.

a.

b. Determine the standard deviation of the number of connections made during a two minute period.

b.

12. According to a recent survey, 75% of all customers will return to the same grocery store. Suppose eight customers are selected at random, what is the probability that:

a. exactly five of the customers will return?

> a.

b. all eight will return?

> b.

c. at least seven will return?

> c.

d. at least one will return?

> d.

e. How many customers would be expected to return to the same store?

> e.

13. Eighty percent of trees planted by a woodlands conservation group survive. What is the probability that:

a. 10 of the 12 trees just planted will survive?

> a.

b. at least 10 of the trees just planted will survive?

> b.

14. Customers use an automatic teller machine at an average rate of 15 per hour. What is the probability that exactly 12 will use the machine in the next hour?

14.

15. On the average two new checking accounts are opened per day at the Farmer's Bank. What is the likelihood that for a particular day:

   a. no new accounts are opened?

   a..

   b. at least one new account is opened?

   b.

16. A management team is comprised of six sales managers and four floor employees. A subcommittee of four is being formed to handle labor negotiations. What is the probability that two sales managers and two floor employees are selected?

16.

17. In a statistics class with 15 males and 13 females, five students are selected to put problems on the board. What is the probability that:

   a. 3 females and 2 males are selected?

   a.

   b. all five students selected are males?

   b.

   c. all five students selected are females?

   c.

   d. at least one male is selected?

   d.

THE NORMAL PROBABILITY DISTRIBUTION

Chapter Goals

After completing this chapter, you will be able to:

1. List the characteristics of a normal probability distribution.

2. Define and calculate z values.

3. Determine the probability that an observation will lie between two points, using the standard normal distribution.

4. Determine the probability that an observation will be above (or below) a given value, using the standard normal distribution.

5. Compare two or more observations that are on different probability distributions.

6. Use the normal distribution to approximate the binomial probability distribution.

Introduction

The previous chapter dealt with discrete probability distributions. Recall that for a discrete distribution, the outcome can assume only a specific set of values. For example, the number of correct responses to ten true-false questions can only be the numbers 0, 1, 2, ..., 10.

This chapter examines an important *continuous probability distribution*—the normal distribution. Recall that a continuous probability distribution can assume an infinite number of values within a given range. As an example, the weight of an engine block could be 54, 54.1, or 54.1437 pounds depending on the accuracy of the measuring device.

Characteristics of the Normal Distribution

The mean of a normal distribution is represented by the Greek letter μ (lower case mu), and standard deviation by the Greek letter σ (lower case sigma).

> *Normal distribution*: A continuous probability distribution that is uniquely determined by μ and σ,

The major characteristics of the normal distribution are:

1. The normal distribution is "*bell-shaped*" and the mean, median, and mode are all equal. Exactly one-half of the observations are larger than this center value, and one-half are smaller.

2. The distribution is *symmetrical*. A vertical line drawn at the mean divides the distribution into two equal halves and these halves possess exactly the same shape.

3. It is *asymptotic*. That is, the "tails of the curve approach the *X-axis* but never actually touch it.

4. A normal distribution is completely described by its mean and standard deviation. This indicates that if the mean and standard deviation are known, a normal distribution can be constructed and its curve drawn.

5. There is a "family" of normal distributions. This means there is a different normal distribution for each combination of μ and σ.

These characteristics are summarized in the following graph.

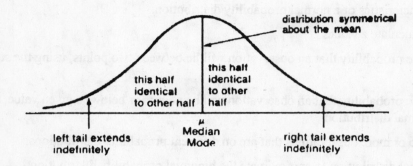

The Standard Normal Distribution

As noted in the previous discussion, there are many normal probability distributions, a different one for each pair of values for a mean and a standard deviation. This principle makes the normal probability distribution applicable to a wide range of real-world situations. However, since there is an infinite number of probability distributions, it would be awkward to construct tables of probabilities for so many different normal distributions. An efficient method for overcoming this difficulty is to standardize each normal distribution.

> *Standard normal distribution*: A normal distribution with a mean of 0 and a standard deviation of 1.

An actual distribution is converted to a standard normal distribution using a z value.

> *z value*: The distance between a selected value designated X, and the population mean, μ, divided by the population standard deviation, σ.

The formula for a specific standardized z value is text formula [7-1]:

$$z = \frac{X - \mu}{\sigma} \qquad [7-1]$$

Where:
X is the value of any particular observation or measurement.
μ is the mean of the distribution
σ is the standard deviation of the distribution
z is the standardized normal value, usually called the z value.

Area Between μ and X

To obtain the probability of a value falling in the interval between the variable of interest (X) and the mean (μ), we first compute the distance between the value (X) and the mean (μ). Then we express that difference in units of the standard deviation by dividing ($X - \mu$) by the standard deviation. This process is called **standardizing.**

To illustrate the probability of a value being between a selected X value and the mean μ, suppose the mean useful life of a car battery is 36 months, with a standard deviation of 3 months. What is the probability that such a battery will last between 36 and 40 months?

The first step is to convert the 40 months to an equivalent standard normal value, using formula 7-1. The computation is:

$$ z = \frac{X - \mu}{\sigma} = \frac{40 - 36}{3} = 1.33 $$

Next refer to Appendix D, a table for the areas under the normal curve. A part of the table in Appendix D is shown below.

z	0.00	0.01	0.02	0.03	0.04	0.05
		•	•	•	•	
		•	•	•	•	
		•	•	•	•	
1.0						
1.1		0.3665	0.3686	0.3708	0.3729	
1.2		0.3869	0.3888	0.3907	0.3925	
1.3		0.4049	0.4066	0.4082	0.4099	
1.4		0.4207	0.4222	0.4236	0.4251	

To use the table, the z value of 1.33 is split into two parts, 1.3 and 0.03, then to obtain the probability go down the left-hand column to 1.3, then move over to the column headed 0.03 and read the probability. It is 0.4082.

The probability that a battery will last between 36 and 40 months is 0.4082. Other probabilities may be calculated, such as more than 46 months, and less than 33 months. Further details are given in Problems 1 through 5.

The Normal Approximation to the Binomial

The binomial table (Appendix A) goes from a sample size of 1 to 20 and 25. What do we do when the sample size is greater than 25? A binomial probability can be estimated using the normal distribution.

> *Normal approximation to the binomial*: A binomial probability can be estimated using the normal distribution.

To apply the normal approximation to the binomial, both n π and $n (1 - \pi)$ must be greater than 5. The sample size, or the number of trials, is designated by n, and π is the probability of a success. The mean and the standard deviation of the binomial are computed by:

$$\mu = n\pi$$
$$\sigma = \sqrt{n\pi(1-\pi)}$$

To illustrate, suppose 60 percent of the applications for an exclusive credit card are approved. In a sample of 200 applications, what is the probability that 130 or more applications are approved?

First verify that both $n\pi$ and $n(1-\pi)$ exceed 5. For $n = 200$ and $\pi = 0.6$

$$n\pi = 200(0.6) = 120 \qquad\qquad n(1-\pi) = 200(1-0.6) = 200(0.4) = 80$$

Thus the normal approximation to the binomial may be used.

The mean and standard deviation are computed as follows:

$$\mu = n\pi = 200(0.60) = 120$$

$$\sigma = \sqrt{n\pi(1-\pi)} = \sqrt{200(0.6)(0.4)} = 6.93$$

This distribution is standardized by formula [7-1] and $\mu = 120$, $\sigma = 6.93$ and letting $X = 129.5$ (Not 130)

$$z = \frac{X - \mu}{\sigma} = \frac{129.5 - 120}{6.93} = 1.37$$

Why is 129.5 used instead of 130? Namely, to "correct" for the fact that a continuous distribution (the normal) is used to approximate a discrete distribution (the binomial). On a continuous scale the value 130 would range from 129.5 to 130.5. On a discrete scale there would be a "gap" between 129 and 130 where there would not be any probability. The 0.50 is called the correction for continuity.

> *Correction for continuity*: A correction factor of 0.5 used to improve the accuracy of the approximation of a binomial probability distribution by the normal curve.

The probability of a z value between 0 and 1.37 is 0.4147 (See Appendix D). Therefore the probability of a z value greater than 1.37 is 0.0853, found by 0.5000 - 0.4147. So, the probability that 130 or more applications will be approved is 0.0853.

Glossary

Normal distribution: A continuous probability distribution that is uniquely determined by μ and σ.

Standard normal distribution: A normal distribution with a mean of 0 and a standard deviation of 1.

z value: The distance between a selected value and the population mean in units of the standard deviation.

Normal approximation to the binomial: A binomial probability can be estimated using the normal distribution.

Correction for continuity: A correction factor of 0.5 used to improve the accuracy of the approximation of a binomial probability distribution by the normal curve.

Chapter Problems

Problem 1

The mean amount of gasoline and services charged by Key Refining Company credit customers is $70 per month. The distribution of amounts spent is approximately normal with a standard deviation of $10. Compute the probability of selecting a credit card customer at random and finding the customer charged between $70 and $83 last month.

Solution

The first step is to convert the area between $70 and $83 to a *z* value using formula [7-1].

$$z = \frac{X - \mu}{\sigma} \qquad [7-1]$$

Where:
X is any value of the random variable ($83 in this problem)
μ   is the arithmetic mean of the normal distribution ($70)
σ   is its standard deviation ($10).

Solving for z:

$$z = \frac{X - \mu}{\sigma} = \frac{\$83 - \$70}{10} = 1.30$$

This indicates that $83 is 1.30 standard deviations to the right of the mean of $70. Showing the problem graphically:

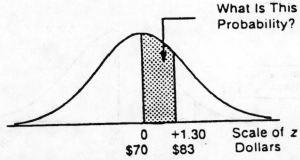

The probability of a *z* value from 0 to 1.30 is given in a table of areas of the normal curve, Appendix D. To obtain the probability, go down the left-hand column to 1.3, then move over to the column headed 0.00, and read the probability. It is 0.4032. To put it another way, 40.32 percent of the credit card customers charge between $70 and $83 per month.

Problem 2

Again using the Key Refinery data from Problem 1, compute the probability of customers charging between $57 and $83 per month.

Solution

As shown in the following graph, the probability of a customer charging between $57 and $70 per month must be combined with the probability of charging between $70 and $83 in a month to obtain the combined probability.

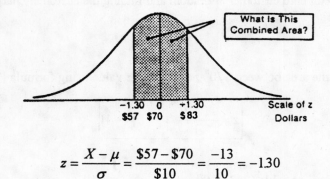

$$z = \frac{X - \mu}{\sigma} = \frac{\$57 - \$70}{\$10} = \frac{-13}{10} = -1.30$$

The probability of between $70 and $83 was computed in Problem 1. Due to the symmetry of the normal distribution, the probability between 0 and 1.30 is the same as the probability between −1.30 and 0. It is 0.4032. The probability that customers will charge between $57 and $83 is 0.8064, found by adding .0·4032 and 0.4032.

Problem 3

Using the Key Refining data from Problem 1, what is the probability that a particular customer charges less than $54?

Solution

The area to be determined is shown below.

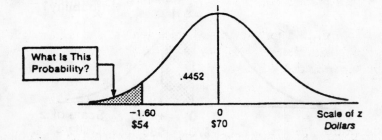

The z value for the area of the normal curve between $70 and $54 is −1.60, found by:

$$z = \frac{X - \mu}{\sigma} = \frac{\$54 - \$70}{\$10} = \frac{-\$16}{\$10} = -1.60$$

Referring to Appendix D, and a z of 1.60, the area of the normal curve between μ ($70) and X ($54) is 0.4452. Recall that for a symmetrical distribution half of the observations are above the mean, and half below it. In this problem, the probability of an observation being below $70 is, therefore, 0.5000. Since the probability of an observation being between $54 and $70 is 0.4452, it follows that 0.5000 − 0.4452 = 0.0548, is the probability that an observation is below $54. To put it another way, 5.48 percent of the customers charge less than $54 per month.

Problem 4

Again using the Key Refining data from Problem 1, compute the probability of a customer charging between $82 and $92.

Solution

The area to be determined is depicted in the following diagram.

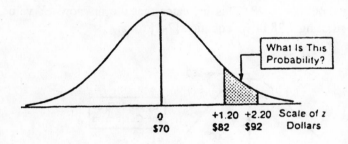

The areas of the normal curve between $70 and $82, and $70 and $92 are determined using formula [7-1].

$$z = \frac{X - \mu}{\sigma} = \frac{\$82 - \$70}{\$10} = -1.20 \qquad z = \frac{X - \mu}{\sigma} = \frac{\$92 - \$70}{\$10} = 2.20$$

The probability corresponding to a z of −1.20 is 0.3849 (from Appendix D).

The probability corresponding to a z of 2.20 is 0.4861 (from Appendix D).

The probability of a credit card customer charging between $82 and $92 a month, therefore, is the difference between these two probabilities. Thus, (0.4861 − 0.3849) = 0.1012. That is, 10.12 percent of the charge account customers charge between $82 and $92 monthly.

Brief Review

In brief there are four situations in which you may find the area under the standard normal distribution.

1. To find the area between 0 and z or (−z) you look up the value directly in the table. We did this in problem 1.

2. To find the area between two points on different sides of the mean determine the two *z* values and add the corresponding areas. We did this in problem 2.

3. To find the area beyond *z* or (–*z*) locate the probability of *z* in the table and subtract that value from 0.500. We did this in problem 3.

4. To find the area between two points on the same side of the mean, determine the two *z* values and subtract the smaller area from the larger area. We did this in problem 4.

Problem 5

Key Refining (Problem 1) decided to send a special financing plan to charge account customers having the highest 10 percent of the money charges. What is the dividing point between the customers who receive the special plan and those who do not?

Solution

The shaded area in the following diagram represents the upper 10 percent who receive the special plan. *X* represents the unknown value that divides the customers into two groups—those who receive the special financing plan (the shaded area), and those who do not receive it. The area from the mean of $70 to this unknown *X* value is 0.4000, found by 0.5000 – 0.1000. From the table of areas of the normal curve (Appendix D), the closest *z* value corresponding to the area 0.4000 is 1.28. This indicates that the unknown *X* value is 1.28 standard deviations above the mean. Substituting 1.28 in the equation [7-1] for *z*:

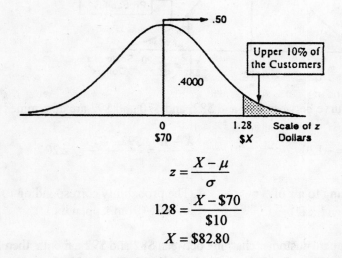

$$z = \frac{X - \mu}{\sigma}$$

$$1.28 = \frac{X - \$70}{\$10}$$

$$X = \$82.80$$

Key Refining should send the special financing plan to those charge account customers having a monthly charge of $82.80 and above.

Check your answers against those in the ANSWER section.

A cola dispensing machine is set to dispense a mean of 2.02 liters into a bottle labeled 2 liters. Actual quantities dispensed vary and the amounts are normally distributed with a standard deviation of 0.015 liters.

a. What is the probability a bottle will contain between 2.02 and 2.04 liters?

b. What is the probability a bottle will contain between 2.00 and 2.03 liters?

c. What is the probability a bottle will contain less than 2 liters?

d. How much cola is dispensed in the largest 4% of the drinks?

Problem 6

The Key Refining Company, referred to in the earlier problems, determined that 15 percent of its customers will not pay their bill by the due date. What is the probability that for a sample of 80 customers, less than 10 will not pay their bill by the due date?

Solution

The answer could be determined by using the binomial distribution where π, the probability of a success, is 0.15, and where n, the number of trials, is 80. However, most binomial tables do not go beyond an n of 25 and the calculations by hand would be very tedious.

As noted previously, the probability can be accurately estimated by using the normal approximation to the binomial. The approximations are quite good when both $n\pi$ and $n(1-\pi)$ are greater than 5.

In this case, $n\pi = (80)(0.15) = 12$, and $n(1-\pi) = (80)(1-0.15) = 68$. Both are greater than 5. Recall the mean and variance of a binomial distribution are computed as follows:

$$\mu = n\pi = (80)(0.15) = 12$$
$$\sigma^2 = n\pi(1-\pi) = (80)(0.15)(0.85) = 10.2$$

The standard deviation is 3.19, found by $\sqrt{10.2}$. The area less than 9.5 is shown on the following diagram. Because we are estimating a discrete distribution using a continuous distribution, the continuity correction factor is needed. In this instance if we were actually using the binomial distribution we would add the probabilities of 0 customers not paying, one customer not paying, and so on, up to nine customers not paying the bill. With the discrete distribution there would be no probability of 8.6 customers not paying their bill.

When we estimate binomial probabilities using the normal distribution, the area for nine corresponds to the area from 8.5 up to 9.5. In this case, we want all the area below (to the left of) 9.5. This area is depicted schematically as:

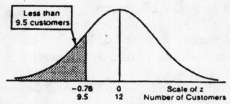

The z value associated with less than 9.5 customers is −0.78, found by

$$z = \frac{9.5 - 12.0}{3.19} = -0.78$$

The area to the left of −0.78 is 0.2177, found by (0.5000 − 0.2823). The probability that less than ten customers will not pay their bill is 0.2177.

A note on the correction factor

We apply the correction factor in only four cases. They are:

1.   For the probability *at least X* occurs, use the area above $(X - 0.5)$

2.   For the probability that *more than X* occurs, use the area above $(X + 0.5)$

3.   For the probability that *X or less* occurs, use the area below $(X + 0.5)$

4.   For the probability that *less than X* occurs, use the area below $(X - 0.5)$

The following output from MINITAB shows the cumulative distribution for the case where $n = 80$ and π = 0.15. Look down the column labeled X to the row for 9 and read the probability. It is 0.2211. That is very close to our estimate of 0.2177.

```
MTB . cdf;
SUBC. binomial 80 .15.

Cumulative Distribution Function

Binomial with n = 80 and p = 0.150000
     x      O(X ,=x)
     1       0.0000
     2       0.0003
     3       0.0013
     4       0.0047
     5       0.0140
     6       0.0345
     7       0.0727
     8       0.1342
     9       0.2211
    10       0.3300
    11       0.4522
    12       0.5762
    13       0.6907
    14       0.7874
    15       0.8625
    16       0.9163
    17       0.9520
    18       0.9741
    19       0.9868
    20       0.9937
    21       0.9971
    22       0.9988
    23       0.9995
    24       0.9998
    25       0.9999
    26       1.0000
```

Exercise 7.2

Check your answers against those in the ANSWER section.

A new drug has been developed that is found to relieve nasal congestion in 90 percent of those with the condition. The new drug is administered to 300 patients with this condition. What is the probability that more than 265 patients will be relieved of the nasal congestion?

CHAPTER 7 ASSIGNMENT

THE NORMAL PROBABILITY DISTRIBUTION

Name _____   Section _____   Score _____

Part I   Select the correct answer and write the appropriate letter in the space provided.

_____ 1. In a normal distribution
   a. the mean and the median are always equal.
   b. the mean and the standard deviation are always equal.
   c. the mean is always larger than the median.
   d. the mean is always smaller than the median.

_____ 2. The normal distribution is
   a. a bell-shaped distribution.
   b. a continuous distribution.
   c. symmetric.
   d. all of the above.

_____ 3. The standard normal distribution
   a. is a special case of the normal distribution.
   b. has a mean equal to 0 and a standard deviation equal to 1.
   c. measures the distance from the mean in units of the standard deviation.
   d. all of the above.

_____ 4. A normal distribution is completely described by
   a. its mean.
   b. its standard deviation.
   c. its mean and standard deviation.
   d. none of the above.

_____ 5. Any normal distribution can be converted to a standard normal distribution by
   a. finding $\mu = n\pi$.
   b. determining that $n\pi$ is greater than 5.

   c. finding $z = \dfrac{x - \mu}{\sigma}$

   d. finding $\sigma = \sqrt{n\pi(1-\pi)}$

_____ 6. A normal distribution
   a. has at least two peaks.
   b .is asymptotic.
   c increases as X increases.
   d is discrete.

_____ 7. The normal distribution can be used to approximate the binomial when
      a. $n\pi$ is at least 25.
      b.   both $n\pi$ and $n(1 - \pi)$ are greater than 5.
      c. $n\pi(1 - \pi p)$ is larger than 5.
      d.   only when the z-score is above 5.

_____ 8. The area under the normal curve between 0 and 1.00 and 0 and -1.00
      a.   is the same.
      b.   is negative.
      c.   equal to zero.
      d.   none of the above.

_____ 9. A z value
      a.   is the standard deviation for the standard normal distribution.
      b.   is a measure of how many standard deviations the mean is from the median.
      c.   is the difference of the mean and the probability of z.
      d.   is a measure of how many standard deviations a particular score is from the mean.

_____ 10. The correction for continuity is used when
      a.   the z-scores are integers.
      b.   the distribution is discrete.
      c.   the z-scores are less than 0.5
      d.   the distribution is continuous.

Part II   Answer the following questions. Be sure to show your work.

11. Fix-It Copiers advertises a mean time of 100 minutes for office calls with a standard deviation of 25 minutes. What percentage of calls are completed:

    a.   between 100 and 120 minutes?

                                                            a.

    b.   in less than 120 minutes?

                                                            b.

    c.   in less than 60 minutes?

                                                            c.

    d.   between 120 and 150 minutes?

                                                            d.

    e.   between 60 and 120 minutes?

                                                            e.

    f.   Twenty percent of their jobs take more than how much time?

                                                            f.

12. Access time to a supercomputer mainframe is normally distributed with an average (mean) of 92 minutes a day with a standard deviation of 11 minutes. Find the probability that on a certain day, the access time is

a. less than 60 minutes.

> a.

b. more than 100 minutes.

> b.

c. between 70 and 90 minutes.

> c.

d. between 1 and 2 hours.

> d.

e. On 15% of the days, the access time is more than how many minutes?

> e.

13. A certain printer ribbon has demonstrated a mean time usage of 9 hours and a standard deviation of 22 minutes. What time usage guarantee (in hours) should the manufacturer advertise in order to ensure that only 4% of the ribbons fail to meet the guaranteed time usage?

> 13.

14. A file cabinet manufacturer estimates that 5% of its file cabinets will have drawers that close improperly. Assume a production run of 40 cabinets is completed.

> a.

a. What is the mean and standard deviation of this distribution?

> b.

b. What is the probability that 3 or more are defective?

> c.

c. What is the probability that exactly 3 cabinets are defective?

> d.

d. What is the probability that there are more than 4 defective file cabinets?

15 A clothing store asserts that 60% of its customers pay by credit. On a particular day, 35 customers purchased items at the store.

    a.   What is the mean and standard deviation of the binomial distribution?

a.

    b.   What is the probability that half (18 or more) of the customers paid by credit?

b.

    c.   What is the probability that 30 or more paid by credit?

c.

    d.   What is the probability that less than 12 paid by credit?

d.

    e.   What is the probability that 12 to 30 paid by credit?

e.

16. It is very difficult for small businesses to be successful. The Small Business Administration estimates that 20 percent will dissolve or go bankrupt within two years. A sample of 50 new businesses is selected.

    a.   What is the mean and standard deviation of this distribution?

a.

    b.   What is the probability that more than 16 in the sample will go bankrupt?

b.

    c.   What is the probability that exactly 14 will go bankrupt?

c.

    d.   What is the probability that between 7 and 9 businesses will go bankrupt?

d.

    e.   What is the probability that between 7 and 15 businesses will go bankrupt?

e.

CHAPTER 8
SAMPLING METHODS AND SAMPLING DISTRIBUTIONS

Chapter Goals

After completing this chapter, you will be able to:

1. Explain why in many situations a sample is the only feasible way to learn about a population.

2. Explain methods for selecting a sample.

3. Distinguish between probability sampling and nonprobability sampling.

4. Define and construct a sampling distribution of sample means.

5. Explain the central limit theorem and its importance.

6. Calculate confidence intervals for means and proportions.

7. Determine an appropriate sample size for attribute and variable sampling.

Introduction

This chapter is the beginning of our study of sampling. Sampling is necessary because we want to make statements about a population but we do not want to (or cannot) examine all the items in that population. Recall from Chapter 1 that a **population** refers to the entire group of objects or persons of interest. The population of interest might be all the persons in the city receiving welfare payments or all the computer chips produced during the last hour. A **sample** is a portion, a part, or a subset of the population. Fifty welfare recipients out of 4,000 receiving payments might constitute the sample, or 20 computer chips might be sampled out of 1,500 produced last hour.

Reasons for Sampling

Why is it necessary to sample? Why can't we just inspect all the items? There are several reasons.

1. *The destructive nature of certain tests*. The manufacturer of fuses cannot test all of them because in the testing the fuse is destroyed and none would be available for sale!

2. *The physical impossibility of checking all the items in the population*. The South Dakota Game Commission, for example, cannot check all the deer, grouse, and other wild game because they are always moving.

3. *The cost of studying all the items in the population is prohibitive*. Some television program ratings are established by analyzing the viewing habits of about 1,200 viewers. The cost of studying all the homes having television would be exorbitant.

4. *The adequacy of sample results*. If the sample results of the viewing habits of 1,200 homes revealed that only 1.1 percent of the homes watched "60 Minutes," no doubt the program would be replaced by another show. Checking the viewing habits of all the homes regarding "60 Minutes" probably would not change the percent significantly.

5. *To contact the whole population would often be very time consuming*. To ask every eligible voter regarding the chances of a senator being re-elected in the forthcoming election would take months. The election would probably be over before the survey was completed.

Probability Sampling Methods

There are two basic types of sampling: probability sampling and nonprobability sampling.

When all the items in the population have a chance to be included in the sample, the method is referred to as *probability sampling*.

> *Probability sample*: A sample selected in such a way that each item or person in the population being studied has a known (nonzero) likelihood of being included in the sample.

When the items included in the sample are based on the judgement of the person selecting the sample, the method is called *nonprobability sampling*.

> *Nonprobability sampling*: A sample selected in such away that **not** all items or people have a chance of being included in the sample.

A sample based on the judgement of the person selecting the sample may be **biased**, meaning that the sample results may not be representative of the population.

Four types of probability sampling are commonly used: *simple random sampling, systematic random sampling, stratified sampling*, and *cluster sampling*.

The must widely used type of sampling is a simple random sample.

> *Simple random sample*: A sample formulated so that each item or person in the population has the same chance of being included in the sample.

Several ways of selecting a simple random sample are:

1. The name or identifying number of each item in the population is recorded on a slip of paper and placed in a box. The slips of paper are shuffled and the required sample size is chosen from the box.

2. Each item is numbered and a *table of random numbers*, such as the one in Appendix E, is used to select the members of the sample.

3. Many computers have routines that randomly select a given number of items from the population.

   Another type of sampling is *a systematic random sample*.

> *Systematic random sample*: The items or individuals of the population are arranged in some way —alphabetically, in a file drawer by date received, or by some other method. A random starting point is selected, and then every k th member of the population is selected for the sample.

In a systematic sample the items in the population are numbered 1, 2, 3,.... Next, a random starting point is selected, let's say 39. Every k th item thereafter, such as every 100th, is selected for the sample. This means that 39, 139, 239, 339, and so on would be a part of the sample.

Another type of probability sample is referred to as *stratified random sampling*.

> *Stratified sample*: A population is first divided into subgroups, called strata, and a sample is selected from each stratum.

For example, if our study involved Army personnel, we might decide to stratify the population (all Army personnel) into generals, other officers, and enlisted personnel. The number selected from each of the three strata could be proportional to the total number in the population for the corresponding strata. Each member of the population can belong to only one of the strata. That is, a military person cannot be a general and a private at the same time.

Another common type of sampling is *cluster sampling*.

> *Cluster sampling*: The population is divided into primary units, and then samples are drawn from the primary units.

Cluster sampling is often used to reduce the cost of sampling when the population is scattered over a large geographic area. Suppose the objective is to study household waste collection in a large city. As a first step you divide the city into smaller units (perhaps precincts). Next, the precincts are numbered and several selected randomly. Finally, households within each of these precincts are randomly selected and interviewed.

Sampling Error

It is not logical to expect that the results obtained from a sample will coincide exactly with those from a population. For example, it is unlikely that the mean welfare payment for a sample of 50 recipients is exactly the same as the mean for all 4,000 welfare recipients.

> *Sampling error*: The difference between a sample statistic and its corresponding population parameter.

Because these errors happen by chance, they are referred to as chance variations.

The Sampling Distribution of the Sample Means

Suppose all possible samples of size n are selected from a specified population, and the mean of each of these samples is computed. The distribution of these sample means is called the *sampling distribution of the sample means*.

> *Sampling distribution of the mean*: A probability distribution consisting of all possible sample means of a given sample size selected from a population and the probability of occurrence associated with each sample mean.

The sampling distribution of the mean is a probability distribution and has the following major characteristics:

1. The mean of all the sample means will be exactly equal to the population mean.

2. If the population from which the samples are drawn is normal, the distribution of sample means is also normally distributed.

3. If the population from which the samples are drawn is not normal, the sampling distribution is approximately normal, provided the samples are "sufficiently" large (usually accepted to include at least 30 observations). This phenomenon is called the *Central Limit Theorem*.

> *Central limit theorem*: If all samples of a particular size are selected from any population, the sampling distribution of the sample means is approximately a normal distribution. This approximation improves with larger samples.

It is interesting to note that we can reason about the distribution of the sample means with absolutely no information about the shape of the original distribution from which the sample was taken.

Point Estimates

A single number used to estimate a population parameter is called a *point estimate*.

> *Point estimate*: The value, computed from sample information, that is used to estimate the population parameter.

The sample mean $\overline{X}$ is a point estimate of the population mean μ, p is a point estimate of π, and s is a point estimate of σ.

For example, a sample of 100 recent accounting graduates revealed a mean starting salary of $30,000. The $30,000 is a point estimate. The sample mean is a point estimate of the mean starting salary of all (population) accounting graduates.

Confidence Interval

Why is the above mentioned central limit theorem so important? It can be used to specify a range of values within which a population parameter, such as the population mean, can be expected to occur. The range of values, within which a population parameter is expected to lie, is usually referred to as the *confidence interval*.

> *Confidence Interval* : A range of values constructed from sample data so that the parameter occurs within that range at a specified probability. The specified probability is called the *level of confidence*.

The end points of the confidence interval are called the *confidence limits*. The measure of the confidence we have that an interval estimate will include the population parameter is called *the level of confidence*.

The Standard Error of the Sample Means

The standard deviation of the sampling distribution of the sample means is called the *standard error of the sample mean* and is denoted by the symbol $\sigma_{\bar{x}}$.

A confidence interval for the population mean is determined by $\sigma_{\bar{x}}$ read "sigma sub X bar."

Standard Error of the Sample Mean: The standard deviation of the sampling distribution of sample means.

The standard error is a measure of the variability of the sampling distribution of the means. It is computed using text formula [8-1]

$$\sigma_{\bar{X}} = \frac{\sigma}{\sqrt{n}} \qquad [8-1]$$

Where:

$\sigma_{\bar{X}}$ is the standard error of the mean

σ is the population standard deviation

n is the sample size

In most situations we do not know the population standard deviation so we replace it with the sample standard deviation. We replace σ with s. Thus we have text formula [8-2]:

$$s_{\bar{X}} = \frac{s}{\sqrt{n}} \qquad [8-2]$$

The size of the standard error is affected by the standard deviation. As the standard deviation increases so does the standard error. The standard error is also affected by the sample size. As the sample size increases the standard error decreases, which indicates that there is less variability in the distribution of the sample means. Obviously we conclude that as we increase the sample size the standard error decreases.

When the sample size (n) is at least 30, it is generally accepted that the Central Limit Theorem will ensure a normal distribution of the sample means. This important consideration allows us to use the standard normal distribution, that is z in our calculation of the confidence interval. In general the confidence interval for the mean of a sample is computed by text formula [8-5].

$$\bar{X} \pm z \frac{s}{\sqrt{n}} \qquad [8-5]$$

Where:

$\overline{X}$ is the sample mean.

z is the value associated with the given level of confidence.

s is the sample standard deviation.

n is the size of the sample.

Confidence Interval for a Population Proportion

The theory and procedure for determining a point estimator and an interval estimator for a population proportion are quite similar. The confidence interval for a population proportion is found by:

$$p \pm z \sqrt{\frac{p(1-p)}{n}} \qquad [8-8]$$

Where:

p is the sample proportion

n is the sample size.

z is the z value for degree of confidence selected.

Finite Correction Factor

If the sampling is done without replacement from a small population, the *finite population correction factor* is used. If the sample constitutes more than 5 percent of the population, the finite correction factor is applied. Its purpose is to account for the fact that a parameter can be more accurately estimated from a small population when a large portion of that population's units are sampled. The correction factor is:

$$\sqrt{\frac{N-n}{N-1}}$$

What is the effect of this term? If N, the number of units in the population, is large relative to n, the sample size, the value of this correction factor is near 1.00.

For example, if N = 10,000 and a sample of 40 is selected, the value of the correction factor is 0.9980, found by $\sqrt{\dfrac{10,000-40}{10,000-1}} = 0.9980$.

However, if N is only 500 the correction factor is 0.9601, found by $\sqrt{\dfrac{500-40}{500-1}} = 0.9601$.

Logically, we can estimate a population parameter with a sample of 40 from a population of 500 more accurately than with a sample of 40 from a population of 10,000.

The standard error of the mean or the standard error of the proportion is multiplied by the correction factor. Because the correction factor will always be less than 1.00, the effect is to reduce the standard error. Stated differently, because the sample constituted a substantial proportion of the population, the standard error is reduced. The confidence interval for the population mean, therefore, is computed as follows:

$$\overline{X} \pm z \frac{s}{\sqrt{n}} \left(\sqrt{\frac{N-n}{N-1}} \right)$$

The confidence interval for a population proportion is:

$$p \pm z \sqrt{\frac{p(1-p)}{n}} \left(\sqrt{\frac{N-n}{N-1}} \right)$$

Choosing an Appropriate Sample Size

Sample size is always a concern when designing a statistical study. Too large a sample could be a waste of time and money collecting the data. Also too small a sample may make the conclusions drawn from the data uncertain. The size of a sample required for a particular study is based on three factors.

1. The desired level of confidence. This is expressed in terms of z.

2. The maximum allowable error E the researcher will tolerate.

3. The variability in the population under study (as measured by s).

The sample size is computed using the formula:

$$n = \left(\frac{z \times s}{E} \right)^2 \qquad [8-11]$$

Where:
n is the size of the sample.
z is the standard normal value corresponding to the desired level of confidence.
s is the estimate of the population standard deviation.
E is the maximum allowable error.

A population with considerable variability (reflected by a large s) will require a larger sample than a population with a smaller standard deviation. E is the maximum allowable error that you, the researcher, are willing to accept. It is the amount that is added and subtracted from the mean to obtain the end points of the confidence limits.

To determine the required sample size for a proportion, three items need to be specified:

1. The desired level of confidence, usually 95 percent or 99 percent.

2. The margin of error in the population proportion that is required.

3. An estimate of the population proportion π.

Text formula [8-12] is used:

$$n = p(1-p) \left(\frac{z}{E} \right)^2 \qquad [8-12]$$

Where:

p is the estimated proportion based on the pilot survey.

z is the z score associated with the degree of confidence selected.

E is the allowable error.

If no estimate of p is available then let $p = 0.50$. The sample size will never be larger than that obtained when $p = 0.50$.

Glossary

Probability sample: A sample selected in such a way that each item or person in the population being studied has a known (nonzero) likelihood of being included in the sample.

Nonprobability sampling: A sample selected in such a way that **not** all items or people have a chance of being included in the sample.

Simple random sample: A sample formulated so that each item or person in the population has the same chance of being included in the sample.

Systematic random sample: The items or individuals of the population are arranged in some way—alphabetically, in a file drawer by date received, or by some other method. A random starting point is selected, and then every k th member of the population is selected for the sample.

Stratified sample: A population is first divided into subgroups, called strata, and a sample is selected from each stratum.

Cluster sampling: The population is divided into primary units, and then samples are drawn from the primary units.

Sampling error: The difference between a sample statistic and its corresponding population parameter.

Sampling distribution of the mean: A probability distribution consisting of all possible sample means of a given sample size selected from a population and the probability of occurrence associated with each sample mean.

Central limit theorem:. If all samples of a particular size are selected from any population, the sampling distribution of the sample means is approximately a normal distribution. This approximation improves with larger samples

Point estimate: The value, computed from sample information, that is used to estimate the population parameter.

Confidence interval: A range of values constructed from sample data so that the parameter occurs within that range at a specified probability. The specified probability is called the *level of confidence*

Standard Error of the Sample Mean: The standard deviation of the sampling distribution of sample means

Chapter Problems

Problem 1

Suppose that a population consists of the six families living in Brentwood Circle. You are studying the number of children in the six families. The population information is:

Family	Number of Children
Clark	1
Walston	2
Dodd	3
Marshall	5
Saner	3
White	4

List the possible samples of size 2 that could be selected from this population and compute the mean of each sample. Organize these sample means into a probability distribution.

Solution

There are 15 different samples. The formula for the number of combinations is used to determine the total number of samples. There are six members of the population and the sample size is two.

$$_6C_2 = \frac{6!}{2!4!} = 15$$

Sample Number	Families in the Sample	Total Number of Children in Sample	Mean Number of Children Per Family in Sample
1	Clark, Walston	3	1.5
2	Clark, Dodd	4	2.0
3	Clark, Marshall	6	3.0
4	Clark, Saner	4	2.0
5	Clark, White	5	2.5
6	Walston, Dodd	5	2.5
7	Walston, Marshall	7	3.5
8	Walston, Saner	5	2.5
9	Walston, White	6	3.0
10	Dodd, Marshall	8	4.0
11	Dodd, Saner	6	3.0
12	Dodd, White	7	3.5
13	Marshall, Saner	8	4.0
14	Marshall, White	9	4.5
15	Saner, White	7	3.5
		Total	45.0

← 3/2

This information is organized into the following probability distribution called the sampling distribution of the means.

Mean Number of Children	Frequency	Probability	
1.5	1	0.067	← 1/15
2.0	2	0.133	
2.5	3	0.200	
3.0	3	0.200	← 3/15
3.5	3	0.200	
4.0	2	0.133	
4.5	1	0.067	
	15	1.000	

Problem 2

Using the Brentwood Circle data in Problem 1, compare the mean of the sampling distribution with the mean of the population. Compare the spread of the sample means with that of the population.

Solution

The mean of the sampling distribution and the mean of the population are the same. The population mean, written μ, is found by $\mu = (1 + 2 + 3 + 5 + 3 + 4)/6 = 3.0$. The mean of the sampling distribution (written $\mu_{\bar{x}}$ because it is the mean of a group of sample means) is also 3.0, found by 45.0/15.

$\overline{X}$ Sample Means	f Frequency	$f\overline{X}$
1.5	1	1.5
2.0	2	4.0
2.5	3	7.5
3.0	3	9.0
3.5	3	10.5
4.0	2	8.0
4.5	1	4.5
	15	45.0

The calculations for the sample means are:

$$\mu_{\bar{x}} = \frac{\Sigma f\overline{X}}{\Sigma f} = \frac{45.0}{15} = 3.0$$

The population mean μ is exactly equal to the mean of the sampling distribution $\mu_{\bar{x}}$ (3.0). This is **always** true.

Note in the following graphs (on the next page), that there is less spread in the sampling distribution of the means (bottom chart) than in the population distribution (top chart). The sample means range from 1.5 to 4.5, whereas the population values ranged from 1 to 5.

Also note that the shape of the population is different than that of the sampling distribution. This phenomenon is described by the central limit theorem. Recall the central limit theorem states that regardless of the shape of the population the sampling distribution will tend toward normal as n increases.

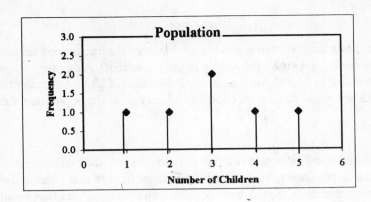

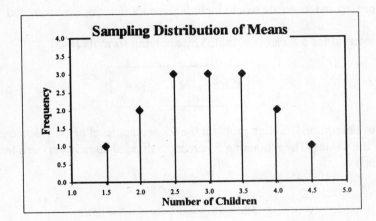

Exercise 8.1

Check your answers against those in the ANSWER section.

The real estate company of Kuhlman and Associates has five sales people. Listed below is the number of homes sold last month by each of the five associates. Bruce Kuhlman, the owner, wants to estimate the population mean number of homes sold based on samples of three.

Associate	Number of Homes Sold
A. Sue Klaus	6
B. John Bardo	2
C. Jean Cannon	5
D. A.J.Kemper	9
E. Carol Ford	3

a. If samples of size 3 are selected, how many different samples are possible?

b. List the various samples and compute the mean of each.

c. Develop a sampling distribution of the means.

d. Draw graphs to compare the variability of the sampling distribution of the mean with that of the population.

Problem 3

Crossett Truck Rental has a large fleet of rental trucks. Many of the trucks need substantial repairs from time to time. Mr. Crossett, the owner, has requested a study of the repair costs. A random sample of 64 trucks is selected. The mean annual repair cost is $1,200, with a standard deviation of $280. Estimate the mean annual repair cost for all rental trucks. Develop the 95 percent confidence interval for the population mean.

Solution

The population parameter being estimated is the population mean—the mean annual repair cost of all Crossett rental trucks. This value is not known, but the best estimate we have of that value is the sample mean of $1,200. Hence, $1,200 is a point estimate of the unknown population parameter. A confidence interval is a range of values within which the population parameter is expected to occur. The 95 percent refers to the approximate percent of time that similarly constructed intervals would include the parameter being estimated.

The confidence interval for a mean is obtained by applying formula [8-5].

$$\overline{X} \pm z\frac{s}{\sqrt{n}} \qquad [8-5]$$

How is the z value determined? In this problem the 95 percent level of confidence is used. This refers to the middle 95 percent of the values. The remaining 5 percent is divided equally between the two tails of curve. (See the following diagram.)

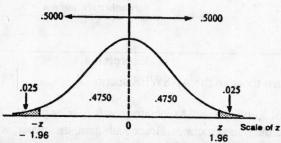

To find z, the standard normal distribution is used. Referring to Appendix D, the first step is to locate the value of 0.4750 in the body of the table, and then read the corresponding row and column values. The z value is 1.96.

Substitute the z value into the equation. The confidence interval is $1,131.40 to $1,268.60

$$\overline{X} \pm z\frac{s}{\sqrt{n}} = \$1,200 \pm 1.96\frac{\$280}{\sqrt{64}}$$
$$= \$1,200 \pm \$68.6$$
$$= \$1,131.40 \quad \text{to} \quad \$1,268.60$$

This indicates that if 100 similar intervals were constructed, about 95 intervals would be expected to include the population mean.

Problem 4

Refer to the information on Crossett Truck Rental in Problem 3. Suppose Crossett's fleet consists of 500 trucks. Develop a 95 percent confidence interval for the population mean.

Solution

When the sample is more than 5 percent of the population, the finite population correction factor is used. In this case the sample size is 64 and the population size is 500. Thus, $n/N = 64/500 = 0.128$ or 12.8 percent. The confidence interval is adjusted as follows.

$$\bar{X} \pm z\frac{s}{\sqrt{n}}\left(\sqrt{\frac{N-n}{N-1}}\right) = \$1,200 \pm 1.96\frac{\$280}{\sqrt{64}}\left(\sqrt{\frac{500-64}{500-1}}\right)$$

$$= \$1,200 \pm \$68.6(0.9347)$$

$$= \$1,200 \pm \$64.12$$

$$= \$1,135.88 \quad \text{to} \quad \$1,264.12$$

Notice that when the correction factor is included the confidence interval becomes smaller. This is logical because the number of items sampled is large relative to the population.

Problem 5

The Independent Department Store wants to determine the proportion of their charge accounts having an unpaid balance of $1500 or more. A sample of 250 accounts revealed that 100 of them had an unpaid balance of $1500 or over. What is the 99 percent confidence interval for the population proportion?

Solution

In the sample of 250 charge accounts, there were 100 with unpaid balances of over $1500. The point estimate of the proportion of charge customers with balances of more than $1500 is 0.40 found by 100/250. The z value corresponding to a 99 percent level of confidence is 2.58 (from Appendix D). The formula for the confidence interval for the population proportion is text formula [8-8]:

$$p \pm z\sqrt{\frac{p(1-p)}{n}} = 0.40 \pm 2.58\sqrt{\frac{(0.40)(1-0.40)}{250}} = 0.40 \pm (2.58)\sqrt{0.00096} = 0.40 \pm 0.08$$

The confidence interval is 0.32 to 0.48. This means that about 99 percent of the similarly constructed intervals would include the population proportion.

Exercise 8.4

Check your answers against those in the ANSWER section.

A random sample of 100 light bulbs is selected. Sixty were found to burn for more than 1,000 hours. Develop a 90 percent confidence interval for the proportion of bulbs that will burn more than 1,000 hours..

Problem 6

Refer to the charge account data of Independent Department Stores in Problem 5. Recall that 250 accounts were sampled. Suppose there is a total of 900 charge customers. Develop a 99 percent confidence interval for the proportion of charge customers with an unpaid account balance of over $1500.

Solution

The finite population correction factor should be used because the sample is 28 percent of the population, found by 250/900. (Note that 28 percent is more than 5% of the population.)

$$p \pm z\sqrt{\frac{p(1-p)}{n}}\left(\sqrt{\frac{N-n}{N-1}}\right) = 0.40 \pm 2.58\sqrt{\frac{(0.40)(1-0.40)}{250}}\left(\sqrt{\frac{900-250}{900-1}}\right)$$

$$= 0.40 \pm 0.08(0.8503)$$

$$= 0.40 \pm 0.068$$

Using the correction factor, the interval is reduced from 0.40 ± 0.08 to 0.40 ± 0.068, or 0.332 to 0.468. Again, this is because Independent Stores has sampled a large proportion (28 percent) of its customers.

Problem 7

The manager of the Jiffy Supermarket wants to estimate the mean time a customer spends in the store. A 95 percent level of confidence is to be used. The standard deviation of the population based on a pilot survey is estimated to be 3.0 minutes. The manager requires the estimate to be within plus or minus 1.00 minute of the population value. What sample size is needed?

Solution

The size of the sample is dependent on three factors.

1. The allowable error (E).
2. The level of confidence (z).
3. The estimated variation in the population, usually measured by s, the sample standard deviation.

In this problem, the store manager has indicated that the estimate must be within 1.0 minute of the population parameter. The level of confidence is 0.95 and the population standard deviation is estimated to be 3.0 minutes. The formula [8-11] for determining the size of the sample is:

$$n = \left(\frac{z \times s}{E} \right)^2 \qquad [8-11]$$

Where:

z refers to the level of confidence

s is the estimated population standard deviation

E the allowable error.

$$n = \left(\frac{(1.96)(3.0)}{1.0} \right)^2 = (5.88)^2 = 34.57 = 35$$

Hence, the manager should randomly select 35 customers and determine the amount of time they spend in the store.

Exercise 8.5

Check your answers against those in the ANSWER section.

A health maintenance organization (HMO) wants to estimate the mean length of a hospital stay. How large a sample of patient records is necessary if the HMO wants to be 99 percent confident of the estimate, and wants the estimate to be within plus or minus 0.2 days? An earlier study showed the standard deviation of the length of stay to be 0.25 days.

Problem 8

The Ohio Unemployment Commission wants to estimate the proportion of the labor force that was unemployed during last year in a certain depressed region. The Commission wants to be 95 percent confident that their estimate is within 5 percentage points (written 0.05) of the population proportion. If the population proportion has been estimated to be 0.15, how large a sample is required?

Solution

Note that the estimate of the population proportion p is 0.15. The allowable error (E) is 0.05. Using the 95 percent level of confidence the z value is 1.96. Applying formula [8-12] to determine the sample size:

$$n = p(1-p)\left(\frac{z}{E} \right)^2 = 0.15(1 - 0.15)\left(\frac{1.96}{0.05} \right)^2 = 195.92 = 196$$

The required sample size is 196.

When no estimate of p is available, 0.50 is used. The size of the sample will never be larger than that obtained when $p = 0.50$. The calculations for the sample size when $p = 0.50$ are:

Chapter 8

$$n = p(1-p)\left(\frac{z}{E}\right)^2 = 0.5(1-0.5)\left(\frac{1.96}{0.05}\right)^2 = 384.16 = 385$$

Note that the required sample size is considerably larger (385 versus 196) when p is set at 0.50.

Exercise 8.6

Check your answers against those in the ANSWER section.

A large bank believes that one-third of its checking customers have used at least one of the bank's other services during the past year. How large a sample is required to estimate the actual proportion within a range of plus and minus 0.04? Use the 98 percent level of confidence.

CHAPTER 8 ASSIGNMENT

SAMPLING METHODS AND SAMPLING DISTRIBUTIONS

Name _____ Section _____ Score _____

Part I   Select the correct answer and write the appropriate letter in the space provided.

_____ 1.   The population proportion is an example of a
a.   sample statistic.
b.   normal population.
c.   sample mean.
d.   population parameter.

_____ 2.   In a probability sample each item in the population has
a.   a chance of being selected.
b.   the same chance of being selected.
c.   a 50 percent chance of being selected.
d.   no chance of being selected.

_____ 3.   In a simple random sample each item in the population has
a.   a chance of being selected.
b.   the same chance of being selected.
c.   a 50 percent chance of being selected.
d.   no chance of being selected.

_____ 4.   The sampling error is
a.   the difference between a sample statistic and a population parameter.
b.   always positive.
c.   the difference between the z value and the mean.
d.   equal to the population value.

_____ 5.   The sample mean is an example of a
a.   sample statistic.
b.   normal population.
c.   weighted mean.
d.   population parameter.

_____ 6.   Suppose we have a negatively skewed population. According to the Central Limit Theorem, the distribution of the sample means of a particular size will
a.   also be negatively skewed.
b.   form a binomial distribution.
c.   approach a normal distribution.
d.   become positively skewed.

_____ 7. If the level of confidence is decreased from 95 percent to 90 percent, the width of the corresponding interval will
a. be increased.
b. be decreased.
c. stay the same.
d. the level of confidence does not have an effect on the width of the interval.

_____ 8. The population is the five employees in a physician's office. The number of possible samples of 2 that could be selected from this population is
a. 5
b. 10
c. 15
d. 60

_____ 9. The finite population correction factor is used when
a. the sample is more than 5 percent of the population.
b. the sample is less than 5 percent of the population.
c. the sample is larger than the population.
d. the population cannot be estimated.

_____ 10. A 90 percent confidence interval for means indicates that 90 out of 100 similarly constructed intervals will include the
a. sample mean.
b. sampling error.
c. *z* value
d. population mean.

Part II   Answer the following questions. Be sure to show essential work.

11. Five bundles of pencils contain the quantities shown at the right.

Bundle	Number of pencils
1	10
2	6
3	10
4	11
5	12

a. How many different samples of 2 bundles each are there?

a.

b. List all possible samples of size 2 and compute the mean of each sample.

c. Calculate the population mean and compare it to the mean of the sampling distribution.

c.

12. As part of a safety check, the Pennsylvania Highway Patrol randomly stopped 65 cars and checked their tire pressure. The sample mean was 32 pounds per square inch with a sample standard deviation of 2 pounds per square inch. Develop a 98 percent confidence interval for the population mean.

12.

13. A survey of 4000 college graduates determined that the mean length of time to earn a bachelor's degree is 5.08 years and the standard deviation is 1.89 years. Construct a 96 percent confidence interval for the mean time required for all graduates to earn a bachelor's degree.

13.

14. Suppose the college in question 13 has only graduated 10,000 students. Construct a 96 percent confidence interval for the mean time required for all graduates to earn a bachelor's degree.

14.

15. Of a random sample of 90 firms with employee stock ownership plans, 50 indicated that the primary reason for setting up the plan was tax related. Develop a 90 percent confidence interval for the population proportion of all such firms with this as the primary motivation.

15.

16. A study of 305 computer chips found that 244 chips functioned properly. Develop a 99 percent confidence interval for the population proportion of properly functioning computer chips.

16. _____

17. A correctional institute would like to report the mean amount of money spent per day on running the facilities. How many days should be considered if a 95 percent confidence is used and the estimate is to be within one hundred dollars? The standard deviation is $400.

17. _____

18. The Corporate Lawyer, a magazine for corporate lawyers, would like to report the mean amount earned by lawyers in their area of specialization. How large a sample is required if the 97 percent level of confidence is used and the estimate is to be within $2500? The standard deviation is $16,000.

18. _____

19. The Customer Relations Department at Commuter Airline, Inc. wants to estimate the proportion of customers that carry only hand luggage. The estimate is to be within 0.03 of the true proportion with 95 percent level of confidence. No estimate of the population proportion is available. How large a sample is required?

19. _____

20. A survey is being conducted on a local mayoral election. If the poll is to have a 98 percent confidence interval and must be within four percentage points, how many people should be surveyed?

20. _____

CHAPTER 9
TESTS OF HYPOTHESIS: LARGE SAMPLES

Chapter Goals

After completing this chapter, you will be able to:

1. Define a hypothesis and hypothesis testing.

2. Describe the five-step hypothesis-testing procedure.

3. Distinguish between a one-tailed and a two-tailed test of hypothesis.

4. Conduct a test of hypothesis about a population mean and a population proportion.

5. Conduct a test of hypothesis about the difference between two population means and two population proportions.

6. Define type I and type II errors.

7. Compute the probability of a Type II error.

Introduction

In the previous chapter we used the normal probability distribution to describe a sampling distribution of means. In this chapter we will extend this knowledge to use sample information to draw conclusions regarding the value of the population parameter.

Recall that a sample is a part or subset of the population, while a parameter is a value calculated from the entire population. In Chapter 8 we estimated a population parameter from a sample statistic. In addition, we developed a range of values, called a confidence interval, within which we expected the population value to be located.

In this chapter, rather than developing a range of values within which we expect the population parameter to occur, we will conduct a test of hypothesis regarding the validity of a statement about a population parameter.

Two statements called hypotheses are made regarding the possible values of population parameters.

What is a Statistical Hypothesis?

A *hypothesis* is a statement about a population.

> *Hypothesis*: A statement about the value of a population developed for the purpose of testing.

In statistical analysis we make a claim, that is, state a hypothesis, then follow up with tests to verify the assertion or to determine that it is untrue.

What is Hypothesis Testing?

The terms *hypothesis testing* and *testing a hypothesis* are used interchangeably. Hypothesis testing starts with a statement about a population parameter such as the mean.

> *Hypothesis testing*: A procedure based on sample evidence and probability theory used to determine whether the hypothesis is a reasonable statement and should not be rejected, or is unreasonable and should be rejected.

For example, one statement about the performance of a new model car is that the mean miles per gallon is 30. The other statement is that the mean miles per gallon is not 30. Only one of these statements is correct.

Five Step Procedure for Testing a Hypothesis

Statistical hypothesis testing is a five-step procedure. These steps are:

1. State the null hypothesis and the alternate hypothesis.

2. Select a level of significance.

3. Identify the test statistic.

4. Formulate a decision rule based on the selected test statistic and level of significance.

5. Take a sample and make a decision whether or not to reject the null hypothesis.

(Each step will be discussed in detail shortly.)

When conducting hypothesis tests we actually employ a strategy of "proof by contradiction." That is, we hope to accept a statement to be true by rejecting or ruling out another statement. The steps involved in hypothesis testing will now be described in more detail.

First we will concentrate on testing a hypothesis about a population mean, or means. Then we will consider one or two population proportions. For a mean or means:

Step 1. State the null hypothesis and the alternate hypothesis.

The first step is to state the hypothesis being tested. It is called the *null hypothesis*, designated H_0, and read H sub zero. The capital letter H stands for hypothesis, and the subscript zero implies "no difference."

> *Null hypothesis*: A statement about the value of a population parameter.

For example, a recent newspaper report made the claim that the mean length of a hospital stay was 3.3 days. You think that the true length of stay is some other length than 3.3 days.

The null hypothesis is written H_0: $\mu = 3.3$, where H_0 is an abbreviation of the null hypothesis. It is the statement about the value of the population parameter, in this case the population mean. The null hypothesis is established for the purpose of testing. On the basis of the sample evidence, it is either rejected or not rejected.

If the null hypothesis is rejected then we accept the alternate hypothesis.

> *Alternate hypothesis*: A statement that is accepted if the sample data provide evidence that the null hypothesis is false.

The alternate hypothesis is written H_1. From the above example the alternate hypothesis is that the mean length of stay is not 3.3 days. It is written H_1: $\mu \neq 3.3$ ($\neq$ is read "not equal to"). H_1 is accepted only if H_0 is rejected. When the "$\neq$" sign appears in the alternate hypothesis, the test is called **a two-tailed test**.

There are two other formats for writing the null and alternate hypotheses. Suppose you think that the mean length of stay is greater than 3.3 days. The null and alternate hypotheses would be written as follows: ($\leq$ is read "equal to or less than").

$$H_0: \mu \leq 3.3$$
$$H_1: \mu > 3.3$$

Notice that in this case the null hypothesis indicates "no change or that μ is less than 3.3." The alternate hypothesis states that the mean length of stay is greater than 3.3 days. Acceptance of the alternate hypothesis would allow us to conclude that the mean length of stay is greater than 3.3 days.

What if you think that the mean length of stay is less than 3.3 days? The null and alternate hypotheses would be written as:

$$H_0: \mu \geq 3.3$$
$$H_1: \mu < 3.3$$

Acceptance of the alternate hypothesis in this instance would allow you to conclude the mean length of stay is less than 3.3 days. When a direction is expressed in the alternate hypothesis, such as $>$ or $<$, the test is referred to as being **one-tailed.**

Step 2. Select the Level of Significance.

After setting up the null hypothesis and alternate hypothesis, the next step is to state the *level of significance*.

> *Level of significance*: The probability of rejecting the null hypothesis when it is actually true.

The level of significance is designated α, the Greek letter alpha. It will indicate when the sample mean is too far away from the hypothesized mean for the null hypothesis to be true. Usually the significance level is set at either 0.01 or 0.05, although other values may be chosen.

Testing a null hypothesis at the 0.05 significance level, for example, indicates that the probability of rejecting the null hypothesis, even though it is true, is 0.05. When a true hypothesis is rejected it is referred to as a *Type I error*.

> *Type I error*: Rejecting the null hypothesis, H_0, when it is actually true.

The decision whether to use the 0.01 or the 0.05 significance level, or some other value, depends on the consequences of making a Type I error. The significance level is chosen before the sample is selected.

If the null hypothesis is not true, but our sample results indicate that it is, we have a *Type II error*.

> **Type II error**: Accepting the null hypothesis when it is actually false.

For example, if H_0 asserts that the mean length of a hospital stay is 3.3 days and we accept this hypothesis when, in fact, the mean length of stay is 4.0 days, then a Type II error is committed.

Step 3. Identify the Test Statistic.

A *test statistic* is a quantity calculated from the sample information and is used as the basis for deciding whether or not to reject the null hypothesis.

> **Test statistic**: A value, determined from sample information, used to determine whether or not to reject the null hypothesis.

Exactly which test statistic to employ is determined by factors such as whether the population standard deviation is known, and the size of the sample.

The standard normal distribution, the z value, is the test statistic used in this chapter. Formula [9-1] is used:

$$z = \frac{\overline{X} - \mu}{\sigma / \sqrt{n}} \qquad [9-1]$$

Where:
$\overline{X}$ is the sample mean.
μ is the population mean.
σ is the population standard deviation.
n is the sample size.
z is the value of the test statistic.

Step 4. Formulate a Decision Rule.

A *decision rule* is based on H_0 and H_1, the level of significance, and the test statistic.

> **Decision rule**: A statement of the conditions under which the null hypothesis is rejected and conditions under which it is not rejected.

The region or area of rejection indicates the location of the values that the probability of their occurrence for a true null hypothesis is rather remote.

> **Critical value**: The dividing point between the region where the null hypothesis is rejected and the region where it is not rejected.

If we are applying a one-tailed test, there is one critical value. If we are applying a two-tailed test, there are two critical values.

The following diagram shows the conditions under which the null hypothesis is rejected, using the 0.05 significance level, a one-tailed test, and the standard normal distribution, the test statistic used in this chapter.

Sampling Distribution for the Statistic z for a One-Tailed Test, 0.05 Level of Significance

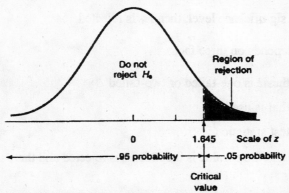

The above diagram portrays the rejection region for a one-tailed test of significance.

1. The area where the null hypothesis is not rejected includes the area to the left of 1.645.

2. The area of rejection is to the right of 1.645.

3. A one-tailed test is being applied. (This will be explained later.)

4. The 0.05 level of significance was chosen.

5. The sampling distribution is of the test statistic z, is normally distributed.

6. The value 1.645 separates the regions where the null hypothesis is rejected and where it is not rejected.

7. The value 1.645 is called the **critical value**.

When is the standard normal distribution used? It is appropriate when the population is normal and the population standard deviation is known. When the population standard deviation is not known, the sample standard deviation is used instead. If the sample is at least 30, then the standard normal distribution is appropriate. If the computed value of z is greater than 1.645, the null hypothesis is rejected. If the computed value of z is smaller than 1.645, the null hypothesis is not rejected.

Step 5. Select the Sample and Make a Decision.

The final step is to select the sample and compute the value of the test statistic. This value is compared to the critical value, or values, and a decision is made whether to reject or not to reject the null hypothesis.

p-value in Hypothesis Testing

In the process of testing a hypothesis, we compared the test statistic to a critical value. We made a decision to either reject the null hypothesis or not to reject it. The question is often asked as to how confident we were in rejecting the null hypothesis.

A **p-value** is frequently compared to the significance level to evaluate the decision regarding the null hypothesis. It is a means of reporting the likelihood that H_0 is not true.

> **p-value**: The probability of observing a sample value as extreme as, or more extreme than, the value observed, given that the null hypothesis is true.

If the *p-value* is greater than the significance level, then H_0 is not rejected.

If the *p-value* is less than the significance level, then H_0 is rejected.

The *p*-value for a given test depends on three factors:

1. whether the alternate hypothesis is one-tailed or two-tailed
2. the particular test statistic that is used
3. the computed value of the test statistic.

For example, if $\alpha = 0.05$ and the *p*-value is 0.0025, H_0 is rejected and there is only a 0.0025 likelihood that H_0 is true.

Testing for Means

Hypothesis tests for two situations will now be considered. One involves a single population; the other, two populations.

Suppose we are concerned with a single population mean. We want to test if our sample mean could have been obtained from a population with a hypothesized mean. For example, we may be interested in testing whether the mean starting salary of recent marketing graduates is equal to $32,000 per year. It is assumed that:

1. The population is normally distributed.
2. The population standard deviation is known.

If σ is not known, the sample standard deviation is substituted for the population standard deviation provided the sample size is 30 or more.

Under these conditions the test statistic is the standard normal distribution with the sample standard deviation s substituted for σ. Thus we use text formula [9-2].

$$z = \frac{\overline{X} - \mu}{s / \sqrt{n}} \qquad [9-2]$$

Where:
z is the value of the test statistic.
$\overline{X}$ is the sample mean.
μ is the population mean.
s is the sample standard deviation.
n is the sample size.

The sample standard deviation s can be substituted for σ providing that the sample size is 30 or more.

If there are two populations, we can compare two sample means to determine if they came from populations with the same or equal means.

For example, a purchasing agent is considering two brands of tires for use on the company's fleet of cars. A sample of 60 Rossford tires indicates the mean useful life to be 45,000 miles. A sample of 50 Maumee tires revealed the useful life to be 48,000 miles. Could the difference between the two sample means be due to chance? The assumption is that for both populations (Rossford and Maumee) the standard deviations are either known or have been computed from samples greater than 30. The test statistic used is the standard normal distribution and its value is computed from text formula [9-3]:

$$z = \frac{\overline{X}_1 - \overline{X}_2}{\sqrt{\dfrac{s_1^2}{n_1} + \dfrac{s_2^2}{n_2}}} \qquad [9-3]$$

Where:

$\overline{X}_1$ and $\overline{X}_2$ refer to the two sample means.

s_1^2 and s_2^2 refer to the two sample variances.

n_1 and n_2,   refer to the two sample sizes.

The following are assumptions necessary for this two-sample test.

1. The populations should be normally distributed.

2. The population standard deviations for both populations should be known.

3. The samples should be from *independent* populations.

Tests Concerning Proportions

We continue our study of hypothesis testing but expand the idea to a *proportion*. What is a proportion?

> *Proportion*: A fraction, ratio, or percentage, that indicates the part of the population or sample having a particular trait of interest.

If we let p stand for the sample proportion then text formula [9-4] is:

$$p = \frac{\text{Number of successes in the sample}}{\text{Number sampled}} \qquad [9-4]$$

For example, we want to estimate the proportion of all home sales made to first time buyers. A random sample of 200 recent transactions showed that 40 were first time buyers. Therefore, we estimate that 0.20, or 20 percent, of all sales are made to first time buyers, found by:

$$p = \frac{40}{200} = 0.20$$

To conduct a test of hypothesis for proportions, the same assumptions required for the binomial distribution must be met. Recall from Chapter 6 that those assumptions are:

1. Each outcome is classified into one of two categories such as, buyers were either first time home buyers or they were not.

2. The number of trials is fixed. In this case it is 200.

3. Each trial is independent, meaning that the outcome of one trial has no bearing on the outcome of any other. Whether the 20th sampled person was a first time buyer does not affect the outcome of any other trial.

4. The probability of a success is fixed. The probability is 0.20 for all 200 buyers in the sample.

Recall from Chapter 7 that the normal distribution is a good approximation of the binomial distribution when $n\pi$ and $n(1-\pi)$ are both greater than 5. In this instance n refers to the sample size and p to the probability of a success. The test statistic that is employed for testing hypotheses about proportions is the standard normal distribution. Text formula [9-6] is used:

$$z = \frac{p - \pi}{\sqrt{\dfrac{\pi(1-\pi)}{n}}} \qquad [9-6]$$

Where:

z is the test statistic
π is the population proportion.
p is the sample proportion.
n is the sample size.

The second test of population compares the proportions of **two populations**. For example, we want to compare the proportion of rural voters planning to vote for the incumbent governor with the proportion of urban voters. The test statistic is formula [9-7]:

$$z = \frac{p_1 - p_2}{\sqrt{\dfrac{p_c(1-p_c)}{n_1} + \dfrac{p_c(1-p_c)}{n_2}}} \qquad [9-7]$$

Where:

p_1 is the proportion from the first sample.
p_2 is the proportion from the second sample.
n_1 is the total number in the first sample.
n_2 is the total number in the second sample.
p_c is the pooled estimate of the population proportion, found by

$$p_c = \frac{X_1 + X_2}{n_1 + n_2} \qquad [9-8]$$

Where:

X_1 is the number possessing the trait in the first sample.

X_2 is the number possessing the trait in the second sample.

Types of Tests of Hypothesis

There are three formats for testing a hypothesis about a proportion. For a one-tailed test there are two possibilities, depending on the intent of the researcher. For example, if we wanted to determine whether more than 25 percent of the sales of homes were sold to first time buyers, the hypotheses would be given as follows:

$$H_0: p \le 0.25$$
$$H_1: p > 0.25$$

If we wanted to find out whether fewer than 25 percent of the homes were sold to first time buyers, the hypotheses would be given as:

$$H_0: p \ge 0.25$$
$$H_1: p < 0.25$$

For a two-tailed test the null and alternate hypotheses are:

$$H_0: p = 0.25$$
$$H_1: p \ne 0.25$$

Where $\ne$ means "not equal to." Rejection of H_0 and acceptance of H_1 allows us to conclude only that the population proportion is "different from" or "not equal to" the population value. It does not allow us to make any statement about the direction of the difference.

Test Statistic

Two tests are considered about proportions. The first is for a *single population*. In the illustration regarding first time home buyers, a sample was drawn and the results tested against a hypothesized population proportion. The test statistic is z and it is found by the formula [9-6]

$$z = \frac{\bar{p} - p}{\sqrt{\dfrac{p(1-p)}{n}}} \qquad [9-6]$$

Where:

$\bar{p}$ is the proportion of "successes".

n is the sample size.

p is the hypothesized population proportion.

Use of these formulas will be examined in the Problem/Solution section.

Glossary

Hypothesis: A statement about the value of a population developed for the purpose of testing

Hypothesis testing: A procedure based on sample evidence and probability theory used to determine whether the hypothesis is a reasonable statement and should not be rejected, or is unreasonable and should be rejected.

Null hypothesis: A statement about the value of a population parameter.

Alternate hypothesis: A statement that is accepted if the sample data provide evidence that the null hypothesis is false.

Level of significance: The probability of rejecting the null hypothesis when it is actually true.

Type I error: Rejecting the null hypothesis, H_0 , when it is actually true.

Type II error: Accepting the null hypothesis when it is actually false.

Test statistic: A value, determined from sample information, used to determine whether or not to reject the null hypothesis.

Decision rule: A statement of the conditions under which the null hypothesis is rejected and conditions under which it is not rejected.

Critical value: The dividing point between the region where the null hypothesis is rejected and the region where it is not rejected.

p-value: The probability of observing a sample value as extreme as, or more extreme than, the value observed, given that the null hypothesis is true.

Proportion: A fraction, ratio, or percentage, that indicates the part of the population or sample having a particular trait of interest.

Chapter Problems

Problem 1

The manufacturer of the new subcompact Clipper claims in their TV advertisements that it will average "40 or more miles per gallon on the open road." Some of the competitors believe this claim is too high. To investigate, an independent testing agency is hired to conduct highway mileage tests. A random sample of 64 Clippers showed their mean miles per gallon to be 38.9, with a sample standard deviation of 4.00 miles per gallon. At the 0.01 significance level can the manufacturer's claim be refuted? Determine the p value. Interpret the result.

Solution

The first step is to state the null and alternate hypotheses. The null hypothesis refers to the "no change" situation. That is, there has been no change in the Clipper's mileage, it is 40 or more mpg. It is written H_0: $\mu \geq 40$ and is read that the population mean is greater than or equal to 40. The alternate hypothesis is that the population mean is less than 40. It is written H_1: $\mu < 40$. If the null hypothesis is rejected, then the alternate is accepted. It would be concluded that the Clipper's mileage is less than 40 mpg.

The second step is to select the level of significance. The testing agency decided on the 0.01 significance level. This is the probability that the null hypothesis will be rejected, when in fact it is true.

The third step is to decide on a test statistic. The use of the standard normal distribution requires that the population standard deviation σ be known. When it is not known, as in this problem, the sample standard deviation designated by s, is used as an estimate of σ. When the sample standard deviation is based on a large sample, the standard normal distribution is still an appropriate test statistic. "Large" is usually defined as being more than 30. To determine z we use formula [9-2].

$$z = \frac{\overline{X} - \mu}{s / \sqrt{n}}$$

Where:
$\overline{X}$ is the sample mean.
μ is the population mean.
s is the standard deviation computed from the sample.
n is the sample size.

The fourth step is to develop the decision rule. The decision rule is a statement of the conditions under which the null hypothesis is rejected. The decision rule is shown in the following diagram. If the computed value of z is to the left of -2.33, the null hypothesis is rejected. The -2.33 is the critical value. How is it determined?

Remember that the significance level stated in the problem is 0.01. This indicates that the area to the left of the critical value under the normal curve is 0.01. For the standard normal distribution the total area to the left of 0 is 0.5000. Therefore, the area between the critical value and 0 is 0.4900, found by $0.5000 - 0.0100$. Now refer to Appendix D, and search the body of the table for a value close to 0.4900. The closest value is 0.4901. Read 2.3 in the left margin and 0.03 in the column containing 0.4901. Thus the z value corresponding to 0.4901 is 2.33.

Recall from Step 1 that the alternate hypothesis is H_1: $\mu < 40$. The inequality sign points in the negative direction. Thus the critical value is -2.33 and the rejection region is all in the lower left tail.

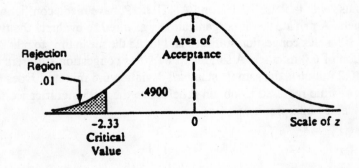

The fifth step is to compute the value of the test statistic, make a decision regarding the null hypothesis, and interpret the results. Since the standard deviation of the population is not known, the sample standard deviation is used as its estimate. Repeating the formula for z:

$$z = \frac{\bar{X} - \mu}{s / \sqrt{n}}$$

Recall that the manufacturer claims 40 mpg and the mean of the sample is 38.9 mpg. Solving for z:

$$z = \frac{38.9 - 40.0}{4.0 / \sqrt{64}} = \frac{-1.1}{0.5} = -2.20$$

The computed value of –2.20 is to the right of –2.33, so the null hypothesis is not rejected. We do not reject the claim of the manufacturer that the Clipper gets at least 40.0 miles per gallon. It is reasonable that the 1.1 miles per gallon between (40.0 and 38.9) could be due to chance.

We do observe, however, that –2.20 is fairly close to the critical value of –2.33. What is the likelihood of a z value to the left of –2.20? It is 0.0139, found by 0.5000 – 0.4861, where 0.4861 is the likelihood of a z value between 0 and 2.20.

The 0.0139 is referred to as the p-value. It is the probability of getting a value of the test statistic (z in this case) more extreme than that actually observed, if the null hypothesis is true. Had the significance level been set at 0.02 instead of .0.01,the null hypothesis would have been rejected. By reporting the p-value we give information on the strength of the decision regarding the null hypothesis.

Exercise 9.1

Check your answers against those in the ANSWER section.

Last year the records of Ski and Golf, Inc., a sporting goods chain, showed the mean amount spent by a customer was $30. A sample of 40 transactions this month revealed the mean amount spent was $33 with a standard deviation of $12. At the 0.05 significance level can we conclude that the mean amount spent has increased? What is the p-value?

Problem 2

Two manufacturers of sinus relief tablets, SINUS and ANTIDRIP, have made conflicting claims regarding the effectiveness of their tablets. A private testing organization was hired to evaluate the two tablets. The testing company tried SINUS on 100 sinus congestion sufferers and found the mean time to relief was 85.0 minutes with a sample standard deviation of 6.0 minutes. A sample of 81 sinus congestion sufferers used ANTIDRIP. The mean time to relief was 86.2 minutes, the sample standard deviation 6.8 minutes. Does the evidence suggest a difference in the amount of time required to obtain relief? Use the 0.05 significance level and the five-step procedure. What is the p-value? Interpret it.

Solution

Note that the testing company is attempting to show only that there is a difference in the time required to affect relief. There is no attempt to show one tablet is "better than" or "worse than" the other. Thus, a two-tailed test is applied.

$$H_0: \mu_1 = \mu_2$$
$$H_1: \mu_1 \neq \mu_2$$

Let μ_1 refer to the mean time to obtain relief using SINUS and μ_2 to the mean time to obtain relief using ANTIDRIP.

The 0.05 significance level is to be used. Because both samples are large (greater than 30) the standard normal distribution is used as the test statistic. The alternate hypothesis does not state a direction, so this is a two-tailed test. The 0.05 significance level is divided equally into two tails of the standard normal distribution. Hence, the area in the left tail is 0.0250 and 0.0250 in the right tail.

The critical values which separate the two rejection regions from the region of acceptance are −1.96 and +1.96. To explain: if the area in a rejection region is 0.0250, the acceptance area is 0.4750, found by 0.5000 − 0.0250. The z value corresponding to an area of 0.4750 is obtained by referring to the table of areas of the normal curve (Appendix D). Search the body of the table for a value as close to 0.4750 as possible and read the corresponding row and column values. The area of 0.4750 is found in the row 1.9 and the column 0.06. Hence, the critical values are + 1.96 or −1.96. This is shown on the following diagram.

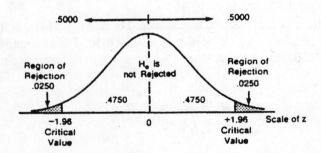

The computed value of z is −1.24, found by using formula [9-3]. Because the population standard deviations are not known, the sample standard deviations are substituted.

$$z = \frac{\overline{X}_1 - \overline{X}_2}{\sqrt{\dfrac{s_1^2}{n_1} + \dfrac{s_2^2}{n_2}}} = \frac{85.0 - 86.2}{\sqrt{\dfrac{(6.0)^2}{100} + \dfrac{(6.8)^2}{81}}} = -1.24$$

The computed value of z is between −1.96 and +1.96. Thus H_0 is not rejected. We conclude that there is no difference in the mean time it takes SINUS and ANTIDRIP to bring relief. The difference of 1.2 minutes (85.0 − 86.2) can be attributed to sampling error (chance).

To determine the p-value we need to find the area to the left of -1.24 and add to it the area to the right of 1.24. Why are we concerned with both tails? Because H_1 is two-tailed. The p-value is 0.2150, found by 2(0.5000 $-$ 0.3925). Since the p-value of 0.2150 is greater than the level of significance of 0.05 do not reject H_0.

Exercise 9.2

Check your answers against those in the ANSWER section.

The county commissioners received a number of complaints from county residents that the Youngsville Fire Department takes longer to respond to fires than the Claredon Fire Department. To check the validity of these complaints, a random sample of 60 fires handled by the Youngsville Fire Department was selected. It was found that the mean response time was 6.9 minutes and the standard deviation of the sample 3.8 minutes. A sample of 70 fires handled by the Claredon Fire Department found the mean response time was 4.9 minutes with a sample standard deviation of 3.0 minutes. Does the data suggest that it takes longer for the Youngsville Department to respond? Use the 0.05 significance level.

Problem 3

The Dean of Students at Scandia Tech believes that 30 percent of the students are employed. You, as President of the Student Government, believe the proportion employed is less than 30 percent and decide to conduct a study. A random sample of 100 students revealed 25 were employed. At the 0.01 significance level, can the Dean's claim be refuted?

Solution

As usual, the first step is to state the null and alternate hypotheses. The null hypothesis is that there is no change in the percent employed. That is, the population proportion is at least 0.30. The alternate hypothesis is that the population proportion is less than 0.30. This is the statement we are trying to test empirically. Symbolically, these statements are written as follows:

$$H_0: p \geq 0.30$$
$$H_1: p < 0.30$$

The 0.01 significance level is to be used. The assumptions of the binomial distribution are met in the problem. That is

1. There are only two outcomes for each trial--the student is either employed or isn't employed.

2. The number of trials is fixed—100 students.

3. Each trial is independent, meaning that the employment of one student selected does not affect another.

4. The probability that any randomly selected student is employed is 0.30.

The normal approximation to the binomial is used because both $n\pi$ and $n(1-\pi)$ exceed 5. That is: $[n\pi = 100(0.30)] = 30$ and $n(1-\pi) = 100(0.70) = 70$. The standard normal distribution, z is the test statistic. To formulate the decision rule, we need the critical value of z. Using the 0.01 significance level, the area is 0.4900, (0.500 $-$ 0.0100).

Search the body of Appendix D for a value as close to 0.4900 as possible. It is 0.4901. The value associated with 0.4901 is 2.33. The alternate hypothesis points in the negative direction, hence the rejection region is in the left tail and the critical value of z is −2.33.

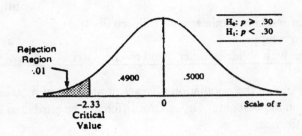

The decision rule is to reject the null hypothesis if the computed value of the test statistic lies in the rejection region to the left of −2.33.

Recall that the sample of 100 Scandia Tech students revealed that 25 were employed. The question is whether the sample proportion of 0.25, found by 25/100, is significantly less than 0.30.

$$z = \frac{p - \pi}{\sqrt{\dfrac{\pi(1-\pi)}{n}}} = \frac{0.25 - 0.30}{\sqrt{\dfrac{(0.30)(1-0.30)}{100}}} = -1.09$$

The computed value of z falls in the region between 0 and −2.33. H_0 is not rejected. There is a difference between the Dean's hypothesized proportion (0.30) and the sample proportion (0.25), but this difference of 0.05 is not sufficient to reject the null hypothesis. The 0.05 can be attributed to sampling (chance). The Dean's claim cannot be refuted.

The p-value is the probability of a z value to the left of −1.09. It is 0.1379, found by (0.5000 − 0.3621). The p-value is larger than the significance level of 0.01, which is consistent with our decision not to reject the null hypothesis.

Exercise 9.3

Check your answers against those in the ANSWER section.

The producer of a TV special expected about 40 percent of the viewing audience to watch a rerun of a 1965 Beatles Concert. A sample of 200 homes revealed 60 to be watching the concert. At the 0.10 significance level, does the evidence suggest that less than 40 percent were watching? Use the usual hypothesis testing format. What is the p-value?

Problem 4

Two different sites are being considered for a day-care center. One is on the south side of the city and the other is on the east side. The decision where to locate the day-care center depends in part on how many mothers work and have children under 5 years old.

A sample of 200 family units on the south side revealed that 88 working mothers have children under 5 years.

A sample of 150 family units on the east side revealed that 57 have children under 5 years and the mother worked. Summarizing the data:

	South Side	East Side
Number of working mothers with children under 5	$X_1 = 88$	$X_2 = 57$
Number in sample	$n_1 = 200$	$n_2 = 150$
Proportion with children under 5 and mothers work	$p_1 = 0.44$	$p_2 = 0.38$

Can we conclude that in the population a larger proportion of mothers on the south side work and have children under 5 than on the east side? Or, can the difference be attributed to sampling variation (chance)? Use the 0.05 level of significance.

Solution

The problem is to examine whether a higher proportion of working mothers of young children live on the south side. The hypotheses will therefore be:

$$H_0: p_1 \le p_2$$
$$H_1: p_1 > p_2$$

The standard normal distribution is the test statistic to be used. The significance level is 0.05. The critical value is 1.645 obtained from Appendix D. The area in the upper tail of the curve is 0.05, therefore the area between $z = 0$ and the critical value is 0.4500, found by (0.5000 – 0.0500). Search the body of the table for a value close to 0.4500. Since 1.64 is equal to 0.4495 and 1.65 is equal to 0.4505, a value between 1.64 and 1.65 or (1.645) is used as the critical value. The null hypothesis is rejected if the calculated value is greater than 1.645. This information is summarized in the following diagram.

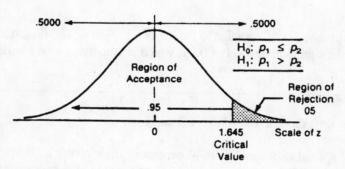

Formula [9-7] for z is repeated below.

$$z = \frac{p_1 - p_2}{\sqrt{\dfrac{p_c(1 - p_c)}{n_1} + \dfrac{p_c(1 - p_c)}{n_2}}} \qquad [9-7]$$

where p_c is a pooled estimate of the population proportion and is computed using formula [9-8].

$$p_c = \frac{X_1 + X_2}{n_1 + n_2}$$

In this problem X_1, and X_2 refer to the number of "successes" in each sample (number of working mothers with children under 5 years), n_1 and n_2 refer to the number of housing units sampled in the south side and east side, respectively.

The pooled estimate of the population proportion is 0.4143, found as follows:

$$p_c = \frac{X_1 + X_2}{n_1 + n_2} = \frac{88 + 57}{200 + 150} = 0.4143$$

Inserting the pooled estimate of 0.4143 in the formula and solving for z in formula [9-7] gives 1.13.

$$z = \frac{p_1 - p_2}{\sqrt{\dfrac{p_c(1 - p_c)}{n_1} + \dfrac{p_c(1 - p_c)}{n_2}}} = \frac{0.44 - 0.38}{\sqrt{\dfrac{(0.4143)(1 - 0.4143)}{200} + \dfrac{(0.4143)(1 - 0.4143)}{150}}} = 1.13$$

The computed value: $z = 1.13$, is less than the critical value of 1.645 so the null hypothesis is not rejected. The difference of 0.06 can be attributed to sampling error (chance). To put it another way, the proportion of mothers who work and have children under 5 on the south side is not significantly greater than the east side. The p-value is 0.1292, found by (0.5000 – 0.3708). So, the probability of finding a value of the test statistic this large or larger is 0.1292.

Exercise 9.4

Check your answers against those in the ANSWER section.

A recent study was designed to compare smoking habits of young women with those of young men. A random sample of 150 women revealed that 45 smoked. A random sample of 100 men indicated that 25 smoked. At the 0.05 significance level does the evidence show that a higher proportion of women smoke? Compute the p-value.

CHAPTER 9 ASSIGNMENT

TESTS OF HYPOTHESIS: LARGE SAMPLES

Name _____ Section _____ Score _____

Part I   Select the correct answer and write the appropriate letter in the space provided.

_____ 1. The null hypothesis is a claim about
 a.   the size of the sample.
 b.   the size of the population.
 c.   the value of a sample statistic.
 d.   the value of a population parameter.

_____ 2. When the null hypothesis is rejected, we conclude that
 a.   the alternate hypothesis is false also.
 b.   the alternate hypothesis is true.
 c.   the sample size is too large.
 d.   we used the wrong test statistic.

_____ 3. A Type I error is committed when
 a. p value is larger than 1.0.
 b.   the significance level is greater than 0.05.
 c.   we reject a true H_0.
 d.   we accept a false H_0.

_____ 4. The condition or conditions under which H_0 is rejected is
 a.   called the decision rule.
 b.   the likelihood of a Type I error.
 c.   called the test statistic.
 d.   called the p-value.

_____ 5. When the p-value is smaller than the significance level
 a.   a Type I error is committed.
 b.   a Type II error is committed.
 c.   the null hypothesis is rejected.
 d.   the critical value is correct.

_____ 6. A Type II error is
 a.   rejecting H_1 when it is true.
 b.   accepting a false H_0.
 c.   reject H_0 when it is true.
 d.   not rejecting a false H_1.

_____ 7. In a test regarding a sample mean, σ is not known. Under which of the following conditions can s be substituted for σ and z used as the test statistic?
   a.   when n is 30 or more.
   b.   when n is less than 30.
   c.   when np and $n(1-p)$ both exceed 5.
   d.   when μ is known.

_____ 8. Under what conditions would a test be considered a one-tailed test.
   a.   When H_0 contains $\neq$.
   b.   When there is more than one critical value.
   c.   When H_1 contains =.
   d.   When H_1 includes a $<$ or $>$.

_____ 9. In a two-tailed test the rejection region is
   a.   all in the upper tail of the standard normal distribution.
   b.   all in the lower tail of the standard normal distribution.
   c.   divided equally between the two tails.
   d.   always equal to -1.96 or 1.96.

_____ 10. To compare a single sample proportion to a population proportion
   a. n must be less than 30.
   b. p must be less than 5.
   c. np and $n(1-p)$ must both be greater than 5.
   d. σ must be given.

Part II   Solve each problem below. Be sure to show essential calculations.

11. For each of the following statements, give the null hypothesis, H_0, and the alternate hypothesis, H_1.

   a.   The mean pulse of lawyers is 90.

a.

   b.   The mean salary of college presidents is at least $162,500.

b.

   c.   The mean IQ score of 20 year olds is more than 100.

c.

   d.   The mean annual income of sales associates is less than $32,000.

d.

12. Identify the Type I and Type II error for each claim in question 11.

a. _____

_____

b. _____

_____

c. _____

_____

d. _____

_____

13. A recent article in a computer magazine suggested that the mean time to fully learn a new software program is 40 hours. A sample of 100 first-time users of a new statistics program revealed the mean time to learn it was 39 hours with the standard deviation of 8 hours. At the 0.05 significance level, can we conclude that users learn the package in less than a mean of 40 hours?

a. State the null and alternate hypotheses.

H_0: _____ H_1: _____

b. State the decision rule.

_____

c. Compute the value of the test statistic.

c. [   ]

d. Compute the p-value.

d. [   ]

e. What is your decision regarding the null hypothesis? Interpret the result.

_____

_____

14. A vinyl siding company claims that the mean time to install siding on a medium size house is at most 20 hours with a standard deviation of 3.7 hours. A random sample of 40 houses sided in the last three years has a mean installation time of 20.8 hours. At the 0.05 significance level, can a claim be made that it takes longer on average than 20 hours to side a house? (Hint: follow the same steps as question 13)

14. _____

15. A financial planner wants to compare the yield of income and growth oriented mutual funds. Fifty thousand dollars is invested in each of a sample of 35 income-oriented and 40 growth-oriented funds. The mean increase for a two year period for the income funds is $1100 with a standard deviation of $45. For the growth-oriented funds the mean increase is $1090 with a standard deviation of $55. At the 0.01 significance level is there a difference in the mean yield of the two funds?

15. _____

16. Last year a survey in the Nashville TV viewing area showed that 20 percent of the viewers watched their news on WBEN, which is channel 13. In an effort to increase their rating, WBEN added several new reporters to cover local stories and events more thoroughly. A survey last week revealed that out of 400 viewers contacted, 94 watched the news on WBEN. Can we conclude that the percent of viewers has increased? Use the 0.05 significance level.

16. _____

17. CherryBerry Soda, Inc. claims that 15 percent of the population can identify its products. In efforts to boost their identity, CherryBerry employs a famous spokesperson to advertise. A survey is then taken to assess the results of the ad campaign. The results show that 17 percent of the 1000 respondents can identify CherryBerry products. Has the advertising campaign increased product identity or is the difference due to chance? Use the 0.10 significance level.

17. _____

18. The Human Resources Director for a large company is studying absenteeism among hourly workers. A sample of 120 day shift employees showed 15 were absent more than five days last year. A sample of 80 afternoon employees showed 18 to be absent five or more times. At the 0.01 significance level can we conclude that there is a higher proportion of absenteeism among afternoon employees?

18. _____

19. At a recent college graduation, a sample of students revealed the following: 95 out of 300 males will go on to graduate school while 64 out of 180 females will go on to graduate school. Is there a significantly higher proportion of women going onto graduate school then men? Use the 0.05 significance level.

19. _____

CHAPTER 10
TESTS OF HYPOTHESIS: SMALL SAMPLES

Chapter Goals

After completing this chapter, you will be able to:

1. Describe the characteristics of Student's t distribution.

2. Understand the difference between dependent and independent samples.

3. Understand the assumptions necessary to conduct a test of hypothesis regarding a population mean, when the number of observations is small.

4. Conduct a test of hypothesis regarding one population mean.

5. Conduct a test of hypothesis regarding the difference in the means of two independent samples.

6. Conduct a test of hypothesis regarding the mean difference between paired observations.

Introduction

In this chapter we continue our study of hypothesis testing. Recall that in Chapter 9 we considered hypothesis tests for means where the population standard deviation was known. If it was not known but we have a sample of more than 30 observations, then the sample standard deviation was substituted for the population standard deviation. The standard normal distribution was used as the test statistic.

What if the standard deviation of the population is not known and the sample size is less than 30? Under these conditions the standard normal distribution is not the appropriate test statistic. The appropriate test statistic is the *Student's t distribution*.

> *Student's t distribution*: A continuous symmetric probability distribution with a mean of 0. The distribution of t differs for each sample size, n. It is flatter and more spread out than the standard normal distribution, z.

William S. Gosset, who wrote under the name "Student" in the early 1900s, first described this distribution.

Characteristics of the t Distribution

The Student's t distribution, also referred to as the t distribution, is similar to the standard normal distribution in some ways, but quite different in others. It has the following major characteristics:

1. It is a continuous distribution, like the standard normal distribution described in Chapter 8.

2. It is bell shaped and symmetrical, again similar to the standard normal distribution.

3. There is a "family" of t distributions. That is, each time the size of the sample changes, a new t distribution is created.

4. The *t* distribution is more spread out (that is, "flatter") at the center than the standard normal distribution.

As noted above, the *t* distribution has a greater spread than the standard normal distribution. Thus, with a stated level of significance, the critical values for *t* are further removed from 0 than they are in the standard normal distribution.

For a one-tailed test with a 0.05 significance level, the following graphs show that values of *t* are larger than those of *z*.

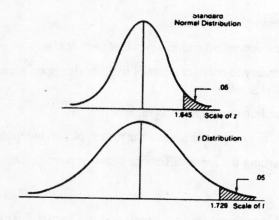

Exactly how these values are obtained will be explained shortly.

Note that when *t* is used as the test statistic instead of the standard normal: (1) The acceptance region will be wider, and (2) A larger value of *t* will be required to reject the null hypothesis.

A further requirement is that the population from which the sample is obtained should be normal or approximately normal.

Degrees of Freedom

To locate the critical value of *t* , we need to know the number of degrees of freedom.

> *Degrees of freedom*: The number of observations in the samples that are free to vary. For a test of hypothesis involving one population mean it is found by $(n-1)$, for two means $(n_1 + n_2 - 2)$, and for a paired difference test $(n-1)$.

For one sample, the number degrees of freedom is found by the number of sample observations minus one $(n-1)$. Thus for a sample of three observations there are two degrees of freedom found by $(3-1) = 2$. Why is this so? Suppose the values of the three sample observations are 5, 7, and 9, the mean of the sample is 7. If any two of these values are changed, then the third is automatically fixed so the mean can remain 7. Suppose the first two are changed to 4 and 5, then the last must be changed to 12 for the three values to have a mean of 7, that is $(4 + 5 + 12)/3 = 7$. Hence, only two of the three values are free to vary and we say there are two degrees of freedom. For a sample of size 15, there are 14 degrees of freedom, found by $(n-1) = (15-1) = 14$.

The decision rule involving the *t* distribution is formulated from Appendix F. This table can be used for both one-tailed and two-tailed tests.

To show how the table is used, suppose we have a sample of six, a one-tailed test, and the 0.05 significance level is to be used.

Step 1. Determine the number of degrees of freedom. There are 5, found by $(n - 1) = (6 - 1) = 5$.

Step 2. Next go down the left-hand column in Appendix F, it is labeled "*df*" to the row of 5.

Step 3. Find the column for a one-tailed test and the 0.05 significance level. The critical value is 2.015.

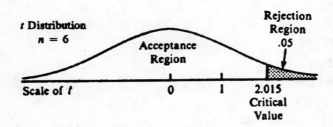

One Sample Test for Means

In this chapter the *t* distribution is used as a test statistic for three tests:

1. for a single population mean
2. for two population means
3. to test for the difference between paired observations.

The value of the *t* statistic for a one-sample test of means is computed by the text formula [10-1]: which is:

$$t = \frac{\overline{X} - \mu}{s / \sqrt{n}} \qquad [10-1]$$

Where:
$\overline{X}$ is the sample mean.
s is the sample standard deviation.
n is the sample size.
μ is the population mean.

This formula is the same as the one presented in Chapter 9 for the standard normal distribution, except s is substituted for μ and the Student's *t* distribution is used to locate the critical value.

Two Sample Test of Means

The *t* distribution may be employed as the test statistic for a test of hypothesis for the difference between two population means. Three assumptions are required:

1. The sampled populations are normally or approximately normally distributed.

2. The two populations are independent.

3. The standard deviations of the two populations are the same.

The t statistic for the two sample cases is similar to that employed in Chapter 9, formula [9-3], for the z statistic, with one additional calculation. The two sample variances must be "pooled" to form a single estimate of the unknown population variance.

This is accomplished by using text formula [10-2]:

$$s_p^2 = \frac{(n_1 - 1)s_1^2 + (n_2 - 1)s_2^2}{n_1 + n_2 - 2} \qquad [10-2]$$

Where:

s_1^2 is the variance in the first sample.

s_2^2 is the variance in the second sample.

n_1 is the number in the first sample.

n_2 is the number in the second sample.

s_p^2 is the pooled estimate of the population variance.

The value of t is then computed using text formula [10-3].

$$t = \frac{\overline{X}_1 - \overline{X}_2}{\sqrt{s_p^2 \left(\frac{1}{n_1} + \frac{1}{n_2} \right)}} \qquad [10-3]$$

$\overline{X}_1$ and $\overline{X}_2$ refer to the sample means.

The degrees of freedom for a two-sample test is found by $(n_1 + n_2 - 2)$.

The Test for Paired Differences

A third hypothesis testing situation occurs when we are concerned with the difference in paired or related observations. Typically, this is a before-and-after situation, where we want to measure the difference.

To illustrate, suppose we administer a reading test to a sample of ten students. Then we have them take a course in speed reading. Thus the test focuses on the reading improvements of each of the ten students. The distribution of the population of differences is assumed to be approximately normal. The test statistic is t, and text formula [10-4] is used.

$$t = \frac{\overline{d}}{s_d / \sqrt{n}} \qquad [10-4]$$

Where:

$\bar{d}$ is the mean of the differences between paired or related observations.

s_d is the standard deviation of the differences between the paired or related observations.

n is the number of paired observations.

For a paired difference test there are $n - 1$ degrees of freedom.

The standard deviation of the differences s_d is computed using text formula [4-9] except that d is substituted for X. The formula is

$$s_d = \sqrt{\frac{\Sigma d^2 - \frac{(\Sigma d)^2}{n}}{n-1}}$$

Glossary

Student's t distribution: A continuous symmetric probability distribution with a mean of 0. The distribution of t differs for each sample size, n. It is flatter and more spread out than the standard normal distribution, z.

Degrees of freedom: The number of observations in the samples that are free to vary. For a test of hypothesis involving one population mean it is found by $(n - 1)$, for two means $(n_1 + n_2 - 2)$, and for a paired difference test $(n - 1)$.

Chapter Problems

Problem 1

Suppose you drive your car to work. The mean driving time is 30 minutes. A fellow worker suggests a different, faster route. As an experiment you recorded these times: 29, 27, 30, 26, and 28 minutes, along the suggested route. You want to use the 0.05 significance level, to decide if the new route takes less driving time.

Solution

The null hypothesis is that the population mean is at least 30 minutes. The alternate hypothesis is that the mean driving time is less than 30 minutes. These hypotheses are written symbolically:

$$H_0: \mu \geq 30$$
$$H_1: \mu < 30$$

To determine the decision rule, we must first assume that the population is normally distributed. Because the population standard deviation is not known, and the sample size is small, the t distribution is used as the test statistic.

The value that will determine whether we should reject the null hypothesis is obtained from Appendix F. Note that in this problem there are 4 degrees of freedom $(n - 1) = (5 - 1) = 4$. We stipulated a 0.05 significance level and a one-tailed test. To obtain the critical value of t, move down the left-hand column of Appendix F to 4 degrees of freedom. Move across that row to the column headed by 0.05 and a one-tailed test. The value given is 2.132. Since the direction of the alternate hypothesis is negative, the critical value is −2.132. The null hypothesis is rejected if the computed t is to the left of -2.132; otherwise, it is not rejected. The decision rule is shown in the following diagram:

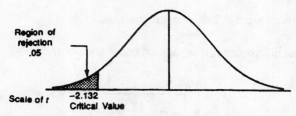

Next the value of the test statistic is computed. Since the mean and standard deviation of the sample are not given, they must be computed from the sample information. The sample mean is computed using formula [3-2], and the standard deviation by taking the square root of formula [4-7]. (Formula [4-7] determines the sample variance.

Sample Times	
X	X²
29	841
27	729
30	900
26	676
28	784
140	3,930

$$\overline{X} = \frac{\Sigma X}{n} = \frac{140}{5} = 28.0$$

$$s = \sqrt{\frac{\Sigma X^2 - \frac{(\Sigma X)^2}{n}}{n-1}} = \sqrt{\frac{3,930 - \frac{(140)^2}{5}}{5-1}} = 1.58$$

These values are inserted into formula [10-1] and the value of the test statistic is computed.

$$t = \frac{\overline{X} - \mu}{s/\sqrt{n}} = \frac{28 - 30}{1.58/\sqrt{5}} = -2.83$$

Since the computed value of -2.83 is to the left of -2.132, the null hypothesis is rejected and the alternate accepted. You conclude that the route suggested by your fellow worker takes less time.

How can we determine the p-value for this test? We cannot get the exact p value as we did in the previous chapters when the standard normal distribution was the test statistic. However, with Appendix F we can estimate the p value. Go to Appendix F and find the row with 4 degrees of freedom (there were four degrees of freedom in this problem), and use the levels of significance for one-tailed tests (this test was one-tailed). Locate a value as close to 2.83, the value of the test statistic, as possible. At the 0.025 significance level the t value is 2.776 and at the 0.01 significance level it is 3.747. The p value is between 0.025 and 0.010, so we can say that the p value is less than 0.025.

Exercise 10.1

Check your answers against those in the ANSWER section.

A supervisor believes employees are taking longer than ten minutes for their breaks. A sample of six employees revealed the following times (in minutes) spent on a break: 9, 12, 14, 15, 10, and 12. At the 0.01 significance level, can it be concluded that employees are taking too long for their breaks? Estimate the p value.

Problem 2

A study of recent graduates from your school revealed that for a sample of ten accounting majors the mean salary was $30,000 per year with a sample variance of $2,000. A sample of eight general business majors revealed a mean salary of $29,000 per year with a variance of $1,500. At the 0.05 significance level can we conclude accounting majors earn more?

Solution

The null hypothesis is that accounting majors earn the same or less than general business majors. The alternate hypothesis is that accounting majors earn more. They are written as follows:

$$H_0: \mu_1 \le \mu_2$$
$$H_1: \mu_1 > \mu_2$$

Where:

μ_1 refers to accounting majors (graduates).
μ_2 refers to general business majors (graduates).

Assuming the two populations follow the normal distribution and that their population standard deviations are equal, then the t distribution is the test statistic. There are 16 degrees of freedom, found by $(n_1 + n_2 - 2) = (10 + 8 - 2) = 16$. The alternate hypothesis is a one-tailed test with the rejection region in the upper tail. From Appendix F, the critical value is 1.746. Hence, H_0 is rejected if the computed value of the test statistic exceeds 1.746.

The first step is to pool the variances, using formula [10-2].

$$s_p^2 = \frac{(n_1 - 1)(s_1^2) + (n_2 - 1)(s_2^2)}{n_1 + n_2 - 2} = \frac{(10 - 1)(2,000)^2 + (8 - 1)(1,500)^2}{10 + 8 - 2} = 3,234,375$$

Next, the value of t is computed, using formula [10-3].

$$t = \frac{\overline{X}_1 - \overline{X}_2}{\sqrt{s_p^2\left(\frac{1}{n_1} + \frac{1}{n_2}\right)}} = \frac{\$30,000 - \$29,000}{\sqrt{(3,234,375)\left(\frac{1}{10} + \frac{1}{8}\right)}} = \frac{1,000}{\sqrt{3,234,375(0.225)}} = \frac{1,000}{853.073} = 1.17$$

Because the computed value of t (1.17) is less than the critical value of 1.746, H_0 is not rejected. The sample evidence does not suggest a difference in the mean salaries of the two groups. The p value, from Appendix F, is greater than 0.10.

A large department store hired a researcher to compare the average purchase amounts for the downtown store with that of its mall store. The following information was obtained:

	Downtown Store	Mall Store
Average purchase amount	$36.00	$40.00
Sample variance	$10.00	$12.00
Sample size	10	10

At the 0.01 significance level can it be concluded that the mean amount spent at the mall store is larger? Estimate the *p*-value.

Problem 3

The Dean of the College of Business at Kingsport University wants to determine if the Grade Point Average (GPA) of business college students decreases during the last semester of their senior year. A sample of six students is selected. Their GPAs for the fall and spring semesters of their senior year are:

Student	Fall Semester	Spring Semester
A	2.7	3.1
B	3.4	3.3
C	3.5	3.3
D	3.0	2.9
E	2.1	1.8
F	2.7	2.4

At the 0.05 significance level, can the Dean conclude that the GPA of graduating seniors declined during their last semester?

Solution

Let μ_d be the mean difference between the fall and spring semester grades for all business students at Kingsport U. in their senior year. Since we want to explore whether grades decrease, a one-tailed test is appropriate.

$$H_0: \mu_d \leq 0$$
$$H_1: \mu_d > 0$$

There are six paired observations; therefore, there are $(n-1) = (6-1) = 5$ degrees of freedom. Using Appendix F with 5 degrees of freedom, the 0.05 significance level and a one-tailed test, the critical value of t is 2.015. H_0 is rejected if the computed value of the test statistic exceeds 2.015.

The value of the test statistic is determined from formula [10-4] below.

$$t = \frac{\bar{d}}{s_d / \sqrt{n}}$$

Where:
$\bar{d}$ is the mean of the differences between fall and spring GPAs.
s_d is the standard deviation of those differences.
n is the number of paired observations.

First, subtract Spring semester grades from fall semester grades. If this difference is positive then a decline has occurred. The sample data is shown below and the values of d and s_d computed:

Student	Fall	Spring	d	d^2
A	2.7	3.1	−0.4	0.16
B	3.4	3.3	0.1	0.01
C	3.5	3.3	0.2	0.04
D	3.0	2.9	0.1	0.01
E	2.1	1.8	0.3	0.09
F	2.7	2.4	0.3	0.09
			0.6	0.40

$$\bar{d} = \frac{\Sigma d}{N} = \frac{0.6}{6} = 0.10$$

$$s_d = \sqrt{\frac{\Sigma d^2 - \frac{(\Sigma d)^2}{n}}{n-1}} = \sqrt{\frac{0.40 - \frac{(0.6)^2}{6}}{6-1}} = 0.2608$$

The t statistic is computed by:

$$t = \frac{\bar{d}}{s_d / \sqrt{n}} = \frac{0.10}{0.2608 / \sqrt{6}} = \frac{0.10}{0.1065} = 0.94$$

Since the computed value of t (0.94) is less than the critical value of 2.015, H_0 is not rejected. The evidence does not suggest a reduction in grades from the fall to the spring semester. The decrease in GPAs can be attributed to chance. The p-value is greater than 0.10.

Exercise 10.2

Check your answers against those in the ANSWER section.

An independent government agency is interested in comparing the heating cost of all- electric homes and those of homes heated with natural gas. A sample of eight all-electric homes is matched with eight homes of similar size and other features that use natural gas. The heating costs for last January are obtained for each home.

Matched Pair	Electric Heat	Gas Heat
1	265	260
2	271	270
3	260	250
4	250	255
5	248	250
6	280	275
7	257	260
8	262	260

At the 0.05 significance level is there reason to believe there is a difference in heating costs?

CHAPTER 10 ASSIGNMENT

TESTS OF HYPOTHESIS: SMALL SAMPLES

Name _____   Section _____   Score _____

Part I   Select the correct answer and write the appropriate letter in the space provided.

_____ 1.   Which of the following statements are true regarding the t distribution?
   a.   it has a mean of 0.
   b.   it is continuous.
   c.   it is more spread out than the z distribution.
   d.   all of the above

_____ 2.   What is a difference between the t distribution and the z distribution?
   a.   The t distribution is only used for samples of 30 or more.
   b.   A larger value of t is needed to reject the null hypotheses.
   c.   The degrees of freedom in the z distribution are larger than those in the t distribution.
   d.   The t distribution has a larger mean than the z distribution.

_____ 3.   Which of the following statements is **not** true regarding the t distribution?
   a.   It is a continuous distribution.
   b.   Each time the degrees of freedom change the t distribution changes.
   c.   The   distribution is flatter than the z distribution.
   d.   It is positively skewed.

_____ 4.   In a two sample test of means for independent samples, $n_1 = 12$ and $n_2 = 10$. There are how many degrees of freedom in the test?
   a.   22
   b.   21
   c.   20
   d.   none of the above

_____ 5.   In the paired t - test, we assume in the null hypothesis that the distribution of the differences between the paired observation has a mean
   a.   equal to 1.
   b.   equal to $n - 1$.
   c.   equal to 0.
   d.   none of the above.

_____ 6.   For a particular significance level and sample size the value of the t for a one-tailed test is
   a.   always less than z.
   b.   always more than z.
   c.   equal to 0.
   d.   equal to z.

_____ 7. Which of the following is **not** an assumption for the two-sample t - test?
   a. equal *sample* variances
   b. independent samples
   c. normal populations
   d. equal *population* standard deviations

_____ 8. Suppose in a one-sample test the sample mean was 10 and the sample size was 15. The sample standard deviation was 3. The appropriate test statistic is
   a. the binomial distribution.
   b. the t distribution.
   c. the z distribution.
   d. none of the above

_____ 9. For tests of hypothesis for a single sample mean, a one-tailed test (rejection region in the upper tail), using the 0.01 significance level, and with n = 12, the critical value is:
   a. 2.179
   b. 2.681
   c. 2.718
   d. 3.106

_____ 10. To determine if a diet supplement is useful for increasing weight, patients are weighed at the start of the program and at the end of the program. This is an example of a(n)
   a. test of paired differences.
   b. independent sample
   c. one sample test for means.
   d. two sample test for means.

Part II   Answer the following questions. Be sure to show essential work.

11. A credit card company wants to evaluate the usage of their card, 20 randomly selected credit card holders were surveyed, and the mean amount they charged in the past twelve months was found to be $2017, while the standard deviation was $867. Use a 0.025 significance level to evaluate the claim that the mean amount charged by all credit card holders was greater than $1750.

   a. State the null and alternate hypotheses.

       H_0: _____ H_1: _____

   b. State the decision rule.

   _____

   c. Compute the value of the test statistic.

c.

d.   Compute the *p*-value.

d.

e.   What is your decision regarding the null hypothesis?

_____

12.   A retail management trade journal reported that the typical shopper spends an average of 1.80 hours per visit in a shopping mall. A sample of 8 shoppers at the Byrnwick Mall in south Toledo revealed the following times. At the 0.01 significance level, can we conclude that shoppers at the Byrnwick Mall spend less than a mean of 1.80 hours?

   1.4   1.7   1.6   2.1   1.6   1.9   1.7   1.7

a.   State the null and alternate hypotheses.

   H_0: _____ H_1: _____

b.   State the decision rule.

_____

c.   Compute the value of the test statistic.

c.

d.   Compute the *p*-value.

d.

e.   What is your decision regarding the null hypothesis?

_____

13. Is the mean salary of accountants who have reached partnership status higher than that for accountants who are not partners? A sample of 15 accountants who have the partnership status showed a mean salary of $62,000 with a standard deviation of $5500. A sample of 12 accountants who were not partners showed a mean of $58,000 with a standard deviation of $6500. At the 0.05 significance level can we conclude that accountants at the partnership level earn larger salaries?

a. State the null and alternate hypotheses.

H_0: _____ H_1: _____

b. State the decision rule.

_____

c. Compute the value of the test statistic.

c. [   ]

d. Compute the p-value.

d. [   ]

e. What is your decision regarding the null hypothesis?

_____

14. The average salary of a sample of 14 teachers in a school building with a Master Degree is $32,741 with a standard deviation of $5800. A sample of 12 teachers in the same building without Master Degrees have an average salary of $27,839 with a standard deviation of $7400. At the 0.01 significance level, do teachers with Master Degrees have higher salaries?

a. State the null and alternate hypotheses.

H_0: _____ H_1: _____

b. State the decision rule.

_____

c. Compute the value of the test statistic.

c.

d. Compute the *p*-value.

d.

e. What is your decision regarding the null hypothesis?

_____

15. The President and CEO of Cliff Hanger International Airlines is concerned about high cholesterol levels of the pilots. In an attempt to improve the situation a sample of seven pilots is selected to take part in a special program, in which each pilot is given a special diet by the company physician. After six months each pilot's cholesterol level is checked again. At the 0.01 significance level can we conclude that the program was effective in reducing cholesterol levels?

Pilot	Before	After	d	d^2
1	255	210		
2	230	225		
3	290	215		
4	242	215		
5	300	240		
6	250	235		
7	215	190		

a. State the null and alternate hypotheses.

H_0: _____ H_1: _____

b. State the decision rule.

_____

c. Compute the value of the test statistic.

c.

d. Compute the *p*-value.

d.

e.   What is your decision regarding the null hypothesis?

_____

16. A group of 5 statistics students receive the following grades on a test: 81, 74, 62, 92, and 76. An
     intervention plan is used and the students increased their scores on a retest to: 85, 79, 75, 95 and 84. At
     the 0.05 significance level, is the intervention plan helpful in increasing the grades?

a.   State the null and alternate hypotheses.

     H_0: _____ H_1: _____

b.   State the decision rule.

_____

c.   Compute the value of the test statistic.

c.

d.   Compute the p-value.

d.

e.   What is your decision regarding the null hypothesis? Interpret the result.

_____

CHAPTER 11
ANALYSIS OF VARIANCE

Chapter Goals

After completing this chapter, you will be able to:

1. Discuss the general idea of analysis of variance.

2. List the characteristics of the F distribution.

3. Conduct a test of hypothesis to determine if two sample variances came from equal populations.

4. Organize data into a one-way and a two-way ANOVA table.

5. Define the terms treatments and blocks

6. Conduct a test of hypothesis among several treatment means.

7. Develop confidence intervals for the difference between two treatment means.

8. Conduct a test of hypothesis among several block means.

Introduction

In Chapter 10 we developed a method to determine whether there is a difference between two population means when the sample sizes are less than 30. What if we wanted to compare more than two populations? The two-sample t test used in Chapter 10 requires that the populations be compared two at a time. This would be very time consuming, would offer the possibility of errors in calculations, but most seriously there would be a build-up of Type I error. That is, the total value of α would become quite large as the number of comparisons increased. In this chapter we will describe a technique that is efficient when simultaneously comparing several sample means to determine if they come from the same or equal populations. This technique is known as *Analysis of Variance (ANOVA).*

> *Analysis of Variance (ANOVA).* A statistical technique for determining whether several populations have the same mean. This is accomplished by comparing the sample variances.

A second test compares two sample variances to determine if the populations are equal. This test is particularly useful in validating that a requirement of the two-sample t tests that both populations have the same standard deviations.

The *F* Distribution

The test statistic used to compare the sample variances and to conduct the ANOVA test is the *F distribution*.

> *F Distribution.* A continuous probability distribution where F is always 0 or positive. The distribution is positively skewed. It is based on two parameters, the number of degrees of freedom in the numerator and the number of degrees of freedom in the denominator.

The major characteristics of the F distribution are:

1. There is a family of F distributions. Each time the number of degrees of freedom in either the numerator or the denominator change, a new F distribution is created.

2. The F distribution is based on two sets of degrees of freedom. One set is for the numerator and the other for the denominator.

3. F cannot be negative and is a continuous distribution.

4. The F distribution is positively skewed and its values may range from 0 to plus infinity. As the values increase, the curve approaches the X-axis but never touches it.

Comparing Two Populations Variances

The F distribution is used to test the hypothesis that the variance of one normal population equals the variance of another normal population. The F distribution can also be used to validate assumptions with respect to certain statistical tests. Regardless of whether we want to determine if one population has more variation than another population does or validate an assumption with respect to a statistical test, we still use the usual five-step hypothesis testing procedure. The value of the test statistic is determined using text formula [11-1].

$$F = \frac{s_1^2}{s_2^2} \qquad [11-1]$$

Where:

s_1^2 is the variance of the first sample.

s_2^2 is the variance of the second sample.

The usual practice is to determine the F ratio by putting the larger of the two variances in the numerator. This will force the F ratio to be larger than 1.00. This allows us to always use the upper tail of the F statistic, thus avoiding the need for more extensive F tables.

Again, the F distribution can be used to determine if the sample variance from one normal population is the same as the variance obtained from another normal population.

For example, if you were comparing the mean starting salaries for this year's marketing graduates to this year's computer science graduates, an assumption required of the two-sample t test is that both populations have the same standard deviation. Therefore, before conducting the test for means, it is essential to show that the two population variances are equal.

The idea behind the test for standard deviations is that if the null hypothesis is true that the two sample variances are equal, then their ratio will be approximately 1.00. If the null hypothesis is false, then the ratio will be much larger than 1.00. The F distribution provides a decision rule to let us know when the departure from 1.00 is too large to have happened by chance.

Assumptions of ANOVA

A use of the F distribution is the analysis of variance (ANOVA) techniques where we compare three or more sample means to determine if they come from equal populations. To employ ANOVA, three conditions must be met:

1. The populations are normally distributed.

2. The populations have equal standard deviations (σ).

3. The samples are selected independently.

When these conditions are met, F is used as the test statistic to measure the variance among means.

The ANOVA Test

The ANOVA test is used to determine if the various sample means came from a single population or populations with different means. The sample means are compared through their variances. The underlying strategy is to estimate the population variance two ways and then find the ratio of these two estimates. If the ratio is about one (1), then the two estimates are the same and we conclude that the sample means are the same. If the ratio is quite different from 1, then we conclude that the sample means are not the same. The F distribution tells when the ratio is too much larger than 1 to have occurred by chance.

The same hypothesis testing procedure used with the standard normal distribution (z) and Student's t is also employed with analysis of variance. The test statistic is the F distribution.

Step 1. State the null hypothesis and the alternate hypothesis.

When three population means are compared, the null and alternate hypotheses are written:

$$H_0: \mu_1 = \mu_2 = \mu_3$$
$$H_1: \text{not all means are equal}$$

Note that rejection of the null hypothesis does not identify which populations differ significantly. It merely indicates that a difference between at least one pair of means exists.

Step 2. Select the level of significance.

The most common values selected are 0.01 or 0.05.

Step 3. Select an appropriate test statistic.

For an analysis of variance problem the appropriate test statistic is F. The F statistic is the ratio of two variance estimates and is computed by the formula:

$$F = \frac{\text{Estimate of the population variance based on the differences between the sample means}}{\text{Estimate of the population variance based on the variation within samples}}$$

There are $(k-1)$ degrees of freedom associated with the numerator of the formula for F, and $(n-k)$ degrees of freedom associated with the denominator, where k is the number of populations and n is the total number of sample observations.

Step 4. Formulate the Decision Rule.

The critical value is determined from the F table found in Appendix G.

To illustrate how the decision rule is established, suppose a package delivery company purchased 14 trucks at the same time. Five trucks were purchased from Ford, four from General Motors (GM), and five from Chrysler. All the trucks were used to deliver packages. The cost of maintaining the trucks for the first year is shown. Is there a significant difference in the mean maintenance cost of the three manufacturers?

Maintenance Cost, By Manufacturer		
Ford	Chrysler	GM
$ 914	$933	$1,004
1,000	874	1,114
1,127	927	1,044
988	983	1,100
947		1,139

The three different manufacturers are called ***treatments***.

Treatments. A specific source of variation in a set of data.

The term is borrowed from agricultural research, where much of the early development of the ANOVA technique took place. Crop yields were compared after different fertilizers (that is, treatments) had been applied to various plots of land.

In the study comparing truck manufacturers there are three treatments. Therefore there are two degrees of freedom in the numerator, found by $(k-1) = (3-1) = 2$. How is the number of degrees of freedom for the denominator determined? Note that in the three samples there are a total of 14 observations. Thus the total number of observations, designated by n, is 14. The number of degrees of freedom in the denominator is 11, found by $(n-k) = (14-3) = 11$.

The critical value of F can be found in Appendix G at the back of the study guide. There are tables for both the 0.01 and the 0.05 significance levels. Using the 0.05 significance level, the degrees of freedom for the numerator are at the top of the table and for the denominator in the left margin. To locate the critical value, move horizontally at the top of the table to 2 degrees of freedom in the numerator, then down that column to the number opposite 11 degrees of freedom in the left margin (denominator). That number is 3.98, which is the critical value of F.

The decision rule is to reject the null hypothesis if the computed value of F exceeds 3.98, otherwise it is not rejected. To reject the null hypothesis and accept the alternate hypothesis allows us to conclude that there is a significant difference between at least one pair of means. If the null hypothesis is not rejected this implies the differences between the sample means could have occurred by chance. Portrayed graphically, the decision rule is shown at the right.

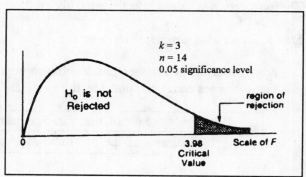

Step 5. Compute F and make a decision.

The value of F is computed from the sample information and a decision is made regarding the null hypothesis. If the computed value of F is 1.98, for example, the null hypothesis is not rejected. If it is greater than 3.98, say 4.26, then the null hypothesis is rejected and the alternate accepted.

The ANOVA Table

A convenient way of organizing the calculations for F is to put them in a table referred to as an ANOVA table.

ANOVA Table				
Source of Variation	Sum of Squares	Degrees of Freedom	Mean Square	F
Treatments	SST	$k-1$	$SST/(k-1) = MST$	MST/MSE
Error	SSE	$n-k$	$SSE/(n-k) = MSE$	
Total	SS Total			

Note in the ANOVA Table that there are three values, called **Sum of Squares**, that are required to compute F. The three values are determined by first calculating SS total and SST, then finding SSE by subtraction. Keep in mind the fact that the SS total term is the total variation, SST is the variation due to the treatments, and SSE is the variation among the treatments.

We work across the table to eventually calculate F. The degrees of freedom are the same as those used to find the critical value of F. The term **mean square** is another expression for estimate of the variance. As seen in the table the **mean square for treatments** (written MST) is SST divided by the degrees of freedom. Also from the table the **mean square error** (written MSE) is SSE divided by the degrees of freedom. To find F we divide MST by MSE. The entire process is explained in Problem 2

Glossary

Analysis of Variance (ANOVA): A statistical technique for determining whether several populations have the same mean. This is accomplished by comparing the sample variances.

F Distribution: A continuous probability distribution where F is always 0 or positive. The distribution is positively skewed. It is based on two parameters, the number of degrees of freedom in the numerator and the number of degrees of freedom in the denominator.

Treatments: A treatment is a specific source, or cause, of variation in a set of data.

Chapter Problems

Problem 1

Tiedke's Department Store accepts three types of credit cards, MasterCard, Visa, and their own store card. The sales manager is interested in finding out whether there is a difference in the mean amounts charged by customers on the three cards. A random sample of 18 credit card purchases (rounded to the nearest dollar) revealed these credit card amounts. At the 0.05 significance level, can we conclude there is a difference in the mean amounts charged per purchase on the three cards?

MasterCard	Visa	Store
$61	$85	$61
28	56	25
42	44	42
33	72	31
51	98	29
56	56	
	72	

Solution

There are three populations involved, the three credit cards. The null and alternate hypotheses are:

$$H_0: \mu_1 = \mu_2 = \mu_3$$

H_1: the means are not all equal

There are three "treatments" or columns. Hence, there are $(k-1) = (3-1) = 2$ degrees of freedom in the numerator. There are 18 observations, therefore $n = 18$. The number of degrees of freedom in the denominator is 15, found by $(n-k) = (18-3)$. The critical value is found in Appendix G. Find the table for the 0.05 significance level and the column headed by 2 degrees of freedom. Then move down that column to the margin row with 15 degrees of freedom and read the value. It is 3.68.

The decision rule is: Reject the null hypothesis if the computed value of F exceeds 3.68, otherwise do not reject H_0. Shown graphically, the decision rule is shown at the right.

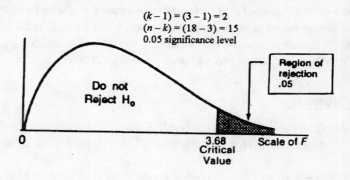

There are two sources of variation in an analysis of variance study. These sources occur between treatments (designated SST) and within treatments (designated SSE). The sum of SST and SSE is the total amount of variation, written SS total; n_c refers to the number of observations in each column (treatments).

The calculations needed for SST, SSE, and SS total are:

	Amounts Charged						
	MasterCard		Visa		Store		Total
	X	X^2	X	X^2	X	X^2	
	$61	3,721	$85	7,225	$61	3,721	
	28	784	56	3,136	25	625	
	42	1,764	44	1,936	42	1,764	
	33	1,089	72	5,184	31	961	
	51	2,601	98	9,604	29	841	
	56	3,136	56	3,136			
Column			72	5,184			
Totals (T_c)	271		483		188		942
Sum of Squares X^2		13,095		35,405		7,912	56,412
Sample size: n_c	6		7		5		18

The sum of squares total, SS total, is computed using formula [11-2].

$$SS\ Total = \Sigma X^2 - \frac{(\Sigma X)^2}{n} = 56,412 - \frac{(942)^2}{18} = 7,114$$

Recall that ΣX^2 refers to the sum of the squares of all observations. However, $(\Sigma X)^2$ is found by summing all the observations and then squaring that sum. The total number of observations is n or 18.

The sum of squares due to treatment (SST) is computed using formula [11-3] where T_c^2 is the square of the column (treatment) totals, and n_c, is the number of samples in each treatment.

$$SST = \Sigma \left(\frac{T_c^2}{n_c} \right) - \frac{(\Sigma X)^2}{n}$$

$$= \left[\frac{(271)^2}{6} + \frac{(483)^2}{7} + \frac{(188)^2}{5} \right] - \frac{(942)^2}{18} = 3,337.9667$$

The sum of squares error (SSE) is computed using formula [11-4] as follows:

$$SSE = SS\ total - SST$$
$$= 7114 - 3,337.9667$$
$$= 3776.0333$$

The next step is to insert these values into the ANOVA table.

Source Variation	Sum of Squares	Degrees of Freedom	Mean Squares
Treatment	SST = 3,337.9667	$(k-1) = (3-1) = 2$	$MST = \dfrac{3,337.9667}{2} = 1,668.9834$
Error	SSE = 3,776.0333	$(n-k) = (18-3) = 15$	$MSE = \dfrac{3,776.0333}{15} = 251.7356$
Total	SS Total = 7,114	17	

Computing F using the formula:

$$F = \frac{MST}{MSE} = \frac{1,668.9834}{251.7356} = 6.63$$

Since the computed value of F (6.63) exceeds the critical value of 3.68, the null hypothesis is rejected at the 0.05 level and the alternate hypothesis is accepted. It is concluded that mean amounts charged by Tiedke's Department Store customers are not the same for the three credit cards.

There are many computer software packages that will perform the ANOVA calculations and output the results. MINITAB, SAS, SPSSX, and Excel are examples. The following output is from the MINITAB system. Notice that computed F is the same as determined previously.

```
ANALYSIS OF VARIANCE
SOURCE      DF        SS           MS          F        P
FACTOR       2       3338         1669        6.63     0.009
ERROR       15       3776          252
TOTAL       17       7114
                                        INDIVIDUAL 95 PCT CI'S FOR MEAN
                                        BASED ON POOLED STDEV
LEVEL        N      MEAN       STDEV    ---------+---------+---------+-------
master       6     45.17       13.08         (------*-----)
visa         7     69.00       18.61                     (------*-----)
store        5     37.60       14.52    (-------*------)
                                        ---------+---------+---------+-------
POOLED STDEV =     15.87                     40        60        80
```

Exercise 11.1

Check your answers against those in the ANSWER section.

The accelerating cost of electricity and gas has caused the management at Arvco Electronics to lower the heat in the work areas. The instructor conducting night classes for employees is concerned that this may have an adverse effect on the employees' test scores. Management agreed to investigate. The employees taking the basic statistics course were randomly assigned to three groups. One group was in a classroom having a temperature of 60^0, another group was placed in a room having a temperature of 70^0, and the third group was in a room having a temperature of 80^0. At the completion of the chapters on tests of hypotheses a common examination was given consisting of ten questions. The number correct for each of the 20 employees was:

Temperature

60^0	70^0	80^0
3	7	4
5	6	6
4	8	5
3	9	7
4	6	6
	8	5
	8	4
		3

At the 0.05 significance level can management conclude that there is a difference in achievement with respect to the three temperatures?

Problem 2

In Problem 1 it was concluded that there was a difference between the mean amounts charged for the three different credit cards, MasterCard, Visa, and the Tiedke's Store card. Between which credit cards is there a significant difference? Use the 0.05 level of significance.

Solution

From the MINITAB Output above note that the mean amount charged using the VISA card was $69.00 and $37.60 for the Department card. Since these means have the largest difference, let's determine if this pair of means differ significantly.

To determine if the means differ, we develop a confidence interval for the difference between the two population means. This confidence interval employs the t distribution and the mean square error (MSE) term. Recall that one of the assumptions for ANOVA is that the standard deviations (or variances) in the sampled populations must be the same. The MSE term is an estimate of this common variance. It is obtained from the MINITAB output. Text formula [11-5] is used:

$$(\overline{X}_1 - \overline{X}_2) \pm t \sqrt{MSE \left(\frac{1}{n_1} + \frac{1}{n_2} \right)} \qquad [11-5]$$

Where:

$\overline{X}_1$ is the mean of the first treatment.

$\overline{X}_2$ is the mean of the second treatment.

t is obtained from the t table in Appendix F. The degree of freedom is equal to $(n - k)$.

MSE   is the mean square error term, which is obtained from the ANOVA table. It is equal to $SSE/(n - k)$ and is an estimate of the common population variance.

n_1 is the number of observations in the first treatment.

n_2 is the number of observations in the second treatment.

If the confidence interval includes 0, there is no difference in the treatment means. However, if both end points of the confidence interval are on the same side of 0 the pair of means differs.

$$(\overline{X}_1 - \overline{X}_2) \pm t \sqrt{MSE\left(\frac{1}{n_1} + \frac{1}{n_2}\right)}$$

$$(69.00 - 37.60) \pm 2.131 \sqrt{252\left(\frac{1}{7} + \frac{1}{5}\right)}$$

$$31.40 \pm 19.81$$

$$\$11.59 \text{ to } \$51.21$$

Where:

$\overline{X}_1$ equals 69.00

$\overline{X}_2$ equals 37.60

n_1 equals 7

n_2 equals 5

t is 2.131 from Appendix F with 15 degrees of freedom and the 95 percent level of confidence.

MSE   is 252, which is in the ANOVA table constructed to calculate F.

Since both end points have the same sign, positive in this case, we conclude that there is a difference in the mean amount charged on VISA and the store card.

Similarly, approximate results can be obtained directly from the MINITAB Output. In the lower right corner of the Output a confidence interval was developed for each mean. The * indicates the mean of the treatment and the parentheses ( ) symbols indicate the endpoints of the confidence interval. In comparing treatment means, if there is any common area between the two, they do not differ. If there is not any common area between the treatment means, they differ. For the credit card example, MasterCard and VISA have common area and do not differ. MasterCard and the store card do not differ, but the store and VISA do differ.

Exercise 11.2

Check your answers against those in the ANSWER section.

In Exercise 1 it was concluded that there was a difference between the mean number correct for the three different temperatures in the work area. The mean score for the 60^0 group is 3.8 and the mean score for the 70^0 group is 7 4. Determine if this pair of means differs significantly.

Problem 3

Lens Grinders, Inc. is an innovative company in terms of employee scheduling. Recently several employees have asked to take only one long break during the day, others have requested several short breaks. In addition, some workers have requested to work four day weeks, others flex time, and still others at random times. The Human Resources Department has decided to conduct a study to determine if the different schedule types and the number of breaks has an effect on output. A sample of 16 employees was obtained. Each employee was randomly assigned to one of the combinations of work schedules and number of breaks. The total output for each worker for a week was then recorded. At the 0.05 significance level is there a difference in the mean output for the various number of breaks and for the different schedules?

Schedule Type	Number of Breaks			
	1	2	3	4
Regular	94	105	96	98
Flex time	97	106	91	90
Four day	96	100	88	88
Random	92	104	86	84

Solution

This is an example of a two-factor ANOVA, often referred to as two-way ANOVA. We are considering variation from three sources: the number of breaks, the type of schedule, and random causes. Two sets of hypotheses are established, one regarding breaks and the other regarding the type of schedules. The breaks are the treatments and the second source of variation, type of schedule, is called the "blocking variable."

Breaks: H_0: The treatment means are the same.

$$\mu_1 = \mu_2 = \mu_3 = \mu_4$$

H_1: The treatment means are not the same.

Schedules: H_0: The block means are the same.

$$\mu_1 = \mu_2 = \mu_3 = \mu_4$$

H_1: The block means are not the same.

The MINITAB system is used to perform the calculations. The output from this problem is as follows:

```
ANALYSIS OF VARIANCE output
SOURCE       DF      SS         MS        F
Breaks       3     495.19    165.06    17.16
Schedule     3     109.69     36.56     3.80
Error        9      86.56      9.62
TOTAL       15     691.44
```

There are four different schedules, so $n = 4$; there are also four different breaks so $k = 4$. Let's consider the treatments, or breaks, first. There are $(k - 1) = (4 - 1) = 3$ degrees of freedom in the numerator and $(n - 1)(k - 1) = (4 - 1)(4 - 1) = 9$ degrees of freedom in the denominator. Using the 0.05 significance level, the critical value of 3.86 is obtained from Appendix G. That is, the null hypothesis that the mean output is the same for the number of breaks is rejected if the computed F exceeds 3.86. The value of F is computed as follows.

$$F = \frac{SST/(k-1)}{SSE/(n-1)(k-1)} = \frac{495.19/3}{86.56/9} = 17.16 \quad \text{or} \quad F = \frac{MST}{MSE} = \frac{165.06}{9.62} = 17.16$$

Since the computed value of 17.16 exceeds the critical value of 3.86, the null hypothesis is rejected. The mean output is not the same for the various number of breaks.

The hypothesis regarding the blocking variable, the schedules, is considered next. There are $(n-1) = (4-1) = 3$ degrees of freedom in the numerator and $(n-1)(k-1) = (4-1)(4-1) = 9$ degrees of freedom in the denominator. Using the 0.05 significance level and Appendix G, the critical value is 3.86. The computed value of F is 3.80.

$$F = \frac{SSB/(n-1)}{SSE/(n-1)(k-1)} = \frac{109.69/3}{86.56/9} = 3.80 \quad \text{or} \quad F = \frac{MSB}{MSE} = \frac{36.56}{9.62} = 3.80$$

The decision is not to reject the null hypothesis. However, 3.80 is very close to the critical value of 3.86. The conclusion is that there is no difference in the output using the various schedules.

Exercise 11.3

Check your answers against those in the ANSWER section.

The following two-way ANOVA table was developed using the MINITAB system. Use the 0.05 significance level.

SOURCE	DF	SS	MS
TREATMENTS	3	45	15
BLOCKS	4	200	50
ERROR	12	144	12

a. How many treatments are there?

b. How many blocks are there?

c. What is the total sample size?

d. Is there a significant difference in the treatment means?

e. Is there a significant difference in the block means?

Problem 4

Teledko Associates is a marketing research firm that specializes in comparative shopping. Teledko is hired by General Motors to compare the selling price of the Pontiac Sunbird with the Chevy Cavalier. Posing as a potential customer, a representative of Teledko visited 8 Pontiac dealerships in Metro City and 6 Chevrolet dealerships and obtained quotes on comparable cars. The standard deviation for the selling prices of 8 Pontiac Sunbirds is $350 and on the six Cavaliers, $290. At the 0.01 significance level is there a difference in the variation in the quotes of the Pontiacs and Chevrolets?

Solution

Let the Sunbird be population 1 and the Cavalier population 2. A two-tailed test is appropriate because we are looking for a difference in the variances. We are not trying to show that one population has a larger variance than the other. The null and alternate hypotheses are:

$$H_o : \sigma_1^2 = \sigma_2^2$$
$$H_1 : \sigma_1^2 \neq \sigma_2^2$$

The F distribution is the appropriate test statistic for comparing two sample variances. For a two-tailed test, the larger sample variance is placed in the numerator. The critical value of F is found by dividing the significance level in half and then referring to Appendix G and the appropriate degrees of freedom. There are $(n-1) = (8-1) = 7$ degrees of freedom in the numerator and $(n-1) = (6-1) = 5$ degrees of freedom in the denominator. From Appendix G, using the 0.01 significance level, the critical value of F is 10.5. If the ratio of the two variances exceeds 10.5, the null hypothesis is rejected and the alternate hypothesis is accepted. The computed value of the test statistic is determined by:

$$F = \frac{s_1^2}{s_2^2} = \frac{(350)^2}{(290)^2} = 1.46$$

The null hypothesis is not rejected. There is no difference in the variation in the price quotes of Pontiac and Chevrolet, because the computed value of F (1.46) is less than the critical F value (10.5).

Exercise 11.4

Check your answers against those in the ANSWER section.

Thomas Economic Forecasting, Inc. and Harmon Econometrics have the same mean error in forecasting the stock market over the last ten years. However, the standard deviation for Thomas is 30 points and 60 points for Harmon. At the 0.05 significance level can we conclude that there is more variation in the forecast given by Harmon Econometrics?

CHAPTER 11 ASSIGNMENT

ANALYSIS OF VARIANCE

Name _____ Section _____ Score _____

Part I   Select the correct answer and write the appropriate letter in the space provided.

_____ 1. The analysis of variance technique is a method for
    a. comparing three or more means.
    b. comparing F distributions.
    c. measuring sampling error.
    d. none of the above.

_____ 2. A treatment is
    a. a normal population.
    b. the explained population.
    c. a source of variation.
    d. the amount of random error.

_____ 3. In a one-way ANOVA, k refers to the
    a. number of observations in each column.
    b. the number of treatments.
    c. the total number of observations.
    d. none of the above.

_____ 4. The F distribution is
    a. continuous distribution.
    b. based on two sets of degrees of freedom.
    c. never negative.
    d. all of the above.

_____ 5. In an ANOVA test there are 5 observations in each of three treatments. The degrees of freedom in the numerator and denominator respectively are:
    a. 2, 4
    b. 3, 15
    c. 3, 12
    d. 2, 12

_____ 6. Which of the following assumptions is **not** a requirement for ANOVA?
    a. dependent samples
    b. normal populations
    c. equal population variances
    d. independent samples

_____ 7. The mean square error term (MSE) is the
    a. estimate of the common population variance.   b. estimate of the population means.
    c. estimate of the sample standard deviation.   d. treatment variation.

_____8. In a one-way ANOVA, the null hypothesis indicates that the treatment means
   a.   are all the same or from equal populations.
   b.   are not from the same populations.
   c.   are all different.
   d.   in at least one pair of means are the same.

_____9. The appropriate test statistic for comparing two sample variances to find out if they came from the same or equal populations is the
   a. t distribution.
   b. z distribution.
   c. F distribution.
   d.   binomial distribution.

_____ 10. What is the probability for an F of more than 6.55 with 3 degrees of freedom in the numerator and 10 in the denominator?
   a.   0.025   b.   0.001   c.   0.01   d.   0.05

Part II   Record your answer in the space provided. Show essential calculations.

11.   The NPC, Inc. is a large mail order company that ships men's shirts all over the United States and Canada. They ship a large number of packages from their warehouse in Delta, Ohio. Their goal is to have 95 percent of the shipments delivered in 4 days. For many years they have used Brown Truck Inc., but recently there have been complaints about slow and inconsistent delivery. A sample of 10 recent shipments handled by Brown Truck showed a standard deviation in delivery time of 1.25 days. A sample of 16 shipments by Rapid Package Service showed a standard deviation in their delivery time of 0.45 days. At the 0.05 significance level is there more variation in the Brown Truck delivery time?

   a.   State the null and alternate hypotheses.
       H_0: _____ H_1: _____

   b.   State the decision rule.
       _____

   c.   Compute the value of the test statistic.

c.

   d.   What is your decision regarding the null hypothesis? Interpret the result.
       _____

12. Jim Ray, an avid golfer, keeps records on his scores for 18 holes of golf. When the temperature is above 65 degrees, the standard deviation of his scores is 5.75 for 25 rounds. When the temperature is below 65 degrees, the standard deviation of his scores is 7.35 for a sample of 21 rounds. At the 0.05 significance level, is there more variation in his scores when the temperature is below 65 degrees?

a. State the null and alternate hypotheses.
   H_0: _____ H_1: _____

b. State the decision rule.

   _____

c. Compute the value of the test statistic.

c.

d. What is your decision regarding the null hypothesis? Interpret the result.

   _____

13. The County Executive for Monroe County is concerned about the response time for the three fire companies in the county. Samples of the response times (in minutes) for each company follow. At the 0.05 significance level is there a difference in the mean response time?

Youngsville	Northeast	Corry
2.2	2.3	0.9
1.2	1.5	0.8
1.9	1.2	1.1
3.1	1.4	1.2
1.8	2.2	0.7
1.5		

a. State the null and alternate hypotheses.

   H_0: _____ H_1: _____

b. State the decision rule.

   _____

c. Compute the value of the test statistic.

c.

d. What is your decision regarding the null hypothesis? Interpret the result.

_____

14. A dentist is trying to decide if there is a difference in the number of weeks three different toothbrushes last. Fifteen patients were randomly assigned to three brands of toothbrushes and the number of weeks that the toothbrushes lasted is given. At the 0.05 significance level, is there a difference in the mean length of time the toothbrushes lasted?

Brand	Weeks of Wear				
A	3	4	6	3	4
B	2	3	2	5	2
C	5	7	5	4	6

a. State the null and alternate hypotheses.
   H_0: _____ H_1: _____

b. State the decision rule.

_____

c. Compute the value of the test statistic.

c.

```
Analysis of Variance
Source    DF     SS      MS
Factor     2   16.93    8.47
Error     12   18.00    1.50
Total     14   34.93
```

d. What is your decision regarding the null hypothesis? Interpret the result.

_____

CHAPTER 12
LINEAR REGRESSION AND CORRELATION

Chapter Goals

After completing this chapter, you will be able to:

1. Draw a scatter diagram.

2. Understand and interpret the terms dependent and independent variable.

3. Calculate and interpret the coefficient of correlation, the coefficient of determination, and the standard error of estimate.

4. Conduct a test of hypothesis to determine whether the population coefficient of correlation is different from zero.

5. Calculate the least squares regression line.

6. Construct and interpret a confidence interval and prediction interval for the dependent variable.

7. Set up and interpret an ANOVA table.

Introduction

We studied hypothesis testing concerning means and proportions where only a single feature of the sampled item was considered. For example, based on sample evidence we concluded that the beginning annual mean salary for accounting graduates is $26,000. With this chapter we begin our study of the relationship between two variables. We may want to determine if there is a relationship between the number of years of company service and the income of executives. Or we may want to explore the relationship between crime in the inner city and the unemployment rate.

To study the relationship between two variables we use two techniques: *correlation analysis* and *regression analysis*.

> *Correlation analysis*: A group of techniques to measure the strength of the association between two variables.

The Scatter Diagram

The purpose of correlation analysis is to find out how strong the relationship is between two variables. One way of looking at the relationship between two variables is to portray the information in a *scatter diagram*.

> *Scatter diagram*: A chart that portrays the relationship between two variables.

The values of the *independent variable* are portrayed on the horizontal axis (*X*-axis) and the *dependent variable* along the vertical axis (*Y*-axis).

> *Dependent variable*: The variable that is being predicted or estimated.

> *Independent variable*: A variable that provides the basis for estimation. It is the predictor variable.

Note in Figure A that as the length of service increases so does income. In Figure B, as employment rises, the crime rate in the inner city declines.

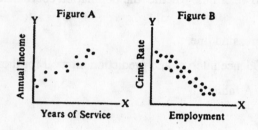

The Coefficient of Correlation

A measure of the linear (straight-line) strength of the association between two variables is given by the *coefficient of correlation*.

> *Coefficient of correlation*: A measure of the strength of the linear relationship between two sets of variables.

It is also called **Pearson's product moment correlation coefficient** or **Pearson's** *r* after its founder Karl Pearson. The correlation coefficient is usually designated by the lower case *r* and may range from −1.00 to +1.00 inclusive. A value of −1.00 indicates perfect negative correlation. A value of +1.00 indicates perfect positive correlation. A correlation coefficient of 0.0 indicates there is no relationship between the two variables under consideration. This information is summarized in the charts that follow.

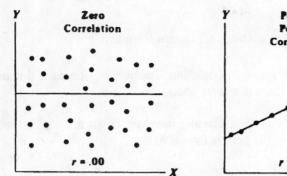
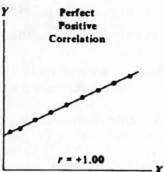
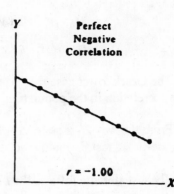

The coefficient of correlation requires that both variables be at least of interval scale.

The degree of strength of the relationship is not related to the sign (direction – or +) of the coefficient of correlation.

For example, an r value of -0.60 represents the same degree of correlation as $+0.60$. An r of -0.70 represents a stronger degree of correlation than 0.40. An r of -0.90 represents a strong negative correlation and $+0.15$ a weak positive correlation.

The coefficient of correlation is computed by text formula [12-1].

$$r = \frac{n(\Sigma XY) - (\Sigma X)(\Sigma Y)}{\sqrt{\left[n(\Sigma X^2) - (\Sigma X)^2\right]\left[n(\Sigma Y^2) - (\Sigma Y)^2\right]}} \qquad [12-1]$$

Where:
n is the number of paired observations.
ΣXY is the sum of the products of X and Y.
ΣX is the X variable summed.
ΣY is the Y variable summed.
ΣX^2 is the X variable squared and the squares summed.
$(\Sigma X)^2$ is the X variable summed and the sum squared.
ΣY^2 is the Y variable squared and the squares summed.
$(\Sigma Y)^2$ is the Y variable summed and the sum squared.
r is the coefficient of correlation.

Testing the Significance of the Correlation Coefficient

A test of significance for the coefficient of correlation may be used to determine if the computed r could have occurred in a population in which the two variables are not related. To put it in the form of a question: Is the correlation in the population zero?

For a two-tailed test the null hypothesis and the alternate hypothesis are written as follows:

$$H_0: \rho = 0 \ \text{(The correlation in the population is zero)}$$

$$H_1: \rho \neq 0 \ \text{(The correlation in the population is different from zero)}$$

The Greek lower case rho, ρ, represents the correlation in the population. The null hypothesis is that there is no correlation in the population, and the alternate that there is a correlation.

From the way H_1 is stated , we know that the test is two tailed. The alternate hypothesis can also be set up as a one-tailed test. It could read "the correlation coefficient is greater than zero."

The test statistic follows the t distribution with $n - 2$ degrees of freedom. Text formula [12-2] is used.

$$t = \frac{r\sqrt{n-2}}{\sqrt{1-r^2}} \qquad [12-2]$$

Regression Analysis

The equation for the straight line used to estimate Y based on X is referred to as the *regression equation*.

> ***Regression Equation***: An equation that defines the relationship between two variables.

The linear relationship between two variables is given by the regression equation:

$$Y' = a + bX \qquad [12-3]$$

Where:
Y' (read Y prime) is the predicted value of the Y variable for a selected X value.
a is the Y intercept. It is the estimated value of Y when $X = 0$.
b is the slope of the line. It measures the change in Y' for each unit change in X. It will always have the same sign as the coefficient of correlation.
X is any value of the independent variable that is selected.

The value of a is the Y intercept and b is the **regression coefficient**. How do we get these values? They are developed mathematically using the *least squares principle*.

> ***Least squares principle***: An equation determined by minimizing the sum of the squares of the vertical distances between the actual Y values and the predicted values of Y'.

Computing and Interpreting the *a* and *b* Values

Suppose the least squares principle was used to develop an equation expressing the relationship between annual salary and years of work experience. The equation is:

$$Y' = a + bX = 20,000 + 500X \ \text{(in dollars)}$$

In the example, annual income is the dependent variable, Y, and is being predicted on the basis of the employee's years of work experience, X, the independent variable. The value of 500, which is b, means that for each additional year of work experience the employee's salary increases by $500. Thus, we would expect an employee with 40 years of work experience to earn $5,000 more than one with 30 years of work experience.

What does the 20,000 dollars represent? It is the value for Y' when $X = 0$. Recall that this is the point where the line intersects the Y-axis. The values of a and b in the regression equation are usually referred to as the regression coefficients. The formulas for computing b and a are:

$$b = \frac{n(\Sigma XY) - (\Sigma X)(\Sigma Y)}{n(\Sigma X^2) - (\Sigma X)^2} \qquad [12-4]$$

$$a = \frac{\Sigma Y}{n} - b\left(\frac{\Sigma X}{n}\right) \qquad [12-5]$$

Where:
X is a value of the independent variable.
Y is a value of the dependent variable.
ΣXY is the sum of the products of the dependent variable and the independent variable.
ΣX is the sum of the independent variables
ΣY is the sum dependent variables
ΣX^2 is the sum of the squares of the independent variable.
n is the number of items the sample.

The Standard Error of Estimate

Rarely does the predicted value of Y' agree exactly with the actual Y value. That is, we expect some prediction error. One measure of this error is called the **standard error of estimate**. It is written $s_{y.x}$.

> **Standard error of estimate**: A measure of the scatter, or dispersion, of the observed values around the line of regression.

A small standard error of estimate indicates that the independent variable is a good predictor of the dependent variable.

The standard error, as it is often called, is similar to the standard deviation described in Chapter 4. Recall that the standard deviation was computed by squaring the difference between the actual value and the mean. This squaring was performed for all n observations. For the standard error of estimate, the difference between the predicted value Y' and the actual value of Y is obtained and that difference squared and summed over all n observations. The text formula [12-6] is:

$$s_{y.x} = \sqrt{\frac{\Sigma(Y - Y')^2}{n - 2}} \qquad [12-6]$$

A more convenient computational form is text formula [12-7]:

$$s_{y \cdot x} = \sqrt{\frac{\Sigma Y^2 - a(\Sigma Y) - b(\Sigma XY)}{n-2}} \qquad [12-7]$$

Where:

a and b are the regression coefficients.

ΣY^2 is the sum of the squares of the dependent variable.

ΣY is the sum of the values of the dependent variables.

ΣXY is the sum of the products of the dependent and independent variable.

n is the sample size.

Regression Assumptions

Linear regression is based on these four assumptions:

1. For each value of X, there is a group of Y values, and these Y values are *normally distributed*.

2. The *means* of these normal distributions of Y values all lie on the straight line of regression.

3. The *standard deviations* of these normal distributions are *equal*.

4. The Y values are statistically *independent*. This means that in the selection of a sample, the Y values chosen for a particular X value do not depend on the Y values for any other X value.

Establishing a Confidence Interval for Y

The standard error is also used to set confidence intervals for the predicted value of Y'. When the sample size is large and the scatter about the regression line is approximately normally distributed, then the following relationships can be expected:

$Y' \pm 1s_{y \cdot x}$ encompasses about 68.0% of the observed values.

$Y' \pm 2s_{y \cdot x}$ encompasses about 95.5% of the observed values.

$Y' \pm 3s_{y \cdot x}$ encompasses about 99.7% of the observed values.

Two types of confidence intervals may be set. The first for the mean value of Y' for a given value of X and the other, called a **prediction interval,** for an individual value of Y' for a given value of X. To explain the difference between the mean predicted value and the individual prediction, suppose we are predicting the salary of management personnel who are 40 years old. In this case we are predicting the mean salary of all management personnel age 40. However, if we want to predict the salary of a particular manager who is 40, then we are making a prediction about a particular individual.

The formula for the confidence interval for the mean value of Y for a given X is:

$$Y' \pm t(s_{y \cdot x}) \sqrt{\frac{1}{n} + \frac{(X - \bar{X})^2}{\Sigma X^2 - \frac{(\Sigma X)^2}{n}}} \qquad [12-8]$$

Where:
Y' is the predicted value for a selected value of X.
X is any selected value of the independent variable.
$\overline{X}$ is the mean of the independent variable X, found by $\Sigma X / n$.
n is the sample size or number of observations.
t is the value of the Student t distribution from Appendix F, with $(n-2)$ degrees of freedom and the given level of significance for a two-tailed test.
$s_{y \cdot x}$ is the standard error of estimate.

The formula is modified slightly for a prediction interval. The number 1 (one) is placed under the radical and the formula becomes:

$$Y' \pm t(s_{y \cdot x}) \sqrt{1 + \frac{1}{n} + \frac{(X - \overline{X})^2}{\Sigma X^2 - \frac{(\Sigma X)^2}{n}}} \qquad [12-9]$$

The Relationship Among Various Measures of Association

The standard error of estimate measures how closely the actual values of Y are to the predicted values of Y'. When the values are close together the standard error is "small." When they are spread out, the standard error will be large. In the calculation of the standard error, the key term is:

$$\Sigma(Y - Y')^2$$

When this term is small, the standard error is also small.

Recall that the coefficient of correlation measured the strength of the association between two variables. When the points on a scatter diagram are close to a straight line, the correlation coefficient tends to be "large." Thus the standard error and the coefficient of correlation reflect the same information but use a different scale to report it. The standard error is in the same units as the dependent variable. The correlation coefficient has a range of -1.00 to $+1.00$.

The *coefficient of determination* also reports the strength of the association.

Coefficient of determination: The proportion of the total variation in the dependent variable Y that is explained or accounted for, by the variation in the independent variable X.

It is the square of the correlation coefficient and has a range 0.00 to 1.00.

A convenient means of showing the relationships among these measures is an ANOVA Table. This is similar to the table developed in the previous chapter. The total variation $\Sigma(Y - \overline{Y})^2$ is divided into two components.

1. The component explained by the regression.
2. The error or unexplained variation.

These two categories are identified in the source column of the following ANOVA table. The column headed *DF* refers to the degrees of freedom associated with each category. The total degrees of freedom is $(n-1)$. The degrees of freedom in the regression is 1 because there is one independent variable. The degrees of freedom associated with the error term is $(n-2)$. The term SS, located in the middle of the table, refers to the variation. These terms are computed as follows:

$$\text{Total variation} \;=\; \text{SS total} \;=\; \Sigma\left(Y-\overline{Y}\right)^{2}$$

$$\text{Error variation} \;=\; \text{SSE} \;=\; \Sigma\left(Y-Y'\right)^{2}$$

$$\text{Regression} \;=\; \text{SSR} \;=\; \Sigma\left(Y'-\overline{Y}\right)^{2}$$

Analysis of Variance

The format for the ANOVA table is:

Source	DF	SS	MS
Regression	1	SSR	SSR/1
Error	n – 2	SSE	SSE/(n – 2)
Total	n – 1	SS total*	

*SS total = SSR + SSE

The coefficient of determination, r^2 can be computed directly from the ANOVA table.

$$r^{2} = \frac{SSR}{SS\,\text{total}} = 1 - \frac{SSE}{SS\,\text{total}} \qquad [12-11]$$

Note that as SSE decreases r^2 increases. The coefficient of correlation is the square root of this value. Hence, both of these values are related to SSE. The standard error of estimate is obtained using the following equation.

$$s_{yx} = \sqrt{\frac{SSE}{n-2}} \qquad [12-12]$$

Note again the role played by the SSE term. A small value of SSE will result in a small standard error of estimate.

Glossary

Correlation analysis: A group of techniques used to measure the strength of the association between two variables.

Scatter diagram: A chart that portrays the relationship between variables.

Dependent variable: The variable that is being predicted or estimated.

Independent variable: A variable that provides the basis for estimation. It is the predictor variable.

Coefficient of correlation: A measure of the strength of the linear relationship between two sets of variables.

Regression equation: An equation that defines the relationship between two variables.

Least squares principle: An equation determined by minimizing the sum of the squares of the vertical distances between the actual Y values and the predicted values of Y'.

Standard error of estimate: A measure of the scatter, or dispersion, of the observed values around the line of regression.

Coefficient of determination: The proportion of the total variation in the dependent variable Y that is explained or accounted for, by the variation in the independent variable X.

Chapter Problems

Problem 1

It is believed that the annual repair cost for the sporty automobile Glockenspiel is related to its age. A sample of 10 automobiles revealed the results in the table at the right.

Repair Cost (in dollars) Y	Age (in years) X
$72	2
99	3
65	1
138	7
170	6
140	8
114	4
83	1
101	2
110	5

a. Plot these data in a scatter diagram. Does it appear there is a relationship between repair cost and age?

b. Compute the coefficient of correlation.

c. Determine at the 0.05 significance level whether the correlation in the population is greater than zero.

Solution

a. The repair cost is the dependent variable and is plotted along the Y-axis. Age is the independent variable and is plotted along the X-axis. To plot the first point, move horizontally on the X-axis to 2 and then go vertically to 72 on the Y-axis and place a dot. This procedure is continued until all paired data are plotted. Note that it appears there is a positive relationship between the two variables. That is, as X, the age of the automobile increases, so does the repair cost. But, the relationship is not perfect as evidenced by the scatter of dots.

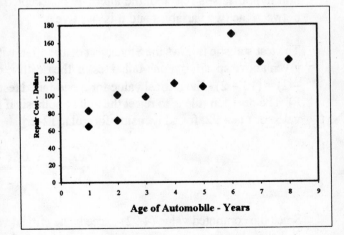

b. The degree of association between age and repair cost is measured by the coefficient of correlation. It is computed by formula [12-1].

$$r = \frac{n(\Sigma XY) - (\Sigma X)(\Sigma Y)}{\sqrt{\left[n(\Sigma X^2) - (\Sigma X)^2\right]\left[n(\Sigma Y^2) - (\Sigma Y)^2\right]}}$$

The calculations in the following table are needed to compute the various totals and squared totals.

The totals are inserted into the formula and the value of r computed:

$$r = \frac{10(4,903) - (39)(1,092)}{\sqrt{\left[10(209) - (39)^2\right]\left[10(128,940) - (1,092)^2\right]}}$$

$$= \frac{6,442}{\sqrt{[569][96,936]}} = 0.867$$

Y	X	XY	X^2	Y^2
72	2	144	4	5,184
99	3	297	9	9,801
65	1	65	1	4,225
138	7	966	49	19,044
170	6	1,020	36	28,900
140	8	1,120	64	19,600
114	4	456	16	12,996
83	1	83	1	6,889
101	2	202	4	10,201
110	5	550	25	12,100
1,092	39	4,903	209	128,940

Recall that 0 indicates no correlation and 1.00 perfect correlation. The r of 0.867 suggests a strong positive correlation between the age of this sports car and annual repair costs. As the age of the car increases so does the annual repair cost.

c. The coefficient of determination is the square of the coefficient of correlation. It is 0.752, found by $(0.867)^2$. This value indicates that 75.2 percent of the variation in repair costs can be explained by the variation in the age of the car.

A test of hypothesis is used to determine if the correlation in the population could be zero. In this instance, suppose we want to show that there is a positive association between the variables. Recall that the Greek letter ρ refers to the correlation in the population. The null and alternate hypotheses are written as follows:

$$H_0 : \rho \leq 0$$
$$H_1 : \rho > 0$$

If the null hypothesis is not rejected, it indicates that the correlation in the population could be zero. If the null hypothesis is rejected, the alternate is accepted. This indicates there is correlation in the population between the two variables and it is positive.

The test statistic follows the Student's t distribution with $(n - 2)$ degrees of freedom. The alternate hypothesis given above specifies a one-tailed test in the positive direction. There are 8 degrees of freedom, found by $(n - 2) = (10 - 2)$. The critical value for a one-tailed test using the 0.05 significance level is 1.860 (Appendix F). The decision rule is to reject the null hypothesis if the computed value of t exceeds 1.860. The computed value of t is 4.92, found by using formula [12-2.]

$$t = \frac{r\sqrt{n-2}}{\sqrt{1-r^2}} = \frac{0.867\sqrt{10-2}}{\sqrt{1-(0.867)^2}} = 4.92$$

Since the computed value (4.92) exceeds the critical value of t, namely 1.860, the null hypothesis is rejected and the alternate accepted. It is concluded that there is a positive association between the age of the automobile and the annual repair cost. The p-value is less than 0.005.

Exercise 12.1

Check your answers against those in the ANSWER section.

A major oil company is studying the relationship between the daily traffic count and the number of gallons of gasoline pumped at company stations. A sample of eight company owned stations is selected and the following information obtained:

Location	Total Gallons of Gas Pumped (000)	Traffic count (hundreds of cars)
West St.	120	4
Willouhby St.	180	6
Mallard Rd.	140	5
Pheasant Rd.	150	5
I-75	210	8
Kinzua Rd.	100	3
Front St.	90	3
Indiana Ave.	80	2

a. Develop a scatter diagram with the amount of gasoline pumped as the dependent variable.

b. Compute the coefficient of correlation

c. Compute the coefficient of determination.

d. Interpret the meaning of the coefficient of determination.

e. Test to determine whether the correlation in the population is zero, versus the alternate hypothesis that the correlation is greater than zero. Use the 0.05 significance level.

Problem 2

In Problem 1 we examined the relationship between the annual repair cost of the Glockenspiel and its age. The correlation between the two variables was 0.867, which we considered to be a strong relationship. We conducted a test of hypothesis and concluded that the relationship between the two variables in the population was greater than zero. The same sample data is repeated below.

Repair Cost (in dollars)	Age (in years)
72	2
99	3
65	1
138	7
170	6
140	8
114	4
83	1
101	2
110	5

a. Use the least squares principle to determine the regression equation.

b. Compute the standard error of estimate.

c. Develop a 95 percent confidence interval for the mean repair cost for all 4-year-old Glockenspiels.

d. Develop a 95 percent prediction interval for the repair cost for Ms. Paul's 4-year-old Glockenspiel.

Chapter 12

Solution

a. The first step is to compute the regression equation. The following calculations are needed.

Y	X	XY	X^2	Y^2
72	2	144	4	5,184
99	3	297	9	9,801
65	1	65	1	4,225
138	7	966	49	19,044
170	6	1,020	36	28,900
140	8	1,120	64	19,600
114	4	456	16	12,996
83	1	83	1	6,889
101	2	202	4	10,201
110	5	550	25	12,100
1,092	39	4,903	209	128,940

Substituting these values into formula [12-4] for b and formula [12-5] for a:

$$b = \frac{n(\Sigma XY) - (\Sigma X)(\Sigma Y)}{n(\Sigma X^2) - (\Sigma X)^2} = \frac{10(4,903) - (39)(1,092)}{10(209) - (39)^2} = \frac{6,442}{569} = 11.32$$

$$a = \frac{\Sigma Y}{n} - b\left(\frac{\Sigma X}{n}\right) = \frac{1,092}{10} - 11.32\left(\frac{39}{10}\right) = 65.05$$

Thus, the regression equation is:

$$Y' = a + bX = 65.05 + 11.32X \text{ (in dollars)}$$

Interpreting, repair costs can be expected to increase $11.32 a year on the average. Stated differently, the repair cost of a 4-year-old Glockenspiel can be expected to cost $11.32 more a year than a 3-year-old Glockenspiel.

b. The standard error of estimate is a measure of the dispersion about the regression line. It is similar to the standard deviation in that it uses squared differences. The differences between the value of Y' and Y are squared and summed over all n observations and then divided by $n-2$. Then find the positive square root of this value. A small value for the standard error of estimate indicates a close association between the dependent and independent variable. The standard error is measured in the same units as the dependent variable. The symbol for the standard error of estimate is $s_{y \cdot x}$.

The standard error is computed using formula [12-7].

$$s_{y \cdot x} = \sqrt{\frac{\Sigma Y^2 - a\Sigma Y - b\Sigma XY}{n-2}} = \sqrt{\frac{128,940 - 65.05(1,092) - 11.32(4,903)}{10-2}} = 17.33$$

c. The regression equation is used to estimate the repair cost of a 4-year-old Glockenspiel. The value of 4 is inserted for X in the equation.

$$Y' = 65.05 + 11.32X$$
$$= 65.05 + 11.32(4)$$
$$= 110.33 \text{ (in dollars)}$$

Thus the expected repair cost for a 4-year-old Glockenspiel is $110.33.

Formula [12-8] is used if we want to develop a 95 percent confidence interval for all four-year-old Glockenspiels.

$$Y' \pm t\left(s_{yx}\right)\sqrt{\frac{1}{n} + \frac{\left(X - \overline{X}\right)^2}{\Sigma X^2 - \frac{(\Sigma X)^2}{n}}}$$

The necessary information for the formula is:

Y' is 110.33 as previously computed.

t is 2.306. There are ($n - 2$) degrees of freedom, or ($n - 2$) = (10 - 2) = 8. From Appendix F, using a two-tailed test and the 0.05 significance level, move down the 0.05 column to 8 df and read the value of t.

n is 10. It is the sample size.

s_{yx} is $17.33, as computed in an earlier section of this problem.

X is 4, the age of the Glockenspiel.

$\overline{X}$ is the mean age of the sampled cars. It is 3.9, found by $\overline{X} = 39/10$.

ΣX is 39, found from the earlier computation in part a.

ΣX^2 is 209, also used in earlier calculations in part a.

Solving for the 95 percent confidence interval:

$$Y' \pm t\left(s_{yx}\right)\sqrt{\frac{1}{n} + \frac{\left(X - \overline{X}\right)^2}{\Sigma X^2 - \frac{(\Sigma X)^2}{n}}} = \$110.33 \pm 2.306(\$17.33)\sqrt{\frac{1}{10} + \frac{(4 - 3.9)^2}{209 - \frac{(39)^2}{10}}}$$

$$= \$110.33 \pm \$12.65$$
$$= \$97.68 \text{ to } \$122.98$$

The 95 percent confidence interval for the mean amount spent on repairs to a 4-year-old Glockenspiel is between $97.68 and $122.98. About 95 percent of the similarly constructed intervals would include the population value.

d.   Recall that Ms. Paul owns a 4-year-old Glockenspiel. The 95 percent prediction interval for her repair costs is computed as follows using formula [12-9].

$$Y' \pm t\left(s_{y \cdot x}\right)\sqrt{1+\frac{1}{n}+\frac{\left(X-\overline{X}\right)^2}{\Sigma X^2 - \frac{\left(\Sigma X\right)^2}{n}}} = \$110.33 \pm 2.306(\$17.33)\sqrt{1+\frac{1}{10}+\frac{\left(4-3.9\right)^2}{209-\frac{\left(39\right)^2}{10}}}$$

$$= \$110.33 \pm \$41.92$$

$$= \$68.41 \text{ to } \$152.25$$

Interpreting we would conclude that Ms. Paul will spend between $68.41 and $152.25 on repairs this year to her four-year-old Glockenspiel. About 95 percent of the similarly constructed intervals would include the population value.

Exercise 12.2

Check your answers against those in the ANSWER section.

In Exercise 1 we studied the relationship between the gasoline pumped in thousands of gallons, and the traffic count at eight company owned stations. The data are repeated below:

Location	Total Gallons of Gas Pumped (000)	Traffic count (hundreds of cars)
West St.	120	4
Willouhby St.	180	6
Mallard Rd.	140	5
Pheasant Rd.	150	5
I-75	210	8
Kinzua Rd.	100	3
Front St.	90	3
Indiana Ave.	80	2

a. Compute the regression equation.

b. Compute the standard error of estimate.

c. Develop a 95 percent confidence interval for the mean amount of gasoline pumped for all stations where the traffic count is 4.

d. Develop a 95 percent prediction interval for the amount of gasoline pumped at the station at Dowling Rd. and I-60, which has a count of 4 (actually 400 cars).

Problem 3

Use the information from Problem 1 to:

a. Develop an ANOVA Table.

b. Compute the coefficient of determination.

c. Compute the coefficient of correlation.

d. Compute the standard error of estimate.

Solution

a. The MINITAB System was used to develop the following output.

Analysis of Variance

SOURCE	DF	SS	MS
Regression	1	7,293.4	7,293.4
Error	8	2,400.2	300.0
Total	9	9,693.6	

b. The coefficient of determination is computed as follows.

$$r^2 = \frac{SSR}{SS\,Total} = \frac{7293.4}{9693.6} = 0.752 \ \ OR \ \ r^2 = \left(1 - \frac{SSE}{SS\,Total}\right) = \left(1 - \frac{2,400.2}{9,693.6}\right) = (1 - 0.248) = 0.752$$

c. The correlation coefficient is 0.867, found by taking the square root of 0.752. These two coefficients 0867 and 0.752) are the same as computed earlier.

d. The standard error of estimate is computed by:

$$s_{y \cdot x} = \sqrt{\frac{SSE}{n-2}} = \sqrt{\frac{2,400.2}{10-2}} = 17.32$$

Note again the role played by the SSE term. A small value of SSE will result in a small standard error of estimate.

Exercise 12.3

Check your answers against those in the ANSWER section.

Refer to Exercise 1, regarding the relationship between the amount of gasoline pumped and the traffic count. The following output was obtained from MINITAB.

Analysis of Variance

SOURCE	DF	SS	MS
Regression	1	14,078	14,078
Error	6	310	51.67
Total	7	14,388	

a. Compute the coefficient of determination.

b. Compute the coefficient of correlation.

c. Compute the standard error of estimate.

Chapter 12

CHAPTER 12 ASSIGNMENT

LINEAR REGRESSION AND CORRELATION

Name _____ Section _____ Score_____

Part I   Select the correct answer and write the appropriate letter in the space provided.

_____ 1. Which of the following statements is **not** correct regarding the coefficient of correlation.
   a. It can range from −1 to 1.
   b. Its square is the coefficient of determination.
   c. It measures the percent of variation explained.
   d. It is a measure of the association between two variables.

_____ 2. The coefficient of determination
   a. is usually written as r^2.
   b. cannot be negative.
   c. is the square of the coefficient of correlation.
   d. all of the above.

_____ 3. The coefficient of correlation was computed to be −0.60. This means
   a. the coefficient of determination is $\sqrt{0.6}$.
   b. as X increase Y decreases.
   c. X and Y are both 0.
   d. as X decreases Y decreases.

_____ 4. Which of the following is a stronger correlation than −0.54?
   a. 0.67   b. 0.45
   c. 0.0   d. −0.45

_____ 5. A regression equation is used to
   a. measure the association between two variables.
   b. estimate the value of the dependent variable based on the independent variable.
   c. estimate the value of the independent variable based on the dependent variable.
   d. estimate the coefficient of determination.

_____ 6. A regression equation was computed to be $Y' = 35 + 6X$. The value of the 35 indicates that
   a. the regression line crosses the Y axis at 35.
   b. the coefficient of correlation is 35.
   c. the coefficient of determination is 35.
   d. an increase of one unit in X will result in an increase of 35 in Y.

_____ 7. The standard error of estimate
   a. is a measure of the variation around the regression line.
   b. cannot be negative.
   c. is in the same units as the dependent variable.
   d. all of the above.

_____ 8. The variable plotted on the horizontal or X-axis in a scatter diagram is called the
      a.   scatter variable.
      b.   independent variable.
      c.   dependent variable.
      d.   correlation variable.

_____ 9. The least squares principle means that
      a. $\Sigma(Y - Y')^2 = 0$.
      b. $\Sigma(Y - \overline{Y})^2$ is maximized.
      c. $\Sigma(Y - Y')^2$ is minimized.
      d. $\Sigma(Y - \overline{Y})^2$ is minimized.

_____ 10. If all the points are on the regression line, then
      a.   the value of b is 0.
      b.   the value of a is 0.
      c.   the correlation coefficient is 0.
      d.   the standard error of estimate is 0.

Part II   Record your answers in the space provided. Show all essential work.

11. The correlation between the number of police on the street and the number of crimes committed, for a sample of 15 comparable sized cities, is 0.45. At the 0.05 significance level is there a positive association in the population between the two variables?

    a.   State the null and alternate hypotheses.

        H_0: _____

        H_1: _____

    b.   State the decision rule.

        _____

    c.   Compute the value of the test statistic.

                                                                         c.

    d.   What is your decision regarding the null hypothesis? Interpret the result.

        _____

12. A study is conducted concerning automobile speeds and fuel consumption rates. The following data is collected:

Speed	45	52	49	60	67	61
MPG	22	26	21	28	33	32

a. Compute the coefficient of correlation.

a. _____

b. Determine at the 0.05 significance level whether the correlation in the population is greater than zero.

b. _____

13. Tem Rousos, president of Rousos Ford, believes there is a relationship between the number of new cars sold and the number of sales people on duty. To investigate he selects a sample of eight weeks and determines the number of new cars sold and the number of sales people on duty for that week.

Week	Sales staff	Cars sold
1	5	53
2	5	47
3	7	48
4	4	50
5	10	58
6	12	62
7	3	45
8	11	60

a. Determine the coefficient of correlation.

a. _____

b. Determine the coefficient of determination. Comment on the strength of the association between the two variables.

b. _____

c. Determine the regression equation.

c.

d. Interpret the regression equation. Where does the equation cross the Y-axis? How many additional cars can the dealer expect to sell for each additional salesperson employed?

_____

_____

_____

e. Determine the standard error of estimate.

e.

f. Develop a 95 percent confidence interval for all the mean car sales for weeks when the sales staff is at 10.

f.

g. In checking the work schedules for next week, Tem finds there are 10 people scheduled. Develop a 95 percent prediction interval for the number of cars sold next week.

g.

CHAPTER 13
MULTIPLE REGRESSION AND CORRELATION ANALYSIS

Chapter Goals

After completing this chapter, you will be able to:

1. Describe the relationship between several independent variables and a dependent variable using a multiple regression equation.

2. Compute and interpret the multiple standard error of estimate and the coefficient of determination.

3. Interpret a correlation matrix.

4. Setup and interpret an ANOVA table.

5. Conduct a test of hypothesis to determine whether regression coefficients differ from zero.

6. Conduct a test of hypothesis on each of the regression coefficients.

Introduction

In the last chapter we began our study of regression and correlation analysis. However, the methods presented considered only the relationship between one dependent variable and one independent variable. The possible effect of other independent variables was ignored. For example, we described how the repair cost of a car was related to the age of the car. Are there other factors that affect the repair cost? Does the size of the engine or the number of miles driven affect the repair cost? When several independent variables are used to estimate the value of the dependent variable it is called *multiple regression*.

> *Multiple Regression*: A set of techniques used to analyze the relationship between two or more independent variables and a dependent variable.

Multiple Regression Analysis

Recall that for one independent variable, the linear regression equation [12-3] from the text, has the form:

$$Y' = a + bX$$

For more than one independent variable, the equation is extended to include the additional variables. For two independent variables we use text formula [13-1]:

$$Y' = a + b_1 X_1 + b_2 X_2 \qquad [13-1]$$

Where:

X_1 is one of the independent variables.

X_2 is the second independent variable.

a is the $Y-$intercept, the point of intercept with the $Y-$axis.

b_1 is the net change in Y for each unit change in X_1, holding X_2 constant.

b_2 is the net change in Y for each unit change in X_2, holding X_1 constant.

The values of b_1, and b_2 are called the **net regression coefficients** or just **regression coefficients**. They indicate the change in the estimated value of the dependent variable for a unit change in one of the independent variables, when the other independent variables are held constant.

This equation can be extended for any number of independent variables.

For example, suppose the National Sales Manager of General Motors wants to analyze regional sales using the number of autos registered in the region (X_1), the average age of the automobiles registered in the region (X_2), and the personal income in the region (X_3). Some of the sample information obtained is:

Region	Sales ($ millions)	Number of autos in region (000)	Average age of autos (years)	Personal Income in Region (billions)
	Y	X_1	X_2	X_3
I	$9.2	842	5.6	$29.5
II	46.8	2,051	5.1	182.6
III	26.2	1,010	5.8	190.7

Suppose the multiple regression equation was computed to be:

$$Y' = a + b_1 X_1 + b_2 X_2 + b_3 X_3$$
$$= 41.0 + 0.0071 X_1 + (-3.19) X_2 + 0.01611 X_3$$

In April of this year the automobile registration bureau announced that in a particular region 1,542,000 autos were registered, and their average age was 6.0 years. Another agency announced that personal income in the region was $150 billion. The sales manager could then estimate, as early as April, annual sales for this year by inserting the value of these independent variables in the equation and solving for Y'

$$Y' = a + b_1 X_1 + b_2 X_2 + b_3 X_3$$
$$= 41.0 + 0.0071(1,542) - 3.19(6.0) + 0.01611(150)$$
$$= \$35.2 \text{ million}$$

What is the meaning of the regression coefficients? The 0.0071 associated with number of autos in the region (in thousands) indicates that for each additional 1,000 autos sold, sales will increase 0.0071 (million), if the other independent variables are held constant. That is, the regression coefficients show change in the dependent variable when the other independent variables are not allowed to change.

Multiple Standard Error of Estimate

It is likely that there is some error in the estimation. This can be measured by the *multiple standard error of estimate*.

> *Multiple standard error of estimate*: Measures the error in the predicted dependent variable.

Like the standard error of estimate described in the previous chapter, it is based on the squared deviations between Y and Y'. Text formula [13-4] is used.

$$s_{y \cdot 12 \cdots k} = \sqrt{\frac{\Sigma(Y - Y')^2}{n - (k+1)}} \qquad [13-4]$$

Where:
Y is the observation.
Y' is the value estimated from the regression equation.
n is the number of observations in the sample.
k is the number of independent variables.
$s_{y \cdot 12 \cdots k}$ is the standard error of estimate. The subscripts indicate the number of independent variables being used to estimate the value of Y.

Assumptions About Multiple Regression and Correlation

As noted in previous chapters, it is generally considered good practice to identify the assumptions related to a topic because if the assumptions are not met fully, the results might be biased. There are six assumptions that must be met in multiple correlation.

1. The independent variables and the dependent variables must have a linear relationship.

2. The dependent variable is continuous and at least interval scale.

3. The variation in the difference between the actual value of the dependent variable and the predicted value is the same for all fitted values of Y. That is, $(Y - Y')$ must be approximately the same for all values of Y'. For example, the $(Y - Y')$ term cannot have a tendency to be larger when Y' is large. The $(Y - Y')$ term is called the residual.

> *Residual*: The difference between the actual and the predicted value of the dependent variable.

When the differences are the same for all fitted values they exhibit homoscedasticity.

> *Homoscedasticity*: The residuals are the same for all estimated values of the dependent variable.

4. The residuals should be approximately normally distributed with a mean of zero. The standard error of estimate is a measure of the dispersion of this distribution.

5. Successive observations of the dependent variable are uncorrelated. Violation of this assumption is called **autocorrelation**.

> **Autocorrelation**: Successive observations of the dependent variable are correlated.

Autocorrelation frequently occurs when the data are collected over successive periods of time.

6. The set of independent variables should not be highly correlated.

> **Multicollinearity**: Correlation among the independent variables.

Seldom in a real world example are all of the conditions fully met. However, the technique of regression still works effectively. If there is concern regarding the violation of one or more of the assumptions, it is suggested that a more advanced statistics book be consulted.

The ANOVA Table

A convenient means of showing the regression output is to use an ANOVA table. This table was first described in Chapter 11 and also mentioned in Chapter 12. The variation in the dependent variable is separated into two components: (1) that explained by the **regression**, that is, the independent variable and (2) the **error** or unexplained variation.

These two categories are identified in the source column of the following ANOVA table. The column headed "DF" refers to the degrees of freedom associated with each category. The total degrees of freedom is $(n-1)$.

The degrees of freedom for regression is k, the number of independent variables. The degrees of freedom associated with the error term is $n-(k+1)$. The SS in the middle of the top row of the ANOVA table refers to the sum of squares, or the variation.

$$\text{Total variation} = SS\,total = \Sigma\left(Y - \overline{Y}\right)^2$$

$$\text{Error variation} = SSE = \Sigma(Y - Y')^2$$

$$\text{Regression variation} = SSR = \left(SS\,Total - SSE\right)$$

The column headed MS refers to the mean square and is obtained by dividing the SS term by the DF term. Thus, MSR, the mean square regression, is equal to SSR/k, and MSE equals SSE/$[n-(k+1)]$. The general format of the ANOVA table is:

Analysis of Variance

Source	DF	SS	MS	F
Regression	k	SSR	MSR = SSR/k	MSR / MSE
Error	$n - (k+1)$	SSE	MSE = SSE/$[n - (k+1)]$	
Total	$n-1$	SS total		

Another measure of the effectiveness of the regression equation is the **coefficient of multiple determination**.

> **Coefficient of multiple determination**: The proportion of the variation in the dependent variable that is explained by the variation in the independent variables.

The coefficient of multiple determination, written R^2, may range from 0 to 1.0. It is the fraction of the variation explained by the regression. The ANOVA table is used to calculate the coefficient of multiple determination. It is the sum of squares due to the regression divided by the sum of squares total.

$$R^2 = \frac{SSR}{SS\,total}$$

In the Automobile Sales example, if the coefficient of multiple determination were 0.81, it would indicate that the three independent variables, considered jointly, explain 81 percent of the variation in millions of sales dollars.

The multiple standard error of estimate may also be found directly from the ANOVA table.

$$s_{y \cdot 12 \cdots k} = \sqrt{\frac{SSE}{n - (k + 1)}}$$

Global Test: Testing Whether the Multiple Regression Model is Valid

The overall ability of the independent variables $X_1, X_2, \ldots X_k$, to explain the behavior of the dependent variable Y can be tested. Two tests of hypotheses are considered in this chapter. The first one is called the *global test*.

> **Global test**: A test used to investigate whether all the independent variables have zero net regression coefficients

It tests the overall ability of the set of independent variables to explain differences in the dependent variable. The null hypothesis is that the net regression coefficients in the population are all zero. If accepted, it would imply that the set of coefficients is of no value in explaining differences in the dependent variable. The alternate hypothesis is that *at least* one of the coefficients is not zero. This test is written in symbolic form for three independent variables as:

$$H_0: \beta_1 = \beta_2 = \beta_3 = 0$$
$$H_1: \text{Not all the } \beta \text{'s are } 0$$

Rejecting H_0 and accepting H_1 implies that one or more of the independent variables is useful in explaining differences in the dependent variable. However, a word of caution, it does not suggest how many or identify which regression coefficients are not zero.

The test statistic used is the F distribution, which was first described in Chapter 10, the ANOVA chapter. To employ the F distribution, two sets of degrees of freedom are required. The degrees of freedom for the numerator are equal to k, the number of independent variables. The degrees of freedom in the denominator are equal to $n - (k + 1)$ where n refers, as usual, to the total number of observations.

Chapter 13

Evaluating Individual Regression Coefficients

The second test of hypothesis identifies which of the set of independent variables are significant predictors of the dependent variable. That is, it tests the independent variables individually rather than as a unit. This test is useful because unimportant variables can be eliminated.

The test statistic is the Student t distribution with $n - (k + 1)$ degrees of freedom. For example, suppose we want to test whether the second independent variable was zero or greater, versus the alternate that it was less than zero. The null and alternate hypotheses would be written as follows.

$$H_0: \beta_2 \geq 0$$
$$H_1: \beta_2 < 0$$

Rejection of the null hypothesis and acceptance of the alternate hypothesis would imply that variable number two is significant and that its sign is negative.

Qualitative Independent Variables

The variables used in regression analysis must be *quantitative variables.*.

> *Quantitative variable*: A numeric variable that is at least interval scale.

Recall that a quantitative variable is a variable that is numerical in nature. However, frequently we want to use variables that are not numeric, such as gender, whether a home has a computer, or whether an answer is yes or no. These variables are called *qualitative variables*.

> *Qualitative variable*: A nonnumeric variable.

Qualitative variables are also called *dummy variables* or indicator variables.

> *Dummy variable*: A variable in which there are only two possible outcomes. For analysis one of the outcomes is coded a 1 and the other outcome is coded 0.

For example, we are interested in estimating the selling price of a used automobile based on its age. Selling price is the dependent variable and age is one independent variable. Another variable is whether or not the car was manufactured in the United States. Note that a particular car can assume only two conditions: either it was built in the U. S. or it was not. To employ a qualitative variable a 0 or 1 coding scheme is used. In the study regarding estimated selling prices of used automobiles, those made in the U.S. are coded 1 and all others as 0.

Analysis of Residuals

We described the assumptions for regression and correlation analysis as:

1. There is a linear relationship between the dependent variable and the independent variables
2. The dependent variable must be continuous and at least interval scale or ratio scale.
3. Successive observations of the dependent variable are not correlated.

4. The residuals, the difference between actual values and the estimated values, are normally distributed.

5. The variation in the residuals is the same for all fitted values of Y'. That is the distribution of $(Y - Y')$ is the same for all values of Y'.

The last two assumptions can be verified by plotting the residuals. We want to confirm that the residuals follow a normal distribution and that the residuals have the same variation whether the Y' value is large or small.

Glossary

Multiple Regression: A set of techniques used to analyze the relationship between two or more independent variables and a dependent variable.

Multiple standard error of estimate: Measures the error in the predicted dependent variable.

Residual: The difference between the actual and the predicted value of the dependent variable.

Homoscedasticity: The residuals are the same for all estimated values of the dependent variable.

Autocorrelation: Successive observations of the dependent variable are correlated.

Multicollinearity: Correlation among the independent variables.

Coefficient of multiple determination: The proportion of the variation in the dependent variable that is explained by variation in the independent variables.

Global test: A test used to investigate whether all of the independent variables have zero net regression coefficients.

Quantitative variable: A numeric variable that is at least interval scale.

Qualitative variable: A nonnumeric variable.

Dummy variable: A variable in which there are only two possible outcomes. For analysis one of the outcomes is coded a 1 and the other outcome is coded 0.

Chapter Problems

Problem 1

The Skaff Appliance Company currently has over 1,000 retail outlets throughout the United States and Canada. They sell name brand electronic products, such as TVs, stereos, VCRs, and microwave ovens. Skaff Appliance is considering opening several additional stores in other large metropolitan areas. Paul Skaff, president, would like to study the relationship between the sales at existing locations and several factors regarding the existing store or its region. The factors are the population and the unemployment in the region, and the advertising expense of the store. Another variable considered is "mall." Mall refers to whether the existing store is located in an enclosed shopping mall or not. A "1" indicates a mall location; a "0" indicates the store is not located in a mall. A random sample of 30 stores is selected.

Sales (000)	Population (000,000)	Percent Unemployed	Advertising Expense (000)	Mall Location
5.17	7.50	5.1	59.0	0
5.78	8.71	6.3	62.5	0
4.84	10.00	4.7	61.0	0
6.00	7.45	5.4	61.0	1
6.00	8.67	5.4	61.0	1
6.12	11.00	7.2	12.5	0
6.40	13.18	5.8	35.8	0
7.10	13.81	5.8	59.9	0
8.50	14.43	6.2	57.2	1
7.50	10.00	5.5	35.8	0
9.30	13.21	6.8	27.9	0
8.80	17.10	6.2	24.1	1
9.96	15.12	6.3	27.7	1
9.83	18.70	0.5	24.0	0
10.12	20.20	5.5	57.2	1
10.70	15.00	5.8	44.3	0
10.45	17.60	7.1	49.2	0
11.32	19.80	7.5	23.0	0
11.87	14.40	8.2	62.7	1
11.91	20.35	7.8	55.8	0
12.60	18.90	6.2	50.0	0
12.60	21.60	7.1	47.6	1
14.24	25.25	0.4	43.5	0
14.41	27.50	4.2	55.9	0
13.73	21.00	0.7	51.2	1
13.73	19.70	6.4	76.6	1
13.80	24.15	0.5	63.0	1
14.92	17.65	8.5	68.1	0
15.28	22.30	7.1	74.4	1
14.41	24.00	0.8	70.1	0

Use the MINITAB system output to:

a. Determine which independent variable has the strongest correlation with sales.
b. Comment on multicollinearity.
c. Conduct a test of hypothesis to determine if any of the regression coefficients are not equal to zero.

Solution

The first step is to determine the correlation matrix. It shows all possible simple coefficients of correlation. The MINITAB output is as follows:

```
          Sales    Popul    %-unemp    Adv
Popul     0.894
%-unemp   -0.198   -0.368
Adv        0.279    0.125    -0.030
Mall       0.155    0.085     0.017    0.259
```

a. Sales is the dependent variable. Of particular interest is which independent variable has the strongest correlation with sales. In this case it is population (0.894). The negative sign between sales and %-unemp indicates that as the unemployment rate increases, sales decrease.

b. A second use of the correlation matrix is to check for multicollinearity. Multicollinearity can distort the standard error of estimate and lead to incorrect conclusions regarding which independent variables are significant. The strongest correlation among the independent variables is between %-unemp and popul (−0.368). A rule of thumb is that a correlation between −0.70 and 0.70 will not cause problems and can be ignored. At this point it does not appear there is a problem with multicollinearity.

c. We want to test the overall ability of the set of independent variables to explain the behavior of the dependent variable. Do the independent variables, population, percent unemployed, advertising expense, and mall explain a significant amount of the variation in sales? This question can be answered by conducting a global test of the regression coefficients. The null and alternate hypotheses are

$$H_0: \beta_1 = \beta_2 = \beta_3 = \beta_4 = 0$$
$$H_1: \text{At least one of the } \beta\text{'s is not zero.}$$

The null hypothesis states that the regression coefficients are all zero. If they are all zero, this indicates they are of no value in explaining differences in the sales of the various stores. If the null hypothesis is rejected and the alternate accepted the conclusion is that at least one of the regression coefficients is not zero. Hence, we would conclude that at least one of the variables is significant in terms of explaining difference in sales.

The F distribution introduced in Chapter 11 is used as the test statistic. The F distribution is based on the degrees of freedom in the numerator and in the denominator. The degrees of freedom associated with the regression, which is the numerator, is equal to the number of independent variables. In this case there are four independent variables, so there are 4 degrees of freedom in the numerator. The degrees of freedom in the error row is $n - (k + 1) = 30 - (4 + 1) = 25$. There are 25 degrees of freedom in the denominator. The critical value of F is obtained from Appendix G. Find the column with 4 degrees of freedom and the row with 25 degrees of freedom in the table for the 0.05 significance level. The value is 2.76. The null hypothesis is rejected if the computed F is greater than 2.76.

The output from MINITAB is as follows.

```
Analysis of Variance
Source        DF      SS        MS        F        P
Regression    4     270.461   67.615    34.71    0.000
Error         25     48.705    1.948
Total         29    319.166
```

The computed value of F is 34.71 as shown above. It is also computed as follows.

$$F = \frac{\dfrac{SSR}{k}}{\dfrac{SSE}{n-(k+1)}} = \frac{\dfrac{270.461}{4}}{\dfrac{48.705}{30-(4+1)}} = \frac{67.615}{1.948} = 34.71$$

Since the computed value of 34.71 exceeds the critical value of 2.76, the null hypothesis is rejected and the alternate accepted. The conclusion is that at least one of the regression coefficients does not equal zero.

Exercise 13.1

Check your answers against those in the ANSWER section.

Todd Heffren, President of Heffren Manufacturing Co., is studying the power usage at his Vanengo Plant. He believes that the amount of electrical power used is a function of the outside temperature during the day, and the number of units produced that day. A random sample of ten days is selected. The power usage in thousands of kilowatt hours of electricity and the production on that date is obtained. The National Weather Service is contacted to obtain the high temperature for the selected dates.

Power Used	Temperature (F)	Units Produced
12	83	120
11	79	110
13	85	128
9	75	101
14	87	105
10	81	108
12	84	110
11	77	107
14	85	112
11	84	119

The MINITAB system was used to compute a correlation matrix and ANOVA table for the Heffren Manufacturing Co. data.

```
              Usage      Temp
Temp          0.838
Output        0.361      0.506

Analysis of Variance
SOURCE       DF          SS          MS
Regression    2        17.069       8.534
Error         7         7.031       1.004
Total         9        24.100
```

a. Do you see any problems with multicollinearity?

b. Test the hypothesis that all the regression equations are zero. Use the 0.05 significance level.

Problem 2

In Problem 1 we found that at least one of the four independent variables had a regression coefficient different from zero.

a. Use the MINITAB system to aid in determining which of the regression coefficients is not equal to zero.
b. Would you consider deleting any of the independent variables?

Solution

The following output is from MINITAB.

The regression equation is:

Sales = $-1.67 + 0.552$ Popul $+ 0.203$ %-unemp $+ 0.0314$ Adv $+ 0.220$ Mall

Predictor	Coef	Stdev	t-ratio	p
Constant	-1.669	1.408	-1.18	0.247
Popul	0.55191	0.05063	10.90	0.000
%-unemp	0.2032	0.1171	1.74	0.095
Adv	0.03135	0.01606	1.95	0.062
Mall	0.2198	0.5400	0.41	0.687

s = 1.396   R-sq = 84.7%   R-sq(adj) = 82.3%

a. The four independent variables explain 84.7% of the variation in sales. For those coefficients where the null hypothesis that the regression coefficients are equal to zero cannot be rejected, we will consider eliminating them from the regression equation. We are actually conducting four tests of hypotheses

For Population	For % Unemployed	For Advertising	For Mall
$H_0: \beta_1 = 0$	$H_0: \beta_2 = 0$	$H_0: \beta_3 = 0$	$H_0: \beta_4 = 0$
$H_1: \beta_1 \neq 0$	$H_1: \beta_2 \neq 0$	$H_1: \beta_3 \neq 0$	$H_1: \beta_4 \neq 0$

We will use the 0.05 significance level and a two-tailed test. The test statistic is the t distribution with n − (k + 1) = 30 − (4 + 1) = 25 degrees of freedom. The decision rule is to reject the null hypothesis if the computed value of t is less than −2.060 or greater than 2.060.

From the MINITAB output, the column labeled "Coef" reports the regression coefficients. The "Stdev" column reports the standard deviation of the slope coefficients. The "t-ratio" column reports the computed value of the test statistic.

The t-ratio for population (10.90) exceeds the critical value, but the computed values for percent unemployed, (1.74) advertising expense (1.95), and mall (0.41) are not in the rejection region. This indicates that the independent variable population should be retained and the other three dropped.

b. However, there is a problem that occurs in many real situations. Note that both percent unemployed and advertising expense are close to being significant. In fact, advertising expense would be significant if we increased the level of significances to 0.10. (The critical value would be −1.708 and 1.708, and 1.95 is outside the critical region.) Another indicator of trouble is a reversal of a sign of the regression coefficient. Earlier in Problem 1, in the correlation matrix, the correlation between percent unemployed and sales was negative. Note, in the above regression equation the sign of the coefficient is positive. (The regression coefficient is 0.203). A reversal of a sign such as this is often an indication of multicollinearity. The earlier conclusion that there was not a problem in this area should be reviewed. Perhaps one or both of the independent variables—either advertising expense or percent unemployment-should be included in the regression equation.

Problem 3

The multiple regression and correlation data for Problem 2 were rerun using the two most significant variables –population and advertising expense

```
The regression equation is
Sales = - 0.08 + 0.521 Popul + 0.0335 Adv
```

Predictor	Coef	StDev	T	P
Constant	-0.079	1.086	-0.07	0.943
Popul	0.52075	0.04806	10.83	0.000
Adv	0.03347	0.001590	2.10	0.045

S = 1.428   R-Sq = 82.8%   R-Sq(adj) = 81.5%

Analysis of Variance

Source	DF	SS	MS	F	P
Regression	2	264.12	132.06	64.78	0.000
Error	27	55.05	2.04		
Total	29	319.17			

a. What is the new multiple regression equation?

b. What is the Y' value for the first store?

c. What is the coefficient of multiple determination? Interpret.

d. Do the residuals approximate a normal distribution?

e. Are the residuals constant for all fitted values of Y' ?

Solution

a. The regression equation is:
$$\text{Sales} = -0.08 + 0.521 \text{ Popul} + 0.0335 \text{ Adv}$$
$$Y' = -0.08 + 0.521 X_1 + 0.0335 X_3$$

b. Y' for the first store is found by substituting the value: $X_1 = 7.5$ and $X_3 = 59.0$ into the Y' equation.

$$Y' = -0.08 + 0.521 X_1 + 0.0335 X_3$$
$$= -0.08 + 0.521(7.5) + 0.0335(59) = 5.804$$

c. The coefficient of multiple determination is R-Sq on the printout. It is 82.8%. A total of 82.8% of the variation in sales is explained by the population and the advertising expense.

d. The MINITAB System was used to develop the fitted values of Y' and the residuals. The fitted values are obtained by substituting the actual values of population and advertising expense in the regression equation. For example, the first store was in a city having 7.5 million populations and advertising expense of 59.0 thousand dollars. We substituted these values in the regression equation and the estimated, or "fitted" values of Y' obtained was 5.804.

The residual is the difference between the actual and the predicted value. For the first store it is –0.634, found by $(Y - Y') = (5.17 - 5.804)$. The residuals are computed for the other 29 stores in a similar fashion. The MINITAB system will perform these time-consuming calculations for us, however the results are slightly different, due to rounding. For example, MINITAB estimates 5.8017 for the first store compared to our estimate of 5.804.

Chapter 13

Row	Sales Y	Fitted Y'	Residual $(Y - Y')$
1	5.17	5.8017	-0.63169
2	5.78	6.5489	-0.76894
3	4.84	7.1705	-2.33050
4	6.00	5.8426	0.15741
5	6.00	6.4779	-0.47790
6	6.12	6.0679	0.05213
7	6.40	7.9830	-1.58299
8	7.10	9.1177	-2.01773
9	8.50	9.3502	-0.85022
10	7.50	6.3270	1.17299
11	9.30	7.7342	1.56581
12	8.80	9.6327	-0.83270
13	9.96	8.7221	1.23788
14	9.83	10.4625	-0.63255
15	10.12	12.3549	-2.23493
16	10.70	9.2153	1.48474
17	10.45	10.7332	-0.28321
18	11.32	11.0019	0.31810
19	11.87	9.5187	2.35131
20	11.91	12.3862	-0.47618
21	12.60	11.4370	1.16304
22	12.60	12.7626	-0.16265
23	14.24	14.5261	-0.28614
24	14.41	16.1129	-1.70287
25	13.73	12.5707	1.15930
26	13.73	12.7439	0.98610
27	13.80	14.6060	-0.80601
28	14.92	11.3919	3.52814
29	15.28	14.0242	1.25579
30	14.41	14.7655	-0.35555

The residuals should approximate a normal distribution. The residuals from the right hand column above are organized into the following histogram. The shape seems to approximate the normal distribution.

```
Histogram of RESI1    N = 30
Midpoint     Count
    -2.5       1   *
    -2.0       2   **
    -1.5       2   **
    -1.0       4   ****
    -0.5       7   *******
     0.0       3   ***
     0.5       1   *
     1.0       5   *****
     1.5       3   ***
     2.0       0
     2.5       1   *
     3.0       0
     3.5       1
```

e. Another assumption, called homoscedasticity, requires that the residuals remain constant for all fitted values of Y'. A scatter diagram can be used to investigate. The horizontal axis is the fitted values, i.e., Y', and the vertical axis reflects the residuals. This assumption seems to be met, according to the following plot.

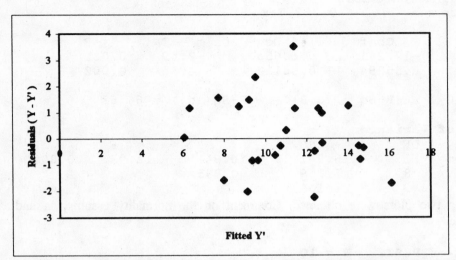

In summary, if Mr. Skaff wants to open new stores, the two variables that are the most effective in explaining differences in sales are the population in the surrounding area and the amount spent on advertising. The basic requirements for the use of regression analysis are met when these variables are used. The unemployment rate and whether or not the store is located in a mall are not important.

Exercise 13.3

Check your answers against those in the ANSWER section.

The multiple regression and correlation data for Exercise 1 and 2 were rerun using the most significant variable temperature. Use the MINITAB output shown on the next page to answer the following questions:

a. What is the new multiple regression equation?

b. What is the Y' value for the first item in the sample?

c. What is the coefficient of multiple determination? Interpret.

d. Do the residuals approximate a normal distribution?

e. Are the residuals constant for all fitted values of Y'?

continued on next page

Chapter 13

Using the independent variable temperature, the following regression equation was developed.

The regression equation is
Usage = - 17.2 + 0.353 Temp

Predictor	Coef	StDev	T	P
Constant	-17.241	6.658	-2.59	0.032
Temp	0.35294	0.08112	4.35	0.002

S = 0.9460   R-Sq = 70.3%   R-Sq(adj) = 66.6%

Analysis of Variance

Source	DF	SS	MS	F	P
Regression	1	16.941	16.941	18.93	0.002
Error	8	7.159	0.895		
Total	9	24.100			

The following two plots were obtained. Comment on the normality assumption and the condition of homoscedasticity.

Histogram of RESI2   N = 10

Midpoint	Count	
-1.6	1	*
-1.2	1	*
-0.8	0	
-0.4	2	**
0.0	1	*
0.4	3	***
0.8	0	
1.2	2	**

```
RESI2   -
        -
        -                                                    x
   1.0+              x
        -
        -                                                        x
        -                   x
        -                                            x
   0.0+   x
        - x
        -                                                x
        -
        -
  -1.0+
        -
        -                        x              x
        -
        -------+---------+---------+---------+---------+---------
+FITS2
           9.60      10.40     11.20     12.00     12.80     13.60
```

CHAPTER 13 ASSIGNMENT

MULTIPLE REGRESSION AND CORRELATION

Name _____   Section _____   Score_____

Part I   Select the correct answer and write the appropriate letter in the space provided.

_____1. In a multiple regression equation there is more than one
   a.   independent variable.
   b.   dependent variable.
   c.   coefficient of correlation.
   d. R^2 value.

_____2. If the coefficient of multiple determination is 1, then the
   a.   net regression coefficients are 0.
   b.   standard error of estimate is 0.
   c. X values are also equal to 0.
   d.   standard error of estimate is also 1.

_____3. A dummy variable
   a.   is also called an indicator variable.
   b.   can only assume values of 0 or 1.
   c.   is used as an independent variable.
   d.   all of the above.

_____4. In the global test of hypothesis
   a.   we use the t distribution as the test statistic.
   b.   we test to see if all of the net regression coefficients are 0.
   c.   we test to insure that each of the independent variables is 0.
   d.   all of the above.

_____5. A residual is
   a.   the independent variable.
   b.   the dependent variable.
   c.   the difference between the actual value and the fitted value.
   d.   equal to R^2.

_____6. The test for individual variables determines which independent variables
   a.   have the most value in determining R^2.
   b.   have nonzero regression coefficients.
   c.   are used to compute the coefficients of correlation.
   d.   are reported in the final equation.

_____7. A correlation matrix shows the
   a.   coefficients of correlation among all the variables.
   b.   net regression coefficients.
   c.   stepwise regression coefficients.
   d.   residuals.

_____8. Homoscedasticity refers to
   a.   residuals that are correlated.
   b.   independent variables that are correlated.
   c.   a nonlinear relationship.
   d.   residuals that are the same for all fitted values of Y'.

_____9. Multicollinearity means that
   a.   the independent variables are correlated.
   b.   time is involved with one of the independent variables.
   c.   the dependent variable is correlated with the independent variables.
   d.   the residuals do not have a constant variance.

_____10. When successive residuals are correlated we refer to this as
   a.   multicollinearity.
   b.   a dummy variable.
   c.   autocorrelation.
   d.   homoscedasticity.

Part II   Record your answer in the space provided. Be sure to show essential calculations.

The following information is used for Problems 11 to 13:

William Clegg is the owner and CEO of Clegg QC Consulting. Mr. Clegg is concerned about the salary structure of his company and has asked the Human Relations Department to conduct a study. Mr. Stan Holt, an analyst in the department, is assigned the project. Stan selects a random sample of 15 employees and gathers information on the salary, number of years with Clegg Consulting, the employee's performance rating for the previous year, and the number of days absent last year.

Salary ($1000)	Years with Firm	Performance Rating	Days Absent
50.3	6	60	8
69.0	9	85	3
50.7	7	60	8
46.9	4	78	12
44.2	5	70	6
50.3	6	73	6
49.2	6	83	6
54.6	5	74	5
52.1	5	85	5
58.3	6	85	4
54.8	4	88	5
63.0	8	78	5
50.1	5	61	6
52.1	4	74	5
36.5	3	65	7

11. The following correlation matrix was developed from the MINITAB System.

   a. Which independent variable has the strongest correlation with salary?

   b. Do you see any problems?

	Salary	Years	Perform
Years	0.768		
Perform	0.514	0.130	
Absent	−0.587	−0.370	−0.435

a.

b.

12. Conduct a test of hypotheses to determine if any of the regression coefficients are not equal to 0. This analysis of variance table was computed as part of the output. Use the 0.05 significance level.

Analysis of Variance

SOURCE	DF	SS	MS	F	p
Regression	3	641.10	213.7	13.91	0.000
Error	11	168.94	15.36		
Total	14	810.04			

a. H_0: _____

   H_1: _____

b. The decision rule is to reject H_0 if _____

c. What is your decision. Interpret.

   _____

   _____

d. Determine the R-square value. _____

   Interpret it.

   _____

   _____

13. Additional information was obtained from MINITAB. Conduct a test of hypothesis to determine if any of the regression coefficients do not equal 0. Use the .05 significance level.

The regression equation is:

```
Salary = 19.2 + 3.10 Years + 0.269 Perform - 0.704 Absent
```

Predictor	Coef	Stdev	t-ratio	p
Constant	19.19	12.15	1.58	0.143
Years	3.0962	0.7061	4.38	0.001
Perform	0.2694	0.1196	2.25	0.046
Absent	-0.7043	0.5859	-1.20	0.255

a. H_0: _____ H_0: _____ H_0: _____

H_1: _____ H_1: _____ H_1: _____

b. The decision rules are to reject H_0 if _____

c. What is your decision? Interpret.

_____

_____

CHAPTER 14
NONPARAMETRIC MEASURES: CHI-SQUARE APPLICATIONS

Chapter Goals

After completing this chapter, you will be able to:

1. List the characteristics of the Chi-square distribution.
2. Conduct a test of hypothesis comparing an observed set of frequencies to an expected distribution.
3. Conduct a test of hypothesis for normality using the Chi-square distribution.
4. Conduct a hypothesis test to determine whether two classification criteria are related.

Introduction

Recall that in Chapters 8 through 11, the level of measurement was assumed to be at least of interval scale and the population from which the sample was drawn was assumed to be normal. What if these conditions cannot be met? In such instances nonparametric or distribution-free tests are used.

> *Nonparametric tests of hypotheses*: Also called distribution-free tests. These tests do not require the population to be normally distributed.

These tests do not require any assumptions about the shape of the population, thus tests of hypothesis can be performed on nominal and ordinal scale data. Recall that the nominal level of measurement requires only that the sample information be categorized, with no order implied. As an example, students are classified by major, such as, business, history, computer science, etc.

This chapter considers tests where only the nominal level of measurement is required, although these tests may be used at a higher level of measurement.

The Chi-Square Distribution

In the previous chapters the standard normal t and F distributions were used as the test statistics. Recall that a test statistic is a quantity, determined from the sample information, used as a basis for deciding whether to reject the null hypothesis. In this chapter another distribution, called chi-square and designated χ^2, is used as the test statistic. It is similar to the t and F distributions in that there is a family of χ^2 distributions, each with a different shape, depending on the number of degrees of freedom. When the number of degrees of freedom is small the distribution is positively skewed, but as the number of degrees of freedom increases it becomes symmetrical and approaches the normal distribution. Chi-square is based on squared deviations between an observed frequency and an expected frequency and, therefore, is always positive.

Goodness-of-Fit Tests

In the *goodness-of-fit test* the χ^2 distribution is used to determine how well an "observed" set of observations "'fits" an "expected" set of observations.

> **Goodness-of-fit test:** A nonparametric test involving a set of observed frequencies and a corresponding set of expected frequencies.

The fundamental purpose of the goodness-of-fit test is to determine if there is a statistical difference between the two sets of data, one of which is observed and the other expected.

For example, an instructor told a class that the grading system would be "uniform." That is, that the same number of A's, B's, C's, D's and F's would be given. Suppose that the grades shown at the right were recorded at the end of the quarter:

Grade	Number
A	12
B	24
C	23
D	30
F	11
	100

The question to be answered is: Do these final grades depart significantly from those that could be expected if the instructor had in fact graded uniformly? The null and alternate hypotheses are:

H_0: The distribution is uniform.
H_1: The distribution is not uniform.

The sampling distribution follows the χ^2 distribution and the value of the test statistic is computed by text formula [14-1]:

$$\chi^2 = \Sigma \left[\frac{(f_o - f_e)^2}{f_e} \right] \qquad [14-1]$$

Where:
f_0 is the observed frequency in a particular category.
f_e is the expected frequency in a particular category.
k is the number of categories with $(k-1)$ degrees of freedom.

It is not necessary that the expected frequencies be equal to apply the goodness-of-fit test. For example, at Scandia Technical Institute, over the years, 50 percent of the students were classified as freshmen, 40 percent sophomores, and 10 percent unclassified.

A sample of 200 students this past semester revealed that 90 were freshmen, 80 were sophomores, and 30 were unclassified. The null and alternate hypotheses are:

H_0: The distribution of students has not changed.
H_1: The distribution of students has changed.

Contingency Tables

The χ^2 distribution is also used to determine if there is a relationship between two criteria of classification. As an example, we are interested in whether there is a relationship between job advancement within a company and the gender of the employee. A sample of 100 employees is selected. The survey results revealed:

Gender	No Advancement	Slow Advancement	Rapid Advancement	Total
Male	7	13	30	50
Female	13	17	20	50
Total	20	30	50	100

Note that an employee is classified two ways: by gender and by advancement. When an individual or item is classified according to two criteria, the resulting table is called a contingency table.

Contingency table: A two-way classification of a particular observation in table form.

The null and alternate hypotheses are expressed as follows:

H_0: There is no relationship between gender and advancement.
H_1: There is a relationship between gender and advancement.

Formula [14-1] is used to compute the value of the test statistics. The expected frequency, f_e is computed by noting that 50/100 or 50 percent of the sample is male. If the null hypothesis is true and advancement is unrelated to the gender of the employee, then it is expected that 50 percent of those who have not advanced will be male. The expected frequency, f_e, for males who have not advanced is 10, found by (0.50)(20). The other expected frequencies are computed similarly. If the difference between the observed and the expected value is too large to have occurred by chance, the null hypothesis is rejected.

There is a limitation to the use of the χ^2 distribution. The value of f_e should be at least 5 for each cell (box). This requirement is to prevent any cell from carrying an inordinate amount of weight and causing the null hypothesis to be rejected.

A Test of Normality

As mentioned previously, the normal probability distribution plays a key role in statistical analysis. In Chapter 7 we devoted an entire chapter to its study. In several other chapters, such as Chapters 9, 10, and 11 we assumed the sampled populations were normally distributed. How can we verify the normality assumption? The chi-square distribution offers a method.

The procedure uses the goodness-of-fit test and formula [14-1]. With the goodness-of-fit procedure the data are already in categories. When we want to test for normality, the usual first step is to organize the data into a frequency distribution. Next, we transform the class limits to a z value by subtracting the class limits from the population mean and dividing by the standard deviation. Thus, we transform the categories of the frequency distribution into deviations from the mean and use the areas in the standard normal distribution to determine the f_e values.

For example, we have the following frequency distribution of biweekly salaries. Assume that $\mu = \$1,200$ and $\sigma = \$200$. The frequency distribution of salaries is converted to a z value, found by $z = (X - \mu)/\sigma$.

Category	Salaries	z values
1	below $800	below −2.00
2	$800 up to 1,000	−2.00 to −1.00
3	1,000 up to 1,200	−1.00 to 0.00
4	1,200 up to 1,400	0.00 to 1.00
5	1,400 up to 1,600	1.00 to 2.00
6	above 1,600	above 2.00

The expected frequencies are computed by determining the area between the z values and multiplying by the sample size. The null hypothesis is that the sampled population is normal, the alternate is that the sampled population is not normal. The degrees of freedom is the number of categories minus 1. Further details of the steps are given in **Problem 4**.

Glossary

Nonparametric tests of hypotheses: Also called distribution-free tests. These tests do not require the population to be normally distributed.

Goodness-of-fit test: A nonparametric test involving a set of observed frequencies and a corresponding set of expected frequencies.

Contingency table: A two-way classification of a particular observation in table for

Chapter Problems

Problem 1

A distributor of personal computers has five locations in the city of Ashland. The sales in units for the first quarter of the year were as follows. At the 0.01 significance level do the records suggest that sales are uniformly distributed among the five locations?

Location	Sales (Units)
North Side	70
Pleasant Township	75
Southwyck	70
I-90	50
Venice Ave.	35
	300

Solution

The first step is to state the null hypothesis and the alternate hypothesis. The null hypothesis is that sales are uniformly distributed. The alternate is that there has been a change and the sales pattern is not uniformly distributed among the five stores. These hypotheses are written as follows:

H_0: Sales are uniformly distributed among the five locations
H_1: Sales are not uniformly distributed among the five locations

The appropriate test statistic is the χ^2 distribution. The critical value is obtained from Appendix H. The number of degrees of freedom is equal to the number of categories minus 1. There are five categories (locations), therefore there are four degrees of freedom found by $(k-1) = (5-1) = 4$. The problem states beforehand that the 0.01 significance level is to be used. To locate the critical value, find the column headed 0.01 and the row where *df*, the degree of freedom, is 4. The value at the intersection of this row and column is 13.277. Therefore, the decision rule is: reject H_0 if the computed value of the test statistic exceeds 13.277, otherwise do not reject the null hypothesis. Graphically, the decision rule is:

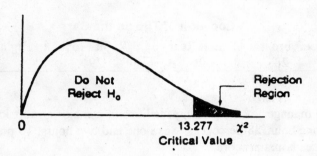

The observed frequencies, f_o are in Column 1 of the following table. The expected frequencies are in Column 2. How are the expected frequencies determined? If the null hypothesis is true (that sales are uniformly distributed among the five locations), then 1/5 of 300, or 60 computers should have been sold at each location.

Location	Col. 1 f_o	Col. 2 f_e	Col. 3 $f_o - f_e$	Col. 4 $(f_o - f_e)^2$	Col. 5 $\dfrac{(f_o - f_e)^2}{f_e}$
North Side	70	60	10	100	1.67
Pleasant Township	75	60	15	225	3.75
Southwyck	70	60	10	100	1.67
I-90	50	60	−10	100	1.67
Venice Ave.	35	60	−25	625	10.42
	300	300	0		19.18

Recall that the value of the test statistic is computed by formula [14-1]

$$\chi^2 = \Sigma \left[\frac{(f_o - f_e)^2}{f_e} \right]$$

The value of the test statistic is determined by first taking the difference between the observed frequency and the expected frequency (Col. 3). Next these differences are squared (Col. 4). Then the result is divided by the expected frequency (Col. 5). This result is then summed over the five locations. The total is 19.18. The value of 19.18 is compared to the critical value of 13.277. Since 19.18 is greater than the critical value, H_0 is rejected and H_1 accepted. We conclude that sales are not uniformly distributed among the five locations.

Check your answers against those in the ANSWER section.

A tire manufacturer is studying the position of tires in blowouts. It seems logical that the tire blowouts will be uniformly distributed among the four positions. For a sample of 100 tire failures, is there any significant difference in that tire's position on the car? Use the 0.05 significance level.

Location of Tire on the Car

Left Front	Left Rear	Right Front	Right Rear
28	20	29	23

Problem 2

From past experience the manager of the parking facilities at a major airport knows that 58 percent of the customers stay less than one hour, 23 percent between one and two hours, 10 percent between two and three hours, and nine percent three hours or more.

The manager wants to update this study. A sample of 500 stamped parking tickets is selected. The results showed 300 stayed less than one hour, 100 from one to two hours, 60 from two to three hours, and 40 parked three hours or more. At the 0.01 significance level does the data suggest there has been a change in the length of time customers use the parking facilities?

Solution

The first step is to state the null hypothesis and alternate hypothesis.

H_0: There has been no change in the distribution of parking times.
H_1: There has been a change in the distribution of parking times

The next step is to determine the decision rule. Note in the table on the next page that there are four categories. The number of degrees of freedom is the number of categories minus 1. In this problem it is $(4 - 1) = 3$ degrees of freedom. Referring to Appendix H, the 0.01 level and 3 degrees of freedom, the critical value of chi-square is 11.345, so H_0 is rejected if χ^2 is greater than 11.345.

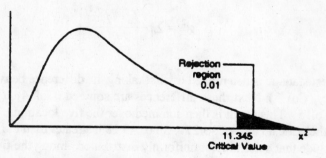

The value of the test statistic is computed as follows:

The observed frequencies from the sample are shown In Column 2 of the following table. Recall that based on past experience 58 percent of the customers parked their car less than one hour. If the null hypothesis is true, then 58% × 500 (in the sample) = 290, the expected frequency. Likewise, 23 percent stayed from one to two hours. Thus, $23\% \times 500$ gives the expected frequency of 115. The complete set of expected frequencies is given in Column 3. Chi-square is computed to be 4.86.

Time in Parking Lot	Col. 1 Percent of Total	Col. 2 Number in Sample f_o	Col. 3 f_e	Col. 4 $f_o - f_e$	Col. 5 $(f_o - f_e)^2$	Col. 6 $\dfrac{(f_o - f_e)^2}{f_e}$
Less than 1 hour	58	300	290	10	100	100/290 = 0.34
1 up to 2 hours	23	100	115	−15	225	225/115 = 1.96
2 up to 3 hours	10	60	50	10	100	100/50 = 2.00
3 hours or more	9	40	45	−5	25	25/45 = 0.56
Total	100	500	500	0		$\chi^2 = 4.86$

Since the computed value of chi-square (4.86) is less than the critical value (11.345), the null hypothesis is not rejected. There has been no change in the lengths of parking time at the airport.

Exercise 14.2

Check your answers against those in the ANSWER section.

In recent years, 42 percent of the American made automobiles sold in the United States were manufactured by General Motors, 33 percent by Ford, 22 percent by Chrysler, and 3 percent by all others.

A sample of the sales of American made automobiles conducted last week revealed that 174 were manufactured by Chrysler, 275 by Ford, 330 by GM, and 21 by all others.

Test the hypothesis at the 0.05 level that there has been no change in the sales pattern.

Problem 3

A study is made by an auto insurance company to determine if there is a relationship between the driver's age and the number of automobile accident claims submitted during a one-year period. From a sample of 300 claims, the following sample information was recorded.

No. of Accidents	Age (Years) Less than 25	25-50	Over 50	Total
0	37	101	74	212
1	16	15	28	59
2 or more	7	9	13	29
Total	60	125	115	300

Use the 0.05 significance level to find out if there is any relationship between the driver's age and the number of accidents.

Chapter 14

Solution

The question under investigation is whether the number of auto accidents is related to the driver's age. The null and alternate hypotheses are.

H_0: There is no relationship between age and the number of accidents.
H_1: There is a relationship between age and the number of accidents.

The critical value is obtained from the chi-square distribution in Appendix H. The number of degrees of freedom is equal to the number of rows minus one, times the number of columns minus one. Hence, the degrees of freedom are $(3 - 1)(3 - 1) = 4$. The significance level, as stated in the problem, is 0.05. The critical value from Appendix H is 9.488. The null hypothesis is rejected if the computed value of χ^2 is greater than 9.488.

Formula [14-1], as cited earlier, is used to determine χ^2.

$$\chi^2 = \Sigma \left[\frac{(f_o - f_e)^2}{f_e} \right]$$

Where:
f_o is the frequency observed.
f_e the expected frequency.

The first step is to determine the expected frequency for each corresponding observed frequency. If the null hypothesis is true (the number of accidents is not related to age) we can expect 212 out of the 300 sampled, or 70.67 percent of the drivers to have had no accidents. Thus, we can expect 70.67 percent of the 60 drivers under 25 years, or 42.40 drivers, to have had no accidents.

Likewise, if the null hypothesis is true, 70.67 percent of the 125 drivers in the 25 to 50 age bracket, or 88.33 drivers, should have had no accidents.

The table below shows the complete set of observed and expected frequencies.

No. of Accidents	Age						
	Less than 25		25-50		Over 50		
	f_o	f_e	f_o	f_e	f_o	f_e	Total
0	37	42.40	101	88.33	74	81.27	212
1	16	11.80	15	24.58	28	22.62	59
2 or more	7	5.80	9	12.08	13	11.12	29
Total	60	60.00	125	125.00	115	115.00	300

Note that some totals were rounded

The expected frequency for any category is found by text formula [14-2]:

$$f_e = \frac{(\text{row total})(\text{column total})}{\text{grand total}}$$

The value for the first row and column is used as an example. There are 212 people who did not have any accidents, 60 persons are less than 25 years old, and there is a total of 300 people. These values are inserted into the formula:

$$f_e = \frac{(\text{row total})(\text{column total})}{\text{grand total}} = \frac{(212)(60)}{300} = 42.40$$

This is the same value computed previously.

The computed value of χ^2 is 11.03.

$$\chi^2 = \Sigma \left[\frac{(f_o - f_e)^2}{f_e} \right] = \frac{(37.00 - 42.40)^2}{42.40} + \frac{(101.00 - 88.33)^2}{88.33} + \ldots + \frac{(13 - 11.12)^2}{11.12} = 11.03$$

Since the computed value of χ^2 is greater than the critical value of 9.488, the null hypothesis is rejected and the alternate accepted. We conclude that there is a relationship between age and the number of accidents.

Exercise 14.3

Check your answers against those in the ANSWER section.

A random sample of 480 male and female adults was asked the amount of time each person spent watching TV last week. Their responses are shown below. At the 0.05 significance level, does it appear that the amount of time spent watching TV is related to the gender of the viewer?

Hours	Gender of Viewer		Total
	Male	Female	
Under 8	70	90	160
8 to 15	100	60	160
15 or more	55	105	160
	225	255	480

Problem 4

The following is the distribution of the number of outpatient surgeries per day for the last 100 days at St. Luke's Hospital, Maumee, Ohio. Assume the population mean is 24 patients per day and the standard deviation is 4 patients per day.

Is it reasonable to assume that the population of the number of patients per day is normally distributed? Use the 0.05 significance level.

Number of Patients	Number of Days
Less than 18	12
18 up to 22	19
22 up to 26	39
26 up to 30	21
30 or more	9
Total	100

Solution

The null hypothesis and the alternate hypothesis are:

H_0 : The population is normal.
H_1 : The population is not normal.

There are 5 categories, so there are $(5 - 1) = 4$ degrees of freedom. From Appendix H, H_0 is rejected if the computed value of chi-square is greater than 9.488.

Next, we compute the expected values. To do this we determine the areas under a normal curve with $\mu = 24$ and $\sigma = 4$. Recall from Chapter 7, to determine the areas we convert from a normal distribution to the standard normal distribution by $z = (X - \mu)/\sigma$. To find the area below 18 patients:

1. The z value corresponding to 18 is -1.50, found by $(18 - 24)/4$.

2. The area between $z = 0.00$ and 1.50 is 0.4332, from Appendix D.

3. The area between -1.50 and 0.00 is also 0.4332, because of symmetry.

4. The area below -1.50 is 0.0668, found by $0.5000 - 0.4332$.

5. If the distribution is normal with $\mu = 24$ and $\sigma = 4$, then we expect $100(0.0668) = 6.68$ days during which there were less than 18 patients.

To determine the expected frequency for 18 up to 22 patients, first find z value for 22 patients. It is -0.50, found by $(22 - 24)/4 = -0.50$. The area between a z value of -0.50 and -1.50 is $0.4332 - 0.1915 = 0.2417$. We therefore expect $100(0.2417) = 24.17$ days to have between 18 and 22 patients.

The remaining expected frequencies are determined similarly.

Number of Patients	z values	f_o	f_e
Less than 18	less than -1.50	12	6.68
18 up to 22	-1.50 up to -0.50	19	24.17
22 up to 26	-0.50 up to 0.50	39	38.30
26 up to 30	0.50 up to 1.50	21	24.17
30 or more	1.50 or more	9	6.68
	Total	100	100.00

To determine the value of chi-square we use formula [14-1]. The computations are as follows:

Number of Patients	f_o	f_e	$\dfrac{(f_o - f_e)^2}{f_e}$
Less than 18	12	6.68	4.2369
18 up to 22	19	24.17	1.1059
22 up to 26	39	38.30	0.0128
26 up to 30	21	24.17	0.4158
3o or more	9	6.68	0.8057
	100	100.00	6.5771

The computed value of chi-square is 6.5771, which is less than the critical value of 9.488. Hence, the null hypothesis is not rejected. We conclude that the sample could have been obtained from a normal population. It is reasonable to conclude that the distribution of days is normally distributed with a mean of 24 and a standard deviation of 4.

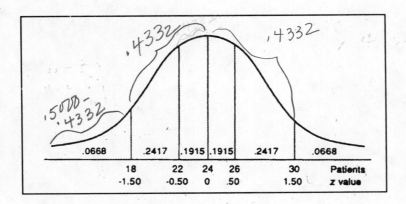

Exercise 14.4

Check your answers against those in the ANSWER section.

Swanton Welding Company fabricates large steel support structures for building and bridge construction. A sample of 400 employees revealed the following distribution of hourly wages. Assume: $\mu = \$12$ and $\sigma = \$3.00$.

Hourly Wage	Frequency
Below $8.00	25
$8.00 up to $10.00	70
$10.00 up to $12.00	110
$12.00 up to $14.00	101
$14.00 up to $16.00	57
Above $16.00	37

At the 0.05 significance level, can we conclude that the population of hourly wages is normally distributed?

CHAPTER 14 ASSIGNMENT

NONPARAMETRIC METHODS: CHI-SQUARE APPLICATIONS

Name _____ Section _____ Score _____

Part I   Select the correct answer and write the appropriate letter in the space provided.

_____1. In a nonparametric test
   a.   the sample size must be at least 30.
   b.   no assumption is made regarding the shape of the population.
   c. σ is always known.
   d.   the interval scale of measurement is required.

_____2. The level of measurement required for the goodness-of-fit test is
   a.   nominal.
   b.   ordinal.
   c.   interval.
   d.   ratio.

_____3. The chi-square distribution is
   a.   positively skewed.
   b.   a continuous distribution.
   c.   based on the number of categories.
   d.   all of the above.

_____4. A two-way classification of the data is called a
   a.   chi-square distribution.
   b.   normal distribution.
   c.   contingency table.
   d.   none of the above.

_____5. In a goodness-of-fit test where f_e values are the same in all four categories
   a.   the degrees of freedom is 3.
   b. $k = 4$.
   c.   the null hypothesis is that the proportion in each category is the same.
   d.   all of the above.

_____6. A sample of 100 undergraduate students is classified by major (3 groups) and gender. How many degrees of freedom are there in the test?
   a.   2
   b.   3
   c.   4
   d.   99

_____7. In a chi-square test the $df = 4$. At the 0.05 significance level the critical value of the chi-square is
   a.   7.779   b.   7.815
   c.   9.488   d.   13.388

_____8. The shape of the chi-square distribution is
   a. based on the degrees of freedom.
   b. based on the level of measurement.
   c. based on the shape of the population.
   d. based on at least 30 observations.

_____9. In a test to find out if the two criteria of classification are related, the expected cell frequencies should be
   a. all less than 5.
   b. at least one less than 5.
   c. at least 5 percent of the population.
   d. at least 5.

_____10. The sum of the observed and the expected frequencies are
   a. always at least 30.   b.   always the same.
   c. always less than 5 percent. d.   always less than 5.

Part II   Record your answer in the space provided. Show essential work.

11. Walter Churchill, owner of Churchill's Super Market, would like to know if there is a preference for the day of the week on which customers do their shopping. A sample of 420 families revealed the following. At the 0.05 significance level, is there a difference in the proportion of customers that prefer each day of the week?

Day of the week	Number of persons
Monday	20
Tuesday	30
Wednesday	20
Thursday	60
Friday	80
Saturday	130
Sunday	80

   a. State the null and alternate hypotheses.

   H_0: _____

   H_1: _____

   b. State the decision rule.

   _____

   c. Compute the value of the test statistic.

c.

   d. What is your decision regarding the null hypothesis? Interpret the result.

   _____

12. A charity solicits donations by phone. From long experience the charity's director reports that 60 percent of the calls will result in refusal to donate, 30 percent will request more information via the mail, and 10 percent will result in an immediate credit card donation. For a sample of 200 calls last week, 140 refused to donate, 50 requested additional information, and 10 made an immediate donation. At the 0.10 significance level was the sample result different from the usual pattern?

a. State the null and alternate hypotheses.

H_0: _____ H_1: _____

b. State the decision rule.

_____

c. Compute the value of the test statistic.

c.

d. What is your decision regarding the null hypothesis? Interpret the result.

_____

_____

13. There are three loan officers at Farmer National Bank. All decisions on mortgage loans are made by one of these officers. The president of the bank would like to be sure that the rejection rate is about the same for the three officers. A sample of 200 recent applications yielded the following results. Is the rejection rate related to the officer that processes the loan? Use the 0.05 significance level.

	Loan Officer		
	Felix	Otis	Foxburrow
Approved	50	70	55
Rejected	10	10	5
Total	60	80	60

a. State the null and alternate hypotheses.

H_0: _____ H_1: _____

b. State the decision rule.

_____

c. Compute the value of the test statistic.

c.

d. What is your decision regarding the null hypothesis? Interpret the result.

_____

_____

14. R & R Electronics manufactures laser printers. The following is the distribution on the repair history of printers repaired under the first six months of the warranty. Assume the population mean is 3.4 months and standard deviation is 1.5 months. Is it reasonable to assume that the population of the number of months are normally distributed? Use the 0.05 significance level.

Number of Months	Number Repaired
under one month	15
1 to 2	18
2 to 3	42
3 to 4	36
4 to 5	21
5 to 6	13
over 6	5
	150

a. State the null and alternate hypotheses.

   H_0: _____ H_1: _____

b. State the decision rule.

   _____

c. Compute the value of the test statistic.

c.

d. What is your decision regarding the null hypothesis? Interpret the result.

   _____

   _____

NONPARAMETRIC METHODS: ANALYSIS OF RANKED DATA

CHAPTER GOALS

After completing this chapter, you will be able to:

1. Conduct the sign test for dependent samples using the binomial and normal distribution as the test statistic.

2. Conduct a test of hypothesis for the population median.

3. Conduct a test of hypothesis for dependent samples using the Wilcoxon signed rank test.

4. Conduct the Wilcoxon rank-sum test for independent samples.

5. Conduct the Kruskal-Wallis test for several independent samples.

6. Conduct and interpret Spearman's coefficient of rank correlation.

7. Conduct a test of hypothesis to determine whether the correlation among the ranks in the population is different from zero.

Introduction

This chapter continues our study of nonparametric tests of hypotheses. Recall that for nonparametric tests no assumption regarding the shape of the population is required. The data can be either the nominal or ordinal scale. In Chapter 14, applications of the chi-square distribution, which requires only the nominal scale of measurement, were presented. In this chapter several tests based on the ordinal scale of measurement are examined.

The first two tests require paired or dependent samples. The sign test is based on only the sign of the difference between paired observations. The Wilcoxon matched-pair signed rank test considers both the sign of the difference and also the magnitude of the difference. The Wilcoxon rank-sum test and the Kruskal-Wallis test are applied to independent samples. Also we look at a coefficient of correlation especially designed for ranked data.

The Sign Test

The *sign test* is based on the sign of a difference between two related observations.

> **Sign test**: A test based on the sign of a difference between two related observations. We usually designate a plus sign (+) for a positive difference between observations and a minus sign (−) for a negative difference between observations.

The sign test has many applications. One is for before and after experiments. It is an alternative to the paired *t* test presented in Chapter 10. The paired *t* test requires that the distribution of the differences in paired observations be normally distributed. If this normality assumption cannot be met, the sign test is employed as an alternative.

The underlying assumption for the sign test is that the number of positive differences should be about the same as the number of negative differences, assuming the treatment or pairing has no effect. The null hypothesis is that the pairing has no effect. If H_0 is true, then any difference in the number of positive and negative differences is due to chance. If the treatment has an effect, then there will be significantly more positive (or negative) differences.

We have concentrated so far on testing a hypothesis about a mean or means. We can also apply the ideas of the sign test to conduct a *median test*, that is, a hypothesis test about the median of a population.

Median test: A test to determine whether the median of a set of sample data is equal to a hypothesized value.

Recall that the median is a value above which half of the observations lie and the other half below it.

For example, we might want to find out whether the median annual salary of quality assurance managers is $52,000, meaning that half the managers earn more than $52,000 and the other half of the managers earn less. In our sample, an annual salary of more than $52,000 is assigned a plus sign, a salary below $52,000 is assigned a minus sign. A salary exactly equal to $52,000 is omitted from further analysis.

The Human Relations Director wants to explore the annual salary of quality assurance managers further. So she first sets up the following null and alternate hypotheses.

$$H_0: \text{Median salary is } \$52,000$$
$$H_1: \text{Median salary is not } \$52,000$$

The way the alternate hypothesis is stated signifies that a two-tailed test is being applied. The solution to this problem is presented in the Problem/Solution section.

The binomial distribution, discussed in Chapter 6, is the test statistic. Recall that there are four conditions for the binomial: only two outcomes, independent trials, a constant probability of success, and a fixed sample size. The null hypothesis, stated in terms of the binomial, is that $\pi = 0.50$. π is the probability of a success. The normal approximation to the binomial is used if both $n\pi$ and $n(1-\pi)$ are greater than 5.

The Wilcoxon Signed-Rank Test

The sign test considers only the sign of the difference between paired observations. Any information regarding the magnitude of the difference is not used. The *Wilcoxon signed-rank test* not only considers the sign of the difference but also the magnitude of the difference.

Wilcoxon Signed rank test: A test for determining whether there is a difference between two sets of data, one of which is based on a "before" situation and the other on an "after" situation. The two sets of data must be related, dependent, or paired.

It is also a replacement for the paired t test when the normality assumption cannot be met. When information on the magnitude of the paired difference is available, the Wilcoxon test is a stronger or a more powerful test because it makes more effective use of the data.

The Wilcoxon Rank-Sum Test

This test is the nonparametric alternative to the Student t test described in Chapter 10. The purpose of Student's t was to determine if two independent populations had the same mean. Recall we assumed that the two independent random samples were selected from normally distributed populations with equal standard deviations. What if the equal standard deviation or the normality assumption cannot be met? The Student t is not appropriate and a nonparametric alternative, the *Wilcoxon rank-sum test*, is used.

> *Wilcoxon rank-sum test*: A test to determine whether there is a difference between two independent populations. No assumption is made regarding the normality of the populations.

The Wilcoxon rank-sum test is based on the sum of the ranks of independent samples. If the populations are the same, then the combined rankings of the two samples will be nearly evenly divided between the two samples and the total of the ranks will be about the same. If the populations are not the same, one of the samples will have a predominance of the larger ranks and its total (rank-sum) will be larger. When both samples are at least 8, the standard normal distribution is used as the test statistic. The formula is:

$$z = \frac{W - \dfrac{n_1(n_1 + n_2 + 1)}{2}}{\sqrt{\dfrac{n_1 n_2(n_1 + n_2 + 1)}{12}}} \qquad [15-4]$$

Where:
W is the sum of the ranks from the first population
n_1 is the number of observations from the first population
n_2 is the number of observations from the second population.

The Kruskal-Wallis Test

The Wilcoxon rank-sum test compares two independent populations. The *Kruskal-Wallis test* allows for the simultaneous comparison of more than two independent populations. It is an alternative to the ANOVA, described in Chapter 11, for comparing more than two population means.

> *Kruskal-Wallis test*: A test to determine whether there is a difference among more than two populations. No assumption regarding the shape of the populations is necessary.

Recall from Chapter 11 that to apply ANOVA it was necessary that:

1. The samples be independent.
2. The populations be normally distributed.
3. The populations have equal standard deviations.

The Kruskal-Wallis test should be used if one or more of these cannot be met. It requires at least five observations in each sample. To employ the Kruskal-Wallis test, we substitute the rankings of the sampled items for the actual values. The test statistic, designated by H is computed using formula [15-5], below.

$$H = \frac{12}{n(n+1)}\left(\frac{(\Sigma R_1)^2}{n_1} + \frac{(\Sigma R_2)^2}{n_2} + \ldots \frac{(\Sigma R_k)^2}{n_k}\right) - 3(n+1) \qquad [15-5]$$

Where:

$\Sigma R_1, \Sigma R_2 \ldots \Sigma R_k$ are the sum of the ranks for the samples designated $1, 2, \ldots, k$.

$n_1, n_2, \ldots n_k$ are the sizes of samples $1, 2, \ldots k$.

n   is the combined number of observations for all samples.

There are $(k-1)$ degrees of freedom (k is the number of populations).

The distribution of the sample H statistic is very close to the Chi-square distribution with $(k-1)$ degrees of freedom *if every sample size is at least 5*. Therefore we use chi-square in formulating the decision rule.

Spearman's Rank Order Correlation

Pearson's coefficient of correlation assumes the data to be of at least interval scale. Charles Spearman, a British statistician, introduced a measure of correlation for ordinal-level data known as *Spearman's rank-order correlation coefficient*.

> *Spearmans Coefficient of rank correlation:* A measure of the relationship between two sets of ranked data.

Spearman's rank-order correlation coefficient, designated r_s, may range between -1.0 and $+1.0$ inclusive with -1.0 and $+1.0$ representing perfect rank correlation. Zero indicates no rank correlation.

Text formula [15-6] is used to compute r_s.

$$r_s = 1 - \frac{6(\Sigma d^2)}{n(n^2 - 1)} \qquad [15-6]$$

Where:

n is the number of paired observations.
d is the difference between the ranks for each pair.

The value of r_s is tested to rule out the possibility that the association was due to chance. For a two-tailed test, the null and alternate hypotheses are stated as follows:

H_0: The rank correlation in the population is zero.
H_1: The rank correlation in the population is not zero.

For large samples where n is 10 or more, the Student's t distribution can be used as the test statistic. There are $(n-2)$ degrees of freedom and the computed t value is found by:

$$t = r_s \sqrt{\frac{n-2}{1-r_s^2}} \qquad [15-7]$$

GLOSSARY

Sign test: A test based on the sign of a difference between two related observations. We usually designate a plus sign (+) for a positive difference between observations and a minus sign (–) for a negative difference between observations

Wilcoxon Signed Rank Test: A test for determining whether there is a difference between two sets of data, one of which is based on a "before" situation and the other an "after" situation. The two sets of data must be related, dependent or paired.

Wilcoxon Rank-Sum test: A test to determine whether there is a difference between two independent populations. No assumption is made regarding the normality of the populations.

Kruskal-Wallis test: A test to determine whether there is a difference among more than two populations. No assumption regarding the shape of the populations is necessary.

Median test: A test to determine whether the median of a set of sample data is equal to a hypothesized value.

Coefficient of rank correlation: A measure of the relationship between two sets of ranked data.

CHAPTER PROBLEMS

Problem I

A sample of ten Army recruits was given a test to determine how well they liked the Army. Later that same day they were taken on a very long and very strenuous march. On their return they were given a similar test to again measure how well they liked the Army. The scores are shown below. At the 0.05 significance level, can we conclude that the recruits liked the Army less after the march?

Recruit	Test Score Before	After
Barrett	132	122
Bier	150	165
Spitler	139	127
Contact	108	101
Walker	106	99
Stasiak	105	92
Soto	133	110
Lopez	157	139
Kies	114	99
Landrum	122	113

Solution

First, note that the samples are dependent That is, we have a score for Barrett before the march and after the march. We are concerned with the distribution of the differences and are not willing to assume that the differences are normally distributed. Thus the paired t test, described in Chapter 10, which requires the normality assumption, cannot be used.

The null hypothesis and the alternate hypothesis are as follows

H_0: There was no change in how well the recruits liked the Army ($\pi \le 0.50$)
H_1: The recruits liked the Army less after the march.($\pi > 0.50$)

Why is the alternate hypothesis $\pi > 0.50$? We subtract the score after the march from the score before the march. Hence, a positive difference indicates that the recruits liked the Army less after the march.

If the null hypothesis is true that there is no change in the view of the recruits toward the Army, then there should be about as many positive differences in the scores as negative. If the recruits liked the Army less after the march, then there should be significantly more positive differences.

The binomial distribution is used as the test statistic. Recall that to apply the binomial:

1. Each outcome is classified into one of two possible outcomes. A difference can only be positive or negative. (If a difference is 0, that observation is dropped from the study.)

2. The probability of a success remains the same from trial to trial. If the null hypothesis is true, that the march had no effect, the probability of the positive difference is 0.50.

3. There is a fixed number of trials. In this case "trials" refers to the sample size. There are ten recruits (trials).

4. Each trial is independent. This means, for example, the scores obtained by Barrett are not related to Landrum's scores.

The following table shows that of the ten recruits, 9 out of 10 liked the Army better before the march.

Recruit	Test X Before	Score Y After	X − Y Sign of Difference
Barrett	132	122	+
Bier	150	165	−
Spitler	139	127	+
Contact	108	101	+
Walker	106	99	+
Stasiak	105	92	+
Soto	133	110	+
Lopez	157	139	+
Kies	114	99	+
Landrum	122	113	+

The normal approximation to the binomial can be used when both $n\pi$ and $n(1-\pi)$ are greater than 5. In this case both are equal to five $(10)(0.5) = 5$ and $10(1-0.5) = 5$, so the binomial distribution will be used as the test statistic. The binomial table is found in Appendix A.

How is the critical value determined? Recall that the alternate hypothesis indicated a one-tailed test. The binomial probability distribution, when $n = 10$ and $\pi = 0.50$, is shown below.

Binomial Probabilities when $n = 10$, $\pi = 0.50$, alpha = 0.05		
Number of Successes	Probability of Success	Cumulative Probability
0	0.001	
1	0.010	
2	0.044	
3	0.117	
4	0.205	
5	0.246	
6	0.205	
7	0.117	
8	0.044	0.055
9	0.010	↑ 0.011
10	0.001	0.001

The decision rule is formulated by adding the probability starting with ten successes (+ signs) in ten trials, then nine successes, and so on, until we come as close to the significance level as possible without exceeding it. In this instance the probability of ten successes in ten trials is 0.001, the probability of nine successes is 0.010, and so on.

The cumulative probabilities are shown in the right-hand column. The probability of nine or more successes is 0.011, and the probability of eight or more successes is 0.055. Since 0.055 is greater than the significance level, of 0.05, the decision rule is to reject the null hypothesis if nine or more plus signs are obtained in the sample.

There are nine plus signs, indicating that nine of the ten recruits liked the Army better before the march. So the null hypothesis is rejected. It is concluded that the recruits liked the Army less after the march.

Chapter 15

Exercise 15.1

Check your answers against those in the ANSWER section.

Twelve persons whose IQs were measured in college between 1960 and 1965 volunteered recently to be retested with an equivalent IQ test. The information is given below

Student	Recent Score	Original Score
John Barr	119	112
Bill Sedwick	103	108
Marica Elmquist	115	115
Ginger Thealine	109	100
Larry Clark	131	120
Jim Redding	110	108
Carol Papalia	109	113
Victor Suppa	113	126
Dallas Paul	94	95
Carol Kozoloski	119	110
Joe Sass	118	117
P. S. Sundar	112	102

At the 0.05 significance level, can we conclude that the IQ scores have increased?

Problem 2

After reviewing the results in Problem 1, the Army ordered an additional study involving a larger number of Army recruits. A sample of 70 recruits were given the test to determine how well they liked the Army and then taken on the long and strenuous march. Then the second test was administered. A total of 50 of the recruits were found to like the Army better before the march. At the 0.05 significance level can we conclude that recruits liked the Army better before the march?

Solution

The null hypothesis and the alternate hypothesis are stated as follows:

$$H_0: \pi \leq 0.50$$
$$H_1: \pi > 0.50$$

Rejection of the null hypothesis and acceptance of the alternate hypothesis allows us to conclude that the recruits like the Army better before the march.

The normal approximation to the binomial is used as the test statistic. Recall that this approximation is used as the test statistic when $n\pi$ and $n(1-\pi)$ both exceed 5. In this instance $n\pi = 70(0.50) = 35$ and $n(1-\pi) = 70(1-0.50) = 35$.

The continuity correction, described in Chapter 7, is appropriate when a continuous distribution, such as the normal, is used to describe a discrete distribution (the binomial). The continuity correction factor includes a value of 0.50 which is either added to or subtracted from X. If the number of plus signs is greater than $n/2$, then 0.50

is subtracted from X. If the number of plus signs is less than $n/2$, then 0.50 is added. In this example, there are 50 pluses which is more than $n / 2 = 70 / 2 = 35.$, thus the formula for the test statistic, [15-2] is:

$$z = \frac{(X - 0.50) - \mu}{\sigma} = \frac{(X - 0.50) - 0.50n}{0.50\sqrt{n}} \qquad [15 - 2]$$

Where:

X is the number of plus (or minus) signs.

n is the number of paired observations (disregarding ties).

μ is the population mean, found by $n\pi$

σ is $0.50 \sqrt{n}$.

z is the z value.

The decision rule is to reject the null hypothesis if the computed value of z exceeds 1.65. This decision rule is based on a one-tailed test, the standard normal distribution, and the 0.05 significance level.

The value of z is computed to be 3.47.

$$z = \frac{(X - 0.50) - \mu}{0.50\sqrt{n}} = \frac{(50 - 0.50) - 70(0.50)}{0.50\sqrt{70}} = 3.47$$

Since the computed value of 3.47 exceeds the critical value of 1.65, the null hypothesis is rejected. It is concluded that the recruits liked the Army less after the march.

Exercise 15.2

Check your answers against those in the ANSWER section.

A sample of 50 adults who were in college between 1960 and 1965 were recently given an IQ test and the scores compared. Thirty of those tested showed an increase in their scores and 20 a decrease. At the .0.05 significance level can we conclude that the scores have increased?

Problem 3

The Human Relations Director at ARCO is wondering whether the median age of executives is 45 years. She selects a sample of 228 executives at random. Of the 228 selected, 3 were exactly 45 years old, 120 were over 45 years, and 105 were less than 45 years of age. At the 0.10 significance level, can we conclude that the median age is different from 45 years?

Solution

The null and the alternate hypotheses are:

$$H_0\text{: Median} = 45$$
$$H_1\text{: Median} \neq 45$$

The three executives who were exactly 45 years old were omitted from the analysis, so the sample size is reduced from 228 to 225. Using a two-tailed test, the 0.10 significance level, and the standard normal distribution

(Appendix D) as the test statistic, the decision rule is to reject H_0 if the computed value of z is less than -1.645 or greater than 1.65.

We will conduct the test for the number of observations greater than 45 years of age. Because the number of observation above the median is more than $n/2$ we use formula [15-2]. There are 120 observations larger than the hypothesized median and $n/2 = 225/2 = 112.5$. The value of z is 0.933, found by

$$z = \frac{(X - 0.50) - 0.50n}{0.50\sqrt{n}} = \frac{(120 - 0.50) - 0.50(225)}{0.50\sqrt{225}} = 0.933$$

Because 0.933 is not in the region beyond 1.65, the null hypothesis is not rejected. We cannot reject the hypothesis that the median age of ARCO executives is 45 years.

Problem 4

Use the Wilcoxon signed-rank test and the sample data in Problem 1, regarding the Army march, to determine if recruits liked the Army better before the march. Again, use the 0.05 significance level.

Solution

The sign test considers only the sign of the difference between paired observations. The Wilcoxon signed-rank test not only considers the sign of the difference between paired observations but also the magnitude of the difference. The null and alternate hypotheses are stated as follows.

H_0: There was no change in how the recruits liked the Army.
H_1: The recruits liked the Army better before the march.

The steps to complete the Wilcoxon signed-rank test are as follows.

1. The difference between each paired of observations is computed. If any difference is 0, it is eliminated and the size of the sample is reduced by the number of zero (0) differences.

2. Determine the absolute value for the values in the difference column.

3. These differences are ranked from lowest to highest, without regard to their signs. If ties occur, the ranks involved are averaged and each tied observation is awarded the mean value.

4. The ranks with a positive difference are assigned to one column and those with a negative difference to another.

5. The sums of the positive (R^+) and negative (R^-) ranks are determined.

6. The smaller of the two sums (R^+) and (R^-) is compared with the critical values found in Appendix J. This critical value is called T.

Appendix J is used to formulate the decision rule. First locate the column headed by 0.05 using a one-tailed test. Next move down that column to the row where $n = 10$. The critical value is 10. The decision is to reject H_0 if the smaller of R^+ and R^- is 10 or less.

The values for R^+ and R^- are as follows:

Recruit	Before	After	Difference	Absolute	Rank	R^+	R^-
Barrett	132	122	10	10	4.0	4.0	
Bier	150	165	−15	15	7.5		7.5
Spitler	139	127	12	12	5.0	5.0	
Contact	108	101	7	7	1.5	1.5	
Walker	106	99	7	7	1.5	1.5	
Stasiak	105	92	13	13	6.0	6.0	
Soto	133	110	23	23	10.0	10.0	
Lopez	157	139	18	18	9.0	9.0	
Kies	114	99	15	15	7.5	7.5	
Landrum	122	113	9	9	3.0	3.0	
						47.5	7.5

Since $R^- = 7.5$, H_0 is rejected and H_1 accepted. It is concluded that recruits liked the Army better before the march.

Exercise 15.3

Check your answers against those in the ANSWER section.

Refer to Exercise 1. Twelve persons whose IQs were measured in college between 1960 and 1965 were located recently and retested with an equivalent IQ test. The information is given below.

Student	Recent Score	Original Score
John Barr	119	112
Bill Sedwick	103	108
Marica Elmquist	115	115
Ginger Thealine	109	100
Larry Clark	131	120
Jim Redding	110	108
Carol Papalia	109	113
Victor Suppa	113	126
Dallas Paul	94	95
Carol Kozoloski	119	110
Joe Sass	118	117
P. S. Sundar	112	102

At the 0.05 significance level can we conclude that the IQ scores have increased in over 20 years? Use the Wilcoxon signed-rank test.

Problem 5

A manufacturer of candy, gum and other snacks wants to compare the daily amounts spent by men and women in vending machines. To investigate, samples of nine men and ten women are selected. Each person is asked to keep a record of the amount they spend in vending machines for a week. The results are as follows:

Amount Spent by Men	Amount Spent by Women
$4.32	$2.81
6.05	3.45
7.21	4.16
8.57	4.32
9.80	5.54
10.10	6.93
12.76	7.54
13.65	8.32
15.87	10.76
	11.21

Assume that the distribution of the amounts spent for men and women is not normally distributed. At the 0.05 significance level can we conclude that men spend more?

Solution

The first step is to determine which test to use. Because the populations are not normally distributed the *t* test for independent samples is not appropriate. The Wilcoxon rank-sum test allows for two independent samples and does not require any assumptions regarding the shape of the population, so it is appropriate.

The next step is to state the null and the alternate hypotheses. A one-tailed test is used because we want to show that the distribution of the amounts spent by the men is larger, or to the right of, that of the women. To put it another way, the median amount spent by the men is larger than the median amount spent by the women.

H_0: The distributions are the same.
H_1: The distribution of the amount spent by men is larger than for women.

When the two independent samples both have at least eight observations, the test statistic is the standard normal distribution. Formula [15-4] for *z* is:

$$z = \frac{W - \dfrac{n_1(n_1 + n_2 + 1)}{2}}{\sqrt{\dfrac{n_1 n_2(n_1 + n_2 + 1)}{12}}}$$

Where:
n_1 is the number of observations from the first population.
n_2 the number of observations from the second population.
W is the sum of the ranks from the first population .

At the 0.05 significance level the null hypothesis is rejected if *z* is greater than 1.65.

The test is based on the sum of the ranks. The two samples are ranked as if they belonged to a single sample. If the null hypothesis is true---that the two populations are the same--then the sum of the ranks for the two groups would be about the same. If the null hypothesis is not true, then there will be a disparity in the rank sums.

The data on the amounts spent by both the men and the women are ranked in the following table and the rank sums determined.

Amount Spent by Men		Amount Spent by Women	
Dollars	Rank	Dollars	Rank
$4.32	4.5	$2.81	1.0
6.05	7.0	3.45	2.0
7.21	9.0	4.16	3.0
8.57	12.0	4.32	4.5
9.80	13.0	5.54	6.0
10.10	14.0	6.93	8.0
12.76	17.0	7.54	10.0
13.65	18.0	8.32	11.0
15.87	19.0	10.76	15.0
		11.21	16.0
	113.5		76.5

The value of z is computed where $W = 113.5$, $n_1 = 9$ and $n_2 = 10$. Note that there was a man and a woman who each spent $4.32. That is, there is a tie for this position. To resolve the tie, the ranks involved are averaged. That is, the ranks of 4 and 5 are averaged and the value of 4.5 is assigned to those involved.

$$z = \frac{W - \dfrac{n_1(n_1 + n_2 + 1)}{2}}{\sqrt{\dfrac{n_1 n_2(n_1 + n_2 + 1)}{12}}} = \frac{113.5 - \dfrac{9(9 + 10 + 1)}{2}}{\sqrt{\dfrac{9(10)(9 + 10 + 1)}{12}}} = 1.919$$

Because the computed value of z (1.919) is greater than the critical value of 1.65, the null hypothesis is rejected. The distribution of the amounts spent by men is larger than that of women. To say it another way, the median of the distribution of the amounts spent by men is larger than the median of the amounts spent by women.

Exercise 15.4

Check your answers against those in the ANSWER section.

The Continental Muffler Company manufactures two different mufflers, the Tough Muffler and the Long Last Muffler. As an experiment, they installed Tough Mufflers on eight of their employees' automobiles and the Long Last on nine cars. The number of miles driven before a muffler needed replacing is recorded below (in thousands of miles).

Tough Muffler	Long Last Muffler
24	35
31	46
37	49
44	52
36	41
30	40
28	32
21	29
	27

Assume the distributions of miles driven are not normal. Does the evidence suggest a difference in the number of miles driven using the two mufflers before replacement? Use the 0.05 significance level.

Problem 6

A study is made regarding the reaction time (in seconds) to danger among four groups of professional drivers: cab drivers, bus drivers, truck drivers, and race car drivers. The results are as follows:

Reaction Time (seconds)			
Cab Drivers	Bus Drivers	Truck Drivers	Race Car Drivers
3.4	4.5	3.7	2.8
3.3	4.0	3.0	2.7
1.9	2.9	2.1	3.8
3.1	3.1	2.9	2.2
2.5	3.7	1.8	1.7
	4.4	3.6	

Assume that the reaction times are not normally distributed. At the 0.05 significance level, is there a difference in reaction times?

Solution

The ANOVA technique described in Chapter 11 for comparing several population means assumed that the populations are normally distributed. In this case the normality assumption cannot be made. Hence a nonparametric alternative, the Kruskal-Wallis test, is used. The null and alternate hypotheses are:

H_0: The distributions of reaction times are the same.
H_1: The distributions of reaction times are not the same.

The χ^2 distribution is the test statistic. For this test there are $k - 1$ degrees of freedom, where $k = 4$ is the number of treatments (groups of professional drivers), so the degrees of freedom is $k - 1 = 4 - 1 = 3$. The critical value from Appendix I is 7.815 given a significance level of 0.05.

The value of the test statistic is computed using formula [15-5].

$$H = \frac{12}{n(n+1)}\left(\frac{\Sigma R_1^2}{n_1} + \frac{\Sigma R_2^2}{n_2} + \ldots \frac{\Sigma R_k^2}{n_k}\right) - 3(n+1)$$

Where:

$\Sigma R_1, \Sigma R_2 \ldots \Sigma R_k$ are the sum of the ranks for the sample designated $1, 2, \ldots, k$.

$n_1, n_2, \ldots .n_k$ are the sizes of samples $1, 2, \ldots k$.

n is the combined number of observations for all samples.

There are $(k - 1)$ degrees of freedom (k is the number of populations).

The value of the test statistic is computed by first ranking the reaction times of the four groups as though they were a single group. Note that there are several instances involving tied ranks. The third bus driver and the fourth truck driver each had a reaction time of 2.9 seconds. These two drivers involve the 9th and 10th ranks. To resolve the tie, the ranks involved are averaged and the average rank assigned to each. Hence both drivers are assigned the rank of 9.5, found by $(9 + 10)/2$. The other ties are resolved in a similar fashion.

Reaction Times and Ranks for Professional Drivers							
Cab Drivers		Bus Drivers		Truck Drivers		Race Car Drivers	
Time	Rank	Time	Rank	Time	Rank	Time	Rank
3.4	15	4.5	22	3.7	17.5	2.8	8
3.3	14	4.0	20	3.0	11	2.7	7
1.9	3	2.9	9.5	2.1	4	3.8	19
3.1	12.5	3.1	12.5	2.9	9.5	2.2	5
2.5	6	3.7	17.5	1.8	2	1.7	1
		4.4	21	3.6	16		
Total	50.5		102.5		60		40

Next, these results are substituted into the formula for H and its value is computed:

$$H = \frac{12}{n(n+1)}\left(\frac{\left(\Sigma R_1\right)^2}{n_1} + \frac{\left(\Sigma R_2\right)^2}{n_2} + \frac{\left(\Sigma R_3\right)^2}{n_3} + \frac{\left(\Sigma R_4\right)^2}{n_4}\right) - 3(n+1)$$

$$= \frac{12}{22(22+1)}\left(\frac{(50.5)^2}{5} + \frac{(102.5)^2}{6} + \frac{(60)^2}{6} + \frac{(40)^2}{5}\right) - 3(22+1)$$

$$= \frac{12}{506}(510.05 + 1751.04 + 600 + 320) - 69 = (75.44 - 69) = 6.44$$

Since the computed value (6.44) is less than the critical value of 7.815, the null hypothesis cannot be rejected The evidence does not suggest a difference in the distribution of reaction times to emergency situations among various types of professional drivers.

Exercise 15.5

Check your answers against those in the ANSWER section.

A travel agency selected samples of hotels from each of three major chains and recorded the occupancy rate for each hotel on a specific date. The occupancy rate is the percentage of the total number of rooms that were occupied the previous night. The results are as follows:

Best Eastern	Comfort Inn	Quality Court
58%	69%	72%
57	67	80
67	62	84
63	69	94
61	77	86
64		

Do these data suggest any difference in the occupancy rates? Use the 0.05 significance level. Assume that the percentages of occupancy rates are not normally distributed.

Problem 7

A sample of 12 auto mechanics was ranked by the supervisor regarding their mechanical ability and their social compatibility. The results are as follows:

Worker	Mechanical Ability	Social Compatibility
1	1	4
2	2	3
3	3	2
4	4	6
5	5	1
6	6	5
7	7	8
8	8	12
9	9	11
10	10	9
11	11	7
12	12	10

Compute the coefficient of rank correlation. Can we conclude that there is a positive association in the population between the ranks of mechanical ability and social compatibility? Use the 0.05 significance level.

Solution

The steps in finding the coefficient of rank correlation are: (1) compute the difference between each set of ranks and then (2) square these differences. The difference is designated d.

Worker	Mechanical Ability	Social Compatibility	d	d^2
1	1	4	-3	9
2	2	3	-1	1
3	3	2	1	1
4	4	6	-2	4
5	5	1	4	16
6	6	5	1	1
7	7	8	-1	1
8	8	12	-4	16
9	9	11	-2	4
10	10	9	1	1
11	11	7	4	16
12	12	10	2	4
			0	74

Applying formula [15-6]:

$$r_s = 1 - \frac{6\left(\Sigma d^2\right)}{n\left(n^2 - 1\right)} = 1 - \frac{6(74)}{12\left(12^2 - 1\right)} = 0.741$$

The value 0.741 indicates a fairly strong positive association between the ranks of mechanical ability and social compatibility. It appears those workers with more mechanical ability also show more social compatibility.

Could this association be due to chance? Use the 0.05 significance level. To answer this question we first state the null and alternate hypotheses.

H_0: The rank correlation in the population is zero.
H_1: The rank correlation in the population is greater than zero.

The alternate hypothesis suggests a one-tailed test. There are ten degrees of freedom, found by $(n - 2) = (12 - 2) = 10$. To locate the critical value refer to Appendix F. For the 0.05 level the critical value of t is 1.812. H_0 is rejected if the computed value of t is greater than 1.812. Using formula [15-7], the computed t is 3.490.

$$t = r_s\sqrt{\frac{n-2}{1-r_s^2}} = 0.74\sqrt{\frac{12-2}{1-(0.741)^2}} = 0.741\sqrt{22.177} = 0.741(4.7092) = 3.4895 = 3.49$$

Since the computed value of 3.49 exceeds the critical value of 1.812, H_0 is rejected and H_1 accepted. It is concluded that there is a positive association between the ranks of social compatibility and mechanical ability among auto mechanics.

Chapter 15

Exercise 15.6

Check your answers against those in the ANSWER section.

The sports editors of the two daily Detroit newspapers predicted the order of finish for the upcoming BigTen football season:

Team	News	Free Press
Penn State	1	2
Ohio State	2	1
Michigan	3	5
Iowa	4	6
Wisconsin	5	3
Michigan State	6	7
Indiana	7	8
Minnesota	8	9
Purdue	9	10
Illinois	10	4
Northwestern	11	11

Compute the coefficient of rank correlation. Interpret.

CHAPTER ASSIGNMENT 15

NONPARAMETRIC METHODS: ANALYSIS OF RANKED DATA

Name _____   Section _____   Score_____

Part I   Select the correct answer and write the appropriate letter in the space provided.

_____1. For nonparametric tests
    a.   the population must be normal.
    b.   there cannot be more than two populations.
    c.   the populations must be independent.
    d.   assumptions regarding the shape of the population are not necessary.

_____2. Which of the following is not an example of a nonparametric test?
    a.   sign test.
    b.   median test.
    c.   one-way ANOVA.
    d.   Kruskal-Wallis test.

_____3. Which of the following tests require paired observations or dependent samples?
    a.   sign test and Kruskal-Wallis
    b.   Wilcoxon's rank-sum and signed-rank tests
    c.   coefficient of rank correlation and Wilcoxon rank-sum test.
    d.   sign test and Wilcoxon signed-rank test.

_____4. The Wilcoxon signed-rank test is stronger than the sign test because the
    a.   Wilcoxon uses interval scale.
    b.   sign test actually uses independent observations.
    c.   sign test has fewer observations.
    d.   Wilcoxon considers the magnitude of the differences.

_____5. Which of the following conditions must be met for the sign test?
    a.   independent samples.
    b.   at least 30 observations.
    c.   dependent samples.
    d.   all of the above.

_____6. The z distribution is used as the test statistic for the Wilcoxon rank-sum test when
    a.   each sample has at least 8 observations.
    b.   the populations are normal.
    c.   the populations have equal standard deviations.
    d.   the samples are dependent.

_____7. The binomial distribution is used as the test statistic for which of the following tests?
    a.   sign test.
    b.   Wilcoxon signed-rank test.
    c.   Wilcoxon rank-sum test.
    d.   Kruskal-Wallis test

_____.8. Which of the following nonparametric tests can be used when comparing more than two populations?
   a.   sign test.
   b.   Kruskal-Wallis test.
   c.   median test.
   d.   Wilcoxon signed-rank test.

_____.9. What is the difference between Pearson's and Spearman's coefficients of correlation.
   a.   Spearman cannot be negative.
   b.   Pearson requires that n be at least 10.
   c.   Spearman uses ranked data.
   d.   Pearson uses nominal data.

_____.10. The Kruskal-Wallis is a nonparametric alternative to
   a.   the chi-square tests.
   b.   the paired t test.
   c.   the independent t test.
   d.   ANOVA

Part II   Record your answer in the space provided. Show essential work.

11.   The National Association of Certified Public Accountants selected a sample of taxpayers with gross incomes of more than $100,000. They asked two major accounting firms to compute the income tax liability for each sampled taxpayer. Use the sign test and the 0.10 significance level to determine if there is a difference in the tax liability.

Taxpayer	Sheet Tax Service	Square Deal				
Schwind	18.9	28.0				
Gankowski	33.1	24.8				
Virost	38.2	28.0				
Williamson	30.2	38.0				
Govito	30.7	31.7				
Trares	30.9	25.7				
Willbond	28.1	30.7				
Fowler	27.2	29.9				
Hawley	30.2	31.0				
Hall	26.2	34.5				
Sanchez	33.4	35.3				
Naymik	33.6	28.2				

   a.   State the null and the alternate hypotheses.

   H_0: _____ H_1: _____

b. State the decision rule.

_____

c. Compute the value of the test statistic. .(Use the space provided in the data table)

c.

d. What is your decision regarding the null hypothesis. Interpret the result.

_____

12. Refer to Problem 11. Rework the problem using the Wilcoxon signed-rank test.

a. State the null and the alternate hypotheses

H_0: _____ H_1: _____

b. State the decision rule.

_____

c. Compute the value of the test statistic. .(Use the space provided in the data table)

c.

d. What is your decision regarding the null hypothesis? Interpret the result.

_____

13. A large Publishing Company wants to compare the annual operating costs of two brands of copying machines. The chief accountant gathered the following information. At the 0.05 significance level is there a difference in the operating costs of the two machines? The distributions of costs are not normally distributed.

Copier A		Copier B	
12,965		4,462	
13,145		4,990	
13,504		5,106	
13,603		5,844	
13,727		7,470	
13,833		7,740	
13,925		8,429	
14,438		9,954	
14,948		10,957	
15,202		12,532	
		13,338	
		14,828	
		21,641	
		23,045	
		28,110	

a. State the null and the alternate hypotheses:

H_0: _____ H_1: _____

b. State the decision rule

_____

c. Compute the value of the test statistic. (Use the space provided in the data table)

c.	

d. What is your decision regarding the null hypothesis? Interpret the result.

_____

14. A retired husband and wife were asked to rate their favorite daytime soaps on a scale of 1 to 20. Their ratings are:

Taxpayer	Husband		Wife			
Mother Knows Best	1		3			
Parlor Games	20		18			
Teddy	3		2			
Sam's Other Sister	5		7			
Time Elapses	4		5			
Sands in the Ocean	16		19			
Laugh, Laugh	10		11			
Hurry Home	3		4			
Stall No More	9		9			
Tidlie, Toodle	6		4			

a. Rank each of the shows for the husband and the wife.

a.

b. Compute the coefficient of rank correlation.

b.

CHAPTER 16
STATISTICAL QUALITY CONTROL

Chapter Goals

After completing this chapter, you will be able to:

1. Discuss the role of quality control in production and service operations.

2. Define and understand the terms: chance causes; assignable causes; in control and out of control; attribute and variable.

3. Construct and interpret a Pareto chart.

4. Construct and interpret a Fishbone diagram.

5. Construct and interpret a mean chart and a range chart.

6. Construct and interpret a percent defective and a c-bar chart.

7. Discuss acceptance sampling.

8. Construct an operating characteristic curve for various sampling plans.

Introduction

Prior to the Industrial Revolution, a craftsman was in complete charge of the quality of the finished product. Before selling a buggy, the craftsman made sure the wheels were round, all the bolts were tight, etc. The Industrial Revolution changed the way clothing, furniture, farm implements, shoes, and other consumer items were manufactured. Employees were organized in assembly lines and each employee performed one or two tasks. To control the quality of the output, all of the finished products were inspected, that is, there was 100 percent inspection after the manufacturing operation was completed.

During the 1930s and 1940s the concept of *statistical quality control* was developed.

> *Statistical quality control*: A concept for controlling the quality of mass-produced items. The objective is to monitor production through many stages of manufacturing.

Instead of 100 percent inspection, a sample of the parts produced is selected and inspected during production and a decision made regarding the quality of the production. The goal is to minimize the amount of defective material produced.

Causes of Variation

On a production line there is no such thing as two identical parts. The difference between two parts may be very small but they are different. The tensile strength of a roll of steel wire varies throughout the length of wire, and not every McDonald's Quarter Pounder has exactly 0.25 lbs. of meat. There are two general categories of variation in a process: *chance variation* and *assignable variation* causes.

> *Chance variations*: Variation that is random in nature. This type of variation cannot be completely eliminated unless there is a major change in the equipment or material used in the process.

A few examples of chance variation include, temperature, humidity, dust in the air, variations in materials, and vibrations from a passing forklift. Chance causes are large in number and random in nature and usually cannot be eliminated. The amount of material or "shot" of plastic used in the injection molding of a plastic product varies due to many conditions. Conditions such as temperature, dust and dirt, etc. are not always constant causing the amount of plastic to vary slightly.

> *Assignable variation*: Variation that is not random. It can be eliminated or reduced by investigating the problem and finding the cause.

An assignable cause of variation is nonrandom variation which can usually be eliminated or greatly reduced. Suppose the sample boxes of breakfast cereal are significantly overweight. An investigation revealed that the lever controlling the weight of the cereal had become loose. Thus, the assignable cause is a loose lever, and it can be easily reset and tightened.

In recent years competition from foreign manufacturers, especially in the automotive industry, has caused American firms to revamp and strengthen their quality control programs.

Diagnostic Charts

Two popular and very useful tools for investigating quality problems to insure that a product is manufactured properly are a *Pareto chart* and a *Fishbone diagram*.

> *Pareto chart*: An analysis technique for tallying the number and type of defects that happen within a product or service.

Pareto, an Italian scientist, noted that most of the "activity" in a process is caused by relatively few of the "factors." His concept, called the 80-20 rule, is that 80 percent of the activity is caused by 20 percent of the factors. The point he makes is that if management concentrates its efforts on 20 percent of the factors, they can attack 80 percent of the problem.

> *Fishbone diagram*: A cause and effect diagram to emphasize the relationship between an effect and a set of possible causes that produce the particular effect.

The fishbone diagram is useful to help organize ideas and to identify relationships that can help us determine factors that are a cause of variability in our process. The usual approach to a fishbone diagram is to consider four problem areas namely: methods, materials, equipment, and personnel.

Fishbone Diagram

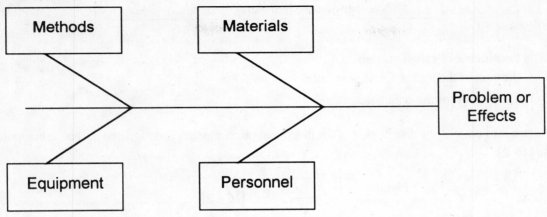

Quality Control Charts

A useful tool for insuring that a product is manufactured properly is a *quality control chart*.

> *Quality control charts*: Portray graphically the results of samples taken during the production period. It is used to identify when assignable causes of variation or changes have entered the process.

Control charts are based on the theory of sampling. We select random samples of the product during the production process and portray the results in chart form. These control charts are useful for separating random causes of variation from those that are assignable to some particular condition.

There are two types of control charts, namely *variable control chart* and *attribute control chart*.

> *Variable control chart*: A control chart that portrays interval or ratio scale measurements.

The variable control chart portrays measurements such as amount of liquid, length of a steel bar, and the time it takes to pack a computer for shipping.

> *Attribute control chart*: A control chart that classifies a product or service as acceptable or unacceptable and is based on the nominal scale of measurement.

The attribute control chart portrays measurements such as the rating of a software program as acceptable or not acceptable.

In order to develop control charts we rely on the sampling theory discussed in connection with the Central Limit Theorem in Chapter 8. In a quality control process we may take several samples every thirty minutes from a production run and compute the mean for each sample. We would then compute the grand mean, that is, the mean of the means. We use formula [16-1].

$$\overline{\overline{X}} = \frac{\Sigma \text{ of the means of the subgroups}}{\text{Number of sample means}} = \frac{\Sigma \overline{X}}{k} \qquad [16-1]$$

Where:

k is the number of sample means.

$\Sigma \overline{X}$ is the sum of the means for each sample.

$\overline{\overline{X}}$ is the symbol for the grand mean.

The standard error of the distribution of the individual sample means is designated $s_{\overline{x}}$ and is computed using formula [16-2].

$$s_{\overline{x}} = \frac{s}{\sqrt{n}} \qquad [16-2]$$

Where:

s is the standard deviation

n is the sample size.

On a chart there is an *in control area* and an *out of control* area. If the plot on the chart representing production is in the "in control" area, it is assumed that the production is satisfactory. If the plot on the chart is in the "out of control" area, it is assumed that the production is unsatisfactory. There is an upper control limit (UCL), and a lower control limit (LCL).

Upper control limit and lower control limit: The two points (lines on the control chart) which separate the in control area from the out of control area.

A typical chart before any plots are made appears as:

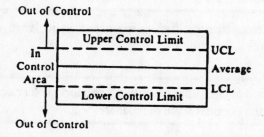

If we are concerned with the mean outside diameter of a pipe and if the manufacturing process is "in control," the sample mean will fall between the UCL and LCL 99.74 percent of the time by chance. This is the same as ± three standard deviations from the arithmetic mean.

Types of Control Charts

There are two basic types of control charts. We use control charts for **variables** when the characteristic under investigation can be measured, such as the outside diameter of a pipe or the weight of the contents of a bottle of cola.

> **Variable**: A reading or measurement that is obtained on the product or service.

Two types of control charts for variables are *the mean chart* and the *range chart*.

> **Mean chart**: The purpose is to portray the fluctuation in the sample means and to identify sample means that indicate that the process is out of control.

The mean chart shows management, production, engineers, machine operators, and others whether the arithmetic mean weight, length, outside diameter, inside diameter, etc., is in control (satisfactory), or out of control (unsatisfactory).

A mean chart has two limits, an upper control limit (UCL) and a lower control limit (LCL). These are computed using formula [16-3].

$$ULC = \overline{\overline{X}} + 3\frac{s}{\sqrt{n}} \quad \text{and} \quad LCL = \overline{\overline{X}} - 3\frac{s}{\sqrt{n}} \qquad [16-3]$$

Where:
s is an estimate of the standard deviation of the population σ.
n is the sample size.

Note that the number 3 appears in both formulas. It represents the 99.74 percent confidence limits. Other levels of confidence can be used.

Rather than calculate the standard deviation from each sample as a measure of variation, it easier to use the range. For small fixed size samples there is a constant relationship between the range and the standard deviation, so we can use the following formulas to determine the 99.74 percent control limits for the mean. It can be shown mathematically that the term $3\frac{s}{\sqrt{n}}$ from formula [16-3] is equivalent to $A_2\overline{R}$ in the following formula [16-4].

$$UCL = \overline{\overline{X}} + A_2\overline{R} \quad \text{and} \quad LCL = \overline{\overline{X}} - A_2\overline{R} \qquad [16-4]$$

Where:
A_2 is a constant used in computing UCL and LCL and is based on the average range $\overline{R}$. See Appendix B.

$\overline{\overline{X}}$ is the grand mean or the mean of the sample means, formula [16-1]: $\overline{\overline{X}} = \dfrac{\Sigma\overline{X}}{k}$.

$\overline{R}$ is the mean of the ranges of the sample, found by $\overline{R} = \dfrac{\Sigma R}{k}$.

A *range chart* has a similar purpose to that of the means chart.

> *Range chart*: Shows the variation in the sample ranges.

Its purpose is to portray the fluctuation in the sample ranges and to identify sample ranges that indicate that the process is out of control. It has been shown, that according to chance, the range of the samples will fall within the limits 99.7 percent of the time (997 out of 1000). When the range falls above the limits we conclude that an assignable cause has affected the operation and an adjustment in the process is needed. Note that for small samples the lower limit is often zero.

As examples, the two charts for variables might appear as:

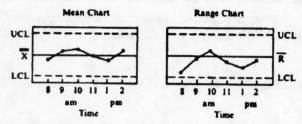

An analysis of the two charts reveals that both the arithmetic mean length of a piece of steel and the range of the lengths of the pieces are satisfactory (in control).

Attribute Control Charts

Some data we collect is the result of counting, rather than measuring. We may have a product or situation, such as a bank loan, that is either granted (acceptable) or not granted (unacceptable). Some products can only be classified as being "acceptable" or "unacceptable." Charts developed for these products are called *attribute charts*.

> *Attributes:* A product or service is classified as acceptable or unacceptable. No reading or measurement is obtained.

For example, a light bulb is either defective or not defective. When this type of classification is used, control charts for these attributes include *the percent defective chart* and *c-bar chart*.

Percent defective chart

When the item recorded is the fraction of unacceptable parts made in a group of parts, the appropriate control chart is the percent defective chart.

> *Percent defective chart*: Shows the percent of production that is defective.

The percent defective chart was drawn to show the percent defective for the manufacturing process for a ball bearing.

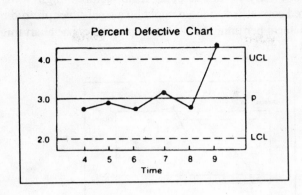

Percent Defective Chart

The process was in control from 4 p.m. until 8 p.m. The 9 p.m. check revealed that the percent defective exceeded the upper control limit of 4 percent. The quality control engineer would no doubt take steps to bring the process back into control (below 4 percent). A percent defective chart is also known as a p chart or $\bar{p}$ chart. The latter is pronounced "p bar chart."

The percent defective chart is based on the binomial distribution, discussed in chapter 6, and proportions, discussed in chapter 10. The center line of the chart is at $\bar{p}$, the mean proportion defective. Formula [16-6] is used.

$$\bar{p} = \frac{\text{Total number defective}}{\text{Total number of items sampled}} \qquad [16-6]$$

The variation in the sample proportion is described by the standard error of a proportion. Formula [16-7] is used.

$$s_p = \sqrt{\frac{\bar{p}(1-\bar{p})}{n}} \qquad [16-7]$$

The standard error of the proportion is used to compute the *UCL* and *LCL* Formula [16-8] is used.

$$LCL, UCL = \bar{p} \pm 3\sqrt{\frac{\bar{p}(1-\bar{p})}{n}} \qquad [16-8]$$

c–Bar Chart

It is difficult for many processes to manufacture all the units without a defect appearing. A chart designed to portray the number of defects per unit is called a *c-bar chart*.

$\bar{c}$ *chart*: An attribute chart that plots the number of defects or failures per unit.

For example, the exterior of an automobile being manufactured might have a paint glob on the hood, the trunk lid might not be centered correctly, and there might be a steel sliver protruding on the left front door. In that case, there would be three defects per unit. For this example, the c–bar chart might appear as:

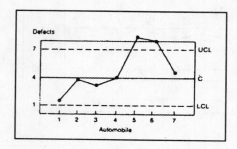

Based on the above chart, between 1 and 7 defects per car is expected. The average is 4. However, the number of defects in car 5 and car 6 exceeded the upper control limit and the process would be declared "out of control." It was brought under control for car 7. That is, the process was back "in control." The purpose of the c-bar chart is to show how many defects are in a unit of production.

We let $\bar{c}$ be the mean number of defects per unit. Recall from Chapter 6 that the standard deviation of a Poisson distribution is the square root of the mean. Thus we can determine the 99.74 percent confidence limits on a c–bar chart by formula [16-9].

$$LCL, UCL = \bar{c} \pm 3\sqrt{\bar{c}} \qquad [16-9]$$

Acceptance Sampling

In any business situation there is concern over the quality of an incoming shipment of a product. For example, a cola manufacturer purchases plastic 2 liter bottles from a blow molding supplier. The plastic bottles are received in lots of 2,400. The manufacturer does not expect each bottle to be perfect, but the manufacturer has an agreement with the supplier regarding the percent of the bottles that are defective. The usual procedure is to check the quality of the incoming product using a statistical sampling plan called *acceptance sampling*.

> *Acceptance sampling*: A method for determining whether an incoming lot of a product meets specified standards.

A random sample of *n* units is selected from the lot of *N* units. If *c* or less units are found defective among the *n* sampled units, the lot is accepted, otherwise it is rejected. The inspection will determine the number of defective parts in the sample. This number is compared to the predetermined number called the *acceptance number*. If the number of defects exceeds the acceptance number, the lot is rejected and returned to the supplier.

> *Acceptance number*: The maximum number of defective units allowed in a sample before the lot is rejected. The number is usually designated as *c*.

As an example, the cola manufacturer selects a random sample of 30 bottles and inspects each. If 3 or less are defective, the entire lot of bottles is accepted. Otherwise, the shipment is returned to the supplier.

Acceptance sampling is a decision-making process. According to the specific sampling plan, the lot is either acceptable or unacceptable. So there are two decisions that can be made. In addition, there are two states of nature. If the lot is acceptable and the sampling process reveals it to be good, or the lot is unacceptable and the sampling process shows the lot to be unacceptable, then a correct decision has been made. However, there are two additional possibilities. The lot may actually contain more defects than it should, but the sampling process reveals it to be acceptable. This is called *consumer's risk*.

Consumer's risk: The likelihood that a lot that should not be accepted is actually accepted.

If the lot is actually within agreed upon limits, but the sampling process reveals that it should be rejected, this is called the *producer's risk*.

Producer's risk: The likelihood that an acceptable lot is rejected.

The following table summarizes the possibilities for the acceptance decisions:

	States of Nature	
Decision	Good Lot	Bad Lot
Accept Lot	Correct	Consumer's Risk
Reject Lot	Producers Risk	Correct

An **operating characteristic** curve is developed to show the probabilities of accepting incoming lots with various quality levels. The binomial distribution is used to determine the probabilities corresponding to the various quality levels.

Glossary

Statistical quality control: A concept for controlling the quality of mass-produced items. The objective is to monitor production through many stages of manufacturing.

Chance variations: Variation that is random in nature. This type of variation cannot be completely eliminated unless there is a major change in the equipment or material used in the process.

Assignable variation: Variation that is not random. It can be eliminated or reduced by investigating the problem and finding the cause.

Pareto chart: An analysis technique for tallying the number and type of defects that happen within a product or service.

Fishbone diagram: A cause and effect diagram to emphasize the relationship between an effect and a set of possible causes that produce the particular effect.

Quality control charts: Portray graphically the results of samples taken during the production period. It is used to identify when assignable causes of variation or changes have entered the process.

Variable control chart: A control chart that portrays interval or ratio scale measurements

Attribute control chart: A control chart that classifies a product or service as acceptable or unacceptable and is based on the nominal scale of measurement

Upper control limit and lower control limit: The two points (lines on the control chart) which separate the in control area from the out of control area.

Variable: A reading or measurement that is obtained on the product or service.

Mean chart: The purpose is to portray the fluctuation in the sample means and to identify sample means that indicate that the process is out of control.

Range chart: Shows the variation in the sample ranges.

Attributes: A product or service is classified as acceptable or unacceptable. No reading or measurement is obtained.

Percent defective chart: Shows the percent of production that is defective.

$\bar{c}$ -chart: An attribute chart that plots the number of defects or failures per unit.

Acceptance sampling: A method for determining whether an incoming lot of a product meets specified standards.

Acceptance number: The maximum number of defective units allowed in a sample before the lot is rejected. The number is usually designated as c.

Consumer's risk: The likelihood that a lot that should not be accepted is actually accepted.

Producer's risk: The likelihood that an acceptable lot is rejected.

CHAPTER PROBLEMS

Problem 1

Custom Comp sells special order computers by taking orders, assembling the computers, and then delivering them to the customer. Each delivery is followed up with a survey seeking to identify ways to improve the service to the customers. Last month's survey showed these results:

a. Develop a Pareto chart.

b. What complaints should management focus on for improved customer satisfaction?

Type of Complaint	Number
Wrong hardware configuration	30
Late delivery	38
Poor technical support	22
Error on invoice	20
Component failure	15
Wrong software package	25

Solution

a. To develop a Pareto chart follow these steps:

Step 1. Calculate the total number of responses. The total is 150

Step 2. Determine what percent each category is of the total by dividing the number in each category by the total. See chart.

Type of Complaint	Number	Percent	Rank	Complaints in rank order	Percent	Cum. %
Wrong hardware configuration	30	20	2	Late delivery	25	25
Late delivery	38	25	1	Wrong Hardware	20	45
Poor technical support	22	15	4	Wrong Software	17	62
Error on invoice	20	13	5	Poor support	15	77
Component failure	15	10	6	Error on invoice	13	90
Wrong software package	25	17	3	Component failure	10	100

Step 3. Rank the frequencies from largest to smallest.

Step 4. Draw the Pareto chart:

Pareto Chart - Type of Complaint

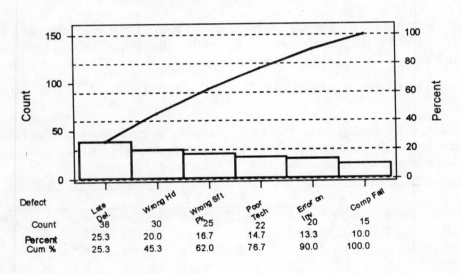

Defect	Late Del.	Wrong Hd	Wrong Sft Pk	Poor Tech	Error on Inv	Comp Fail
Count	38	30	25	22	20	15
Percent	25.3	20.0	16.7	14.7	13.3	10.0
Cum %	25.3	45.3	62.0	76.7	90.0	100.0

Problem 2

A machine set to fill a bottle with 60.0 grams of liquid was started at 7 a.m. today. Slight variations (called chance variations) were expected. The quality control inspector made her initial check of the weights at 8 a.m. She selected five bottles from the first hour of production and weighed the contents of each bottle. The results of the first seven inspections follow:

Time	1	2	3	4	5
8 a.m.	60.0	59.9	60.0	60.0	60.1
9 a.m.	60.0	60.2	60.1	60.2	60.0
10 a.m.	60.1	60.1	60.0	59.8.	60.0
11 a.m.	60.0	59.8	60.0	60.0	60.2
12 noon	60.2	60.0	59.8	60.1	59.8
1 p.m.	60.3	60.1	59.9	60.1	59.8.
2 p.m.	60.1	59.8.	59.7	59.9.	59.8.

a. Develop a control chart for the sample means.

b. Develop a control chart for the sample ranges.

Solution

a. The upper and lower control limits for the mean are determined using formula [16-3].

$$UCL \text{ and } LCL = \overline{\overline{X}} \pm A_2 \overline{R} \qquad [16-3]$$

Where:

$\overline{\overline{X}}$ is the mean of the sample means.

$\overline{R}$ is the mean of the ranges.

A_2 is a factor which is related to the standard deviation. A_2 is based on the number of observations taken each hour, that is, the sample size.

Statistical theory has shown that there is a constant relationship between the range and the standard deviation for a given sample size. A_2 expresses this constant relationship. To obtain the specific value for A_2, refer to Appendix B. Move down the "Number of items in the sample" column to 5. Read across the row to the A_2 column and read the value. It is 0.577.

To find the mean and the average range, refer to the table below. The sample values for 8 a.m. are 60.0, 59.9, 60.0, 60.0 and 60.1 grams, respectively. The sum of those five values is 300.0, so the mean is 60.0 grams (found by 300.0 / 5). The means for all remaining hours are computed. The sum of the seven means is 419.98 and the mean of these seven means $\left(\overline{\overline{X}}\right)$ is 59.997, found by: $\overline{\overline{X}} = \dfrac{\Sigma \overline{X}}{n} = \dfrac{419.98}{7} = 59.997$.

For the 8 a.m. check, the highest weight is 60.1 grams, the lowest 59.9 grams. The difference between the highest and lowest (the range) is 0.2. The sum of the seven ranges is 2.4 and the mean is 0.343, found by 2.4/7. This information is summarized in the following table.

Time	1	2	3	4	5	ΣX	$\overline{X}$	R	
8 a.m.	60.0	59.9	60.0	60.0	60.1	300.0	60.00	0.2	$\overline{\overline{X}} = \dfrac{419.98}{7} = 59.997$
9 a.m.	60.0	60.2	60.1	60.2	60.0	300.5	60.10	0.2	
10 a.m.	60.1	60.1	60.0	59.8.	60.0	300.0	60.00	0.3	
11 a.m.	60.0	59.8	60.0	60.0	60.2	300.0	60.00	0.4	$\overline{R} = \dfrac{2.4}{7} = 0.343$
12 noon	60.2	60.0	59.8	60.1	59.8	299.9	59.98	0.4	
1 p.m.	60.3	60.1	59.9	60.1	59.8.	300.2	60.04	0.5	
2 p.m.	60.1	59.8.	59.7	59.9.	59.8	299.3	59.86	0.4	
							419.98	2.4	

As noted, the control limits for the hourly sample means are determined using formula [16-3].

$$UCL \text{ and } LCL = \overline{\overline{X}} \pm A_2 \overline{R}$$
$$= 59.997 \pm 0.577(0.343)$$
$$= 59.997 \pm 0.198$$

So the lower control limit is set at 59.799 and the upper control limit is set at 60.195. The MINITAB software system was used to generate the following control chart. Note that subgroup 1 is 8:00 a.m., subgroup 2 is 9:00 a.m., etc. There is a small difference in the limits due to rounding, but it is clear that the process is in control until 2 p.m. At that time the sample mean drops to 59.86 grams. This is still greater than the lower limit on the chart of 59.80 grams. However, this rather dramatic downward shift is likely an indicator of trouble and should be investigated.

Control Chart for Bottle Weight

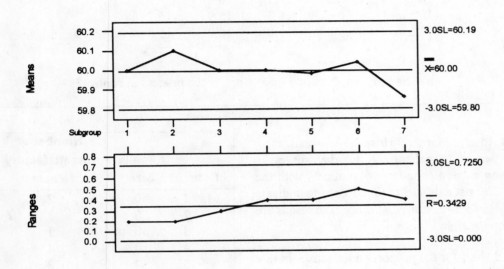

b. For the 8 a.m. check, the highest weight is 60.1 grams, the lowest 59.9. The difference between the highest and lowest (the range) is 0.2. The sum of the seven ranges is 2.4 and the mean 0.343, found by 2.4 / 7. This information is summarized in the previous table.

The LCL and UCL of the control chart for ranges is constructed using formula [16-4].

$$\text{Upper control limit UCL} = D_4\overline{R}$$

$$\text{Lower control limit LCL} = D_3\overline{R}$$

The factors D_3 and D_4 (like A_2) are developed from the constant relationship between the range and the standard deviation. The factors D_3 and D_4 are also obtained from Appendix B. To obtain the values go down the left column to the number in the sample (5) and then go across to the columns headed D_3 and D_4. The factor $D_4 = 2.115$ and $D_3 = 0$. To determine the UCL and LCL for the range chart:

$$\text{Upper control limit UCL} = D_4\overline{R} = 2.115(0.343) = 0.725$$

$$\text{Lower control limit LCL} = D_3\overline{R} = 0(0.343) = 0$$

The process appears to be in control for variability.

Check your answers against those in the ANSWER section.

At the Snyder Pretzel Factory a machine that is set to fill a bag with 16 ounces of pretzels was started at 7:00 a.m. today. Slight variations are expected. The Quality Control Inspector checked the weights as shown below.

		Bag		
Time	1	2	3	4
8 a.m.	16.1	16.0	15.9	16.1
9 a.m.	16.2	16.1	16.0	15.9
10 a.m.	16.0	15.8	15.9	15.7
11 a.m.	15.8	15.9	16.0	15.8

Develop a chart for the:

a. Sample means   b. Sample ranges   c. Is the process in control?

Problem 3

The Administration at Rossford General Hospital is investigating the quality of meals served to patients. A ten-day survey is conducted by submitting a questionnaire to 50 patients with the noon meal each day. The patients are required only to indicate whether the meal was satisfactory or unsatisfactory. The results are as shown in the table on the right:

Construct a control chart for the proportion defective. In this case, the chart is really measuring the proportion of the patients dissatisfied with the meal.

Date	Sample Size	Number of Unsatisfactory Meals
May 1	50	2
2	50	3
3	50	1
4	50	4
5	50	8
6	50	2
7	50	5
8	50	4
9	50	7
10	50	4

Solution

This problem requires the use of an attribute chart because a meal is classified only as satisfactory or unsatisfactory. No "measurement" is obtained.

The upper and lower control limits are determined using formula [16-8].

$$UCL \text{ and } LCL = \bar{p} \pm 3\sqrt{\frac{\bar{p}(1-\bar{p})}{n}} \qquad [16-8]$$

Where:
$\bar{p}$ is the proportion defective over all the samples.
n is the number in each sample.

The value of $\bar{p}$, the proportion unsatisfactory, is computed by first determining the proportion of unsatisfactory meals for each sample.

Date	Sample Size	Number of Unsatisfactory Meals	Proportion of Unsatisfactory Meals
May 1	50	2	0.04
2	50	3	0.06
3	50	1	0.02
4	50	4	0.08
5	50	8	0.16
6	50	2	0.04
7	50	5	0.10
8	50	4	0.08
9	50	7	0.14
10	50	4	0.08
			0.80

Then, to compute the mean percent defective:

$$\bar{p} = \frac{\text{Sum of percent defective}}{\text{Number of samples}} = \frac{0.80}{10} = 0.08$$

$$UCL \, and \, LCL = \bar{p} \pm 3\sqrt{\frac{\bar{p}(1-\bar{p})}{n}}$$

$$= 0.08 \pm 3\sqrt{\frac{0.08(1-0.08)}{50}}$$

$$= 0.08 \pm 0.115$$

$$= 0 \text{ and } 0.195$$

Thus, the control limits for the proportion of unsatisfactory meals are set at 0 and 0.195. The lower control limit could not logically be a negative number. The following MINITAB chart indicates that the proportion of unsatisfactory meals is well within the control limit.

Control Chart for Unsatisfactory Meals

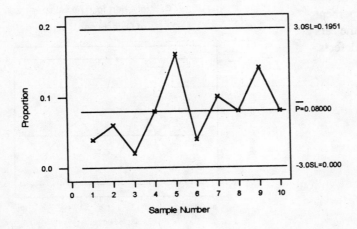

Chapter 16

Check your answers against those in the ANSWER section.

The manager of the campus Subway Sandwich Shop is investigating the quality of the noon special sandwich for the week of April 1. The five-day survey requested that customers indicate if a sandwich is satisfactory or unsatisfactory. The results are shown at the right. Develop a control chart for the proportion of customers dissatisfied with the sandwich

Day	Sample Size	Number Unsat.
1	40	2
2	40	3
3	40	1
4	40	2
5	40	4

Problem 4

A new automobile assembly line was put into operation. The number of defects on the exterior of the first ten cars off the assembly line was 3, 5, 4, 6, 2, 3, 5, 4, 2, and 4. Construct a $\bar{c}$ chart for the number of defects per unit.

Solution

The upper and lower limits for a $\bar{c}$ chart are determined using formula [16-7].

$$UCL \text{ and } LCL = \bar{c} \pm 3\sqrt{\bar{c}} \qquad [16-7]$$

The total number of defects in the first ten cars is 38, found by $3 + 5 + 4 + 6 + 2 + 3 + 5 + 4 + 2 + 4$. The mean number of defects per car ($\bar{c}$) is:

$$\bar{c} = \frac{\Sigma \text{of the number of defects}}{\text{Total number of cars}} = \frac{38}{10} = 3.8$$

The upper and lower control limits are:

$$UCL \text{ and } LCL = \bar{c} \pm 3\sqrt{\bar{c}} = 3.8 \pm 3\sqrt{3.8} = 3.8 \pm 5.848$$

$$UCL = 9.648, LCL = 0 (\text{since the number of defects cannot be less than } 0)$$

Based on the sample data for the $\bar{c}$ bar chart, more than 99 percent (99.73% to be more precise) of the cars will have between 0 and 9.648 defects.

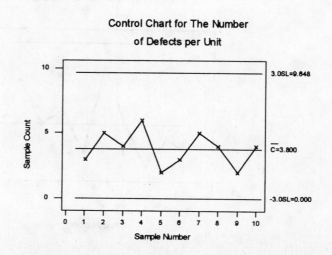

Control Chart for The Number of Defects per Unit

Problem 5

The Berry Cola Company processes a soft drink with a blueberry flavor added to the cola. It is packaged in 2-liter plastic bottles. The bottles are purchased from Persall Plastics in lots of 2,400. Berry Cola has agreed to select a sample of 25 incoming bottles and inspect them for all quality characteristics. If 2 or less defective bottles are found in the sample, the lot is considered acceptable. Suppose we want to develop an operating characteristic curve showing the likelihood that lots will be accepted that are 5%, 10%, or 20% defective.

Solution

This is an example of attribute sampling, because each bottle sampled is classified as either acceptable or not acceptable. No measurement or "reading" is obtained on the bottle.

The binomial distribution is used to compute the various probabilities. Recall that to employ the binomial distribution four requirements must be met.

1. There are only two possible outcomes. A bottle is either acceptable or not acceptable.

2. There are a fixed number of trials. The number of trials is the sample size, 25 in this case.

3. There is constant probability of success. A success is the probability of finding a defective part. In this case, Berry Cola is concerned about lots that are 5 percent, 10 percent and 20 percent defective.

4. The trials are independent. The probability the fifth bottle is defective is not related to the probability the eighth bottle is defective.

The binomial probabilities are given in Appendix A.

First, let's assume the lot is actually 5% defective, so $\pi = 0.05$, n, the size of the sample, is 25, and the acceptance number is 2. We usually let c refer to the acceptance number, so here $c = 2$.

Next, to find the probability turn to Appendix A, an n of 25, and the column where $\pi = 0.05$. Berry Cola will allow 0, 1, or 2 defects in the sample of 25.

Then, find the row where x, the number of defects, is 0 and read the probability. It is 0.277. The probability of 1 defect in a sample of 25 where $\pi = 0.05$ is 0.365. The probability of 2 defects is 0.231.

Adding these three probabilities (0, 1, and 2) gives the probability of accepting a lot that is actually 5 percent defective. The result is 0.873, found by (0.277 + 0.365 + 0.231). Hence, the probability of accepting a lot that is actually 5 percent defective is 0.873. This is often written in the following shorthand form.

$$P(x \le 2|\pi = 0.05 \text{ and } n = 25) = 0.873$$

Where:

x is the number of defects.

| means "given that."

To find the probability of 2 or fewer defects, when $\pi = 0.10$:

$$P(x \le 2|\pi = 0.10 \text{ and } n = 25) = (0.072 + 0.199 + 0.266) = 0.537$$

The probability of 2 or fewer defects when $\pi = 0.20$ is 0.099, found by (0.004 + 0.024 + 0.071).

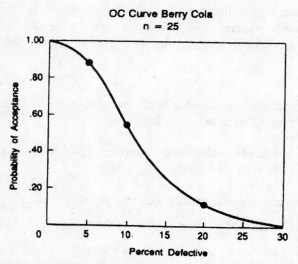

The above OC curve shows the various values of π and their corresponding probability of accepting a lot of that quality. The management of Berry Cola will be able to quickly evaluate the acceptance probabilities for the various quality levels. Other probabilities can be developed by using the normal approximation to the binomial distribution, (not discussed here).

Exercise 16.3

Check your answers against those in the ANSWER section.

Use the sampling plan developed above and compute the probability that a lot which is 30% defective is accepted

---

CHAPTER 16 ASSIGNMENT

STATISTICAL QUALITY CONTROL

Name _____ Section _____ Score _____

Part I   Select the correct answer and write the appropriate letter in the space provided.

_____1.   Statistical quality control means
     a.   inspecting all members of the population.
     b.   inspecting a sample of the population.
     c.   limiting the size of the population.
     d.   finding every defective item in the population.

_____2.   Chance causes are
     a.   random in nature.
     b.   due to some specific cause, like a worn tool.
     c.   the result of the use of control charts.
     d.   used in hypothesis testing.

_____3.   A variable control chart is
     a.   based on a measurement or reading.
     b.   used to estimate the probability of acceptance.
     c.   based on whether the product is acceptable or unacceptable.
     d.   used to estimate the standard deviation.

_____4.   Which of the following is a variable control chart?
     a. c-bar chart
     b.   percent defective chart
     c.   mean and range chart
     d.   all of the above

_____5.   In acceptance sampling
     a.   the sample size is n.
     b.   the binomial distribution is used.
     c.   the letter c is the acceptance number.
     d.   all of the above

_____6.   How far away from the mean are the upper and lower control limits?
     a.   99.73 percent
     b.   plus or minus two standard deviations
     c.   plus or minus three standard deviations
     d.   half the range

_____7.   A particular sampling plan consists of 20 items. The lot is considered acceptable if there are 0 or
     1 defects found in the sample.
     a. c is equal to 1   b.   the probability of accepting a lot 20 percent defective is 0.070
     c. n is equal to 20   d.   all of the above

_____ 8. Refer to question 7. If the acceptance number is increased from 1 to 2, the probability of accepting a lot 20 percent defective will
   a. stay the same.
   b. increase.
   c. decrease.
   d. cannot tell from the information given

_____ 9. An operating characteristic curve shows the probability of
   a. finding a particular sample size.
   b. finding a particular value for c.
   c. rejecting a lot.
   d. accepting a lot with a given percent defective.

_____ 10. The producer's risk is
   a. the likelihood an acceptable lot is rejected.
   b. the likelihood an acceptable lot is accepted.
   c. a new value for c.
   d. the size of the sample.

Part II Record the answers in the space provided. Show essential calculations.

11. The North Central Insurance Company is studying recent claim history. A sample of 5 claims (in $000) for each of the last 5 months is obtained.

Month	Samples					Total	Mean	Range
	1	2	3	4	5			
Jan	1.1	0.9	1.3	1.5	1.2			
Feb	0.5	1.4	1.4	1.3	1.1			
March	0.4	0.3	0.9	0.9	1.0			
April	1.3	1.6	1.6	1.5	0.6			
May	1.2	0.3	1.1	0.7	0.6			

a. Determine the upper and lower control limits for the mean.

a.

b. Determine the upper and lower control limits for the range.

b.

12. A high-speed machine produces a small plastic spacer. To check on the machine's performance, a sample of 30 spacers is selected each hour and the number of defects in the sample determined. On the basis of the samples taken yesterday, determine the control limits for the percent defective chart.

Sample Number	Number in Sample	Number of Defects
1	30	1
2	30	5
3	30	5
4	30	1
5	30	5
6	30	9
7	30	5
8	30	10
9	30	7
10	30	3

13. Dr. Sundar is chairman of the Sociology Department at Southeast State University. He is studying the number of students who drop a sociology course after they have initially registered. The following is the number of drops per section for the 15 courses offered last semester in the department:

4   9   3   4   4   4   8   6   8   2   1   2   2   3   5

What are the control limits for the c-bar chart of the number of drops?

13.

14. The Mills Hardware Company purchases various types of pliers, in lots of 5000, for sale in the Home Improvement Department. The Purchasing Department inspects 20 pliers at random before accepting each lot. If 2 or less of the pliers are defective, the lot is accepted. If 3 or more of the sample are defective, the lot is returned to the manufacturer.

a. Determine the probability of accepting a lot that is 10 percent defective.

a.

b. Determine the probability of finding a lot that is 20 percent defective.

b.

15. A company produces steel rods for various machines. The rods must meet strict specifications in order to function; otherwise they are unusable. Seven recent lots were examined and each rod was checked to see if it met the specifications. The data in the table at the right was observed:

Lot Number	Sample Size	Number of unusable rods
1	100	6
2	100	3
3	100	9
4	100	8
5	100	4
6	100	4
7	100	5

a. Determine the control limits for the percent defective chart.

a.

b. Based on this sample, what would the largest number of unusable rods per 100 be?

b.

16. The company in problem # 15 also undergoes a daily inspection of the lengths of the steel rods produced. The data in the table at the right is collected during a daily inspection:

	Sample lengths			
Time	1	2	3	4
9:00 a.m.	1.27 m	1.26 m	1.30 m	1.28 m
11:00 a.m.	1.26	1.29	1.26	1.27
1:00 p.m.	1.30	1.28	1.28	1.26
3:00 p.m.	1.26	1.29	1.26	1.28
5:00 p.m.	1.27	1.30	1.29	1.27

a. Determine the upper and lower control limits for the mean.

a.

b. Determine the upper and lower control limits for the range.

b.

Chapter Goals

After completing this chapter, you will be able to:

1. Describe an index.

2. Understand the difference between a weighted index and an unweighted index.

3. Construct and interpret a Laspeyres Price index.

4. Construct and interpret a Paasche Price index.

5. Construct and interpret a value index.

6. Explain how the Consumer Price index is constructed and used.

Introduction

There are thousands of indexes published on a regular basis by the federal government, foreign governments, the United Nations, magazines devoted to business such as *Forbes*, universities, and so on. You have most likely heard of such *index numbers* as the **Consumer Price Index**, the **Dow Jones Industrial Average**, and **Nasdaq**. What is an index number?

> ***Index number***: A number that expresses the relative change in price, quantity, or value from one time period to another.

The main use of index numbers is to describe the percent change in price, quantity, or value from one time period (called the ***base period***) to another time period.

> ***Base period***: Usually one year, such as 1982, which is used as a reference period. Changes in price, quantity, or value are measured from the base period to another period, called the given period.

The ***base*** of most indexes is 100.

> ***Base***: The number in the denominator used to compute the index. Most indexes have the base of 100.

At this writing, the base period for the Consumer Price Index (CPI) is the period 1993 – 95. It is written 1993-95 = 100. If the CPI for this month is 149.2, it indicates that the overall price of goods and services purchased by American consumers increased 49.2 percent from the 1993-95 base to the present month. Likewise, if the index measuring the quantity of pig iron exported is presently 90.0 with a base in 1986 of 100, it indicates that the quantity of exports decreased 10 percent from 1986 to the present.

Construction of Index Numbers

Simple indexes are calculated by dividing the number in the given period by the number in the base period. For a price index, P is found by formula [17-1].

$$P = \frac{p_t}{p_o}(100) \qquad [17-1]$$

Where:

P is the price index for any given period.

p_t is the price in the given period (any period other than the base period).

p_o is the price in the base period.

As an example, suppose the wholesale price of tomatoes in 1988 (selected as the base period and written $1988 = 100$), was 32¢ a pound, and currently they are 69¢ a pound. The index of tomato prices for the given period is 215.6, found by

$$P = \frac{p_t}{p_o}(100) = \frac{69}{32}(100) = 215.625 = 215.6$$

This reveals that the price of tomatoes increased 115.6 percent from 1988 to the present time.

Unweighted Indexes

In many situations we wish to combine several items and develop an index to compare the cost of a group of items in two different time periods. We might be interested in an index for the items that relate to the cost of driving a sport utility vehicle. This index would include items such as insurance prices, fuel prices, the cost of oil changes, license fees, and so on.

Simple Average of the Price Relatives

The simple average of the price relatives is an arithmetic mean of the simple indexes for a group of items. It is computed using text formula [17-2].

$$P = \frac{\Sigma P_i}{n} \qquad [17-2]$$

Where:

ΣP_i is the sum of the indexes for each of the items.

n is the number of items.

To illustrate, suppose the prices of several items for 1985 and 1998 and the simple index for each item is as shown.

The simple average of the price relatives is found using formula [17-2]

Commodity	Unit	1985	1998	Simple Index
Battery	Each	$ 60.00	$ 70.00	166.6667
Tires	Set of 4	240.00	380.00	158.3333
Gasoline	gallon	1.23	1.12	91.0569
			Total	366.0569

$$P = \frac{\Sigma P_i}{n} = \frac{366.0569}{3} = 122.01896 = 122.02$$

This indicates that the mean of the group of indexes increased 22.02 percent from 1985 to 1998.

A distinct advantage of the simple average of the price relatives is that the impact an item has on the average is not related to the units. A negative feature of this index is that it does not consider the relative importance of the items included in the index.

Simple Aggregate Index

A slightly more complex problem would be to compute the **simple aggregate index** for several commodities. The formula is text formula [17-3]

$$P = \frac{\Sigma p_t}{\Sigma p_o} \times 100 \qquad [17-3]$$

Where:

Σp_t is the sum of the prices for the given period.

Σp_o is the sum of the prices for the base period.

To illustrate using the previous example, suppose the prices of several items for 1985 and 1998 are shown in the table at the right:

A simple aggregate price index is computed using formula [17-3].

Commodity	Unit	1985	1998
Battery	Each	$ 60.00	$ 70.00
Tires	Set of 4	240.00	380.00
Gasoline	gallon	1.23	1.12
Total		$301.23	$451.12

$$P = \frac{\Sigma p_t}{\Sigma p_o}(100) = \frac{\$451.12}{\$301.23}(100) = 149.759 = 149.8$$

This indicates there has been a 49.8 percent increase in the prices over the 13-year period from 1985 to 1998.

This method of computing a price index has two major disadvantages. It fails to consider the relative importance (weights) of the items, and it does not take into account the differing units. The index would be different, for example, if we considered one tire instead of a set of four tires.

Weighted Price Index

In the previous example we indicated that relative importance or weights of the items were not taken into account. A way to appropriately weight various items is with a **weighted price index**. There are two common methods of computing a weighted price index.

Laspeyres Price Index

The most commonly used weighted price index is the *Laspeyres Price Index* named after its originator.

> **Laspeyres Price Index**: A weighted aggregate price index that uses the quantities in the *base* period as weights.

It uses *base-year* quantities as weights. In essence, it assumes that consumption of the items selected for the index does not change from the base period to the current period. Thus, only price is allowed to change and the index for the current period reflects this price change.

Text formula [17-4] is used:

$$P = \frac{\Sigma p_t q_o}{\Sigma p_o q_o}(100) \qquad [17-4]$$

Where:
p_t is the price in the current period.
p_o is the price in the base period.
q_o is the quantity consumed in the current period.

The Laspeyres method, with some modifications, is the method used for most weighted price indexes.

Paasche Price Index

Another weighted price index is the *Paasche Price Index* which uses the current quantity weights and adjusts the base each time a new period is considered.

> **Paasche Price Index**: A weighted aggregate price index that uses the quantities in the *current* year as the weights.

Text formula [17-5] is used:

$$P = \frac{\Sigma p_t q_t}{\Sigma p_o q_t}(100) \qquad [17-5]$$

Where:
p_t is the price in the current period.
p_o is the price in the base period.
q_t is the quantity consumed in the base period.

How do we decide which index to use? Both the Laspeyres index and the Paasche's index have limitations, as indicated in the following table:

	Advantages	**Disadvantages**
Laspeyres	Requires quantity data from only the base period. This allows a more meaningful comparison over time. The changes in the index can be attributed to changes in the price.	Does not reflect changes in buying patterns over time, thus may overweight goods whose prices increase over time.
Paasche's	Uses quantities from the current period, thus reflects current buying habits.	Requires quantity data for each year, which may be difficult to obtain. Because different quantities are used each year, it is impossible to attribute changes in the index to changes in price alone. Tends to overweight the goods whose prices have declined. Requires the prices to be recomputed each year.

Fisher's Ideal Index

Fisher's Ideal Index is an index that attempts to overcome the shortcomings of both the Laspeyres and Paasche's index.

Fisher's Ideal Index: The geometric mean of the Laspeyres and Paasche's indexes.

Recall that a geometric mean is calculated by taking the k root of the product of k positive integers.

Fisher's ideal index is computed using formula [17-6] from the text.

$$\text{Fisher's ideal index} = \sqrt{(\text{Laspeyres' Index})(\text{Paasche's Index})} \qquad [17-6]$$

It appears that Fishers Ideal Index is perfect since it combines the best features of both Laspeyres and Paasche, however it has the same basic flaws as the Paasche index. It requires a new set of quantities each year.

Value Index

A *value index* is an index computed for a group of items, such as computers, software, printers, and paper from one time period to another.

Value index: Measures the changes in both the price and quantities involved.

Text formula [17-7] is used:

$$V = \frac{\Sigma p_t q_t}{\Sigma p_o q_o}(100) \qquad [17-7]$$

Chapter 17

Where:
p_t is the price in the current period.
q_t is the quantity consumed in the current period.
p_o is the price in the base period.
q_o is the quantity consumed in the base period.

Note that we need the original base year prices, the base year quantities, the current year prices, and the current year quantities.

The Consumer Price Index

The *Consumer Price Index* (CPI) is the most well known price index.

> *Consumer Price Index*: Measures the change in the price of a fixed market basket of goods and services from one period to another.

Actually there are currently two consumer price indexes being published by the federal government every month. The Consumer Price Index—All Urban Consumers is applicable for about 80 percent of the total population. The other CPI, the Consumer Price Index for City Wage Earners and Clerical Worker Families covers about 32 percent of the population in the United States.

They are designed to measure the price changes in a fixed "market basket" of goods and services purchased by most American consumers using the base period 1993-95. Included are such diverse items as the price of gasoline, bread, dental fees, taxes, and soft drinks. It has been published regularly since 1921.

The CPI is not just one index. Separate indexes are published for food and beverages, transportation, medical care, entertainment, rent, and apparel. In addition, there are CPIs for most large cities, such as Dallas, Detroit, and Seattle.

Real Income

Both consumer price indexes have a number of other applications. The CPI can be used to determine *real income*.

> *Real income*: A person's income adjusted for changes in price. It allows a person to determine whether his or her standard of living has increased, stayed the same, or decreased since the base period.

The computation of real income allows a person to evaluate whether his or her take-home pay has been keeping up with price increases. If prices are rising faster than the increase in take-home pay (called money income) a person's standard of living is decreasing, meaning that she or he cannot purchase the same amount of goods and services as in the base period. Text formula [17-8] for real income is:

$$\text{Real Income} = \frac{\text{Money income}}{\text{CPI}}(100) \qquad [17-8]$$

Purchasing Power of the Dollar

The CPI can also be used to compute *the purchasing power of the dollar*.

> *Purchasing power of the dollar*: The value of one dollar in a given period compared with the value of a dollar in the base period.

As the name implies, it shows how much purchasing power the dollar has today compared with the base period. For a particular time period it is computed using text formula [17-10]:

$$\text{Purchasing power of dollar} = \frac{\$1}{\text{CPI}}(100) \qquad [17-10]$$

Glossary

Index number: A number that expresses the relative change in price, quantity, or value from one time period to another.

Base period: Usually one year, such as 1982, which is used as a reference period. Changes in price, quantity, or value are measured from the base period to another period, called the given period.

Base: The number in the denominator used to compute the index. Most indexes have the base of 100.

Laspeyres Price Index: A weighted aggregate price index that uses the quantities in the *base* period as weights.

Paasche Price Index: A weighted aggregate price index that uses the quantities in the *current* year as the weights.

Fisher's Ideal Index: The geometric mean of the Laspeyres and Paasche's indexes.

Value Index: Measures the changes in both the price and quantities involved.

Consumer Price Index: Measures the change in the price of a fixed market basket of goods and services from one period to another.

Real income: A person's income adjusted for changes in price. It allows a person to determine whether his or her standard of living has increased, stayed the same, or decreased since the base period.

Purchasing power of the dollar: The value of one dollar in a given period compared with the value of a dollar in the base period.

CHAPTER PROBLEMS

Problem 1

The hourly earnings for registered nurses at St. Luke's Hospital for selected years between 1986 and 1998 is shown. Using 1986 as the base period, develop an index that shows the changes in hourly earnings during the period. Interpret.

Year	Hourly Earnings
1986	$10.45
1988	12.66
1990	14.22
1992	15.91
1994	17.02
1998	17.57

Chapter 17

Solution

The wage in a selected period is divided by the wage in the base period and the result is multiplied by 100 (formula [17-1]). The calculations are shown below. The usual practice is to report the index either to the nearest tenth or the nearest hundredth.

Year	Hourly Earnings	Index	Found by
1986	$10.45	100.0	($10.45/$10.45)(100)
1988	12.66	121.1	($12.66/$10.45)(100)
1990	14.22	136.1	($14.22/$10.45)(100)
1992	15.91	152.2	($15.91/$10.45)(100)
1994	17.02	162.9	($17.02/$10.45)(100)
1998	17.57	168.1	($17.57/$10.45)(100)

The hourly earnings of the nurses increased by 68.1 percent from 1986 to 1998, found by (168.1 − 100.0).

Exercise 17.1

Check your answers against those in the ANSWER section.

The federal minimum hourly wage rates for selected years between 1975 and 1998 are shown. Using 1975 as the base period, develop an index that shows the changes in hourly wages.

Year	Hourly Wage
1975	$2.10
1980	3.10
1985	3.35
1990	3.80
1995	4.25
1996	4.75
1997	5.15
1998	5.75

Problem 2

An index is to be constructed to show the changes in the price of selected hardware items sold from 1986 to 1998. The prices and quantities consumed in the two periods are shown at the right. Using 1986 as the base period, compute:

Item	1986 Price	1986 Quantity	1998 Price	1998 Quantity
Hammer (each	$6.00	100	$9.00	120
Linseed oil (qt.)	2.00	1,000	2.00	1,100
Sandpaper (sheet)	0.10	800	0.08	900
½ hp. motor (each)	30.00	10	45.00	15

a. A simple aggregate price index.

b. The Laspeyres price index.

c. The Paasche price index,

Solution

a. First the simple aggregate price index is computed. The prices of the four items for the base year (1986) and the current year are totaled.

Item	1986 Price	1996 Price
Hammer (each	$6.00	$9.00
Linseed oil (qt.)	2.00	2.00
Sandpaper (sheet)	0.10	0.08
½ hp. motor (each)	30.00	45.00
Total	$38.10	$56.08

The formula for the simple price index is:

$$P = \frac{\Sigma p_t}{\Sigma p_o}(100) = \frac{\$56.08}{\$38.10}(100) = 147.2$$

The simple aggregate index shows the price has increased 47.2 percent in the ten-year period.

b. The simple, or unweighted index, does not take into account any of the quantities involved. For example, the price of sandpaper decreased by $0.02, but this will have little impact compared to the $3.00 increase in hammers or the $15.00 increase in the motor. A more meaningful measure is to consider the quantities consumed. The Laspeyres index assumes that the quantities in the base period are still representative in the current period and uses them as weights. Recall that the formula [17-4] for the Laspeyres price index is:

$$P = \frac{\Sigma p_t q_o}{\Sigma p_o q_o}(100)$$

The calculations for the Laspeyres weighted-price index are shown below:

Item	1986 Price p_o	Quantity q_o	$p_o q_o$	1998 Price p_t	$p_t q_o$
Hammer (each	$6.00	100	$600	$9.00	$900
Linseed oil (qt.)	2.00	1,000	2,000	2.00	2,000
Sandpaper (sheet)	0.10	800	80	0.08	64
½ hp. motor (each)	30.00	10	300	45.00	450
Total	$38.10		$2,980		$3,414

Applying formula [17-4]:

$$P = \frac{\Sigma p_t q_o}{\Sigma p_o q_o}(100) = \frac{\$3,414}{\$2,980}(100) = 114.6$$

The quantity sold in the base period q_o is held constant, that is, it appears both in the denominator and in the numerator. Since the quantity sold is held constant, the only factor affecting the index is price. The price of these selected hardware items increased 14.6 percent between 1986 and 1998.

c. Note in the previous table involving hammers, linseed oil, etc. that the quantities sold changed from 1986 to 1998. Paasche's index reflects these changes. Computing the price index using the Paasche method gives 116.4.

Item	1986 Price p_o	1996 Quantity q_t	$p_o q_t$	1996 Price p_t	1996 Quantity q_t	$p_t q_t$
Hammer (each	$6.00	120	$720.00	$9.00	120	$1,080.00
Linseed oil (qt.)	2.00	1,100	2,200.00	2.00	1,100	2,200.00
Sandpaper (sheet)	0.10	900	90.00	0.08	900	72.00
½ hp. motor (each)	30.00	15	450.00	45.00	15	675.00
Total			$3,460.00			$4,027.00

Formula [17-5] is used and the essential calculations are:

$$P = \frac{\Sigma p_t q_t}{\Sigma p_o q_t}(100) = \frac{\$4,027}{\$3,460}(100) = 116.4$$

Thus, the price of these selected items using current quantities consumed as weights increased 16.4 percent between 1986 and 1998. The Paasche method has one serious drawback. As the time period changes from 1993, 1994, 1995, etc., the quantity consumed for each one of those years must be collected and all the calculations redone.

Exercise 17.2

Check your answers against those in the ANSWER section.

The manager of a small marine discount store believes that prices of marine products have risen dramatically since 1988. Others disagree. To investigate, he selected a few items and recorded the prices and quantities sold the first week of April, 1988 and the first week of April, 1998.

Item	1988 Price p_o	Quantity q_o	$p_o q_o$	1998 Price p_t	q_t	$p_t q_t$
Battery	$25	32	$800	$40	30	$1,200
Cable	22	8	176	30	8	240
Bimini top	325	2	650	500	2	1,000
Depth finder	300	2	600	450	2	900
Total	$672		$2,226	$1,020		$3,340

a. Compute a simple aggregate price index.

b. Determine the weighted price index using the Laspeyres method.

c. Determine the weighted price index using the Paasche method

---

Problem 3

Hannah Simpson, an accountant, graduated from college in 1985 and received a starting salary of $22,000. By 1998 her salary had increased to $60,000. The consumer price index (1982 – 84 = 100) in 1985 was 107.6 and in 1998 it was 158.9. Convert her salary to 1985 dollars and determine her real income. What conclusion would you make?

Solution

By converting her actual yearly income of $22,000 and $60,000 to real incomes, changes in her standard of living between two time periods can be evaluated. If money income is increasing faster than the consumer price index, then a person's standard of living is higher than the base period. This would mean, in Hannah's case, she could buy more goods and services in 1998 than in 1985. Conversely, if consumer prices are rising at a faster rate than her money income, then her standard of living is declining. That is, she could buy less. Real income is computed using formula [17-8], which is:

$$\text{Real Income} = \frac{\text{Money income}}{\text{CPI}}(100)$$

$$\text{For 1985 Real Income} = \frac{\$22,000}{107.6}(100) = \$20,446.09 = \$20,446$$

$$\text{For 1996 Real Income} = \frac{\$60,000}{158.9}(100) = \$37,759.59 = \$37,760$$

Thus in terms of constant 1982-84 base period dollars, Hannah's salary increased $17,314, found by ($37,760 − $20,446). This is an increase in real income of 84.7%, found by ($17,314/$20,446)(100).

Problem 4

The Consumer Price Index in the base period of 1993-95 is set at 100. The CPI was 158.9 in January 1998. What is the purchasing power of the dollar for the base period and January 1998?

Solution

The purchasing power of the dollar for a particular time period is found by.

$$\text{Purchasing power of the dollar} = \frac{\$1}{\text{CPI}}(100)$$

$$\text{For the base period} = \frac{\$1}{100.0}(100) = \$1.00$$

$$\text{For January 1968} = \frac{\$1}{158.9}(100) = \$0.629 = \$0.63$$

Assume that a hamburger and an order of French fries cost $1 in the base period of 1993-95. Thus if you had $1,000 you could buy 1,000 orders. However, in January 1998 that same $1,000 could only purchase 630 orders (because the price of a burger and French fries had increased).

Exercise 17.3

Check your answers against those in the ANSWER section.

Carl Eger had an annual income in the base period of $40,000 and by 1998 his income had increased to $50,000. During the same period the consumer price index rose from 100 to 158.9.

a.   What was Carl's real income in 1998?

b.   Did his income keep pace with inflation?

c.   Compare the value of $1.00 in the base period with that of the year 1998.

CHAPTER 17 ASSIGNMENT

INDEX NUMBERS

Name _____ Section _____ Score _____

Part I   Select the correct answer and write the appropriate letter in the space provided.

_____1.   The base period is
   a.   always 1982-84.
   b.   usually a year such as 1990, or a group of years such as 1982-84.
   c.   always reported as dollars.
   d.   a number such as 104.67

_____2.   A given period refers to
   a.   any other period than the base period.
   b.   the year 1967.
   c.   a dollar value such as $25,000.
   d.   the smaller of two values.

_____3.   A Laspeyres Price Index uses as its weights
   a.   given period quantities.
   b.   base period quantities.
   c.   base period prices.
   d.   given period prices.

_____4.   In an aggregate price index
   a.   the prices of several commodities are added.
   b.   no consideration is given to the units.
   c.   it does not consider the quantities involved.
   d.   all of the above.

_____5.   The Paasche Price index uses as its weights the
   a.   given period quantities.
   b.   base period quantities.
   c.   base period prices.
   d.   given period prices.

_____6.   The current base period for the Consumer Price Index is
   a.   1994-96.
   b.   1982-84.
   c.   1982.
   d.   1984.

_____7.   The Index of Industrial Production for 1996 is 135.4, (1982-84 = 100). This means that production
   a.   increased $35.40 in 1996.   b.   declined 35.4 percent since 1982.
   c.   increased 35.4 percent since 1982-84.   d.   decreased 35.4 percent in 1996.

_____8. A firm sold $50,000 of a particular product in 1992 and $60,000 in 1998. Using 1992 as the base, what is the index for 1998?
   a. $10,000
   b. 20 percent
   c. 120 percent.
   d. 83.3 percent

_____9. An index has 1980 has its base. The index reported in 1990 was 127.2 and in 1998 it was 186.7. The percent increase from 1990 to 1998 is
   a. 46.8 percent.
   b. 27.2 percent.
   c. 59.5 percent.
   d. none of the above.

_____10. Which of the following price indexes uses *current* period quantities in its base?
   a. a value index
   b. a simple index
   c. Laspeyres Price Index
   d. Paasche Price Index

Part II: Record your answer in the space provided. Show essential work.

11. The earnings per share for Energen Corporation. from the 1997 Annual Report are given at the right. Develop an index showing the change in earnings for the given years. Use 1993 as the base period.

Year	Earnings per share	Index
1993	$1.77	
1994	2.19	
1995	1.77	
1996	1.95	
1997	2.31	

12. Professor Jim Martin had an annual income in the base period of $30,000. In 1998 his annual income was $61,100. During the same period the CPI rose from 100 to 158.9. What was his real income in 1998?

12.

13. The following table shows the prices and quantities consumed by a family of four for selected food commodities for 1990 and 1998. Use 1990 as the base period.

Commodity	1990		1998	
	Price	Quantity	Price	Quantity
Ground beef (per lb)	$1.39	80	$1.99	110
Milk (1 gallon)	1.69	100	1.89	120
Cookies (dozen)	1.29	95	1.69	100
Steak (per pound)	4.99	50	5.99	40

a. Determine the simple index for steak for 1998.

```
a.
```

b. Determine the simple aggregate price index for 1998.

```
b.
```

c. Determine the Laspeyres price index for 1998.

```
c.
```

d. Determine the Paasche price index for 1998.

```
d.
```

e. Determine a value index for 1998.

```
e.
```

14. The table below reports the net profit for Heban Tool and Die, Inc. for the years 1990 and 1998 Also reported is the tool and die index for the same years (1985 = 100).

Year	Net profit	Index
1990	$45,380	120
1998	65,035	150

a. What was the percent increase in the index from 1990 to 1998?

a.

b. Convert the index to a 1990 base. What is the new index for 1998?

b.

c. Determine the net profit for 1998 in terms of the 1990 base. Comment on the change.

c.

Chapter Goals

After completing this chapter, you will be able to:

1. Define the four components of a time series.

2. Determine a linear trend equation.

3. Compute a moving average.

4. Compute the trend equation for a nonlinear trend.

5. Use trend equations to forecast future time periods and to develop seasonally adjusted forecasts.

6. Determine and interpret a set of seasonal indexes.

7. Deseasonalize data using a seasonal index.

Introduction

It is often necessary to analyze past sales, and/or production data, in order to estimate future events. A collection of data over a period of time is called a *time series*.

> *Time series*: A collection of data recorded over a period of time — weekly, monthly, quarterly, or annually.

The collection of time series data is generally done yearly, quarterly, monthly, or weekly. As an example of time series, Team Sports, a sporting goods store that opened in 1978, reports sales each month. Another example would be the employment data by quarter for the Atlantic City, New Jersey hotels since 1990. Analysis of historical data is useful to management in current decision making as well as intermediate and long-range estimates.

Components of a Time Series

A time series value consists of four components: the trend, cyclical variation, seasonal variation, and irregular variation. The first component of a time series is the *secular trend*.

> *Secular Trend*: The smooth long-term direction of a time series.

The trend or direction may be upward such as the sales at Team Sports. The trend may be downward. The manager of your bookstore would attest that the sales of slide rules have declined since 1975 to virtually zero today (because calculators and home computers have replaced slide rules in business and universities).

The second component of a time series is the *cyclical variation*.

> *Cyclical variation*: The rise and fall of a time series over periods longer than one year.

While the long-run direction of the time series may be increasing, there may be "ups and downs" that seem to follow the business cycle. These periods of prosperity and recession are referred to as cyclical variation.

The third component of a time series is the *seasonal variation*.

> *Seasonal variation*: Patterns of change in a time series within a year. These patterns tend to repeat themselves each year.

Many sales, production, and other time series fluctuate with the season. Sales of toys are highest during the Christmas season, and rentals of skis at a ski resort are higher in February and nonexistent in July.

The fourth component of a time series, **irregular variation**, may be divided into two components, *episodic fluctuations* and *residual fluctuations*.

> *Episodic fluctuations*: Unpredictable variation in a time series that is due to unusual causes that can be identified such as strikes, tornado damage, or fire.

Episodic variations are unpredictable, but they can be identified. Major floods, hurricanes, or strikes are examples of unpredictable events but it is possible to identity the time period in which they happened.

> *Residual fluctuations*: Unpredictable variation in a time series that cannot be identified.

Residual variation is the random variation that is present in a time series after the episodic variations have been removed from the data.

Types of Trend Equations

Linear Equations

If sales, employment, production, and other business series increase or decrease over a period of time and approximate a *straight line*, the equation for this growth is given by formula [18-1], the linear trend equation.

$$Y' = a + bt \qquad [18-1]$$

Where:
Y' is the projected value of the Y variable for a selected value of t.
a is the Y-intercept. It is the estimated value of Y when $t = 0$.
b is the slope of the line, or the average change in Y' for each change of one unit (increase or decrease) in t.
t is any value of time that is selected.

Least Squares Method

The *least squares method* of computing the equation for a straight line through the data of interest gives the "best fitting" line. The following equations are used to calculate a and b.

$$b = \frac{\Sigma tY - (\Sigma y)(\Sigma t)/n}{\Sigma t^2 - (\Sigma t)^2/n} \qquad [18-3]$$

$$a = \frac{\Sigma Y}{n} - b\left(\frac{\Sigma t}{n}\right) \qquad [18-4]$$

If the sales, production, or other data tend to approximate a linear trend, the equation developed by the least squares method can be used to estimate sales, etc. for some future period.

Nonlinear Trends

If the general trend of a time series does not follow a straight line when plotted on arithmetic graph paper, the least squares trend equation should not be used to approximate past trends or to estimate future values. A series that appears curvilinear when plotted on arithmetic graph paper should be fitted with a logarithmic trend equation. The general equation for the logarithmic trend equation is:

$$\log Y' = \log a + \log b(t) \qquad [18-5]$$

There are many other types of equations that may be fitted to the data, such as second and third degree polynomials. A good first step in determining which equation to use is to plot the data with time on the horizontal axis and sales, production, or the variable of interest on the vertical axis.

Seasonal Variation

Seasonal variations is another component of time series. Business series such as lawn care service firms, automobile sales, and highway construction, have periods of above average and below average activities each year. A *seasonal index* is used for analysis of the trends of seasonally affected businesses.

> *Seasonal index*: A value that identifies the effects of various seasons. The index is usually reported monthly or quarterly.

As the name seasonal implies, climatic conditions are often responsible for the variation in the time series. Construction activities, sales of skis and suntan lotion, and the production of corn are examples of products whose production and consumption are related to the weather. Retail sales increase around holidays such as Easter, Christmas, and the start of the new school year. Techniques are available to isolate the seasonal component of a time series in order to make better estimates. One reason for measuring a seasonal pattern is to understand the pattern and to compare it to other years.

For example, we may want to compare the sales this March with the sales in March for previous years. Another reason for determining an index is to use it for short-term planning. A firm in the lawn care business in the Great Lakes region, for example, will want to begin hiring seasonal employees early in April when the weather starts to get warm. The ratio-to-moving-average method of isolating the seasonal component will be examined in the Problem section.

Glossary

Time series: A collection of data recorded over a period of time — weekly, monthly, quarterly, or annually

Secular trend: The smooth long-term direction of a time series.

Cyclical variation: The rise and fall of a time series over periods longer than one year.

Seasonal variation: Patterns of change in a time series within a year. These patterns tend to repeat themselves each year.

Episodic fluctuations: Unpredictable variation in a time series that is due to unusual causes that can be identified such as strikes, tornado damage, or fire.

Residual fluctuations: Unpredictable variation in a time series that cannot be identified

Seasonal index: A value that identifies the effects of various seasons. The index is usually reported monthly or quarterly.

CHAPTER PROBLEMS

Problem 1

The sales (in $ millions) for the years 1994 to 1998 of Grape Juice, Inc. are shown.

a. Determine the least squares trend equation.

b. Estimate the sales for 2000, using the trend equation.

c. Plot the data on a chart.

Year	Sales ($ million)
1994	736
1995	781
1996	889
1997	942
1998	974

Solution

a. To simplify the calculations, the years are replaced by codes. In this problem we'll let the year 1994 be 1, 1995 be 2, and so on. This will reduce the size of the terms used in computing the trend equation. The trend equation is of the form $Y' = a + bt$, where Y' is the estimated sales, a is the Y intercept, b is the slope of the trend equation, and t is the coded time value. The computations needed are shown in the table at the right.

Year	Sales ($ million) Y	t	Yt	t^2
1994	736	1	736	1
1995	781	2	1,562	4
1996	889	3	2,667	9
1997	942	4	3,768	16
1998	974	5	4,870	25
	4,322	15	13,603	55

The values of a and b are determined using the formulas [18-3] and [18-4]. To emphasize that time is used as the independent variable t is used in place of X.

$$b = \frac{\Sigma tY - (\Sigma Y)(\Sigma t)/n}{\Sigma t^2 - (\Sigma t)^2/n} = \frac{13,603 - 4,322(15)/5}{55 - (15)^2/5} = \frac{637}{10} = 63.7$$

$$a = \frac{\Sigma Y}{n} - b\left(\frac{\Sigma t}{n}\right) = \frac{4,322}{5} - 63.7\left(\frac{15}{5}\right) = (864.4 - 191.1) = 673.3$$

The trend equation is $Y' = 673.3 + 63.7t$. How do we interpret this equation? The value of 673.3 is the intersection with the Y-axis. This is the estimated sales when the coded year is 0. The value 63.70 is the rate of change. That is, sales are increasing at a rate of $63.7 million dollars per year.

b. To estimate sales for 2000 the first step is to determine the code for that year. The code is 7 found by subtracting: (2000 – 1993). Note that 1993 would be year zero in the coding system. Next 7 is substituted for *t* in the trend equation and the value of Y' determined.

$$Y' = 673.3 + 63.7t = \left[673.3 + 63.7(7)\right] = (673.3 + 445.9) = 1119.2$$

The estimated sales for 2000 are $1,119.2 million.

c. Chart with trend line for sales data.

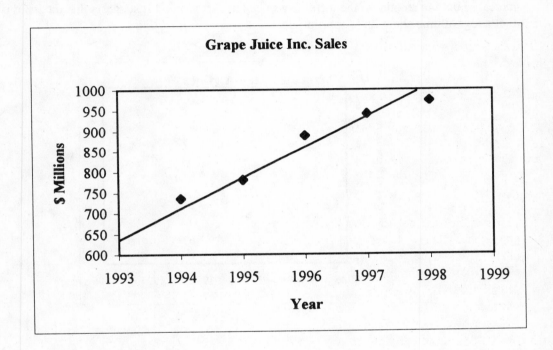

The following table reports the earnings per share (in dollars) for the Piedmont Natural Gas Company from 1992 to 1998.

Year	Average Shareholders' Equity					
1992	1993	1994	1995	1996	1997	1998
1.40	1.45	1.35	1.45	1.67	1.85	1.95

a. Plot the data.
b. Develop a linear trend equation.
c. Estimate the earnings per share for 1999.

Problem 2

The number of passengers carried by Northeastern Airlines from 1988 to 1994 is shown at the right.

a. Plot the data on a chart.

b. Determine a trend equation.

c. Estimate the number of passengers for 1996.

Year	Passengers (000)
1988	3.3
1989	4.1
1990	4.9
1991	6.4
1992	9.0
1993	12.8
1994	16.9

Solution

a. The data on the number of passengers carried by Northeastern Airlines is shown in the following chart. The number of passengers is increasing, but not in a linear fashion. In fact, the number of passengers not only increased but the amount of the increase was larger each year. This suggests that the trend is not linear, and that a logarithmic equation is appropriate.

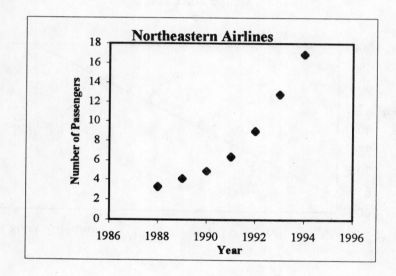

The MINITAB system is used to determine the logarithmic equation. The first step is to enter the years, next the codes for the years, and finally the number of passengers. The LET command is used to determine the logs of the number of passengers. Finally the REGRESSION procedure is used, with the log of the number of passengers as the dependent variable and the coded years as the independent variable. The output is as follows:

```
MTB > set cl
DATA> 1988:1994
DATA> end
MTB > set c2
DATA> 1:7
DATA> end
MTB > set c3
DATA> 3.3,4.1,4.9,6.4,9,12.8,16.9
DATA> end
MTB > name cl 'Year' c2 'Code' c3 'Pass-ger' c4 'Log-pass'
MTB > logten c3 c4
MTB > print cl-c4

     ROW   year  Code  Pass-ger    Log-pass
       1   1988  1         3.3     0.51851
       2   1989  2         4.1     0.61278
       3   1990  3         4.9     0.69020
       4   1991  4         6.4     0.80618
       5   1992  5         9.0     0.95424
       6   1993  6        12.8     1.10721
       7   1994  7        16.9     1.22789

MTB > Regress 'Log-pass' 1 'Code';
SUBC> Constant

Regression analyses

The regression equation is
Log-pass = 0.362 + 0.121 Code

Predictor    Coef       Stdev        t-ratio    p
Constant     0.36229    0.02678      13.53      0.000
Code         0.120751   0.005987     20.17      0.000

s = 0.03168      R-sq = 98.8%      R-sq(adj) = 98.5%

Analysis of Variance

SOURCE        DF      SS         MS         F         P
Regression    1       0.40826    0.40826    406.75    0.000
Error         5       0.00502    0.00100
Total         6       0.41328
```

The number of passengers for 1996 can be estimated using the logarithmic equation. The code for 1996 is 9, found by 1996 − 1987. Substituting $t = 9$ into the equation:

$$Y' = 0.36229 + 0.120751t = 0.36229 + 0.120751(9) = 1.449049$$

Since Y' is a logarithmic equation, we need the antilog of 1.449049. It is 28.122. Thus, the estimated number of passengers in 1996 is 28.122 thousand.

Chapter 18

Step 4. Determine the specific seasonal. The specific seasonal index for each quarter is then computed by dividing the quarterly enrollment in column 1 by the centered four-quarter moving average in column 4 and multiplying the result by 100. The specific seasonal for the summer quarter of 1995 is 32.3, found by (0.8/2.4750)(100). The specific seasonals are in column 5.

Year	Quarter	1 Enrollment	2 Four quarter moving Total	3 Four-quarter moving Avg.	4 Centered moving average Avg	5 Specific Seasonal
1992	Winter	3.2				
	Spring	2.8				
			10.0	2.500		
	Summer	0.8			2.4750	32.3
			9.8	2.450		
	Fall	3.2			2.4500	130.6
			9.8	2.450		
1993	Winter	3.0			2.4625	121.8
			9.9	2.475		
	Spring	2.8			2.5125	111.4
			10.2	2.550		
	Summer	0.9			2.6125	34.4
			10.7	2.675		
	Fall	3.5			2.7500	127.3
			11.3	2.825		
1994	Winter	3.5			2.8250	123.9
			11.3	2.825		
	Spring	3.4			2.9000	117.2
			11.9	2.975		
	Summer	0.9			3.0375	29.6
			12.4	3.100		
	Fall	4.1			3.1500	130.2
			12.8	3.200		
1995	Winter	4.0			3.2125	124.5
			12.9	3.225		
	Spring	3.8			3.2500	116.9
			13.1	3.275		
	Summer	1.0				
	Fall	4.3				

Step 5. Determine the mean of the specific seasonals. The specific seasonals are organized into a table and the mean specific seasonal for each quarter is determined. For the winter quarter the mean is 123.4.

Chapter 18

		Quarter			
Year	**Winter**	**Spring**	**Summer**	**Fall**	
1992			32.3	130.6	
1993	121.8	111.4	34.4	127.3	
1994	123.9	117.2	29.6	130.2	
1995	<u>124.5</u>	<u>116.9</u>	_____	____	
Total	370.2	345.5	96.3	388.1	**Total**
Mean	123.4	115.2	32.1	129.4	400.1
Typical Index	123.37	115.17	32.09	129.37	400.0

Step 6. Adjust the means. The total of the four means should theoretically be 400.0 because the average of the four quarters is designated as 100.0. However, the total may not be equal to 400.0 due to rounding. A correction factor, therefore, is applied to each mean to arrive at the typical seasonal indexes. It is computed by.

$$\text{Correction factor} = \frac{400.0}{\text{Total of means}}$$

$$\text{For this problem} = \frac{400.0}{400.1} = 0.99975$$

Multiplying each of the means by the correction factor of 0.99975 gives the four typical seasonal indexes

Winter	123.37
Spring	115.17
Summer	32.09
Fall	129.37

Note that enrollment is traditionally high in the fall and winter, and drops off sharply in the summer. The summer enrollment is typically only 32.09 percent of the mean enrollment, or nearly 70 percent below the mean enrollment for the year.

Exercise 18.3

Check your answers against those in the ANSWER section.

The quarterly sales for the Norton Company are given in millions of dollars for four years. Compute the quarterly seasonal index using the ratio-to-moving-average method.

		Quarter		
Year	**I**	**II**	**III**	**IV**
1995	2	8	10	2
1996	4	10	10	4
1997	4	12	14	4
1998	6	16	20	4

Problem 4

The Kinzua Boat Rental Company estimates that 24,000 boat rentals will be made this coming year. The seasonal index for the month of July is 130. What are the estimated rentals for July?

Solution

If there were no seasonal variation, 2,000 boats would be rented each month, found by 24,000/12. However, the index of 130 for July indicates that rentals are 30 percent above average for that month. To determine the projected rentals for July, we increase the average rental by 30 percent. This is computed by 2,000 (1.30) [or 2,000 (130/100)] which equals 2,600 rentals.

Exercise 18.4

Check your answers against those in the ANSWER section.

Refer to Problem 4. Suppose the seasonal index for June was computed to be 120 and 47 for November.

a. Determine the seasonally adjusted sales for June.

b. Determine the seasonally adjusted sales for November.

Problem 5

The Director of Admissions at Starbrick Tech needs an estimate of enrollment for each quarter of 1999. Use the enrollment data for the years 1995 to 1998 and the seasonal indexes determined in Problem 3 to find a trend equation for enrollment. Use the trend equation and the seasonal values to estimate enrollment for each quarter of 1998.

Solution

First we need to determine the seasonally adjusted trend equation. In the following table the actual enrollment for each quarter is shown in the "Students" column and the seasonal index is shown in the "Index" column. To determine the deseasonalized trend value, the actual enrollment is divided by the seasonal index. For example, the actual enrollment in the winter quarter of 1995 was 3.2 students (in thousands) and the seasonal index is 123.37 for the winter quarter. The deseasonalized enrollment is 2.5938, found by 3.2 / 1.2337.

Year	Quarter	Code	Students	Index	Deseasonalized
1995	Winter	1	3.2	1.2337	2.59382
	Spring	2	2.8	1.1517	2.43119
	Summer	3	0.8	0.3209	2.49299
	Fall	4	3.2	1.2937	2.47353
1996	Winter	5	3.0	1.2337	2.43171
	Spring	6	2.8	1.1517	2.43119
	Summer	7	0.9	0.3209	2.80461
	Fall	8	3.5	1.2937	2.70542
1997	Winter	9	3.5	1.2337	2.83699
	Spring	10	3.4	1.1517	2.95216
	Summer	11	0.9	0.3209	2.80461
	Fall	12	4.1	1.2937	3.16920
1998	Winter	13	4.0	1.2337	3.24228
	Spring	14	3.8	1.1517	3.29947
	Summer	15	1.0	0.3209	3.11624
	Fall	16	4.3	1.2937	3.32380

The MINITAB system is used to determine the trend equation with the seasonal effect removed. From the MINITAB output, which follows, the deseasonalized trend equation is $Y' = 2.2787 + 0.0636\,t$. This trend equation indicates that over the 16 quarters the deseasonalized growth rate was about 64 students per quarter. (Recall that the enrollment data was reported in thousands.)

```
MTB > regr c4 1 cl

The regression equation is
Deseason = 2.28 + 0.0636 Code

Predictor      Coef      Stdev     t-ratio       p
Constant     2.27871    0.07132    31.95      0.000
Code         0.063602   0.007376    8.62      0.000
```

Assuming that the 16 periods of historical data are reasonably good predictors of future enrollment at Starbrick Tech, we can use the trend equation to project 1999 enrollment. The winter quarter of 1999 is period 17, so $t = 17$ is substituted in the trend equation.

$$Y' = 2.2787 + 0.0636\,t = 2.2787 + 0.0636(17) = 3.3599$$

The estimated enrollment for the winter quarter is 3.3599, or 3,360 students, without considering the seasonal effect. The index for winter is 123.37, which indicates that winter is 23.37 percent above the typical quarter, so the actual enrollment for the winter quarter is estimated at 4.145, or 4,145 students, found by 3.3599 (1.2337). The estimates for the other quarters are determined in a similar fashion and this information is summarized in the table at the right.

Year	Quarter	Code	Deseasonalized Enrollment	Seasonal Index	Forecast
1999	Winter	17	3.3599	123.37	4,145
	Spring	18	3.4235	115.17	3,943
	Summer	19	3.4871	32.09	1,119
	Fall	20	3.5507	129.37	4,594

The enrollment for the fall quarter is normally the highest, and the smallest for the summer. This is also true for the estimates in 1999.

Exercise 18.5

Check your answers against those in the ANSWER section.

The quarterly sales for the Norton Company were reported in Exercise 3 and a seasonal index was computed for each quarter.

a. Deseasonalize the data and determine the trend equation.

b. Estimate the seasonally adjusted sales for the four quarters of 1999..

CHAPTER 18 ASSIGNMENT

TIME SERIES AND FORECASTING

Name _____ Section _____ Score _____

Part I   Select the correct answer and write the appropriate letter in the space provided.

_____ 1. A listing of values over a period of time is called a
    a. trend.   b. time series.
    c. seasonal index.   d. residual.

_____ 2. The long-term behavior of a variable over an extended period of time is called
    a. the seasonal index.
    b. the cyclical variation.
    c. the trend.
    d. episodic variation.

_____ 3. A period of prosperity followed by recession is called the
    a. cyclical variation.
    b. trend.
    c. seasonal variation.
    d. irregular variation.

_____ 4. When we plot a trend equation, the variable plotted along the horizontal axis is
    a. the dependent variables.
    b. sales.
    c. time.
    d. log of time.

_____ 5. The variation within a year, such as retail sales during the Christmas holidays, is called the
    a. trend.
    b. seasonal variation.
    c. irregular variation.
    d. cyclical variation.

_____ 6. In June of 1998 the Youngsville TrueValue Hardware store suffered severe damage to its contents during a flood. This is an example of
    a. residual variation.
    b. cyclical variation.
    c. seasonal variation because it happened during the summer.
    d. episodic variation.

_____ 7. The purpose of determining the ratio-to-moving average when computing a seasonal index is to eliminate the
    a. random variation.   b. trend.
    c. episodic variation.   d. none of the above.

8. The reason for centering a moving average is to
   a. convert the average to an index.
   b. remove the random variation.
   c. find the correction factor.
   d. align the time periods.

_____ 9. A monthly index is being developed for the company sales. The moving total will consist of
   a. four quarterly sales values.
   b. logs of sales.
   c. logs of quarters.
   d. twelve monthly sales values.

_____ 10. The index for October for imports by Wines, Inc. is 90. The actual imports for October were $450,000. The seasonally adjusted imports are
   a. $405,000.
   b. $450,000.
   c. $500,000.
   d. none of the above.

Part II Record the answers in the space provided. Show essential calculations.

11. The earnings per share for Whirlpool Corporation as shown in the 1997 annual report are given. (Source: 1997 Whirlpool's Annual Report)

   a. Develop a least squares trend equation. Code the year 1993 as 1.

Year	Earning per share			
1993	$3.19			
1994	2.10			
1995	2.80			
1996	2.08			
1997	3.15			
1998	3.47			

1998 is estimated

a.

   b. Estimate the earnings per share for 1999.

b.

12. The following table shows the number of homes built by Custom Builders, Inc. in the last four years by quarter. Develop a seasonal index for each quarter using the ratio-to-moving average method. (Use the form on the next page).

Year	I	II	III	IV
1992	5	9	8	8
1993	6	9	9	8
1994	6	10	10	7
1995	6	10	9	8

Year	Qtr.	Homes	4-Qtr. Moving Total	4-Qtr. Moving Avg.	Centered Moving Avg.	Specific Seasonal
1992	I					
	II					
	III					
	IV					
1993	I					
	II					
	III					
	IV					
1994	I					
	II					
	III					
	IV					
1995	I					
	II					
	III					
	IV					

Quarter					
Year	I	II	III	IV	
1992					
1993					
1994					
1995					
Total					Total
Mean					
Typical Index					

CHAPTER 19
AN INTRODUCTION TO DECISION MAKING

CHAPTER GOALS

After completing this chapter, you will be able to:

1. Define the terms *state of nature, event, act,* and *payoff.*

2. Organize information into a payoff table or a decision tree.

3. Determine the expected payoff of an act.

4. Compute opportunity loss and expected opportunity loss.

5. Assess the value of information.

Introduction

The approach to decision making in the previous chapters was to set up a null hypothesis and an alternate hypothesis, formulate a decision rule, take a sample from the population, and then on the basis of the sample information make a decision about the null hypothesis. This is the classical approach to decision making. This chapter considers a slightly different approach to decision making called decision theory. In decision theory various alternative courses of action are considered. However, the monetary values of these courses of action are taken into account for the purpose of determining the optimum course of action.

Elements of a Decision

Under conditions of certainty there are several courses of action available to the decision-maker, and the decision-maker knows the result of each course of action. The purchasing agent at a hospital may need to purchase 1,000 new bed sheets. The agent checks with several suppliers and obtains prices for sheets of comparable quality and then makes the purchase from the supplier offering the best price. Note that no uncertainty regarding future events exists.

Decision making under conditions of uncertainty also entails several courses of action, but in addition there is uncertainty regarding future events. For example, a businessman has $100,000 to invest and he is considering investing it in drilling oil wells.

If he strikes oil, he makes a profit ten times his original investment. If it is a dry well, he loses his money. Note, therefore, there is a condition of uncertainty. The unknown future outcomes are called the *states of nature*.

States of nature: The uncontrollable future events.

The state of nature is not under the control of the decision-maker. In the oil drilling problem there are two states of nature, either the well will produce oil or it will not. The investor has two courses of action, or alternatives, either to invest or not to invest. Thus the *acts* are the courses of action available to the decision-maker.

> *Acts*: Two or more possible actions available to the decision-maker.

For each combination of a state of nature and a course of action there is a *payoff* or outcome.

> *Payoff*: The result of a particular combination of an act and a state of nature.

These terms are summarized in the following **payoff table** showing the problems facing the investor.

Payoff Table		
	State of Nature	
Act	**Strike Oil**	**Does Not Strike Oil**
Invest in oil well	$1,000,000	−$100,000
Do not invest in oil well	0	0

The payoff from the act "Investing in the oil well" and the state of nature "strike oil" is $1,000,000.

Usually the payoff table is not the only information available. In fact a decision based solely on the payoff table might, in many situations, ignore valuable historical records. In our oil-drilling problem, we might do some research and find out that only 5 of 100 drillings result in an oil strike. It could be said that the probability of striking oil is 0.05 while the probability of not striking oil is 0.95.

If we combine our payoff table with the probabilities we can arrive at an **expected payoff**. Expected payoff is also called **expected monetary value**, shortened to EMV. It is also called the **mean payoff**. Text formula [19-1] is used to calculate EMV.

$$ EMV(A_i) = \Sigma[P(S_j) \cdot V(A_i, S_j)] \qquad [19-1] $$

Where:

$EMV(A_i)$ refers to the expected value of the various decision alternatives. There may be several decision possibilities. We will let 1 stand for the first alternative, 2 for the second, and so on. The lowercase letter i represents the range of decision alternatives.

$P(S_j)$ refers to the probability of the various states of nature. There can be an unlimited number, so we'll let j represent the various possible outcomes.

$V(A_i, S_j)$ refers to the value of the various payoffs. Note that each payoff is the result of a combination of a decision alternative and a state of nature

Opportunity Loss Table

The difference between what a decision-maker could have made had he /she known the state of nature and what he /she actually made is referred to as regret or *opportunity loss*.

> *Opportunity loss*: The difference between the payoff a decision-maker receives for a chosen action and the maximum that the decision-maker could have received for choosing the action yielding the highest payoff for the state of nature that occurred.

A payoff table is easily converted to an opportunity loss table by finding the maximum payoff for each state of nature and subtracting all other entries in the column from the maximum value. In the oil drilling problem if the state of nature is to strike oil the opportunity loss for selecting the event "do not invest" is $1,000,000, found by $1,000,000 (the optimum event) minus 0 (the payoff for selecting the course of action "do not invest").

The following table is an opportunity loss table for the oil well problem.

Opportunity Loss Table		
	State of Nature	
Event	Strike Oil	Does Not Strike Oil
Invest in oil well	0	$100,000
Do not invest in oil well	$1,000,000	0

In an opportunity loss table values cannot be negative.

Evaluating Courses of action

Under conditions of uncertainty the various courses of action can be compared if the probability of the various states of nature can be estimated. These estimates may be obtained from an analysis of historical data, or on the basis of subjective estimates. Suppose geological studies indicated the probability of striking oil was 0.05, and the probability of not striking oil was 0.95. That is $P(S_1) = 0.05$ and $P(S_2) = 0.95$. The expected payoff called the EMV for the act of investing can be obtained as follows:

State of Nature	Payoff	Probability of State of Nature	Expected Value
Strike oil S_1	$1,000,000	0.05	$50,000
Do not strike oil S_2	-$100,000	0.95	-$95,000
			-$45,000

The expected payoff is the probability of each state of nature times the payoff for the particular combination of act and state of nature. In the previous examples the expected payoff is a -$45,000, a loss of $45,000 for the act of investing. The expected payoff for the act of investing is compared with that of not investing.

State of Nature	Payoff	Probability of State of Nature	Expected Value
Strike oil S_1	0	0.05	$0
Do not strike oil S_2	0	0.95	0
			0

The expected payoff for not investing is $0. Using the expected value of the various outcomes as the decision criterion, the decision rule would be to select the largest expected value. If you were the investor would you rather lose $45,000 or lose $0. Undoubtedly you would select to lose $0.

The Value of Perfect Information

The concept of **perfect information** refers to the value of knowing with certainty, which state of nature will occur. In the oil well problem, the investor would know beforehand which state of nature would happen, that is whether the oil well is dry or not. The *expected value of perfect information* (EVPI) is calculated by determining the difference between the maximum payoff under conditions of certainty and the maximum payoff under uncertainty. It may be thought of as the cost of uncertainty. Text formula [19-3] is used.

$$\text{EVPI} = \left(\begin{array}{c}\text{Expected value under}\\\text{conditions of certainty}\end{array}\right) - \left(\begin{array}{c}\text{Optimal decision under}\\\text{conditions of uncertainity}\end{array}\right) \qquad [19-3]$$

GLOSSARY

State of nature: The unknown future event. The state of nature is not under the control of the decision-maker.

Acts: Two or more possible actions available to the decision-maker.

Payoff: The result of a particular combination of an act and a state of nature.

Opportunity loss: The difference between the payoff a decision-maker receives for a chosen action and the maximum that the decision-maker could have received for choosing the action yielding the highest payoff for the state of nature that occurred.

CHAPTER PROBLEMS

Problem 1

Jan's Cake Shop is a small bakery that specializes in decorating cakes. These cakes are baked early each morning for sale that day. Any cakes not sold the same day they are baked must be discarded. Jan knows, from her records, that she can always sell between 11 and 14 cakes, but she would like to know how many to bake each day to maximize her profit. From the last 50 business days she is able to develop the following probability distribution. The table shows that 11 cakes were sold on 10 days or 20% of the days. Also, 12 cakes were sold on 25 days, or 50%

Number of Cakes Sold	Days	Probability
11	10	0.20
12	25	0.50
13	10	0.20
14	5	0.10
	50	1.00

of the days, etc. Suppose each cake is sold for $10.00, and the cost to bake plus the ingredients and labor is $6.00.

a. Develop a payoff table.

b. Using the expected monetary value criterion make a recommendation as to the number of cakes to bake.

c. What is the value of perfect information?

Solution

a. The first step is to develop a payoff table. There are four acts, or alternative decisions, open to Jan. She can bake 11, 12, 13 or 14 cakes each day. There are also four states of nature, and one of these will happen each day. The four states of nature are that 11, 12, 13, or 14 cakes are demanded.

The payoff for the act of baking 11 cakes and the state of nature of 11 cakes being demanded is a payoff of $44, found by:

$$\text{(number sold} \times \text{selling price)} - \text{(number baked} \times \text{cost)} = (11 \times \$10) - (11 \times \$6) = \$44$$

So the entry in the first row and the first column is $44. What is the profit if the demand is 14 cakes but only 11 are baked? Only 11 cakes were baked and hence only 11 can be sold. So the profit (payoff) is $44 found by 11 × $4. How about the payoff for baking 14 cakes and a demand of 11? Note that in this case Jan has 3 unsold cakes at a value of 3 × $6 =

Act	State of Nature (Demand)			
	S_1	S_2	S_3	S_4
Cakes Baked	11	12	13	14
11 A_1	$44	$44	$44	$44
12 A_2	38	48	48	48
13 A_3	32	42	52	52
14 A_4	26	36	46	56

$18, which must be deducted from the total amount sold. The same equation is used to determine the payoff:

$$\text{(number sold} \times \text{selling price)} - \text{(number baked} \times \text{cost)} = (11 \times \$10) - (14 \times \$6) = \$26$$

The other entries in the payoff table are developed similarly.

The expected payoff or expected monetary value, written EMV (A_i) for each act (alternative course of action) is computed using the historical sales. For the act of baking 14 cakes, the expected payoff is $38, as shown below

These calculations are summarized as follows:

State of Nature Demand	Payoff $V(A_4, S_j)$	Probability $P(S_j)$	Expected Value
11 cakes S_1	$26	0.20	$5.20
12 cakes S_2	36	0.50	18.00
13 cakes S_3	46	0.20	9.20
14 cakes S_4	56	0.10	5.60
		EMV(A_4)→	$38.00

$$\boxed{EMV(A_i) = \Sigma[P(S_j) \cdot V(A_i, S_j)] \qquad [19-1]}$$

Where:

$EMV(A_i)$ refers to the expected monetary value of the various decision alternatives. There may be several decision possibilities. We will let 1 stand for the first alternative, 2 for the second, and so on. The lowercase letter i represents the range of decision alternatives.

$P(S_j)$ refers to the probability of the various states of nature. There can be an unlimited number, so we'll let j represent the various possible outcomes.

$V(A_i, S_j)$ refers to the value of the various payoffs. Note that each payoff is the result of a combination of a decision alternative and a state of nature.

Chapter 19

The $EMV(A_4)$, the expected monetary value for the decision alternative of baking 14 cakes is computed using formula [19-1].

$$EMV(A_4) = P(S_1) \cdot V(A_4 S_1) + P(S_2) \cdot V(A_4 S_2) + P(S_3) \cdot V(A_4 S_3) + P(S_4) \cdot V(A_4 S_4)$$
$$= 0.20(\$26.00) + 0.50(\$36.00) + 0.20(\$46.00) + 0.10(\$56.00)$$
$$= \$5.20 + \$18.00 + \$9.20 + \$5.60$$
$$= \$38.00$$

The expected payoffs for all four acts are shown below.

$EMV(A_i)$	Number of Cakes	Expected Payoff
1	11	$44.00
2	12	46.00
3	13	43.00
4	14	38.00

b.   The act of baking 12 cakes has the largest expected profit of $46.00. In the long run if Jan baked 12 cakes each day her profit would be the largest. We recommend that Jan bake 12 cakes.

c.   Suppose an old prospector came by the bakery and said he could predict, without error, the demand (state of nature) for the day. This information would be available before she started to bake the cakes. How much should Jan be willing to pay him for the information? In essence, the old prospector is removing the uncertainty from the decision making process. The expected payoff under conditions of certainty, written in EVPI, is computed as follows:

Column 1	Column 2	Column 3	Column 4
State of Nature	Payoff	Probability	Payoff
Demand	$V(A^*, S_j)$	$P(S_j)$	$P(S_j) \, V(A^*, S_j)$
11 cakes	44	0.20	$8.80
12 cakes	48	0.50	24.00
13 cakes	52	0.20	10.40
14 cakes	56	0.10	5.60
			$48.80

The symbol $V(A^*,S_j)$ refers to the best alternative for a given state of nature.

If the prospector said the demand today will be 12, Jan would bake 12 cakes because that will maximize her profit. This will occur 50 percent of the time, which is obtained from Column 3 of the probability distribution. If Jan always knew her demand, she could make $48.80 per day. Using the expected value criterion she can make $46 per day.

The value of perfect information EVPI is $2.80, found by $48.80 – $46.00. Jan should be willing to pay up to $2.80 to remove the uncertainty from her decision making process.

Check your answers against those in the ANSWER section.

A bank is trying to decide whether to make a one-year loan of $100,000 to Sharkey Chevy. Past experience has shown that one of three outcomes will occur if the loan is made:

1. The loan is repaid plus the 10 percent interest without a problem.

2. The customer, Sharkey Chevy in this case, has difficulty paying the loan. However, the bank is finally repaid with 10 percent interest, but collection fees cost the bank $2,000.

3. The customer goes bankrupt and the bank only collects 70 percent of the amount loaned.

If the bank does not make the loan it can make eight percent interest for the year elsewhere. Historical records reveal the following probabilities for the various states of nature.

States of Nature	Probability
Repaid	0.85
Repaid with difficulty	0.10
Bankrupt	0.05
	1.00

a. Develop a payoff table.

b. Determine the optimum act using the expected monetary value criterion.

c. Compute the value of perfect information

Problem 2

Using the data from Jan's Cake Shop in Problem 1, develop an opportunity loss table and compute the expected opportunity loss.

Solution

A loss table is generated from a payoff table. Recall the payoff table for this problem was part of Problem 1. The opportunity loss is the difference between what could have been made had the decision-maker known the state of nature and thus selected the maximum payoff, the payoff for the other acts. For Jan's Cake Shop, had she known the state of nature was that 11 cakes would be sold, designated S_1, she would have obviously selected to bake 11 cakes. Hence, $44 – $44 = $0, so the opportunity loss would have been $0. Had the state of nature been 11 and Jan decided to bake 12 cakes, the opportunity loss would be $6, found by $44 – $38.

Had the demand been 13, but Jan decided to bake 11 cakes, the opportunity loss would be $8, found by $52 – $44. The full table is shown at the right.

The expected opportunity loss is determined in the same way as expected payoff. For example, the expected opportunity loss for the act of baking 13 cakes is computed as follows:

Opportunity Loss Table State of Nature (demand)			
Act	11	12	13	14
11	$0	$4	$8	$12
12	6	0	4	8
13	12	6	0	4
14	18	12	6	0

Opportunity Loss For Baking 13 Cakes			
State of Nature	Opportunity Loss	Probability of State of Nature	Expected Opportunity Loss
11 Cakes baked	$12	0.20	$2.40
12 Cakes baked	6	0.50	3.00
13 Cakes baked	0	0.20	0.00
14 Cakes baked	4	0.10	0.40
			$5.80

The calculations are summarized as follows:

$$EOL(A_i) = \Sigma\left[P(S_j)\cdot R(A_i,S_j)\right] \qquad [19-2]$$

Where:

$EOL(A_1)$ refers to the expected opportunity loss for a particular decision alternative.

$P(S_j)$ refers to the probability associated with the various states of nature.

$R(A_i, S_j)$ refers to the regret or loss for a particular combination of a state of nature and a decision alternative.

The $EOL(A_3)$, the regret or opportunity loss for selecting the alternative of baking 13 cakes, is computed as follows using formula [19-2].

$$EOL(A_3) = P(S_1)\cdot R(A_2,S_1) + P(S_2)\cdot R(A_2,S_2) + P(S_3)\cdot R(A_2,S_3) + P(S_4)\cdot R(A_2,S_4)$$
$$= 0.20(\$12.00) + 0.50(\$6.00) + 0.20(\$0) + 0.10(\$4.00)$$
$$= \$5.80$$

The expected opportunity loss is the smallest for the act of baking 12 cakes. In fact, it is exactly the same as the value of perfect information. The expected opportunity loss measures the uncertainty in the decision-making process.

Expected Opportunity Loss	
Act	Expected Opportunity
11 cakes baked	$4.80
12 cakes baked	2.80
13 cakes baked	5.80
14 cakes baked	10.80

Exercise 19.2

Check your answers against those in the ANSWER section.

Using the bank loan problem in Exercise 1, develop an opportunity loss table and compute the expected opportunity loss for each decision alternative.

CHAPTER ASSIGNMENT 19

AN INTRODUCTION TO DECISION MAKING

Name _____ Section _____ Score _____

Part I Select the correct answer and write the appropriate letter in the space provided.

_____1. In decision theory there is uncertainty regarding .
   a. course of action.
   b. payoffs.
   c. states of nature.
   d. the value of perfect information.

_____2. The term "decision theory" refers to
   a. classical hypothesis testing.
   b. subjective probability.
   c. the alternate hypothesis.
   d. two or more decision alternatives.

_____3. The unknown future outcomes are called
   a. courses of action.
   b. states of nature.
   c. the opportunity loss.
   d. the value of perfect information.

_____4. For each combination of course of action and state of nature there is
   a. a payoff.
   b. an expected value of perfect information.
   c. an expected value.
   d. none of the above.

_____5. The expected value of perfect information and the expected opportunity loss
   a. are always equal.
   b. have no relationship with each other.
   c. have the same standard deviation
   d. equal the particular state of nature

_____6. Two or more courses of action available to the decision-maker are called
   a. states of nature.
   b. decision alternatives or acts.
   c. the expected value.
   d. none of the above.

_____7. The difference between the optimum decision and any other decision is called
   a. an expected value.
   b. a payoff.
   c. an opportunity loss.
   d. the expected value of perfect information.

_____8. A decision-maker does not have control over
    a. the payoff table.
    b. the decision alternatives.
    c. the states of nature.
    d. the opportunity loss table.

_____9. An opportunity loss table reports the amount of opportunity loss for each state of nature and
    a. course of action.
    b. payoff.
    c. expected value.
    d. expected value of perfect information.

_____10. When all the facts are known in a decision situation, it can be said that the decision was made under
    a. uncertainty.
    b. certainty.
    c. opportunity.
    d. subjectivity.

Part II   Record your answer in the space provided. Show all essential work.

16. Ralph Higgins, the owner of the Spaghetti Warehouse, is considering expansion. He owns the land nearby and could build his own building on that land. If he decides to build the new building and the economy improves, he estimates that his first year profits will be $100,000. If he builds his own building and there is a recession, he will lose $40,000. He could expand the current restaurant. If he selects this alternative, he estimates he will make an additional $25,000 if the economy improves, and lose $5,000 if there is a recession. He could also do nothing, in which case there is no additional profit or loss. The probability the economy will improve is 0.25, and the probability of a recession is 0.75.

    a. Develop a payoff table for the various acts and states of nature.

Acts	States of Nature	
	Economy improves	Recession
Build new		
Expand		
Do nothing		

b. Compute the expected payoff for each alternative.

b. A_1

b. A_2

b. A_3

c. Determine the expected value of perfect information.

c.

d. Convert the payoff to an opportunity loss table.

Acts	States of Nature	
	Economy improves	Recession
Build new		
Expand		
Do nothing		

e. What course of action would you recommend?

_____

_____

DESCRIBING DATA: FREQUENCY DISTRIBUTIONS AND GRAPHIC PRESENTATION

Exercise 2.1

Frequency distribution:

Miles per Gallon	Tallies	Number of Engines
15 up to 20	//	2
20 up to 25	////	4
25 up to 30	### /	6
30 up to 35	###	5
35 up to 40	///	3

Exercise 2.2

Histogram

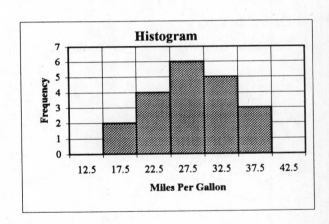

Exercise 2.3

Frequency polygon

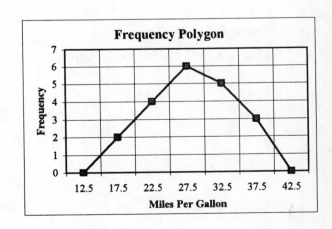

Exercise 2.4.

Stem and leaf chart

Stem	Leaf
1	89
2	0013577899
3	00022679

Exercise 2.5.

a. Less-than-Cumulative Frequency Polygon

b. About 60% of the automobiles are getting less than 30 miles per gallon

c. About 20% of the automobiles are getting 20 miles per gallon

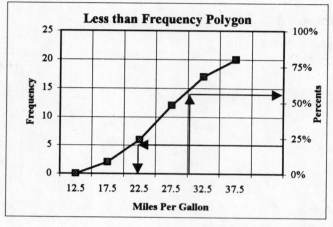

Exercise 2.6.

Line chart for 1991 to 1997 expenditures.

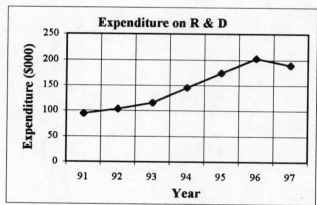

Exercise 2.7.

Bar chart for 1991 to 1997 expenditures

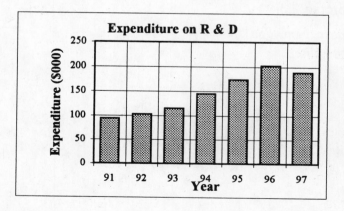

Exercise 2.8.

Two directional bar chart.

High Rise	+5%
Multi Family	+8.3%
Single Family	-15.6%
Mobile	+50%
Condos	+25%

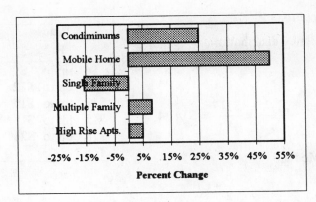

Exercise 2.9.

Pie chart for new cars sold

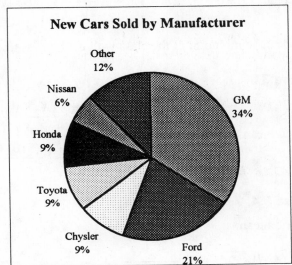

CHAPTER 3

DESCRIBING DATA: MEASURES OF LOCATION

Exercise 3.1

a. Mean: $\overline{X} = \dfrac{\Sigma X}{n} = \dfrac{8+5+4+10+8+3+4}{7} = \dfrac{42}{7} = 6$

b. Median = 5. Middle data value.   3, 4, 4, 5, 8, 8, 10
$\Uparrow$

c. Mode = 4 and 8

Exercise 3.2

Frequency distribution:

Wage Rate	Frequency f	Class Midpoint X	fX	CF
$6 up to $9	2	$7.50	$15.00	2
$9 up to $12	8	10.50	84.00	10
$12 up to $15	20	13.50	270.00	30
$15 up to $18	14	16.50	231.00	44
$18 up to $21	6	19.50	117.00	50
Total	50		$717.00	

a. Mean:

$$\overline{X} = \frac{\Sigma fX}{n} = \frac{\$717}{50} = \$14.34$$

b. Median:

$$\text{Median} = L + \frac{\frac{n}{2} - CF}{f}(i) = \$12 + \frac{\frac{50}{2} - 10}{20}(\$3.00) = \$12 + \frac{15}{20}(\$3.00) = \$12 + \$2.25 = \$14.25$$

c. Mode: The midpoint of the class with the highest frequency, $13.50

Exercise 3.3

Weighted mean:

$$\overline{X} = \frac{w_1 X_1 + w_2 X_2 + w_3 X_3 + w_4 X_4}{w_1 + w_2 + w_{31} + w_4}$$

$$= \frac{31(\$30) + 42(\$10) + 47(\$20) + 63\$24)}{31 + 42 + 47 + 63} = \frac{\$3802}{183} = \$20.78$$

Exercise 3.4

Geometric mean:

$$GM = \sqrt[15]{\frac{1850}{475}} - 1 = (\sqrt[15]{3.894736} - 1) = (1.094876 - 1) = 0.094876 = 9.49\%$$

CHAPTER 4

DESCRIBING DATA: MEASURES OF DISPERSION

Exercise 4.1

a. Range = $27 - $10 = $17

b. $$\overline{X} = \frac{\Sigma X}{n} = \frac{80}{5} = 16$$

$$MD = \frac{\Sigma |X - \overline{X}|}{n} = \frac{22}{5} = 4.4$$

X	$|X - \overline{X}|$				Absolute deviation	X^2
10	$| 10 - 16 |$	=	$| -6 |$	=	6	100
12	$| 12 - 16 |$	=	$| -4 |$	=	4	144
15	$| 15 - 16 |$	=	$| -1 |$	=	1	225
16	$| 16 - 16 |$	=	$| 0 |$	=	0	256
27	$| 27 - 16 |$	=	$| 11 |$	=	11	729
80			Σ	=	22	1454

c. Variance

$$s^2 = \frac{\Sigma X^2 - \frac{(\Sigma X)^2}{n}}{n-1} = \frac{1454 - \frac{(80)^2}{5}}{5-1} = 43.5$$

d. Standard deviation $s = \sqrt{43.5} = 6.595 = 6.6$

Exercise 4.2

Weekly Income	f	Class Midpoint X	fX	fX²	CF
100 up to 150	5	125	625	78,125	5
150 up to 200	9	175	1575	275,625	14
200 up to 250	20	225	4500	1,012,500	34
250 up to 300	18	275	4950	1,361,250	52
300 up to 350	5	325	1625	528,125	57
350 up to 400	3	375	1125	421,875	60
	60		14,400	3,677,500	

a. Standard deviation:

$$s = \sqrt{\frac{\Sigma fX^2 - \frac{(\Sigma fX)^2}{n}}{n-1}} = \sqrt{\frac{3,677,500 - \frac{(14,400)^2}{60}}{60-1}} = 61.27$$

b. First quartile:

$$Q_1 = L + \frac{\frac{n}{4} - CF}{f}(i) = 200 + \frac{\frac{60}{4} - 14}{20}(50) = \$202.50$$

Third quartile:

$$Q_3 = L + \frac{\frac{3n}{4} - CF}{f}(i) = 250 + \frac{\frac{3(60)}{4} - 34}{18}(50) = \$280.56$$

Quartile deviation: $Q.D. = \frac{Q_3 - Q_1}{2} = \frac{\$280.56 - \$202.50}{2} = \frac{\$78.06}{2} = \$39.03$

Exercise 4.3

a. Percent:

$$k = \frac{X - \overline{X}}{s} = \frac{\$885 - \$990}{\$70} = -1.5$$

$$k = \frac{X - \overline{X}}{s} = \frac{\$1095 - \$990}{\$70} = 1.5$$

Applying Chebyshev's Theorem: $1 - \frac{1}{k^2} = (1 - \frac{1}{1.5^2}) = (1 - \frac{1}{2.25}) = (1 - 0.4444) = 0.5556 = 55.6\%$

This means that at least 56% of the salespersons earn between $885 and $1095 in commission.

b. Positive skewness since the mean 990 is larger than the median 950.

c. Coefficient of skewness: $sk = \frac{3(\overline{X} - median)}{s} = \frac{3(990 - 950)}{70} = 1.71$

Exercise 4.4

The data is first put into an ordered array.

| $25 | $28 | $39 | $50 | $61 | $65 | $81 | $82 | $85 | $85 |
| $85 | $86 | $90 | $92 | $120 | $137 | $140 | $142 | $148 | $152 |

a. First Quartile: Let $P = 25$ and $L_p = (n+1)\dfrac{P}{100} = (19+1)\dfrac{25}{100} = 5$

Then locate the 5th observation in the array, which is 61. Thus $Q_1 = 61$ or $61,000.

b. Third quartile: Let $P = 75$ and $L_p = (n+1)\dfrac{P}{100} = (19+1)\dfrac{75}{100} = 16$

Then locate the 16th observation in the array, which is 137. Thus $Q_3 = 137$ or $137,000.

c. The median: Let $P = 50$ and $L_p = (n+1)\dfrac{P}{100} = (19+1)\dfrac{50}{100} = 10$

Then locate the 10th observation in the array, which is 85. Thus $Q_2 =$ the median = 85 or $85,000.

d. Box plot: The five essential pieces of data are:

Minimum value = 25, $Q_1 = 61$, $Q_2 = 85$ $Q_3 = 137$,   Maximum value = 152

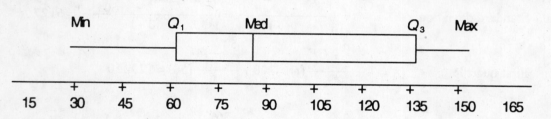

CHAPTER 5

A SURVEY OF PROBABILITY CONCEPTS

Exercise 5.1

a. Visits twice a year: $\dfrac{90}{300} = 0.30$

b. Visits: $\dfrac{60}{300} + \dfrac{90}{300} + \dfrac{120}{300} = \dfrac{270}{300} = 0.90$

Exercise 5.2

Proportion of students: $0.60 + 0.20 - 0.12 = 0.68$

Exercise 5.3

a. All three: $P(3) = (0.10)(0.10)(0.10) = 0.001$

b. None: P(none) = (0.90)(0.90)(0.90) = 0.729

c. At least one: 1 − P(none) = (1 − 0.729) = 0.271

Exercise 5.4

a. Both female: $P(\text{both female}) = \dfrac{6}{10} \times \dfrac{5}{9} = 0.33$

b. At least one male: $P(\text{At least one male}) = \left(\dfrac{4}{10} \times \dfrac{3}{9}\right) + \left(\dfrac{4}{10} \times \dfrac{6}{9}\right) + \left(\dfrac{6}{10} \times \dfrac{4}{9}\right) = 0.67$

                                            m *m*   *m* *f*   *f* *m*

Exercise 5.5

a. Had Heart attack or is heavy smoker:

$$P(\text{Heart attack or heavy smoker}) = \frac{180}{500} + \frac{125}{500} - \frac{90}{500} = 0.43$$

b. Heavy Smoker no heart attack: $P(\text{Heavy smoker no heart attack}) = \dfrac{35}{500} = 0.07$

Exercise 5.6

a.

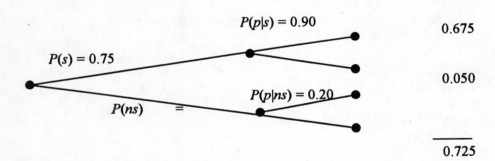

$$P(s|p) = \frac{0.75 \times 0.90}{(0.75)(0.90) + (0.25)(0.20)} = \frac{0.675}{0.725} = 0.931$$

Exercise 5.7

Number of different flights: 5 × 10 = 50

Exercise 5.8

Number of different ways: $_nP_r = \dfrac{n!}{(n-r)!} = \dfrac{8!}{4!} = 8 \times 7 \times 6 \times 5 = 1680$

Exercise 5.9

Number of different trip combinations: $_nC_r = \dfrac{n!}{r!(n-r)!} = \dfrac{8!}{5!3!} = \dfrac{8 \times 7 \times 6}{3 \times 2} = 56$

357   **Answer Section**

CHAPTER 6

DISCRETE PROBABILITY DISTRIBUTIONS

Exercise 6.1

Number of Accidents per Month X	Probability P(X)	xP(x)	$(X-\mu)$	$(X-\mu)^2$	$(X-\mu)^2 P(X)$
0	0.60	0	0 – 0.5	–0.5	(0.25)(0.6) = 0.150
1	0.30	0.3	1 – 0.5	0.5	(0.25)(0.3) = 0.075
2	0.10	0.2	2 – 0.5	1.5	(2.25)(0.1) = 0.225
Σ	1.0	0.5			Σ = 0.450

a. Mean: $\mu = \Sigma[xP(x)] = 0.5$ **b.** Variance: $\sigma^2 = \Sigma[(x-\mu)^2 P(x)] = 0.45$

Exercise 6.2

a. Rules of probability:

R,R,NR	(0.60)(0.60)(0.40)	=	0.144
R,NR,R	(0.60)(0.40)(0.60)	=	0.144
NR,R,R	(0.40)(0.60)(0.60)	=	0.144
	Σ	=	0.432

b. $P(x) = \dfrac{n!}{x!(n-x)!}(\pi)^x(1-\pi)^{n-x}$

$= \dfrac{3!}{2!(3-2)!}(0.60)^2(0.40)^1 = 0.432$

Exercise 6.3

Use Appendix A and $n = 12$

a. $P(0) = 0.014$

b. $P(x \geq 5) = 0.158 + 0.079 + 0.029 + 0.008 + 0.001 + 0 + 0 + 0 = 0.275$

c. $P(2 \leq x \geq 4) = 0.168 + 0.240 + 0.231 = 0.639$

Exercise 6.4

$\mu = np = (1000)(0.002) = 2.00$ and Appendix C, $\mu = 2$ and $x = 0$

a. $P(0) = 0.1353$

b. $P(x \geq 2) = \{1 - [P(0) + P(1)]\} = \{1 - [0.1353 + 0.2707]\} = \{1 - 0.406\} = 0.594$

Exercise 6.5

Two are defective: $N = 30,\ S = 5, n = 4, x = 2$

$$P(x) = \frac{\left({}_sC_x\right)\left({}_{N-S}C_{n-x}\right)}{\left({}_NC_n\right)} = \frac{\left({}_5C_2\right)\left({}_{30-5}C_{4-2}\right)}{\left({}_{30}C_4\right)} = \frac{\dfrac{5!}{2!3!} \times \dfrac{25!}{2!23!}}{\dfrac{30!}{4!26!}} = 0.109$$

CHAPTER 7

THE NORMAL PROBABILITY DISTRIBUTION

Exercise 7.1

a. Probability a bottle will contain between 2.02 and 2.04 liters: $z = \dfrac{X - \mu}{\sigma} = \dfrac{2.04 - 2.02}{0.015} = 1.33$

Appendix D value is 0.4082; thus the probability a bottle will contain between 2.02 and 2.04 liters is 0.4082.

b. Probability a bottle will contain between 2.00 and 2.03 liters:

$z = \dfrac{2.00 - 2.02}{0.015} = -1.33$ $z = \dfrac{2.03 - 2.02}{0.015} = 0.67$ Appendix D values are 0.2486 and 0.4082.

The two probabilities are added (0.4082 +0.2486 =0.6568), thus the probability of a bottle containing between 2.00 and 2.03 liters is 0.6568.

c. Probability a bottle will contain less than 2.00 liters $z = \dfrac{2.00 - 2.02}{0.015} = -1.33$

Appendix D value is 0.4082, thus (0.5000 – 0.4082 = 0.0918). The probability a bottle will contain less than 2 liters is 0.0918.

d. Cola dispensed in the largest 4%. First subtract (0.50 – 0.04) = 0.46, then find the z value such that 0.4600 of the area is between 0 and z. That value is z = 1.75. Then solve for .

$z = \dfrac{X - \mu}{\sigma}$ $1.75 = \dfrac{X - 2.02}{0.015}$ $X = 0.02625 + 2.02 = 2.05\,\text{liters}$

Thus the largest 4% of the bottles contain 2.05 liters or more.

Exercise 7.2

Probability that more than 265 will be relieved.

$$\mu = 300 \times 0.90 = 270$$

$$\sigma = \sqrt{300(0.90)(0.10)} = \sqrt{27} = 5.20$$

$$z = \frac{265.5 - 270}{5.20} = -0.87$$

$$P(X > 265.5) = 0.3078 + 0.5000 = 0.8078$$

CHAPTER 8

SAMPLING METHODS AND SAMPLING DISTRIBUTIONS

Exercise 8.1

a. $\quad _5C_3 = \dfrac{5!}{3!2!} = 10$

b. Various samples and the mean.

Sample Number	Homes Sold	Total Homes Sold	Mean Number of Homes Sold
1	ABC	13	4.33
2	ABD	17	5.67
3	ABE	11	3.67
4	BCD	16	5.33
5	BCE	10	3.33
6	CDE	17	5.67
7	CDA	20	6.67
8	DEA	18	6.00
9	DEB	14	4.67
10	ACE	14	4.67

c. Sampling distribution of the means.

Mean Sold	Frequency	Probability
3.33	1	0.1
3.67	1	0.1
4.33	1	0.1
4.67	2	0.2
5.33	1	0.1
5.67	2	0.2
6.00	1	0.1
6.67	1	0.1
	10	1.0

d. Sampling distribution of the population.

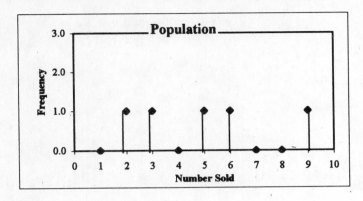

d. Sampling distribution of the means.

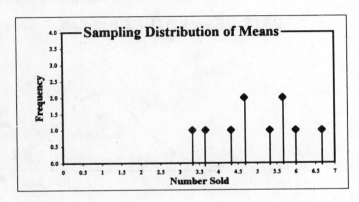

Exercise 8.2

The z value is 2.33, found by Appendix D and locating the value 0.4901 in the body of the table, and reading the corresponding row and column values.

$$\bar{X} \pm z\frac{s}{\sqrt{n}} = \$150 \pm 2.33\left(\frac{\$20}{\sqrt{36}}\right) = \$150 \pm \$7.77 = \$142.23\,\text{to}\,\$157.77$$

Exercise 8.3

$$\$150 \pm 2.33\left(\frac{\$20}{\sqrt{36}}\right)\left(\sqrt{\frac{200-36}{200-1}}\right) = \$150 \pm \$7.05 = \$142.95\,\text{to}\,\$157.05$$

Exercise 8.4

The z value is 1.65, found by Appendix D and locating the value 0.4500 in the body of the table, and reading the corresponding row and column values. Note that 0.4500 is exactly half way between 0.4495 and 0.4505.

$$0.60 \pm 1.645 \sqrt{\frac{(0.60)(1-0.60)}{100}} = 0.60 \pm 0.08 = 0.52 \text{ and } 0.68$$

Exercise 8.5

$$n = \left[\frac{z \times s}{E}\right]^2 = \left[\frac{(2.58)(0.25)}{0.20}\right]^2 = 10.4 = 11$$

Exercise 8.6

$$n = p(1-p)\left(\frac{z}{E}\right)^2 = (0.33)(1-0.33)\left(\frac{2.33}{0.04}\right)^2 = 750.2 = 751$$

CHAPTER 9

TESTS OF HYPOTHESIS: LARGE SAMPLES

Exercise 9.1

$H_0: \mu \leq \$30 \qquad H_1: \mu > \$30$

H_0 is rejected if z is greater than 1.645.

$$z = \frac{\$33 - \$30}{\$12 / \sqrt{40}} = 1.58$$

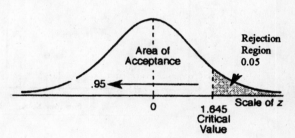

H_0 is not rejected. No increase in the mean amount spent.

p-value $= P(z > 1.58) = 0.5000 - 0.4429 = 0.0571$. The p-value of $0.0571 \geq 0.05$, do not reject H_0.

Exercise 9.2

Let Youngsville be population 1.

$H_0: \mu_1 \leq \mu_2 \qquad H_1: \mu_1 > \mu_2$

H_0 is rejected if z is greater than 1.645.

$$z = \frac{6.9 - 4.9}{\sqrt{\frac{(3.8)^2}{60} + \frac{(3.0)^2}{70}}} = 3.29$$

H_0 is rejected. It takes Youngsville longer to respond to fires.

Exercise 9.3

$H_0: \rho \geq 0.40 \qquad H_1: \rho < 0.40$

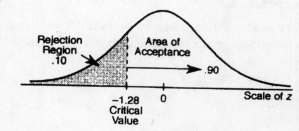

H_0 is rejected if z is less than -1.28.

$$z = \frac{\dfrac{60}{200} - 0.40}{\sqrt{\dfrac{(0.40)(1-0.40)}{200}}} = -2.89$$

H_0 is rejected. Less than 40% of the viewing audience watched the concert.

p-value $= P(z < -2.89) = (0.5000 - 0.4981) = 0.0019$, which is less than the level of significance of 0.10, thus we reject H_0.

Exercise 9.4

Let population 1 be women.

$$H_0 : \rho_1 \le \rho_2 \qquad H_1 : \rho_1 > \rho_2$$

H_0 is rejected if z is greater than 1.645.

$$\rho_c = \frac{45 + 25}{150 + 100} = 0.28$$

$$z = \frac{0.30 - 0.25}{\sqrt{\dfrac{(0.28)(1-0.28)}{150} + \dfrac{(0.28)(1-0.28)}{100}}} = 0.86$$

H_0 is not rejected. The proportion of smokers is the same.

p-value $= P(z > 0.86) = (0.5000 - 0.3051) = 0.1949$, The p-value of $0.1949 \ge 0.05$, do not reject H_0.

CHAPTER 10

TESTS OF HYPOTHESIS: SMALL SAMPLES

Exercise 10.1

$$H_0 : \mu \le 10 \qquad H_1 : \mu > 10$$

H_0 is rejected if t is greater than 3.365.

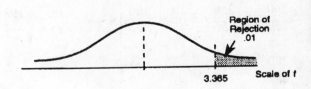

X	X²
9	81
12	144
14	196
15	225
10	100
12	144
72	890

$$\overline{X} = \frac{72}{6} = 12$$

$$s = \sqrt{\frac{890 - \frac{(72)^2}{6}}{5}} = 2.28$$

$$t = \frac{12 - 10}{2.28 / \sqrt{6}} = 2.15$$

Since t is less than 3.365, H_0 is not rejected. Employee breaks are not longer than ten minutes. The p-value is between 0.050 and 0.025.

Exercise 10.2

Let population 1 refer to the mall.

$H_0 : \mu_1 \le \mu_2$ $H_1 : \mu_1 > \mu_2$ H_0 is rejected if z is greater than 2.552.

$$s_p^2 = \frac{(10-1)(12)^2 + (10-1)(10)^2}{10 + 10 - 2} = 122$$

$$t = \frac{40 - 36}{\sqrt{122\left(\frac{1}{10} + \frac{1}{10}\right)}} = 0.81$$

Reject H_0 if $t > 2.552$.

H_0 is not rejected. There is no difference in mean amount spent at the mall and downtown store. p-value is greater than 0.10.

Exercise 10.3

$H_0 : \mu_d = 0$ $H_1 : \mu_d \ne 0$

Reject H_0 if t is less than -2.365 or greater than 2.365.

Electric	Gas	d	d²
265	260	5	25
271	270	1	1
260	250	10	100
250	255	−5	25
248	250	−2	4
280	275	5	25
257	260	−3	9
262	260	2	4
		13	193

$$\overline{d} = \frac{13}{8} = 1.625$$

$$s_d = \sqrt{\frac{193 - \frac{(13)^2}{8}}{7}} = 4.96$$

$$t = \frac{1.625}{4.96 / \sqrt{8}} = 0.93$$

H_0 is not rejected. There is no difference in the heating cost.

Exercise 11.1

$H_0: \mu_1 = \mu_2 = \mu_3$; $\qquad$ H_1: Not all means are equal.

H_0 is rejected if F is greater than 3.59. df in numerator = (3 – 1) = 2, df in denominator = (20 – 3) = 17

	60^0		70^0		80^0		
	X	X^2	X	X^2	X	X^2	Total
	3	9	7	49	4	16	
	5	25	6	36	6	36	
	4	16	8	64	5	25	
	3	9	9	81	7	49	
	4	16	6	36	6	36	
			8	64	5	25	
			8	64	4	16	
					3	9	
T_c	19		52		40		111
ΣX^2		75		394		212	681
n_c	5		7		8		20

$$SS\,\text{Total} = \Sigma X^2 - \frac{(\Sigma X)^2}{n}$$

$$= 681 - \frac{111^2}{20}$$

$$= 681 - 616.05 = 64.95$$

$$SST = \Sigma\left(\frac{T_c^2}{n_c}\right) - \frac{(\Sigma X)^2}{n}$$

$$= \left[\frac{19^2}{5} + \frac{52^2}{7} + \frac{40^2}{8}\right] - \frac{111^2}{20}$$

$$= [72.2 + 386.29 + 200] - 616.05$$

$$= 658.49 - 616.05 = 42.44$$

$$SSE = SS\,total - SST$$

$$= 64.95 - 42.41$$

$$= 22.51$$

Source	SS	df	MS	F
Between	42.44	2	21.22	16.03
Error	22.51	17	1.32	
	64.95	19		

$$F = \frac{\dfrac{42.44}{2}}{\dfrac{22.51}{17}} = \frac{21.22}{1.32} = 16.03$$

H_0 is rejected. There is a difference in the mean number correct (achievement).

Exercise 11.2

The means differ, found by using formula [11-5] and:

Answer Section

$\overline{X}_1 = 7.4 \qquad n_1 = 7$

$\overline{X}_2 = 3.8 \qquad n_2 = 5$

$t = 2.110$ from Appendix F: $(n - k) = (20 - 3) = 17$ degrees of freedom and the 95 percent level of confidence.

$MSE = 1.32$ from $SSE/(n - k) = 22.51/17 = 1.32$

$$(\overline{X}_1 - \overline{X}_2) \pm t \sqrt{MSE\left(\frac{1}{n_1} + \frac{1}{n_2}\right)}$$

$$(7.4 - 3.8) \pm 2.110 \sqrt{1.32\left(\frac{1}{7} + \frac{1}{5}\right)}$$

$$3.6 \pm 1.42$$

$$2.18 \text{ to } 5.02$$

The means differ since both end points of the confidence interval are of the same sign, positive in this problem.

Exercise 11.3

a. There are 4 treatments, found by: If $(k - 1) = 3$, then $k = 4$

b. There are 5 blocks, found by, . If $(b - 1) = 4$, then $b = 5$

c.. Total sample size is 20, found by,. If $(n - 1) = 19$, then $n = 20$

d. $H_0: \mu_1 = \mu_2 = \mu_3$
   $H_1:$ Not all means are equal
   H_0 is rejected if $F > 3.49$

   $$F = \frac{MST}{MSE} = \frac{15}{12} = 1.25 \qquad H_0 \text{ is not rejected. No difference in the treatment means.}$$

e. $H_0: \mu_1 = \mu_2 = \mu_3 = \mu_4$
   $H_1:$ Not all means are equal
   H_0 is rejected if $F > 3.26$

   $$F = \frac{MSB}{MSE} = \frac{50}{12} = 4.17 \qquad H_0 \text{ is rejected. The block means differ.}$$

Exercise 11.4

$$H_0: \sigma_H^2 \leq \sigma_T^2; \qquad H_1: \sigma_H^2 > \sigma_T^2$$

At the 0.05 level of significance and 9 degrees of freedom for both the numerator and the denominator, using Appendix G. H_0 is rejected if $F > 3.18$.

$$F = \frac{(60)^2}{(30)^2} = 4.00 \qquad H_0 \text{ is rejected. There is more variation in the Harmon forecast.}$$

CHAPTER 12

LINEAR REGRESSION AND CORRELATION

Exercise 12.1

a. Scatter diagram:

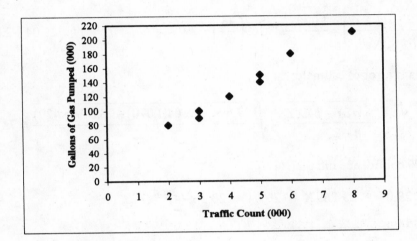

b. Coefficient of correlation:

Y	X	XY	X^2	Y^2
120	4	480	16	14,400
180	6	1,080	36	32,400
140	5	700	25	19,600
150	5	750	25	22,500
210	8	1,680	64	44,100
100	3	300	9	10,000
90	3	270	9	8,100
80	2	160	4	6,400
1,070	36	5,420	188	157,500

$$r = \frac{8(5,420) - (36)(1,070)}{\sqrt{\left[8(188) - (36)^2\right]\left[8(157,500) - (1,070)^2\right]}} = \frac{43,360 - 38,520}{\sqrt{(208)(115,100)}} = \frac{4840}{4892.93} = 0.989$$

c. Coefficient of determination: $\qquad r^2 = (0.989)^2 = 0.978$.

d. About 97.8 percent of the variation in gasoline pumped is explained by the traffic count.

e. $H_0: \rho \le 0$
$H_1: \rho > 0$ H_0 is rejected if t is greater than 1.943. $\quad t = \dfrac{0.989\sqrt{6}}{\sqrt{1-(0.989)^2}} = 16.38$

H_0 is rejected. There is positive correlation in the population.

Exercise 12.2

a. Regression equation:

$$b = \frac{n(\Sigma XY)-(\Sigma X)(\Sigma Y)}{n(\Sigma X^2)-(\Sigma X)^2} = \frac{8(5{,}420)-36(1{,}070)}{8(188)-(36)^2} = 23.269$$

$$a = \frac{\Sigma Y}{n} - b\left(\frac{\Sigma X}{n}\right) = \frac{1{,}070}{8} - 23.269\left(\frac{36}{8}\right) = 29.04 \qquad\qquad Y' = 29.04 + 23.269\,X$$

b. Standard error of estimate:

$$s_{y\cdot x} = \frac{\sqrt{\Sigma Y^2 - a\Sigma Y - b\Sigma XY}}{n-2} = \sqrt{\frac{157{,}500 - 29.04(1{,}070) - 23.269(5{,}420)}{8-2}} = 7.179$$

c. A 95% confidence interval:

$$Y' = 29.04 + 23.269\,X = 29.04 + 23.269(4) = 122.116$$

$$Y' \pm t(s_{y\cdot x})\sqrt{\frac{1}{n} + \frac{(X-\overline{X})^2}{\Sigma X^2 - \dfrac{(\Sigma X)^2}{n}}} = 122.116 \pm 2.447(7.179)\sqrt{\frac{1}{8} + \frac{(4-4.5)^2}{188 - \dfrac{(36)^2}{8}}}$$

$$= 122.116 \pm 6.445$$
$$= 115.71 \,\text{to}\, 128.56$$

d. A 95% prediction interval:

$$Y' \pm t(s_{y\cdot x})\sqrt{1 + \frac{1}{n} + \frac{(X-\overline{X})^2}{\Sigma X^2 - \dfrac{(\Sigma X)^2}{n}}} = 122.116 \pm 2.447(7.179)\sqrt{1 + \frac{1}{8} + \frac{(4-4.5)^2}{188 - \dfrac{(36)^2}{8}}}$$

d.
$$= 122.116 \pm 18.712$$
$$= 103.4 \,\text{to}\, 140.83$$

Exercise 12.3

a. Coefficient of determination:

$$r^2 = \frac{SSR}{SS\,Total} = \frac{14{,}078}{14{,}388} = 0.9785 \quad OR \quad 1 - \frac{SSE}{SS\,Total} = 1 - \frac{310}{14{,}388} = (1 - 0.0215) = 0.9785$$

b. Coefficient of correlation: $r = \sqrt{r^2} = \sqrt{0.9785} = 0.9892$

c. Standard error of estimate: $s_{y.x} = \sqrt{\dfrac{SSE}{n-2}} = \sqrt{\dfrac{310}{8-2}} = 7.188$

MULTIPLE REGRESSION AND CORRELATION ANALYSIS

Exercise 13.1

No problem with multicollinearity since the correlation of 0.506 between the independent variable temperature and output is in the rule of thumb range of -0.70 to $+0.70$.

$H_0: \beta_1 = \beta_2 = 0$ $H_0:$ Not all βs are zero

H_0 is rejected if $F > 4.74$, found by Appendix G, $\alpha = 0.05$, $df_n = 2$, $df_d = 7$

$$F = \frac{\dfrac{17.069}{2}}{\dfrac{7.03}{7}} = \frac{8.534}{1.004} = 8.5$$

H_0 is rejected. At least one regression coefficient is not equal to zero.

Exercise 13.2

For temperature: For Output

$H_0: \beta_1 = 0$ $H_0: \beta_2 = 0$

$H_1: \beta_1 \neq 0$ $H_1: \beta_2 \neq 0$

Reject H_o if $t < -2.365$ or $t > 2.365$

For temperature $t = 3.72$, thus H_0 for β_1 is rejected. It appears temperature is related to usage.

For output $t = -0.36$, thus H_0 for β_2 is not rejected. It appears that output is not related to usage.

Exercise 13.3

a. The regression equation is:
$$\text{Usage} = -17.2 + 0.353\ \text{Temp}$$
$$Y' = -17.2 + 0.353\ X_1$$

b. Y' for the first sample item is found by substituting the value: $X_1 = 83$ into the equation.

$$Y' = -17.2 + 0.353 X_1$$
$$= -17.2 + 0.353(83) = 12.099 = 12.10$$

c. The coefficient of multiple determination is R-Sq on the printout. It is 70.3%. A total of 70.3% of the variation in power usage is explained by the temperature.

d. The MINITAB System was used to develop the fitted values of Y' and the residuals. The residuals should approximate a normal distribution. The residuals were organized into the histogram as shown. The shape seems to be somewhat like the normal distribution.

e. The scatter diagram is used to investigate homoscedasticity. The horizontal axis is the fitted values, i.e., Y', and the vertical axis reflects the residuals. Homoscedasticity requires that the residuals remain constant for all fitted values of Y'. This assumption seems to be met, according to the plot.

CHAPTER 14

NONPARAMETRIC METHODS: CHI-SQUARE APPLICATIONS

Exercise 14.1.

H_0: Tire failures are uniformly distributed. H_1: Tire failures are not uniformly distributed.

Reject H_0 if the computed value of χ^2 is greater than 7.815, found by Appendix H, 0.05 level of significance and 3 df.

Location	Col. 1 f_o	Col. 2 f_e	Col. 3 $f_o - f_e$	Col. 4 $(f_o - f_e)^2$	Col. 5 $\dfrac{(f_o - f_e)^2}{f_e}$
Left Front	28	25	3	9	0.36
Left Rear	20	25	−5	25	1.00
Right Front	29	25	4	16	0.64
Right Rear	23	25	−2	4	0.16
	100	100	0		2.16

H_0 is not rejected. There is no difference in the failure rate.

Exercise 14.2

H_0: There has been no change in the distribution. H_1: There has been a change in the distribution..

Reject H_0 if the computed value of χ^2 is greater than 7.815, found by Appendix H, 0.05 level of significance and 3 df.

	Col. 1	Col. 2	Col. 3	Col. 4	Col. 5	Col. 6
Company	Percent of Total	Number in Sample f_o	f_e	$f_o - f_e$	$(f_o - f_e)^2$	$\dfrac{(f_o - f_e)^2}{f_e}$
GM	42	330	336	−6	36	36/336 = 0.107
Ford	33	275	264	11	121	121/264 = 0.458
Chrysler	22	174	176	−2	4	4/176 = 0.023
Other	3	21	24	−3	9	9/24 = 0.375
Total	100	800	800	0		$\chi^2 = 0.963$

H_0 is not rejected. There has been no change in the distribution.

Exercise 14.3

H_0: There is no relationship between gender and amount of time spent watching TV.

H_1: There is a relationship between gender and amount of time spent watching TV.

Reject H_0 if the computed value of χ^2 is greater than 5.991, found by Appendix H, 0.05 level of significance and 2 df.

$$f_e = \frac{(\text{row total})(\text{column total})}{\text{grand total}} = \frac{160 \times 225}{480} = 75, \quad \frac{160 \times 255}{480} = 85$$

Hours	Male			Female			Total
	f_o	f_e	$\dfrac{(f_o - f_e)^2}{f_e}$	f_o	f_e	$\dfrac{(f_o - f_e)^2}{f_e}$	
Under 8	70	75	0.333	90	85	0.294	160
8 up to 15	100	75	8.333	60	85	7.353	160
15 or more	55	75	5.333	105	85	4.706	160
Total	225	225	13.999	255	255	12.353	480

$$\chi^2 = \Sigma \left[\frac{(f_o - f_e)^2}{f_e} \right] = 13.999 + 12.353 = 26.352$$

H_0 is rejected because χ^2 is greater than 5.991. There is a relationship between gender and the amount of time spent watching TV.

Exercise 14.4

H_0: The distribution is normal. H_1 The distribution is not normal.

Reject H_0 if the computed value of χ^2 is greater than 11.070.

Wage	Area	f_e	f_o	$f_o - f_e$	$(f_o - f_e)^2$	$(f_o - f_e)^2 / f_e$
below $8	0.0918	36.72	25	−11.72	137.3584	3.7407
8 up to 10	0.1596	63.84	70	6.16	37.9456	0.5944
10 up to 12	0.2486	99.44	110	10.56	111.5136	1.1214
12 up to 14	0.2486	99.44	101	1.56	2.4336	0.0245
14 up to 16	0.1596	63.84	57	−6.84	46.7856	0.7329
16 or more	0.0918	36.72	37	0.28	0.0784	0.0021
Total	1.000	400.00	400			6.2160

The computed value of χ^2 is 6.2160, which is less than the critical value of 11.070. Hence, the null hypothesis is not rejected. We conclude that the sample could have been obtained from a normal population.

CHAPTER 15

NONPARAMETRIC METHODS: ANALYSIS OF RANKED DATA

Exercise 15.1.

Student	Recent Score	Original Score	Sign of Difference
John Barr	119	112	+
Bill Sedwick	103	108	−
Marica Elmquist	115	115	0
Ginger Thealine	109	100	+
Larry Clark	131	120	+
Jim Redding	110	108	+
Carol Papalia	109	113	−
Victor Suppa	113	126	−
Dallas Paul	94	95	−
Carol Kozoloski	119	110	+
Joe Sass	118	117	+
P. S. Sundar	112	102	+

H_0: There is no change in IQ scores ($\pi \leq 0.50$)
H_1: Recent IQ scores have increased over the scores in the 1960's ($\pi > 0.50$)

There are 12 observations, but there is one case where the difference is 0 (Marcia Elmquist), so $n = 11$. Because $P(X \geq 9) = (0.000 + 0.005 + 0.027) = 0.032$ and $P(X \geq 8) = (0.000 + 0.005 + 0.027 + 0.081) = 0.113$. H_0 is rejected if there are 9 or more plus signs. Since there are only 7, H_0 cannot be rejected. IQ's have not increased.

Exercise 15.2

H_0: $\pi \leq 0.50$
H_1: $\pi > 0.50$

H_0 is rejected if $z > 1.65$. $z = \dfrac{(30 - 0.50) - 25.0}{0.5\sqrt{50}} = 1.27$ H_0 cannot be rejected. IQ scores have not increased.

Exercise 15.3

H_0: There is no difference in the IQ scores.
H_1: The IQ scores have increased.
H_0 is rejected if the smaller of R^+ and R^- is 13 or less.

Student	Recent Score	Original Score	Diff.	Absol.	Rank	R^+	R^-
Barr	119	112	7	7	6.0	6.0	
Sedwick	103	108	−5	5	5.0		5.0
Elmquist	115	115	0				
Thealine	109	100	9	9	7.5	7.5	
Clark	131	120	11	11	10.0	10.0	
Redding	110	108	2	2	3.0	3.0	
Papalia	109	113	−4	4	4.0		4.0
Suppa	113	126	−13	13	11.0		11.0
Paul	94	95	−1	1	1.5		1.5
Kozoloski	119	110	9	9	7.5	7.5	
Sass	118	117	1	1	1.5	1.5	
Sundar	112	102	10	10	9.0	9.0	
						44.5	21.5

Since 21.5 is not less than or equal to 13, H_0 is not rejected. There has been no change in IQ scores.

Exercise 15.4

H_0: The two populations are the same.
H_1: The two populations are not the same.
Reject H_0 if $z < -1.96$ or $z > 1.96$.

Tough		Long Last	
Miles	Rank	Miles	Rank
24	2	35	9
31	7	46	15
37	11	49	16
44	14	52	17
36	10	41	13
30	6	40	12
28	4	32	8
21	1	29	5
	55	27	3
			98

$$z = \frac{55 - \dfrac{8(8+9+1)}{2}}{\sqrt{\dfrac{8(9)(8+9+1)}{12}}} = -1.636$$

H_0 is not rejected. The distributions of miles driven are the same.

Exercise 15.5

H_0: The distributions of occupancy rates are the same.
H_1: The distributions of occupancy rates are not the same.
H_0 is rejected if χ^2 is greater than 5.991.

Occupancy Rates of Three Hotels							
Best Eastern		Comfort Inn		Quality Court			
%	Rank	%	Rank	%	Rank		
58	2	69	9.5	72	11		
57	1	67	7.5	80	13		
67	7.5	62	4	84	14		
63	5	69	9.5	94	16		
61	3	77	12	86	15		
64	6						
	24.5		42.5		69		

$$H = \frac{12}{16(17)}\left(\frac{(24.5)^2}{6} + \frac{(42.5)^2}{5} + \frac{(69.0)^2}{5}\right) - 3(17)$$

$$= \frac{12}{272}(100.04 + 361.25 + 952.2) - 51 = (62.36 - 51) = 11.36$$

H_0 is rejected. The occupancy rates are not the same.

Exercise 15.6

Team	News	Free Press	d	d^2
Penn State	1	2	−1	1
Ohio State	2	1	1	1
Michigan	3	5	−2	4
Iowa	4	6	−2	4
Wisconsin	5	3	2	4
Michigan State	6	7	−1	1
Indiana	7	8	−1	1
Minnesota	8	9	−1	1
Purdue	9	10	−1	1
Illinois	10	4	6	36
Northwestern	11	11	0	0
				54

$$r_s = 1 - \frac{6(54)}{11(11^2 - 1)} = 0.754$$ There is a strong positive correlation between the ratings.

Exercise 16.1.

a. Sample means

Time	Bag 1	2	3	4	ΣX	$\overline{X}$	R	
8 a.m.	16.1	16.0	15.9	16.1	64.1	16.03	0.2	$\overline{\overline{X}} = \dfrac{63.81}{4} = 15.95$
9 a.m.	16.2	16.1	16.0	15.9	64.2	16.05	0.3	
10 a.m.	16.0	15.8	15.9	15.7	63.4	15.85	0.3	$\overline{R} = \dfrac{1}{4} = 0.25$
11 a.m.	15.8	15.9	16.0	15.8	63.5	<u>15.88</u>	<u>0.2</u>	
						63.81	1.0	

$$UCL \text{ and } LCL = 15.95 \pm 0.729(0.25)$$
$$= 15.95 \pm 0.18$$
$$UCL = 16.13 \text{ and } LCL = 15.77$$

b. Sample ranges:
$$UCL = D_4\overline{R} = 2.282(0.25) = 0.57$$
$$LCL = D_3\overline{R} = 0(0.25) = 0$$

c. The process appears to be in control.

Exercise 16.2

Day	Sample Size	Number Unsatisfactory	Proportion Unsat.
1	40	2	0.050
2	40	3	0.075
3	40	1	0.025
4	40	2	0.050
5	40	4	<u>0.100</u>
			0.300

$$\overline{p} = \frac{0.3}{5} = 0.06$$

$$UCL \text{ and } LCL = \overline{p} \pm 3\sqrt{\frac{\overline{p}(1-\overline{p})}{n}}$$
$$= 0.06 \pm 3\sqrt{\frac{0.06(1-0.06)}{40}}$$
$$= 0.06 \pm 0.11 = 0 \text{ and } 0.17$$

Exercise 16.3

$$\bar{c} = \frac{2+4+5+3+2+1+5+2+3+1}{10} = \frac{28}{10} = 2.8$$

$$
\begin{aligned}
UCL \text{ and } LCL &= \bar{c} \pm 3\sqrt{\bar{c}} \\
&= 2.8 \pm 3\sqrt{2.8} \\
&= 2.8 \pm 5.02 \\
UCL &= 7.82 \\
LCL &= 0
\end{aligned}
$$

Exercise 16.4

$P(x \le 2 | \pi = 0.30 \text{ and } n = 25) = 0.008$ from Appendix A where

$c = 2, n = 25, \pi = 0.30$ and $(0.000 + 0.001 + 0.007 = 0.008)$

CHAPTER 17

INDEX NUMBERS

Exercise 17.1.

Wage	Index	
$2.10	100.00	found by (2.10/2.10) 100
$3.10	147.6	found by (3.10/2.10) 100
$3.35	159.5	found by (3.35/2.10) 100
$3.80	181.0	found by (3.80/2.10) 100
$4.25	202.4	found by (4.25/2.10) 100
$4.75	226.2	found by (4.75/2.10) 100
$5.15	245.2	found by (5.15/2.10) 100
$5.75	273.8	found by (5.75/2.10) 100

Exercise 17.2

a. Simple aggregate index: $\dfrac{\$1,020}{\$672}(100) = 151.79$

b. Laspeyres index:

Item	1988 Price p_0	Quantity q_0	$p_0 q_0$	1998 Price p_t	$p_t q_0$
Battery	$25	32	$800	$40	$1280
Cable	22	8	176	30	240
Bimini top	325	2	650	500	1000
Depth finder	300	2	600	450	900
Total	$672		$2226	$1020	$3420

Laspeyres index: $P = \dfrac{\$3,420}{\$2,226}(100) = 153.64$

b. Paasche's index:

Item	1988 Price p_0	1996 Quantity q_t	$p_0 q_t$	1996 Price p_t	$p_t q_t$
Battery	$25	30	$750	$40	$1200
Cable	22	8	176	30	240
Bimini top	325	2	650	500	1000
Depth finder	300	2	600	450	900
Total	$672		$2176	$1020	$3340

Paasche's index: $P = \dfrac{\$3,340}{\$2,176}(100) = 153.49$

Exercise 17.3.

1996 real income: $\dfrac{\$50,000}{158.9}(100) = \$31,466$

His salary decreased $8,534 in real dollars, found by ($31,446 - $40,000)

1998 purchasing power $\dfrac{\$1}{158.9}(100) = \$0.629 = \$0.63$

Exercise 18.1.

a. Chart.

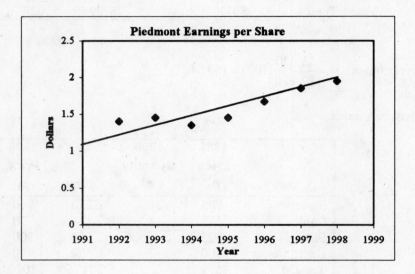

b. Trend equation.

Year	Y	t	Yt	t^2
1992	1.40	1	1.40	1
1993	1.45	2	2.90	4
1994	1.35	3	4.05	9
1995	1.45	4	5.80	16
1996	1.67	5	8.35	25
1997	1.85	6	11.10	36
1998	1.95	7	13.65	49
Total	11.12	28	47.25	140

$$b = \frac{47.25 - (11.12)\left(\dfrac{28}{7}\right)}{140 - \dfrac{(28)^2}{7}} = \frac{2.77}{28} = 0.0989$$

$$a = \frac{11.12}{7} - 0.098\left(\frac{28}{7}\right) = 1.1966$$

b. $Y' = 1.197 + 0.098(t)$

c. $Y' = 1.197 + 0.098(t) = 1.197 + 0.098(8) = 1.981$

Exercise 18.2

a. The equation is developed using the MINITAB output.

```
MTB >  print c1-c4

        ROW    year    Code    Pass-ger      Log-pass
         1     1991     1         2.0        0.301030
         2     1992     2         3.0        0.477121
         3     1993     3         4.4        0.643453
         4     1994     4         6.0        0.778151
         5     1995     5         8.5        0.929419



MTB >  Regress 'Log-Impt' 1 'Code';
SUBC>  Constant

Regression analyses

The regression equation is
Log-Impt = 0.158 + 0.156 Code

Predictor        Coef        Stdev        t-ratio        p
Constant       0.15849      0.01497        10.59       0.002
Code           0.155781     0.004514       34.51       0.000
```

b. The prediction for 1996 is:

$$Y' = 0.15849 + 0.155781\,t$$
$$= 0.15849 + 0.155781\,(6)$$
$$= 1.093176$$

The antilog of 1.093176 is 12.393, so the prediction for 1996 is 12.393 million.

Exercise 18.3

Table for computing quarterly seasonal index.

Year	Qtr.		Moving Total	Moving Avg.	Centered Moving Avg.	Specific Seasonal
1995	I	2				
	II	8				
			22	5.50		
	III	10			5.750	173.913
			24	6.00		
	IV	2			6.250	32.000
			26	6.50		
1996	I	4			6.500	61.538
			26	6.50		
	II	10			6.750	148.148
			28	7.00		
	III	10			7.000	142.857
			28	7.00		
	IV	4			7.250	55.172
			30	7.50		
1997	I	4			8.000	50.000
			34	8.50		
	II	12			8.500	141.176
			34	8.50		
	III	14			8.750	160.000
			36	9.00		
	IV	4			9.500	42.105
			40	10.00		
1998	I	6			10.750	55.814
			46	11.50		
	II	16			11.500	139.130
			46	11.50		
	III	20				
	IV	4				

		Quarter			
Year	I	II	III	IV	
1995			173.913	32.000	
1996	61.538	148.148	142.857	55.172	
1997	50.000	141.176	160.000	42.105	
1998	55.814	139.130			
Total	167.352	428.454	476.770	129.277	Total
Mean	55.784	142.818	158.923	43.092	400.617
Typical Index	55.698	142.598	158.678	43.026	400.000

Exercise 18.4

a. June = 2,000 (1.20) = 2,400   b.   November = 2,000 (0.47) = 940

Exercise 18.5

a. Using MINITAB the trend equation is:

$Y' = 4.0434 + 0.46079 (t)$,   First quarter of 1995 = 1, thus first quarter of 1998 is 17.

b.   Seasonally adjusted sales.

Quarter	Trend	Seasonal	Forecast
17	11.87683	55.69809	6.615167
18	12.33762	142.598	17.5932
19	12.79841	158.6782	20.30829
20	13.25920	43.02563	5.704855

Note: Slight variations in the prediction equation may occur depending on the computer software used.

CHAPTER 19

AN INTRODUCTION TO DECISION MAKING

Exercise 19.1

a.   Payoff table.

	Repaid	Difficulty	Bankrupt
Loan	$110,000	$108,000	$70,000
No loan	108,000	108,000	108,000

(Loan)   EMV(A₁) = 0.85 ($110,000) + 0.10 ($108,000) + 0.05 ($70,000) = $107,800

(No loan)   EMV(A₂) = $108,000

Since $108,000 is greater than $107,800 the banker should not make the loan.

b. EMV = 0.85 ($110,000) + 0.10 ($108,000) + 0.05 ($108,000) = $109,700

c. EVPI = $109,700 − $108,000 = $1,700

Exercise 19.2

	Repaid	Difficulty	Bankrupt
Loan	0	0	$38,000
No loan	$2,000	0	0

EOL(A₁) (Loan)   = 0.05 ($38,000) = $1,900

EOL(A₂) (No loan) = 0.85 ($2,000) = $1,700

The expected opportunity loss is the smallest for the act of no loan and the same as the value of perfect information ($1,200).

APPENDIXES

Tables

APPENDIX A

BINOMIAL PROBABILITY DISTRIBUTION

$n = 1$
PROBABILITY

r	0.05	0.10	0.20	0.30	0.40	0.50	0.60	0.70	0.80	0.90	0.95
0	0.950	0.900	0.800	0.700	0.600	0.500	0.400	0.300	0.200	0.100	0.050
1	0.050	0.100	0.200	0.300	0.400	0.500	0.600	0.700	0.800	0.900	0.950

$n = 2$
PROBABILITY

r	0.05	0.10	0.20	0.30	0.40	0.50	0.60	0.70	0.80	0.90	0.95
0	0.903	0.810	0.640	0.490	0.360	0.250	0.160	0.090	0.040	0.010	0.003
1	0.095	0.180	0.320	0.420	0.480	0.500	0.480	0.420	0.320	0.180	0.095
2	0.003	0.010	0.040	0.090	0.160	0.250	0.360	0.490	0.640	0.810	0.903

$n = 3$
PROBABILITY

r	0.05	0.10	0.20	0.30	0.40	0.50	0.60	0.70	0.80	0.90	0.95
0	0.857	0.729	0.512	0.343	0.216	0.125	0.064	0.027	0.008	0.001	0.000
1	0.135	0.243	0.384	0.441	0.432	0.375	0.288	0.189	0.096	0.027	0.007
2	0.007	0.027	0.096	0.189	0.288	0.375	0.432	0.441	0.384	0.243	0.135
3	0.000	0.001	0.008	0.027	0.064	0.125	0.216	0.343	0.512	0.729	0.857

$n = 4$
PROBABILITY

r	0.05	0.10	0.20	0.30	0.40	0.50	0.60	0.70	0.80	0.90	0.95
0	0.815	0.656	0.410	0.240	0.130	0.063	0.026	0.008	0.002	0.000	0.000
1	0.171	0.292	0.410	0.412	0.346	0.250	0.154	0.076	0.026	0.004	0.000
2	0.014	0.049	0.154	0.265	0.346	0.375	0.346	0.265	0.154	0.049	0.014
3	0.000	0.004	0.026	0.076	0.154	0.250	0.346	0.412	0.410	0.292	0.171
4	0.000	0.000	0.002	0.008	0.026	0.063	0.130	0.240	0.410	0.656	0.815

$n = 5$
PROBABILITY

r	0.05	0.10	0.20	0.30	0.40	0.50	0.60	0.70	0.80	0.90	0.95
0	0.774	0.590	0.328	0.168	0.078	0.031	0.010	0.002	0.000	0.000	0.000
1	0.204	0.328	0.410	0.360	0.259	0.156	0.077	0.028	0.006	0.000	0.000
2	0.021	0.073	0.205	0.309	0.346	0.313	0.230	0.132	0.051	0.008	0.001
3	0.001	0.008	0.051	0.132	0.230	0.313	0.346	0.309	0.205	0.073	0.021
4	0.000	0.000	0.006	0.028	0.077	0.156	0.259	0.360	0.410	0.328	0.204
5	0.000	0.000	0.000	0.002	0.010	0.031	0.078	0.168	0.328	0.590	0.774

$n = 6$
PROBABILITY

r	0.05	0.10	0.20	0.30	0.40	0.50	0.60	0.70	0.80	0.90	0.95
0	0.735	0.531	0.262	0.118	0.047	0.016	0.004	0.001	0.000	0.000	0.000
1	0.232	0.354	0.393	0.303	0.187	0.094	0.037	0.010	0.002	0.000	0.000
2	0.031	0.098	0.246	0.324	0.311	0.234	0.138	0.060	0.015	0.001	0.000
3	0.002	0.015	0.082	0.185	0.276	0.313	0.276	0.185	0.082	0.015	0.002
4	0.000	0.001	0.015	0.060	0.138	0.234	0.311	0.324	0.246	0.098	0.031
5	0.000	0.000	0.002	0.010	0.037	0.094	0.187	0.303	0.393	0.354	0.232
6	0.000	0.000	0.000	0.001	0.004	0.016	0.047	0.118	0.262	0.531	0.735

APPENDIX A

Bᴵɴᴏᴍⁱᴀʟ Pʀᴏʙᴀʙⁱʟⁱᴛʏ Dⁱꜱᴛʀⁱʙᴜᴛⁱᴏɴ (*continued*)

$n = 7$
PROBABILITY

r	0.05	0.10	0.20	0.30	0.40	0.50	0.60	0.70	0.80	0.90	0.95
0	0.698	0.478	0.210	0.082	0.028	0.008	0.002	0.000	0.000	0.000	0.000
1	0.257	0.372	0.367	0.247	0.131	0.055	0.017	0.004	0.000	0.000	0.000
2	0.041	0.124	0.275	0.318	0.261	0.164	0.077	0.025	0.004	0.000	0.000
3	0.004	0.023	0.115	0.227	0.290	0.273	0.194	0.097	0.029	0.003	0.000
4	0.000	0.003	0.029	0.097	0.194	0.273	0.290	0.227	0.115	0.023	0.004
5	0.000	0.000	0.004	0.025	0.077	0.164	0.261	0.318	0.275	0.124	0.041
6	0.000	0.000	0.000	0.004	0.017	0.055	0.131	0.247	0.367	0.372	0.257
7	0.000	0.000	0.000	0.000	0.002	0.008	0.028	0.082	0.210	0.478	0.698

$n = 8$
PROBABILITY

r	0.05	0.10	0.20	0.30	0.40	0.50	0.60	0.70	0.80	0.90	0.95
0	0.663	0.430	0.168	0.058	0.017	0.004	0.001	0.000	0.000	0.000	0.000
1	0.279	0.383	0.336	0.198	0.090	0.031	0.008	0.001	0.000	0.000	0.000
2	0.051	0.149	0.294	0.296	0.209	0.109	0.041	0.010	0.001	0.000	0.000
3	0.005	0.033	0.147	0.254	0.279	0.219	0.124	0.047	0.009	0.000	0.000
4	0.000	0.005	0.046	0.136	0.232	0.273	0.232	0.136	0.046	0.005	0.000
5	0.000	0.000	0.009	0.047	0.124	0.219	0.279	0.254	0.147	0.033	0.005
6	0.000	0.000	0.001	0.010	0.041	0.109	0.209	0.296	0.294	0.149	0.051
7	0.000	0.000	0.000	0.001	0.008	0.031	0.090	0.198	0.336	0.383	0.279
8	0.000	0.000	0.000	0.000	0.001	0.004	0.017	0.058	0.168	0.430	0.663

$n = 9$
PROBABILITY

r	0.05	0.10	0.20	0.30	0.40	0.50	0.60	0.70	0.80	0.90	0.95
0	0.630	0.387	0.134	0.040	0.010	0.002	0.000	0.000	0.000	0.000	0.000
1	0.299	0.387	0.302	0.156	0.060	0.018	0.004	0.000	0.000	0.000	0.000
2	0.063	0.172	0.302	0.267	0.161	0.070	0.021	0.004	0.000	0.000	0.000
3	0.008	0.045	0.176	0.267	0.251	0.164	0.074	0.021	0.003	0.000	0.000
4	0.001	0.007	0.066	0.172	0.251	0.246	0.167	0.074	0.017	0.001	0.000
5	0.000	0.001	0.017	0.074	0.167	0.246	0.251	0.172	0.066	0.007	0.001
6	0.000	0.000	0.003	0.021	0.074	0.164	0.251	0.267	0.176	0.045	0.008
7	0.000	0.000	0.000	0.004	0.021	0.070	0.161	0.267	0.302	0.172	0.063
8	0.000	0.000	0.000	0.000	0.004	0.018	0.060	0.156	0.302	0.387	0.299
9	0.000	0.000	0.000	0.000	0.000	0.002	0.010	0.040	0.134	0.387	0.630

BINOMIAL PROBABILITY DISTRIBUTION (continued)

$n = 10$
PROBABILITY

r	0.05	0.10	0.20	0.30	0.40	0.50	0.60	0.70	0.80	0.90	0.95
0	0.599	0.349	0.107	0.028	0.006	0.001	0.000	0.000	0.000	0.000	0.000
1	0.315	0.387	0.268	0.121	0.040	0.010	0.002	0.000	0.000	0.000	0.000
2	0.075	0.194	0.302	0.233	0.121	0.044	0.011	0.001	0.000	0.000	0.000
3	0.010	0.057	0.201	0.267	0.215	0.117	0.042	0.009	0.001	0.000	0.000
4	0.001	0.011	0.088	0.200	0.251	0.205	0.111	0.037	0.006	0.000	0.000
5	0.000	0.001	0.026	0.103	0.201	0.246	0.201	0.103	0.026	0.001	0.000
6	0.000	0.000	0.006	0.037	0.111	0.205	0.251	0.200	0.088	0.011	0.001
7	0.000	0.000	0.001	0.009	0.042	0.117	0.215	0.267	0.201	0.057	0.010
8	0.000	0.000	0.000	0.001	0.011	0.044	0.121	0.233	0.302	0.194	0.075
9	0.000	0.000	0.000	0.000	0.002	0.010	0.040	0.121	0.268	0.387	0.315
10	0.000	0.000	0.000	0.000	0.000	0.001	0.006	0.028	0.107	0.349	0.599

$n = 11$
PROBABILITY

r	0.05	0.10	0.20	0.30	0.40	0.50	0.60	0.70	0.80	0.90	0.95
0	0.569	0.314	0.086	0.020	0.004	0.000	0.000	0.000	0.000	0.000	0.000
1	0.329	0.384	0.236	0.093	0.027	0.005	0.001	0.000	0.000	0.000	0.000
2	0.087	0.213	0.295	0.200	0.089	0.027	0.005	0.001	0.000	0.000	0.000
3	0.014	0.071	0.221	0.257	0.177	0.081	0.023	0.004	0.000	0.000	0.000
4	0.001	0.016	0.111	0.220	0.236	0.161	0.070	0.017	0.002	0.000	0.000
5	0.000	0.002	0.039	0.132	0.221	0.226	0.147	0.057	0.010	0.000	0.000
6	0.000	0.000	0.010	0.057	0.147	0.226	0.221	0.132	0.039	0.002	0.000
7	0.000	0.000	0.002	0.017	0.070	0.161	0.236	0.220	0.111	0.016	0.001
8	0.000	0.000	0.000	0.004	0.023	0.081	0.177	0.257	0.221	0.071	0.014
9	0.000	0.000	0.000	0.001	0.005	0.027	0.089	0.200	0.295	0.213	0.087
10	0.000	0.000	0.000	0.000	0.001	0.005	0.027	0.093	0.236	0.384	0.329
11	0.000	0.000	0.000	0.000	0.000	0.000	0.004	0.020	0.086	0.314	0.569

$n = 12$
PROBABILITY

r	0.05	0.10	0.20	0.30	0.40	0.50	0.60	0.70	0.80	0.90	0.95
0	0.540	0.282	0.069	0.014	0.002	0.000	0.000	0.000	0.000	0.000	0.000
1	0.341	0.377	0.206	0.071	0.017	0.003	0.000	0.000	0.000	0.000	0.000
2	0.099	0.230	0.283	0.168	0.064	0.016	0.002	0.000	0.000	0.000	0.000
3	0.017	0.085	0.236	0.240	0.142	0.054	0.012	0.001	0.000	0.000	0.000
4	0.002	0.021	0.133	0.231	0.213	0.121	0.042	0.008	0.001	0.000	0.000
5	0.000	0.004	0.053	0.158	0.227	0.193	0.101	0.029	0.003	0.000	0.000
6	0.000	0.000	0.016	0.079	0.177	0.226	0.177	0.079	0.016	0.000	0.000
7	0.000	0.000	0.003	0.029	0.101	0.193	0.227	0.158	0.053	0.004	0.000
8	0.000	0.000	0.001	0.008	0.042	0.121	0.213	0.231	0.133	0.021	0.002
9	0.000	0.000	0.000	0.001	0.012	0.054	0.142	0.240	0.236	0.085	0.017
10	0.000	0.000	0.000	0.000	0.002	0.016	0.064	0.168	0.283	0.230	0.099
11	0.000	0.000	0.000	0.000	0.000	0.003	0.017	0.071	0.206	0.377	0.341
12	0.000	0.000	0.000	0.000	0.000	0.000	0.002	0.014	0.069	0.282	0.540

BINOMIAL PROBABILITY DISTRIBUTION *(continued)*

$n = 13$
PROBABILITY

r	0.05	0.10	0.20	0.30	0.40	0.50	0.60	0.70	0.80	0.90	0.95
0	0.513	0.254	0.055	0.010	0.001	0.000	0.000	0.000	0.000	0.000	0.000
1	0.351	0.367	0.179	0.054	0.011	0.002	0.000	0.000	0.000	0.000	0.000
2	0.111	0.245	0.268	0.139	0.045	0.010	0.001	0.000	0.000	0.000	0.000
3	0.021	0.100	0.246	0.218	0.111	0.035	0.006	0.001	0.000	0.000	0.000
4	0.003	0.028	0.154	0.234	0.184	0.087	0.024	0.003	0.000	0.000	0.000
5	0.000	0.006	0.069	0.180	0.221	0.157	0.066	0.014	0.001	0.000	0.000
6	0.000	0.001	0.023	0.103	0.197	0.209	0.131	0.044	0.006	0.000	0.000
7	0.000	0.000	0.006	0.044	0.131	0.209	0.197	0.103	0.023	0.001	0.000
8	0.000	0.000	0.001	0.014	0.066	0.157	0.221	0.180	0.069	0.006	0.000
9	0.000	0.000	0.000	0.003	0.024	0.087	0.184	0.234	0.154	0.028	0.003
10	0.000	0.000	0.000	0.001	0.006	0.035	0.111	0.218	0.246	0.100	0.021
11	0.000	0.000	0.000	0.000	0.001	0.010	0.045	0.139	0.268	0.245	0.111
12	0.000	0.000	0.000	0.000	0.000	0.002	0.011	0.054	0.179	0.367	0.351
13	0.000	0.000	0.000	0.000	0.000	0.000	0.001	0.010	0.055	0.254	0.513

$n = 14$
PROBABILITY

r	0.05	0.10	0.20	0.30	0.40	0.50	0.60	0.70	0.80	0.90	0.95
0	0.488	0.229	0.044	0.007	0.001	0.000	0.000	0.000	0.000	0.000	0.000
1	0.359	0.356	0.154	0.041	0.007	0.001	0.000	0.000	0.000	0.000	0.000
2	0.123	0.257	0.250	0.113	0.032	0.006	0.001	0.000	0.000	0.000	0.000
3	0.026	0.114	0.250	0.194	0.085	0.022	0.003	0.000	0.000	0.000	0.000
4	0.004	0.035	0.172	0.229	0.155	0.061	0.014	0.001	0.000	0.000	0.000
5	0.000	0.008	0.086	0.196	0.207	0.122	0.041	0.007	0.000	0.000	0.000
6	0.000	0.001	0.032	0.126	0.207	0.183	0.092	0.023	0.002	0.000	0.000
7	0.000	0.000	0.009	0.062	0.157	0.209	0.157	0.062	0.009	0.000	0.000
8	0.000	0.000	0.002	0.023	0.092	0.183	0.207	0.126	0.032	0.001	0.000
9	0.000	0.000	0.000	0.007	0.041	0.122	0.207	0.196	0.086	0.008	0.000
10	0.000	0.000	0.000	0.001	0.014	0.061	0.155	0.229	0.172	0.035	0.004
11	0.000	0.000	0.000	0.000	0.003	0.022	0.085	0.194	0.250	0.114	0.026
12	0.000	0.000	0.000	0.000	0.001	0.006	0.032	0.113	0.250	0.257	0.123
13	0.000	0.000	0.000	0.000	0.000	0.001	0.007	0.041	0.154	0.356	0.359
14	0.000	0.000	0.000	0.000	0.000	0.000	0.001	0.007	0.044	0.229	0.488

APPENDIX A

BINOMIAL PROBABILITY DISTRIBUTION (*continued*)

$n = 15$
PROBABILITY

r	0.05	0.10	0.20	0.30	0.40	0.50	0.60	0.70	0.80	0.90	0.95
0	0.463	0.206	0.035	0.005	0.000	0.000	0.000	0.000	0.000	0.000	0.000
1	0.366	0.343	0.132	0.031	0.005	0.000	0.000	0.000	0.000	0.000	0.000
2	0.135	0.267	0.231	0.092	0.022	0.003	0.000	0.000	0.000	0.000	0.000
3	0.031	0.129	0.250	0.170	0.063	0.014	0.002	0.000	0.000	0.000	0.000
4	0.005	0.043	0.188	0.219	0.127	0.042	0.007	0.001	0.000	0.000	0.000
5	0.001	0.010	0.103	0.206	0.186	0.092	0.024	0.003	0.000	0.000	0.000
6	0.000	0.002	0.043	0.147	0.207	0.153	0.061	0.012	0.001	0.000	0.000
7	0.000	0.000	0.014	0.081	0.177	0.196	0.118	0.035	0.003	0.000	0.000
8	0.000	0.000	0.003	0.035	0.118	0.196	0.177	0.081	0.014	0.000	0.000
9	0.000	0.000	0.001	0.012	0.061	0.153	0.207	0.147	0.043	0.002	0.000
10	0.000	0.000	0.000	0.003	0.024	0.092	0.186	0.206	0.103	0.010	0.001
11	0.000	0.000	0.000	0.001	0.007	0.042	0.127	0.219	0.188	0.043	0.005
12	0.000	0.000	0.000	0.000	0.002	0.014	0.063	0.170	0.250	0.129	0.031
13	0.000	0.000	0.000	0.000	0.000	0.003	0.022	0.092	0.231	0.267	0.135
14	0.000	0.000	0.000	0.000	0.000	0.000	0.005	0.031	0.132	0.343	0.366
15	0.000	0.000	0.000	0.000	0.000	0.000	0.000	0.005	0.035	0.206	0.463

$n = 16$
PROBABILITY

r	0.05	0.10	0.20	0.30	0.40	0.50	0.60	0.70	0.80	0.90	0.95
0	0.440	0.185	0.028	0.003	0.000	0.000	0.000	0.000	0.000	0.000	0.000
1	0.371	0.329	0.113	0.023	0.003	0.000	0.000	0.000	0.000	0.000	0.000
2	0.146	0.275	0.211	0.073	0.015	0.002	0.000	0.000	0.000	0.000	0.000
3	0.036	0.142	0.246	0.146	0.047	0.009	0.001	0.000	0.000	0.000	0.000
4	0.006	0.051	0.200	0.204	0.101	0.028	0.004	0.000	0.000	0.000	0.000
5	0.001	0.014	0.120	0.210	0.162	0.067	0.014	0.001	0.000	0.000	0.000
6	0.000	0.003	0.055	0.165	0.198	0.122	0.039	0.006	0.000	0.000	0.000
7	0.000	0.000	0.020	0.101	0.189	0.175	0.084	0.019	0.001	0.000	0.000
8	0.000	0.000	0.006	0.049	0.142	0.196	0.142	0.049	0.006	0.000	0.000
9	0.000	0.000	0.001	0.019	0.084	0.175	0.189	0.101	0.020	0.000	0.000
10	0.000	0.000	0.000	0.006	0.039	0.122	0.198	0.165	0.055	0.003	0.000
11	0.000	0.000	0.000	0.001	0.014	0.067	0.162	0.210	0.120	0.014	0.001
12	0.000	0.000	0.000	0.000	0.004	0.028	0.101	0.204	0.200	0.051	0.006
13	0.000	0.000	0.000	0.000	0.001	0.009	0.047	0.146	0.246	0.142	0.036
14	0.000	0.000	0.000	0.000	0.000	0.002	0.015	0.073	0.211	0.275	0.146
15	0.000	0.000	0.000	0.000	0.000	0.000	0.003	0.023	0.113	0.329	0.371
16	0.000	0.000	0.000	0.000	0.000	0.000	0.000	0.003	0.028	0.185	0.440

APPENDIX A

BINOMIAL PROBABILITY DISTRIBUTION (*continued*)

$n = 17$
PROBABILITY

r	0.05	0.10	0.20	0.30	0.40	0.50	0.60	0.70	0.80	0.90	0.95
0	0.418	0.167	0.023	0.002	0.000	0.000	0.000	0.000	0.000	0.000	0.000
1	0.374	0.315	0.096	0.017	0.002	0.000	0.000	0.000	0.000	0.000	0.000
2	0.158	0.280	0.191	0.058	0.010	0.001	0.000	0.000	0.000	0.000	0.000
3	0.041	0.156	0.239	0.125	0.034	0.005	0.000	0.000	0.000	0.000	0.000
4	0.008	0.060	0.209	0.187	0.080	0.018	0.002	0.000	0.000	0.000	0.000
5	0.001	0.017	0.136	0.208	0.138	0.047	0.008	0.001	0.000	0.000	0.000
6	0.000	0.004	0.068	0.178	0.184	0.094	0.024	0.003	0.000	0.000	0.000
7	0.000	0.001	0.027	0.120	0.193	0.148	0.057	0.009	0.000	0.000	0.000
8	0.000	0.000	0.008	0.064	0.161	0.185	0.107	0.028	0.002	0.000	0.000
9	0.000	0.000	0.002	0.028	0.107	0.185	0.161	0.064	0.008	0.000	0.000
10	0.000	0.000	0.000	0.009	0.057	0.148	0.193	0.120	0.027	0.001	0.000
11	0.000	0.000	0.000	0.003	0.024	0.094	0.184	0.178	0.068	0.004	0.000
12	0.000	0.000	0.000	0.001	0.008	0.047	0.138	0.208	0.136	0.017	0.001
13	0.000	0.000	0.000	0.000	0.002	0.018	0.080	0.187	0.209	0.060	0.008
14	0.000	0.000	0.000	0.000	0.000	0.005	0.034	0.125	0.239	0.156	0.041
15	0.000	0.000	0.000	0.000	0.000	0.001	0.010	0.058	0.191	0.280	0.158
16	0.000	0.000	0.000	0.000	0.000	0.000	0.002	0.017	0.096	0.315	0.374
17	0.000	0.000	0.000	0.000	0.000	0.000	0.000	0.002	0.023	0.167	0.418

$n = 18$
PROBABILITY

r	0.05	0.10	0.20	0.30	0.40	0.50	0.60	0.70	0.80	0.90	0.95
0	0.397	0.150	0.018	0.002	0.000	0.000	0.000	0.000	0.000	0.000	0.000
1	0.376	0.300	0.081	0.013	0.001	0.000	0.000	0.000	0.000	0.000	0.000
2	0.168	0.284	0.172	0.046	0.007	0.001	0.000	0.000	0.000	0.000	0.000
3	0.047	0.168	0.230	0.105	0.025	0.003	0.000	0.000	0.000	0.000	0.000
4	0.009	0.070	0.215	0.168	0.061	0.012	0.001	0.000	0.000	0.000	0.000
5	0.001	0.022	0.151	0.202	0.115	0.033	0.004	0.000	0.000	0.000	0.000
6	0.000	0.005	0.082	0.187	0.166	0.071	0.015	0.001	0.000	0.000	0.000
7	0.000	0.001	0.035	0.138	0.189	0.121	0.037	0.005	0.000	0.000	0.000
8	0.000	0.000	0.012	0.081	0.173	0.167	0.077	0.015	0.001	0.000	0.000
9	0.000	0.000	0.003	0.039	0.128	0.185	0.128	0.039	0.003	0.000	0.000
10	0.000	0.000	0.001	0.015	0.077	0.167	0.173	0.081	0.012	0.000	0.000
11	0.000	0.000	0.000	0.005	0.037	0.121	0.189	0.138	0.035	0.001	0.000
12	0.000	0.000	0.000	0.001	0.015	0.071	0.166	0.187	0.082	0.005	0.000
13	0.000	0.000	0.000	0.000	0.004	0.033	0.115	0.202	0.151	0.022	0.001
14	0.000	0.000	0.000	0.000	0.001	0.012	0.061	0.168	0.215	0.070	0.009
15	0.000	0.000	0.000	0.000	0.000	0.003	0.025	0.105	0.230	0.168	0.047
16	0.000	0.000	0.000	0.000	0.000	0.001	0.007	0.046	0.172	0.284	0.168
17	0.000	0.000	0.000	0.000	0.000	0.000	0.001	0.013	0.081	0.300	0.376
18	0.000	0.000	0.000	0.000	0.000	0.000	0.000	0.002	0.018	0.150	0.397

BINOMIAL PROBABILITY DISTRIBUTION (*continued*)

$n = 19$
PROBABILITY

r	0.05	0.10	0.20	0.30	0.40	0.50	0.60	0.70	0.80	0.90	0.95
0	0.377	0.135	0.014	0.001	0.000	0.000	0.000	0.000	0.000	0.000	0.000
1	0.377	0.285	0.068	0.009	0.001	0.000	0.000	0.000	0.000	0.000	0.000
2	0.179	0.285	0.154	0.036	0.005	0.000	0.000	0.000	0.000	0.000	0.000
3	0.053	0.180	0.218	0.087	0.017	0.002	0.000	0.000	0.000	0.000	0.000
4	0.011	0.080	0.218	0.149	0.047	0.007	0.001	0.000	0.000	0.000	0.000
5	0.002	0.027	0.164	0.192	0.093	0.022	0.002	0.000	0.000	0.000	0.000
6	0.000	0.007	0.095	0.192	0.145	0.052	0.008	0.001	0.000	0.000	0.000
7	0.000	0.001	0.044	0.153	0.180	0.096	0.024	0.002	0.000	0.000	0.000
8	0.000	0.000	0.017	0.098	0.180	0.144	0.053	0.008	0.000	0.000	0.000
9	0.000	0.000	0.005	0.051	0.146	0.176	0.098	0.022	0.001	0.000	0.000
10	0.000	0.000	0.001	0.022	0.098	0.176	0.146	0.051	0.005	0.000	0.000
11	0.000	0.000	0.000	0.008	0.053	0.144	0.180	0.098	0.017	0.000	0.000
12	0.000	0.000	0.000	0.002	0.024	0.096	0.180	0.153	0.044	0.001	0.000
13	0.000	0.000	0.000	0.001	0.008	0.052	0.145	0.192	0.095	0.007	0.000
14	0.000	0.000	0.000	0.000	0.002	0.022	0.093	0.192	0.164	0.027	0.002
15	0.000	0.000	0.000	0.000	0.001	0.007	0.047	0.149	0.218	0.080	0.011
16	0.000	0.000	0.000	0.000	0.000	0.002	0.017	0.087	0.218	0.180	0.053
17	0.000	0.000	0.000	0.000	0.000	0.000	0.005	0.036	0.154	0.285	0.179
18	0.000	0.000	0.000	0.000	0.000	0.000	0.001	0.009	0.068	0.285	0.377
19	0.000	0.000	0.000	0.000	0.000	0.000	0.000	0.001	0.014	0.135	0.377

$n = 20$
PROBABILITY

r	0.05	0.10	0.20	0.30	0.40	0.50	0.60	0.70	0.80	0.90	0.95
0	0.358	0.122	0.012	0.001	0.000	0.000	0.000	0.000	0.000	0.000	0.000
1	0.377	0.270	0.058	0.007	0.000	0.000	0.000	0.000	0.000	0.000	0.000
2	0.189	0.285	0.137	0.028	0.003	0.000	0.000	0.000	0.000	0.000	0.000
3	0.060	0.190	0.205	0.072	0.012	0.001	0.000	0.000	0.000	0.000	0.000
4	0.013	0.090	0.218	0.130	0.035	0.005	0.000	0.000	0.000	0.000	0.000
5	0.002	0.032	0.175	0.179	0.075	0.015	0.001	0.000	0.000	0.000	0.000
6	0.000	0.009	0.109	0.192	0.124	0.037	0.005	0.000	0.000	0.000	0.000
7	0.000	0.002	0.055	0.164	0.166	0.074	0.015	0.001	0.000	0.000	0.000
8	0.000	0.000	0.022	0.114	0.180	0.120	0.035	0.004	0.000	0.000	0.000
9	0.000	0.000	0.007	0.065	0.160	0.160	0.071	0.012	0.000	0.000	0.000
10	0.000	0.000	0.002	0.031	0.117	0.176	0.117	0.031	0.002	0.000	0.000
11	0.000	0.000	0.000	0.012	0.071	0.160	0.160	0.065	0.007	0.000	0.000
12	0.000	0.000	0.000	0.004	0.035	0.120	0.180	0.114	0.022	0.000	0.000
13	0.000	0.000	0.000	0.001	0.015	0.074	0.166	0.164	0.055	0.002	0.000
14	0.000	0.000	0.000	0.000	0.005	0.037	0.124	0.192	0.109	0.009	0.000
15	0.000	0.000	0.000	0.000	0.001	0.015	0.075	0.179	0.175	0.032	0.002
16	0.000	0.000	0.000	0.000	0.000	0.005	0.035	0.130	0.218	0.090	0.013
17	0.000	0.000	0.000	0.000	0.000	0.001	0.012	0.072	0.205	0.190	0.060
18	0.000	0.000	0.000	0.000	0.000	0.000	0.003	0.028	0.137	0.285	0.189
19	0.000	0.000	0.000	0.000	0.000	0.000	0.000	0.007	0.058	0.270	0.377
20	0.000	0.000	0.000	0.000	0.000	0.000	0.000	0.001	0.012	0.122	0.358

APPENDIX A

BINOMIAL PROBABILITY DISTRIBUTION (concluded)

$n = 25$
PROBABILITY

r	0.05	0.10	0.20	0.30	0.40	0.50	0.60	0.70	0.80	0.90	0.95
0	0.277	0.072	0.004	0.000	0.000	0.000	0.000	0.000	0.000	0.000	0.000
1	0.365	0.199	0.024	0.001	0.000	0.000	0.000	0.000	0.000	0.000	0.000
2	0.231	0.266	0.071	0.007	0.000	0.000	0.000	0.000	0.000	0.000	0.000
3	0.093	0.226	0.136	0.024	0.002	0.000	0.000	0.000	0.000	0.000	0.000
4	0.027	0.138	0.187	0.057	0.007	0.000	0.000	0.000	0.000	0.000	0.000
5	0.006	0.065	0.196	0.103	0.020	0.002	0.000	0.000	0.000	0.000	0.000
6	0.001	0.024	0.163	0.147	0.044	0.005	0.000	0.000	0.000	0.000	0.000
7	0.000	0.007	0.111	0.171	0.080	0.014	0.001	0.000	0.000	0.000	0.000
8	0.000	0.002	0.062	0.165	0.120	0.032	0.003	0.000	0.000	0.000	0.000
9	0.000	0.000	0.029	0.134	0.151	0.061	0.009	0.000	0.000	0.000	0.000
10	0.000	0.000	0.012	0.092	0.161	0.097	0.021	0.001	0.000	0.000	0.000
11	0.000	0.000	0.004	0.054	0.147	0.133	0.043	0.004	0.000	0.000	0.000
12	0.000	0.000	0.001	0.027	0.114	0.155	0.076	0.011	0.000	0.000	0.000
13	0.000	0.000	0.000	0.011	0.076	0.155	0.114	0.027	0.001	0.000	0.000
14	0.000	0.000	0.000	0.004	0.043	0.133	0.147	0.054	0.004	0.000	0.000
15	0.000	0.000	0.000	0.001	0.021	0.097	0.161	0.092	0.012	0.000	0.000
16	0.000	0.000	0.000	0.000	0.009	0.061	0.151	0.134	0.029	0.000	0.000
17	0.000	0.000	0.000	0.000	0.003	0.032	0.120	0.165	0.062	0.002	0.000
18	0.000	0.000	0.000	0.000	0.001	0.014	0.080	0.171	0.111	0.007	0.000
19	0.000	0.000	0.000	0.000	0.000	0.005	0.044	0.147	0.163	0.024	0.001
20	0.000	0.000	0.000	0.000	0.000	0.002	0.020	0.103	0.196	0.065	0.006
21	0.000	0.000	0.000	0.000	0.000	0.000	0.007	0.057	0.187	0.138	0.027
22	0.000	0.000	0.000	0.000	0.000	0.000	0.002	0.024	0.136	0.226	0.093
23	0.000	0.000	0.000	0.000	0.000	0.000	0.000	0.007	0.071	0.266	0.231
24	0.000	0.000	0.000	0.000	0.000	0.000	0.000	0.001	0.024	0.199	0.365
25	0.000	0.000	0.000	0.000	0.000	0.000	0.000	0.000	0.004	0.072	0.277

APPENDIX B

FACTORS FOR CONTROL CHARTS

Number of Items in Sample	Chart for Averages	Chart for Ranges		
	Factors for Control Limits	Factors for Central Line	Factors for Control Limits	
	A_2	d_2	D_3	D_4
2	1.880	1.128	0	3.267
3	1.023	1.693	0	2.575
4	0.729	2.059	0	2.282
5	0.577	2.326	0	2.115
6	0.483	2.534	0	2.004
7	0.419	2.704	0.076	1.924
8	0.373	2.847	0.136	1.864
9	0.337	2.970	0.184	1.816
10	0.308	3.078	0.223	1.777
11	0.285	3.173	0.256	1.744
12	0.266	3.258	0.284	1.716
13	0.249	3.336	0.308	1.692
14	0.235	3.407	0.329	1.671
15	0.223	3.472	0.348	1.652

Source: Adapted from American Society for Testing and Materials. Manual on Quality Control of Materials. 1951, Table B2, p. 115. For detailed table and explanation, see Acheson J. Duncan, Quality Control and Industrial Statistics, 3d ed. (Homewood, Il.: Richard D. Irwin, 1974). Table M, p. 927

APPENDIX C

POISSON DISTRIBUTION

μ

X	0.1	0.2	0.3	0.4	0.5	0.6	0.7	0.8	0.9
0	0.9048	0.8187	0.7408	0.6703	0.6065	0.5488	0.4966	0.4493	0.4066
1	0.0905	0.1637	0.2222	0.2681	0.3033	0.3293	0.3476	0.3595	0.3659
2	0.0045	0.0164	0.0333	0.0536	0.0758	0.0988	0.1217	0.1438	0.1647
3	0.0002	0.0011	0.0033	0.0072	0.0126	0.0198	0.0284	0.0383	0.0494
4	0.0000	0.0001	0.0003	0.0007	0.0016	0.0030	0.0050	0.0077	0.0111
5	0.0000	0.0000	0.0000	0.0001	0.0002	0.0004	0.0007	0.0012	0.0020
6	0.0000	0.0000	0.0000	0.0000	0.0000	0.0000	0.0001	0.0002	0.0003
7	0.0000	0.0000	0.0000	0.0000	0.0000	0.0000	0.0000	0.0000	0.0000

μ

X	1.0	2.0	3.0	4.0	5.0	6.0	7.0	8.0	9.0
0	0.3679	0.1353	0.0498	0.0183	0.0067	0.0025	0.0009	0.0003	0.0001
1	0.3679	0.2707	0.1494	0.0733	0.0337	0.0149	0.0064	0.0027	0.0011
2	0.1839	0.2707	0.2240	0.1465	0.0842	0.0446	0.0223	0.0107	0.0050
3	0.0613	0.1804	0.2240	0.1954	0.1404	0.0892	0.0521	0.0286	0.0150
4	0.0153	0.0902	0.1680	0.1954	0.1755	0.1339	0.0912	0.0573	0.0337
5	0.0031	0.0361	0.1008	0.1563	0.1755	0.1606	0.1277	0.0916	0.0607
6	0.0005	0.0120	0.0504	0.1042	0.1462	0.1606	0.1490	0.1221	0.0911
7	0.0001	0.0034	0.0216	0.0595	0.1044	0.1377	0.1490	0.1396	0.1171
8	0.0000	0.0009	0.0081	0.0298	0.0653	0.1033	0.1304	0.1396	0.1318
9	0.0000	0.0002	0.0027	0.0132	0.0363	0.0688	0.1014	0.1241	0.1318
10	0.0000	0.0000	0.0008	0.0053	0.0181	0.0413	0.0710	0.0993	0.1186
11	0.0000	0.0000	0.0002	0.0019	0.0082	0.0225	0.0452	0.0722	0.0970
12	0.0000	0.0000	0.0001	0.0006	0.0034	0.0113	0.0263	0.0481	0.0728
13	0.0000	0.0000	0.0000	0.0002	0.0013	0.0052	0.0142	0.0296	0.0504
14	0.0000	0.0000	0.0000	0.0001	0.0005	0.0022	0.0071	0.0169	0.0324
15	0.0000	0.0000	0.0000	0.0000	0.0002	0.0009	0.0033	0.0090	0.0194
16	0.0000	0.0000	0.0000	0.0000	0.0000	0.0003	0.0014	0.0045	0.0109
17	0.0000	0.0000	0.0000	0.0000	0.0000	0.0001	0.0006	0.0021	0.0058
18	0.0000	0.0000	0.0000	0.0000	0.0000	0.0000	0.0002	0.0009	0.0029
19	0.0000	0.0000	0.0000	0.0000	0.0000	0.0000	0.0001	0.0004	0.0014
20	0.0000	0.0000	0.0000	0.0000	0.0000	0.0000	0.0000	0.0002	0.0006
21	0.0000	0.0000	0.0000	0.0000	0.0000	0.0000	0.0000	0.0001	0.0003
22	0.0000	0.0000	0.0000	0.0000	0.0000	0.0000	0.0000	0.0000	0.0001

APPENDIX D

AREAS UNDER THE NORMAL CURVE

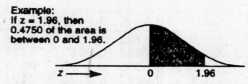

Example:
If z = 1.96, then
0.4750 of the area is
between 0 and 1.96.

Z	0.00	0.01	0.02	0.03	0.04	0.05	0.06	0.07	0.08	0.09
0.0	0.0000	0.0040	0.0080	0.0120	0.0160	0.0199	0.0239	0.0279	0.0319	0.0359
0.1	0.0398	0.0438	0.0478	0.0517	0.0557	0.0596	0.0636	0.0675	0.0714	0.0753
0.2	0.0793	0.0832	0.0871	0.0910	0.0948	0.0987	0.1026	0.1064	0.1103	0.1141
0.3	0.1179	0.1217	0.1255	0.1293	0.1331	0.1368	0.1406	0.1443	0.1480	0.1517
0.4	0.1554	0.1591	0.1628	0.1664	0.1700	0.1736	0.1772	0.1808	0.1844	0.1879
0.5	0.1915	0.1950	0.1985	0.2019	0.2054	0.2088	0.2123	0.2157	0.2190	0.2224
0.6	0.2257	0.2291	0.2324	0.2357	0.2389	0.2422	0.2454	0.2486	0.2517	0.2549
0.7	0.2580	0.2611	0.2642	0.2673	0.2704	0.2734	0.2764	0.2794	0.2823	0.2852
0.8	0.2881	0.2910	0.2939	0.2967	0.2995	0.3023	0.3051	0.3078	0.3106	0.3133
0.9	0.3159	0.3186	0.3212	0.3238	0.3264	0.3289	0.3315	0.3340	0.3365	0.3389
1.0	0.3413	0.3438	0.3461	0.3485	0.3508	0.3531	0.3554	0.3577	0.3599	0.3621
1.1	0.3643	0.3665	0.3686	0.3708	0.3729	0.3749	0.3770	0.3790	0.3810	0.3830
1.2	0.3849	0.3869	0.3888	0.3907	0.3925	0.3944	0.3962	0.3980	0.3997	0.4015
1.3	0.4032	0.4049	0.4066	0.4082	0.4099	0.4115	0.4131	0.4147	0.4162	0.4177
1.4	0.4192	0.4207	0.4222	0.4236	0.4251	0.4265	0.4279	0.4292	0.4306	0.4319
1.5	0.4332	0.4345	0.4357	0.4370	0.4382	0.4394	0.4406	0.4418	0.4429	0.4441
1.6	0.4452	0.4463	0.4474	0.4484	0.4495	0.4505	0.4515	0.4525	0.4535	0.4545
1.7	0.4554	0.4564	0.4573	0.4582	0.4591	0.4599	0.4608	0.4616	0.4625	0.4633
1.8	0.4641	0.4649	0.4656	0.4664	0.4671	0.4678	0.4686	0.4693	0.4699	0.4706
1.9	0.4713	0.4719	0.4726	0.4732	0.4738	0.4744	0.4750	0.4756	0.4761	0.4767
2.0	0.4772	0.4778	0.4783	0.4788	0.4793	0.4798	0.4803	0.4808	0.4812	0.4817
2.1	0.4821	0.4826	0.4830	0.4834	0.4838	0.4842	0.4846	0.4850	0.4854	0.4857
2.2	0.4861	0.4864	0.4868	0.4871	0.4875	0.4878	0.4881	0.4884	0.4887	0.4890
2.3	0.4893	0.4896	0.4898	0.4901	0.4904	0.4906	0.4909	0.4911	0.4913	0.4916
2.4	0.4918	0.4920	0.4922	0.4925	0.4927	0.4929	0.4931	0.4932	0.4934	0.4936
2.5	0.4938	0.4940	0.4941	0.4943	0.4945	0.4946	0.4948	0.4949	0.4951	0.4952
2.6	0.4953	0.4955	0.4956	0.4957	0.4959	0.4960	0.4961	0.4962	0.4963	0.4964
2.7	0.4965	0.4966	0.4967	0.4968	0.4969	0.4970	0.4971	0.4972	0.4973	0.4974
2.8	0.4974	0.4975	0.4976	0.4977	0.4977	0.4978	0.4979	0.4979	0.4980	0.4981
2.9	0.4981	0.4982	0.4982	0.4983	0.4984	0.4984	0.4985	0.4985	0.4986	0.4986
3.0	0.4987	0.4987	0.4987	0.4988	0.4988	0.4989	0.4989	0.4989	0.4990	0.4990

APPENDIX E

TABLE OF RANDOM NUMBERS

02711	08182	75997	79866	58095	83319	80295	79741	74599	84379
94873	90935	31684	63952	09865	14491	99518	93394	34691	14985
54921	78680	06635	98689	17306	25170	65928	87709	30533	89736
77640	97636	37397	93379	56454	59818	45827	74164	71666	46977
61545	00835	93251	87203	36759	49197	85967	01704	19634	21898
17147	19519	22497	16857	42426	84822	92598	49186	88247	39967
13748	04742	92460	85801	53444	65626	58710	55406	17173	69776
87455	14813	50373	28037	91182	32786	65261	11173	34376	36408
08999	57409	91185	10200	61411	23392	47797	56377	71635	08601
78804	81333	53809	32471	46034	36306	22498	19239	85428	55721
82173	26921	28472	98958	07960	66124	89731	95069	18625	92405
97594	25168	89178	68190	05043	17407	48201	83917	11413	72920
73881	67176	93504	42636	38233	16154	96451	57925	29667	30859
46071	22912	90326	42453	88108	72064	58601	32357	90610	32921
44492	19686	12495	93135	95185	77799	52441	88272	22024	80631
31864	72170	37722	55794	14636	05148	54505	50113	21119	25228
51574	90692	43339	65689	76539	27909	05467	21727	51141	72949
35350	76132	92925	92124	92634	35681	43690	89136	35599	84138
46943	36502	01172	46045	46991	33804	80006	35542	61056	75666
22665	87226	33304	57975	03985	21566	65796	72915	81466	89205
39437	97957	11838	10433	21564	51570	73558	27495	34533	57808
77082	47784	40098	97962	89845	28392	78187	06112	08169	11261
24544	25649	43370	28007	06779	72402	62632	53956	24709	06978
27503	15558	37738	24849	70722	71859	83736	06016	94397	12529
24590	24545	06435	52758	45685	90151	46516	49644	92686	84870
48155	86226	40359	28723	15364	69125	12609	57171	86857	31702
20226	53752	90648	24362	83314	00014	19207	69413	97016	86290
70178	73444	38790	53626	93780	18629	68766	24371	74639	30782
10169	41465	51935	05711	09799	79077	88159	33437	68519	03040
81084	03701	28598	70013	63794	53169	97054	60303	23259	96196
69202	20777	21727	81511	51887	16175	53746	46516	70339	62727
80561	95787	89426	93325	86412	57479	54194	52153	19197	81877
08199	26703	95128	48599	09333	12584	24374	31232	61782	44032
98883	28220	39358	53720	80161	83371	15181	11131	12219	55920
84568	69286	76054	21615	80883	36797	82845	39139	90900	18172
04269	35173	95745	53893	86022	77722	52498	84193	22448	22571
10538	13124	36099	13140	37706	44562	57179	44693	67877	01549
77843	24955	25900	63843	95029	93859	93634	20205	66294	41218
12034	94636	49455	76362	83532	31062	69903	91186	65768	55949
10524	72829	47641	93315	80875	28090	97728	52560	34937	79548
68935	76632	46984	61772	92786	22651	07086	89754	44143	97687
89450	65665	29190	43709	11172	34481	95977	47535	25658	73898
90696	20451	24211	97310	60446	73530	62865	96574	13829	72226
49006	32047	93086	00112	20470	17136	28255	86328	07293	38809
74591	87025	52368	59416	34417	70557	86746	55809	53628	12000
06315	17012	77103	00968	07235	10728	42189	33292	51487	64443
62386	09184	62092	46617	99419	64230	95034	85481	07857	42510
86848	82122	04028	36959	87827	12813	08627	80699	13345	51695
65643	69480	46598	04501	40403	91408	32343	48130	49303	90689
11084	46534	78957	77353	39578	77868	22970	84349	09184	70603

APPENDIX F

STUDENT'S t DISTRIBUTION

df	Level of significance for one-tailed test					
	.10	.05	.025	.01	.005	.0005
	Level of significance for two-tailed test					
	.20	.10	.05	.02	.01	.001
1	3.078	6.314	12.706	31.821	63.657	636.619
2	1.886	2.920	4.303	6.965	9.925	31.599
3	1.638	2.353	3.182	4.541	5.841	12.924
4	1.533	2.132	2.776	3.747	4.604	8.610
5	1.476	2.015	2.571	3.365	4.032	6.869
6	1.440	1.943	2.447	3.143	3.707	5.959
7	1.415	1.895	2.365	2.998	3.499	5.408
8	1.397	1.860	2.306	2.896	3.355	5.041
9	1.383	1.833	2.262	2.821	3.250	4.781
10	1.372	1.812	2.228	2.764	3.169	4.587
11	1.363	1.796	2.201	2.718	3.106	4.437
12	1.356	1.782	2.179	2.681	3.055	4.318
13	1.350	1.771	2.160	2.650	3.012	4.221
14	1.345	1.761	2.145	2.624	2.977	4.140
15	1.341	1.753	2.131	2.602	2.947	4.073
16	1.337	1.746	2.120	2.583	2.921	4.015
17	1.333	1.740	2.110	2.567	2.898	3.965
18	1.330	1.734	2.101	2.552	2.878	3.922
19	1.328	1.729	2.093	2.539	2.861	3.883
20	1.325	1.725	2.086	2.528	2.845	3.850
21	1.323	1.721	2.080	2.518	2.831	3.819
22	1.321	1.717	2.074	2.508	2.819	3.792
23	1.319	1.714	2.069	2.500	2.807	3.768
24	1.318	1.711	2.064	2.492	2.797	3.745
25	1.316	1.708	2.060	2.485	2.787	3.725
26	1.315	1.706	2.056	2.479	2.779	3.707
27	1.314	1.703	2.052	2.473	2.771	3.690
28	1.313	1.701	2.048	2.467	2.763	3.674
29	1.311	1.699	2.045	2.462	2.756	3.659
30	1.310	1.697	2.042	2.457	2.750	3.646
40	1.303	1.684	2.021	2.423	2.704	3.551
60	1.296	1.671	2.000	2.390	2.660	3.460
120	1.289	1.658	1.980	2.358	2.617	3.373
∞	1.282	1.645	1.960	2.326	2.576	3.291

APPENDIX G

CRITICAL VALUES OF THE F DISTRIBUTION AT A 5 PERCENT LEVEL OF SIGNIFICANCE, $\alpha = 0.05$

Degrees of Freedom for the Numerator

	1	2	3	4	5	6	7	8	9	10	12	15	20	24	30	40	60	120	∞
1	161	200	216	225	230	234	237	239	241	242	244	246	248	249	250	251	252	253	254
2	18.5	19.0	19.2	19.2	19.3	19.3	19.4	19.4	19.4	19.4	19.4	19.4	19.4	19.5	19.5	19.5	19.5	19.5	19.5
3	10.1	9.55	9.28	9.12	9.01	8.94	8.89	8.85	8.81	8.79	8.74	8.70	8.66	8.64	8.62	8.59	8.57	8.55	8.53
4	7.71	6.94	6.59	6.39	6.26	6.16	6.09	6.04	6.00	5.96	5.91	5.86	5.80	5.77	5.75	5.72	5.69	5.66	5.63
5	6.61	5.79	5.41	5.19	5.05	4.95	4.88	4.82	4.77	4.74	4.68	4.62	4.56	4.53	4.50	4.46	4.43	4.40	4.37
6	5.99	5.14	4.76	4.53	4.39	4.28	4.21	4.15	4.10	4.06	4.00	3.94	3.87	3.84	3.81	3.77	3.74	3.70	3.67
7	5.59	4.74	4.35	4.12	3.97	3.87	3.79	3.73	3.68	3.64	3.57	3.51	3.44	3.41	3.38	3.34	3.30	3.27	3.23
8	5.32	4.46	4.07	3.84	3.69	3.58	3.50	3.44	3.39	3.35	3.28	3.22	3.15	3.12	3.08	3.04	3.01	2.97	2.93
9	5.12	4.26	3.86	3.63	3.48	3.37	3.29	3.23	3.18	3.14	3.07	3.01	2.94	2.90	2.86	2.83	2.79	2.75	2.71
10	4.96	4.10	3.71	3.48	3.33	3.22	3.14	3.07	3.02	2.98	2.91	2.85	2.77	2.74	2.70	2.66	2.62	2.58	2.54
11	4.84	3.98	3.59	3.36	3.20	3.09	3.01	2.95	2.90	2.85	2.79	2.72	2.65	2.61	2.57	2.53	2.49	2.45	2.40
12	4.75	3.89	3.49	3.26	3.11	3.00	2.91	2.85	2.80	2.75	2.69	2.62	2.54	2.51	2.47	2.43	2.38	2.34	2.30
13	4.67	3.81	3.41	3.18	3.03	2.92	2.83	2.77	2.71	2.67	2.60	2.53	2.46	2.42	2.38	2.34	2.30	2.25	2.21
14	4.60	3.74	3.34	3.11	2.96	2.85	2.76	2.70	2.65	2.60	2.53	2.46	2.39	2.35	2.31	2.27	2.22	2.18	2.13
15	4.54	3.68	3.29	3.06	2.90	2.79	2.71	2.64	2.59	2.54	2.48	2.40	2.33	2.29	2.25	2.20	2.16	2.11	2.07
16	4.49	3.63	3.24	3.01	2.85	2.74	2.66	2.59	2.54	2.49	2.42	2.35	2.28	2.24	2.19	2.15	2.11	2.06	2.01
17	4.45	3.59	3.20	2.96	2.81	2.70	2.61	2.55	2.49	2.45	2.38	2.31	2.23	2.19	2.15	2.10	2.06	2.01	1.96
18	4.41	3.55	3.16	2.93	2.77	2.66	2.58	2.51	2.46	2.41	2.34	2.27	2.19	2.15	2.11	2.06	2.02	1.97	1.92
19	4.38	3.52	3.13	2.90	2.74	2.63	2.54	2.48	2.42	2.38	2.31	2.23	2.16	2.11	2.07	2.03	1.98	1.93	1.88
20	4.35	3.49	3.10	2.87	2.71	2.60	2.51	2.45	2.39	2.35	2.28	2.20	2.12	2.08	2.04	1.99	1.95	1.90	1.84
21	4.32	3.47	3.07	2.84	2.68	2.57	2.49	2.42	2.37	2.32	2.25	2.18	2.10	2.05	2.01	1.96	1.92	1.87	1.81
22	4.30	3.44	3.05	2.82	2.66	2.55	2.46	2.40	2.34	2.30	2.23	2.15	2.07	2.03	1.98	1.94	1.89	1.84	1.78
23	4.28	3.42	3.03	2.80	2.64	2.53	2.44	2.37	2.32	2.27	2.20	2.13	2.05	2.01	1.96	1.91	1.86	1.81	1.76
24	4.26	3.40	3.01	2.78	2.62	2.51	2.42	2.36	2.30	2.25	2.18	2.11	2.03	1.98	1.94	1.89	1.84	1.79	1.73
25	4.24	3.39	2.99	2.76	2.60	2.49	2.40	2.34	2.28	2.24	2.16	2.09	2.01	1.96	1.92	1.87	1.82	1.77	1.71
30	4.17	3.32	2.92	2.69	2.53	2.42	2.33	2.27	2.21	2.16	2.09	2.01	1.93	1.89	1.84	1.79	1.74	1.68	1.62
40	4.08	3.23	2.84	2.61	2.45	2.34	2.25	2.18	2.12	2.08	2.00	1.92	1.84	1.79	1.74	1.69	1.64	1.58	1.51
60	4.00	3.15	2.76	2.53	2.37	2.25	2.17	2.10	2.04	1.99	1.92	1.84	1.75	1.70	1.65	1.59	1.53	1.47	1.39
120	3.92	3.07	2.68	2.45	2.29	2.18	2.09	2.02	1.96	1.91	1.83	1.75	1.66	1.61	1.55	1.50	1.43	1.35	1.25
∞	3.84	3.00	2.60	2.37	2.21	2.10	2.01	1.94	1.88	1.83	1.75	1.67	1.57	1.52	1.46	1.39	1.32	1.22	1.00

Degrees of Freedom for the Denominator

CRITICAL VALUES OF THE F DISTRIBUTION AT A 1 PERCENT LEVEL OF SIGNIFICANCE, $\alpha = 0.01$

Degrees of Freedom for the Numerator

	1	2	3	4	5	6	7	8	9	10	12	15	20	24	30	40	60	120	∞
1	4052	5000	5403	5625	5764	5859	5928	5981	6022	6056	6106	6157	6209	6235	6261	6287	6313	6339	6366
2	98.5	99.0	99.2	99.2	99.3	99.3	99.4	99.4	99.4	99.4	99.4	99.4	99.4	99.5	99.5	99.5	99.5	99.5	99.5
3	34.1	30.8	29.5	28.7	28.2	27.9	27.7	27.5	27.3	27.2	27.1	26.9	26.7	26.6	26.5	26.4	26.3	26.2	26.1
4	21.2	18.0	16.7	16.0	15.5	15.2	15.0	14.8	14.7	14.5	14.4	14.2	14.0	13.9	13.8	13.7	13.7	13.6	13.5
5	16.3	13.3	12.1	11.4	11.0	10.7	10.5	10.3	10.2	10.1	9.89	9.72	9.55	9.47	9.38	9.29	9.20	9.11	9.02
6	13.7	10.9	9.78	9.15	8.75	8.47	8.26	8.10	7.98	7.87	7.72	7.56	7.40	7.31	7.23	7.14	7.06	6.97	6.88
7	12.2	9.55	8.45	7.85	7.46	7.19	6.99	6.84	6.72	6.62	6.47	6.31	6.16	6.07	5.99	5.91	5.82	5.74	5.65
8	11.3	8.65	7.59	7.01	6.63	6.37	6.18	6.03	5.91	5.81	5.67	5.52	5.36	5.28	5.20	5.12	5.03	4.95	4.86
9	10.6	8.02	6.99	6.42	6.06	5.80	5.61	5.47	5.35	5.26	5.11	4.96	4.81	4.73	4.65	4.57	4.48	4.40	4.31
10	10.0	7.56	6.55	5.99	5.64	5.39	5.20	5.06	4.94	4.85	4.71	4.56	4.41	4.33	4.25	4.17	4.08	4.00	3.91
11	9.65	7.21	6.22	5.67	5.32	5.07	4.89	4.74	4.63	4.54	4.40	4.25	4.10	4.02	3.94	3.86	3.78	3.69	3.60
12	9.33	6.93	5.95	5.41	5.06	4.82	4.64	4.50	4.39	4.30	4.16	4.01	3.86	3.78	3.70	3.62	3.54	3.45	3.36
13	9.07	6.70	5.74	5.21	4.86	4.62	4.44	4.30	4.19	4.10	3.96	3.82	3.66	3.59	3.51	3.43	3.34	3.25	3.17
14	8.86	6.51	5.56	5.04	4.69	4.46	4.28	4.14	4.03	3.94	3.80	3.66	3.51	3.43	3.35	3.27	3.18	3.09	3.00
15	8.68	6.36	5.42	4.89	4.56	4.32	4.14	4.00	3.89	3.80	3.67	3.52	3.37	3.29	3.21	3.13	3.05	2.96	2.87
16	8.53	6.23	5.29	4.77	4.44	4.20	4.03	3.89	3.78	3.69	3.55	3.41	3.26	3.18	3.10	3.02	2.93	2.84	2.75
17	8.40	6.11	5.18	4.67	4.34	4.10	3.93	3.79	3.68	3.59	3.46	3.31	3.16	3.08	3.00	2.92	2.83	2.75	2.65
18	8.29	6.01	5.09	4.58	4.25	4.01	3.84	3.71	3.60	3.51	3.37	3.23	3.08	3.00	2.92	2.84	2.75	2.66	2.57
19	8.18	5.93	5.01	4.50	4.17	3.94	3.77	3.63	3.52	3.43	3.30	3.15	3.00	2.92	2.84	2.76	2.67	2.58	2.49
20	8.10	5.85	4.94	4.43	4.10	3.87	3.70	3.56	3.46	3.37	3.23	3.09	2.94	2.86	2.78	2.69	2.61	2.52	2.42
21	8.02	5.78	4.87	4.37	4.04	3.81	3.64	3.51	3.40	3.31	3.17	3.03	2.88	2.80	2.72	2.64	2.55	2.46	2.36
22	7.95	5.72	4.82	4.31	3.99	3.76	3.59	3.45	3.35	3.26	3.12	2.98	2.83	2.75	2.67	2.58	2.50	2.40	2.31
23	7.88	5.66	4.76	4.26	3.94	3.71	3.54	3.41	3.30	3.21	3.07	2.93	2.78	2.70	2.62	2.54	2.45	2.35	2.26
24	7.82	5.61	4.72	4.22	3.90	3.67	3.50	3.36	3.26	3.17	3.03	2.89	2.74	2.66	2.58	2.49	2.40	2.31	2.21
25	7.77	5.57	4.68	4.18	3.85	3.63	3.46	3.32	3.22	3.13	2.99	2.85	2.70	2.62	2.54	2.45	2.36	2.27	2.17
30	7.56	5.39	4.51	4.02	3.70	3.47	3.30	3.17	3.07	2.98	2.84	2.70	2.55	2.47	2.39	2.30	2.21	2.11	2.01
40	7.31	5.18	4.31	3.83	3.51	3.29	3.12	2.99	2.89	2.80	2.66	2.52	2.37	2.29	2.20	2.11	2.02	1.92	1.81
60	7.08	4.98	4.13	3.65	3.34	3.12	2.95	2.82	2.72	2.63	2.50	2.35	2.20	2.12	2.03	1.94	1.84	1.73	1.60
120	6.85	4.79	3.95	3.48	3.17	2.96	2.79	2.66	2.56	2.47	2.34	2.19	2.03	1.95	1.86	1.76	1.66	1.53	1.38
∞	6.63	4.61	3.78	3.32	3.02	2.80	2.64	2.51	2.41	2.32	2.18	2.04	1.88	1.79	1.70	1.59	1.47	1.32	1.00

Degrees of Freedom for the Denominator

Appendix G

APPENDIX H

WILCOXON *T* VALUES

N	2α .15 α .075	.10 .050	.05 .025	.04 .020	.03 .015	.02 .010	.01 .005
4	0						
5	1	0					
6	2	2	0	0			
7	4	3	2	1	0	0	
8	7	5	3	3	2	1	0
9	9	8	5	5	4	3	1
10	12	10	8	7	6	5	3
11	16	13	10	9	8	7	5
12	19	17	13	12	11	9	7
13	24	21	17	16	14	12	9
14	28	25	21	19	18	15	12
15	33	30	25	23	21	19	15
16	39	35	29	28	26	23	19
17	45	41	34	33	30	27	23
18	51	47	40	38	35	32	27
19	58	53	46	43	41	37	32
20	65	60	52	50	47	43	37
21	73	67	58	56	53	49	42
22	81	75	65	63	59	55	48
23	89	83	73	70	66	62	54
24	98	91	81	78	74	69	61
25	108	100	89	86	82	76	68
26	118	110	98	94	90	84	75
27	128	119	107	103	99	92	83
28	138	130	116	112	108	101	91
29	150	140	126	122	117	110	100
30	161	151	137	132	127	120	109
31	173	163	147	143	137	130	118
32	186	175	159	154	148	140	128
33	199	187	170	165	159	151	138
34	212	200	182	177	171	162	148
35	226	213	195	189	182	173	159
40	302	286	264	257	249	238	220
50	487	466	434	425	413	397	373
60	718	690	648	636	620	600	567
70	995	960	907	891	872	846	805
80	1,318	1,276	1,211	1,192	1,168	1,136	1,086
90	1,688	1,638	1,560	1,537	1,509	1,471	1,410
100	2,105	2,045	1,955	1,928	1,894	1,850	1,779

SOURCE: Abridged from Robert L. McCormack, "Extended Tables of the Wilcoxon Matched-Pair Signed Rank Statistic," *Journal of the American Statistical Association*, September 1965, pp. 866–67.

APPENDIX I

CRITICAL VALUES OF CHI-SQUARE

This table contains the values of χ^2 that correspond to a specific right tail area and specific numbers of degrees of freedom df.

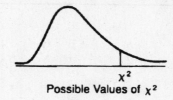

Possible Values of χ^2

DEGREES OF FREEDOM df	RIGHT-TAIL AREA			
	0.10	0.05	0.02	0.01
1	2.706	3.841	5.412	6.635
2	4.605	5.991	7.824	9.210
3	6.251	7.815	9.837	11.345
4	7.779	9.488	11.668	13.277
5	9.236	11.070	13.388	15.086
6	10.645	12.592	15.033	16.812
7	12.017	14.067	16.622	18.475
8	13.362	15.507	18.168	20.090
9	14.684	16.919	19.679	21.666
10	15.987	18.307	21.161	23.209
11	17.275	19.675	22.618	24.725
12	18.549	21.026	24.054	26.217
13	19.812	22.362	25.472	27.688
14	21.064	23.685	26.873	29.141
15	22.307	24.996	28.259	30.578
16	23.542	26.296	29.633	32.000
17	24.769	27.587	30.995	33.409
18	25.989	28.869	32.346	34.805
19	27.204	30.144	33.687	36.191
20	28.412	31.410	35.020	37.566
21	29.615	32.671	36.343	38.932
22	30.813	33.924	37.659	40.289
23	32.007	35.172	38.968	41.638
24	33.196	36.415	40.270	42.980
25	34.382	37.652	41.566	44.314
26	35.563	38.885	42.856	45.642
27	36.741	40.113	44.140	46.963
28	37.916	41.337	45.419	48.278
29	39.087	42.557	46.693	49.588
30	40.256	43.773	47.962	50.892